The Workers' and Peasants' State

MANCHESTER
UNIVERSITY PRESS

The Workers' and Peasants' State

Communism and society
in East Germany under Ulbricht
1945–71

edited by
Patrick Major and Jonathan Osmond

Manchester University Press
Manchester and New York

distributed exclusively in the USA by Palgrave

Copyright © Manchester University Press 2002

While copyright in the volume as a whole is vested in Manchester University Press, copyright in individual chapters belongs to their respective authors, and no chapter may be reproduced wholly or in part without the express permission in writing of both author and publisher.

Published by Manchester University Press
Oxford Road, Manchester M13 9NR, UK
and room 400, 175 Fifth Avenue, New York, NY 10010, USA
www.manchesteruniversitypress.co.uk

Distributed exclusively in the USA by
Palgrave, 175 Fifth Avenue, New York,
NY 10010, USA

Distributed exclusively in Canada by
UBC Press, University of British Columbia, 2029 West Mall,
Vancouver, BC, Canada V6T 1Z2

British Library Cataloguing-in-Publication Data
A catalogue record for this book is available from the British Library

Library of Congress Cataloging-in-Publication Data applied for

ISBN 0 7190 6288 8 hardback
      0 7190 6289 6 *paperback*

First published 2002

10 09 08 07 06 05 04 03 02   10 9 8 7 6 5 4 3 2 1

Typeset in Photina
by Action Publishing Technology Ltd, Gloucester
Printed in Great Britain
by Bookcraft (Bath) Ltd, Midsomer Norton

Contents

	List of contributors	vii
	Preface	xi
	List of abbreviations	xiii
1	Introduction *Patrick Major*	1

I State

2	The leadership of the Socialist Unity Party of Germany under Ulbricht *Peter Grieder*	22
3	Ulbricht's secret police: the Ministry of State Security *Jens Gieseke* (Translated from the German by Mary Carlene Forszt and Patrick Major)	41
4	The people's police and the people in Ulbricht's Germany *Richard Bessel*	59
5	'Protecting the accomplishments of socialism'? The (re)militarisation of life in the German Democratic Republic *Corey Ross*	78

II Society

6	Popular opinion *Mark Allinson*	96
7	Workers and the Socialist Unity Party of Germany in the summer of 1953 *Gareth Pritchard*	112
8	From *Junker* estate to co-operative farm: East German agrarian society 1945–61 *Jonathan Osmond*	130

Contents

9 Squaring the circle: the dilemmas and evolution of women's policy   *Donna Harsch*   151

10 The limits of repression and reform: youth policy in the early 1960s   *Mark Fenemore*   171

11 Going west: the open border and the problem of *Republikflucht*   *Patrick Major*   190

III Culture

12 The evangelical church in the German Democratic Republic   *Merrilyn Thomas*   210

13 The fifth column: dance music in the early German Democratic Republic   *Toby Thacker*   227

14 National paradigm and legitimacy: uses of academic history writing in the 1960s   *Stefan Berger*   244

15 History in the academy: objectivity and partisanship in the Marxist historiography of the German Democratic Republic   *Heiko Feldner*   262

IV Conclusion

16 Retheorising 'state' and 'society' in the German Democratic Republic   *Mary Fulbrook*   280

Index   299

Contributors

Mark Allinson lectures in German and Austrian history at the University of Bristol. He has recently published a book on the early history of the German Democratic Republic (GDR), *Politics and Popular Opinion in East Germany, 1945–1968* (Manchester, 2002). He is also the editor of *Contemporary Germany* (London, 2002) and author of *Germany and Austria 1814–2000* (London, 2000) for students of modern languages. His current research work centres on interwar Austria.

Stefan Berger is Professor of Modern and Contemporary History at the University of Glamorgan. He has recently published *Social Democracy and the Working Class in Nineteenth- and Twentieth-Century Germany* (London, 2000); *Writing National Histories* (London, 1999), and *Nationalism, Labour and Ethnicity* (Manchester, 1999). He is currently working on the historiographical relations between Britain and Germany in the nineteenth and twentieth centuries, as well as on relations between the British left and the GDR. He is also currently preparing a monograph on German national identity, and is co-editor for Edward Arnold's *Writing History* series on historiography and historical theory.

Richard Bessel is Professor of Twentieth-Century History at the University of York. His publications include *Political Violence and the Rise of Nazism* (New Haven, 1984); (ed.) *Life in the Third Reich* (Oxford, 1987); *Germany after the First World War* (Oxford, 1993); (ed.) *Fascist Italy and Nazi Germany: Comparisons and Contrasts* (Cambridge, 1996); (ed., with Ralph Jessen) *Die Grenzen der Diktatur: Staat und Gesellschaft in der DDR* (Göttingen, 1996); and (ed., with Clive Emsley) *Patterns of Provocation: Police and Public Disorder* (New York and Oxford, 2000). He is also Co-Editor of the journal *German History*.

Heiko Feldner is Lecturer in Modern German History in the School of European Studies at Cardiff University. His research interests lie broadly in German intellectual history since the eighteenth century, and in the history and theory of historical writing. He is the author of *Das Erfahrnis der Ordnung* (Frankfurt am Main, 1999) and co-editor of the forthcoming series for Edward Arnold, *Writing History*, and of its first volume, *Writing History: Theory and Practice*.

Mark Fenemore has recently completed a PhD at the University of London on 'Nonconformity on the borders of dictatorship: youth subcultures in the GDR' and is currently teaching at the University of Galway, Ireland.

Mary Fulbrook, educated at the universities of Cambridge and Harvard, is Professor of German History at University College London. She has published very widely in German and comparative European history, including several edited volumes. Her books include: *A Concise History of Germany* (Cambridge, 1990); *Anatomy of a Dictatorship: Inside the GDR, 1949–1989* (Oxford, 1995); *German National Identity after the Holocaust* (Cambridge, 1999); *Interpretations of the Two Germanies, 1945–1990* (2nd edn, Basingstoke, 2000); *The Divided Nation: A History of Germany, 1918–2000* (2nd edn, London, 2001); and *Historical Theory* (London, 2002). She is currently working on the social history of the GDR.

Jens Gieseke, is a historian working in the Department of Education and Research of the Federal Commissioner for the Stasi Records in Berlin. His research focuses on the history of rule and society in the GDR and other Communist countries. He recently published: *Mielke-Konzern: Die Geschichte der Stasi 1945–1990* (Munich and Stuttgart, 2001); *Die hauptamtlichen Mitarbeiter der Staatssicherheit: Personalstruktur und Lebenswelt 1950–1989/90* (Berlin, 2000); *The GDR State Security: Shield and Sword of the Party* (Berlin, forthcoming).

Peter Grieder is Lecturer in Twentieth-Century History at the University of Hull. He specialises in the history of the GDR, his most significant publication being *The East German Leadership, 1946–1973: Conflict and Crisis* (Manchester, 1999). His next book will be about the impact of glasnost and perestroika on the Socialist Unity Party of Germany (SED) between 1985 and 1989.

Donna Harsch is an Associate Professor in History at Carnegie Mellon University in Pittsburgh, Pennsylvania, USA. She has published *German Social Democracy and the Rise of Nazism, 1928–1933* (Chapel Hill, NC, 1993). Since the mid-1990s, her research has focused on women in the early GDR. Among other articles, she has published, 'Society, the state, and abortion in East Germany, 1950–1972', *American Historical Review*, 102 (1997). Her book-in-progress, *The Revenge of the Domestic: East German Women and the Construction of State Socialism, 1945–1970* (Princeton, NJ, forthcoming), will survey the history of women's experiences as workers, mothers, wives, consumers and citizens.

Patrick Major lectures in contemporary history at the University of Warwick. He has published *The Death of the KPD: Communism and Anti-Communism in West Germany, 1945–1956* (Oxford, 1997), and is currently completing *Behind the Berlin Wall: East Germany and the Frontiers of Power* (Oxford, 2003). He is also turning his attention to the popular culture of the Cold War in a comparative East–West context, including the role of spy novels and science fiction, as well as sport and music, in shaping postwar identities.

Jonathan Osmond is Professor of Modern European History at Cardiff University. He has published *German Reunification: A Reference Guide and Commentary* (London, 1992) and *Rural Protest in the Weimar Republic: The Free Peasantry in the Rhineland and Bavaria* (Basingstoke, 1993). His essays on agriculture in the Soviet Zone/GDR appear in two German collections (Götttingen and Stuttgart, 1996), and his essays on the end of the GDR in collections edited by Mary Fulbrook (London, 1997 and 2001) and by Moira Donald and Tim Rees (Basingstoke, 2001). He has also published on visual art in the GDR, and this is the starting point for his current major project on art and politics in modern Germany.

Gareth Pritchard is a Lecturer in the Department of History at the University of Wales, Swansea. He has recently published a monograph on *The Making of the GDR: From Antifascism to Stalinism 1945–53* (Manchester, 2000). He has also published articles on national identity in contemporary Germany, female labour in the Soviet zone and young people in postwar East Germany. He is currently writing a book that explores the interaction between occupation policies and German politics in all four Zones of Occupation in the key year of 1945.

Corey Ross is Lecturer in Modern History at the University of Birmingham. His first book, *Constructing Socialism at the Grass-Roots: The Transformation of East Germany, 1945–65* (Basingstoke, 2000), is a 'bottom-up' social history of the GDR's two formative decades, focusing on the interplay between regime policies, popular opinion and social change. He has recently completed the first historiographic overview of the GDR, *The East German Dictatorship: Problems and Perspectives in the Interpretation of the GDR* (London, 2002).

Toby Thacker has completed a doctoral thesis on politics and music in Germany, 1945–1955, with Jonathan Osmond at Cardiff University. He is preparing articles for publication on the censorship of music in the GDR, 1951–53, on musicians and *Republikflucht* in the GDR and on the introduction of American music in Germany after 1945. He spoke about the Bach Year (1950) in a divided Germany at the American Historical Association conference in San Francisco in January 2002.

Merrilyn Thomas has been researching the role of the Protestant Church in the GDR. She has completed a doctoral thesis at University College London on the relationship between Church and state during the 1960s, both domestically and in terms of the GDR's relations with Britain. Her contribution to *Britain and the GDR: Relations and Perceptions in a Divided World* will be published by the Arbeitskreis für deutsche Englandforschung

(Berlin, 2002). In 1965, Thomas lived in the GDR for several months, later graduating from the University of East Anglia in European Studies and working as a journalist for many years. She is the author of a book on the American death penalty entitled *Life on Death Row* (London, 1989).

Preface

Most of the chapters in this volume originated in the conference on 'Ulbricht's Germany', held at Cardiff University in March 1999 under the auspices of the Cardiff Centre for Modern German History and the German History Society. The latter was generous in providing financial support, for which the editors and contributors are grateful. Thanks are also due to all those who participated in the discussions at the conference (particularly Arnd Bauerkämper and Thomas Lindenberger who joined us from Potsdam), to Bonny Harvey for her help in organisation, to Barbara Docherty for copy-editing, to Rachel Armstrong, Jonathan Bevan, Rachael Bolden and Alison Whittle at Manchester University Press for their assistance and patience during the production of the volume, and to the archivists and librarians in Germany who have helped us all with our research.

This book aims to open up to an English-speaking readership the wealth of original research which has been undertaken in recent years on the Soviet Occupation Zone and the early German Democratic Republic. It does not claim to be comprehensive, but it does represent many important facets of East Germany in the years 1945–71. There are certainly many further challenges in terms of research topics, methodologies and new sources, but it is hoped that they will be met in future, in the same way that the population of the GDR undoubtedly rose to the challenge of the laudable appeal made to them by the authorities in the 1950s to 'Reduce forest fires by 33.6 per cent!'

Jonathan Osmond

Abbreviations

ABV	Abschnittsbevollmächtigte(r) ('Section Plenipotentiary')
ADGB	Allgemeiner Deutscher Gewerkschaftsbund (General German Trade Union Association)
AFA	Antifaschistische Frauenausschüsse (Antifascist Women's Committees)
BAB	Bundesarchiv Berlin (Federal Archive, Berlin)
BAK	Bundesarchiv Koblenz (Federal Archive, Koblenz)
BLHA	Brandenburgisches Landeshauptarchiv (Brandenburg Main State Archive)
BPA	Bezirksparteiarchiv (Regional Party Archive)
BStU	Bundesbeauftragte(r) für die Unterlagen der Staatssicherheit (Federal Commissioner for the State Security Records)
BT	Bezirkstag (Regional Parliament)
CDU	Christlich-Demokratische Union (Christian Democratic Union)
CDUD	Christlich-Demokratische Union Deutschlands (Christian Democratic Union of Germany)
CPSU	Communist Party of the Soviet Union
DBD	Demokratische Bauernpartei Deutschlands (Democratic Peasants' Party of Germany)
DEFA	Deutsche Film – AG (German film company = state-sponsored cinema)
DFD	Demokratischer Frauenbund Deutschlands (Democratic Women's League of Germany)
DSF	Gesellschaft für Deutsch–Sowjetische Freundschaft (Society for German–Soviet Friendship)
DVdI	Deutsche Verwaltung des Innern (German Administration of the Interior)
EDC	European Defence Community

List of abbreviations

EDG	Kleine Enzyklopädie Deutsche Geschichte (Short Encyclopedia of German History)
EKD	Evangelische Kirche in Deutschland (Evangelical Church in Germany)
EKU	Evangelische Kirche der Union (Evangelical Church of the Union)
FDGB	Freier Deutscher Gewerkschaftsbund (Free German Trade Union Association)
FDJ	Freie Deutsche Jugend (Free German Youth)
FDP	Freie Demokratische Partei (Free Democratic Party)
FRG	Federal Republic of Germany (West Germany)
GDR	German Democratic Republic (East Germany)
GG	*Geschichte und Gesellschaft* (*History and Society*)
GSSD	Gruppe der sowjetischen Streitkräfte in Deutschland (Group of Soviet Armed Forces in Germany)
GST	Gesellschaft für Sport and Technik (Society for Sport and Technology)
HA	Hauptabteilung (Main Department of the Stasi)
HVDVP	Hauptverwaltung der Deutschen Volkspolizei (Main Administration of the German People's Police)
IM	Inoffizieller Mitarbeiter (Unofficial collaborator with the Stasi)
KGB	Commissariat of State Security (Soviet Union)
KL	Kreisleitung (District Leadership)
KMS	Karl-Marx-Stadt (Chemnitz)
KPD	Kommunistische Partei Deutschlands (Communist Party of Germany)
KVP	Kasernierte Volkspolizei (People's Police in Barracks)
LAM	Landesarchiv Merseburg (State Archive, Merseburg)
LDP(D)	Liberal-Demokratische Partei Deutschlands (Liberal-Democratic Party of Germany)
LPA	Landesparteiarchiv (State Party Archive)
LPG	Landwirtschaftliche Produktionsgenossenschaft (Agricultural Production Co-operative)
MAS	Maschinen-Ausleih-Station (Machine Lending Station)
MfS	Ministerium für Staatssicherheit (Ministry of State Security or Stasi)
MTS	Maschinen-Traktoren-Station (Machine Tractor Station)
NATO	North Atlantic Treaty Organisation
NDPD	National-Demokratische Partei Deutschlands (National Democratic Party of Germany)
NKGB	People's Commissariat of State Security (Soviet Union)
NKVD	People's Commissariat of Internal Affairs (Soviet Union)
NÖS	Neues Ökonomisches System (New Economic System)
NPD	Nationaldemokratische Partei Deutschlands (National Democratic Party of Germany)

List of abbreviations

NVA	Nationale Volksarmee (National People's Army)
OibE	Offiziere im besonderen Einsatz (Officers on Special Assignment (Stasi))
PB	Politbüro (Political Office of the Central Committee)
PGH	Produktionsgenossenschaft des Handwerks (trade or production co-operative)
PID	Politisch-ideologische Diversion ('Political–ideological diversion')
RdB	Rat des Bezirkes (Regional Council)
RIAS	Radio in the American Sector
SAGs	Sowjetische Aktiengesellschaften (Soviet companies)
SAPMO	Stiftung Archiv der Parteien und Massenorganisationen der DDR (Archive Foundation of the Parties and Mass Organisations of the GDR)
SBZ	Sowjetische Besatzungszone (Soviet Occupation Zone)
SED	Sozialistische Einheitspartei Deutschlands (Socialist Unity Party of SfKF Staatssekretariat für Kirchenfragen (Ministry) of Church Affairs) Germany
SfKF	Staatssekretariat für Kirchenfragen (Ministry of Church Affairs)
SMAD	Sowjetische Militäradministration in Deutschland (Soviet Military Administration in Germany)
SPD	Sozialdemokratische Partei Deutschlands (Social Democratic Party of Germany)
SPK	Staatliche Plankommission (State Planning Commission)
SStAC	Sächsisches Staatsarchiv Chemnitz (Saxon State Archive, Chemnitz)
SStAL	Sächsisches Staatsarchiv Leipzig (Saxon State Archive, Leipzig)
ThHStAW	Thüringisches Hauptstaatsarchiv Weimar (Thuringian Main State Archive, Weimar)
VdgB	Vereinigung der gegenseitigen Bauernhilfe (Association for Mutual Peasant Aid)
VDK	Verband Deutscher Komponisten (Association of German Composers)
VEB	Volkseigener Betrieb (People's Own Factory)
VEG	Volkseigene Güter (People's Own Estates)
VELK	Vereinigte Evangelisch-Lutherische Kirche in Deutschland (United Evangelical Lutheran Church in Germany)
VVN	Vereinigung der Verfolgten des Naziregimes (Union of the Victims of the Nazi Regime)
ZA	Zentralarchiv (Central Archive)
ZAIG	Zentrale Auswertungs- und Informationsgruppe (Central Evaluation and Information Group)
ZfG	*Zeitschrift für Geschichtswissenschaft* (*Journal of Historical Science*)
ZK	Zentralkomitee (Central Committee)

1

Introduction

Patrick Major

With the fall of the Berlin Wall and the subsequent collapse of the German Democratic Republic (GDR), what was once the stuff of political science and area studies has become history. East Germany was a system which liked to generate paper, and officialdom reported on almost every aspect of its citizenry. As part of the reckoning with the defunct state, a flood of literature has appeared in Germany, currently eclipsing even that on the Third Reich.[1] Amid the many specialist monographs and case-studies a number of overviews have also begun to emerge, but often reaching radically different conclusions.[2] English-speaking historians have also been making important contributions to East German history, following Mary Fulbrook's pioneering lead.[3] It was decided to gather their findings in a single volume for a synthesis of recent work on political, social and cultural history, covering a quarter century of continuity and change. Most papers were heard at the Cardiff conference in 1999, sponsored by the German History Society; others were commissioned specially. What follows is a brief introduction to the main historical events and recent German debates for those new to the GDR, with suggestions for further reading from the growing German literature.

Postwar Allied Zones of Occupation in Germany were already agreed in 1944, but at the time observers did not realise that five years later the Soviet Zone would become a separate state, the GDR, confronting the Federal Republic (FRG) in the West. Everything pointed at first to provisionality. Unlike other eastern European states, which sooner or later became people's democracies, the Soviet Occupation Zone, or SBZ, inhabited a half-way position in Kremlin thinking. Considerable tensions existed between metropolitan decision-makers in Moscow, such as Beria, intent on mining Saxon uranium for a Soviet bomb, and later apparently prepared to do a deal over a united Germany, and military government officials such as Tiul'panov, propaganda chief in the SBZ. The latter has been seen as a champion of a viable eastern state, not to be crippled by 'smash-and-grab' reparations but strengthened as a bulwark of socialism. Others, like Semionov, the Political Adviser, mediated between all-German negotiators and hardliners. Indeed, policy on the ground cannot be understood without reference to the high politics of Moscow's Cold War. Although the very top levels of Soviet Communist Party (CPSU) decision-making are still rather murky, Soviet foreign policy is slowly coming to light.[4]

Research on the Soviet Military Administration (SMAD) itself has also been somewhat hampered by lack of access to Moscow's archives. Norman Naimark was among the first to view SMAD materials before renewed restrictions were applied, providing a good 'feel' for the Occupation.[5] A number of more institutional studies have also appeared, trying to reimpose order on the seemingly chaotic flood of SMAD decrees.[6] Most recently, G. P. Kynin and Jochen Laufer have been editing Russian-language editions of key documents.[7] These highlight how important reparations were to the Soviets, whose priority was economic exploitation of the SBZ, rather than political reconfiguration. The apparatus itself was labour-intensive and top-heavy, involving many departments, some overlapping in jurisdiction, ruling by a mixture of preferment and food parcels on the one hand, and the threat of arrest by the secret police from the People's Commissariat of Internal Affairs (NKVD) on the other. The quality of Occupation officers has been rated as high to indifferent. Some were cultured Germanophiles; others preferred to milk their personal fiefdoms.

According to the 1945 Potsdam Agreement, pending unification and a peace treaty, Germany would have no central government. The SBZ thus consisted of five *Länder* (later in the GDR fifteen *Bezirke*), carved out of central Prussia and Saxony, which never quite overcame their differences, while East Berlin technically belonged under the quadripartite control of all four Allies. Provincial administrations arose, with posts such as the interior usually in Communist hands, but often under non-Communist ministers-president. The Communist Party (KPD) was soon subsumed, however, alongside the Social Democrats within a united workers' party, the SED. The circumstances surrounding this merger in April 1946, whether forced from above by SMAD, or carried on a wave of Social Democratic Party (SPD)/KPD reconciliation in the wake of Nazi persecution, have generated heated debate.[8] Pursuing a bottom-up approach, as do many contributors in this volume, Gareth Pritchard has shown how disorientated rank-and-file members became in these disputes.[9] The newly opened archives have also allowed an inside view of the Stalinisation process of the late 1940s and 1950s, a time when even Politbüro leaders were purged prior to abortive show trials, but also grass-roots activists made way for younger apparatchiks.[10] Close examination of the rank-and-file reveals how undisciplined SED members could be. The mass influx in the mid-1940s had included many opportunists, who 'wavered' during crises such as 1953 or 1958–61. Indeed, one cannot draw a sharp dividing line between party and society

Introduction

when 10 per cent of the adult population were SED members, with one foot in the apparat and one in the community.

Unlike the one-party Soviet state, the SBZ professed to be a multi-party system, including Christian and Liberal Democrats (CDUD and LDPD), and from 1948 a Peasants' Party (DBD) and a National Democratic Party (NDPD) appealing to moderate ex-Nazis. All parties were linked from the summer of 1945 in a series of 'antifascist blocs', both at the centre and in the localities. It was clear from the outset, however, that the KPD/SED was determined to be the driving force, especially once its majority claims were exposed in the October 1946 local elections, the first and last such competitive polls. Thereafter, Communist power rested on the committee rather than the ballot. The National Front, which grew out of the blocs in 1949, became the basis for the single lists which confronted East German electors. Cubicles were provided, but use of them was frowned upon – the only choice for voters was to strike out names of unacceptable candidates. Non-voters, such as priests, were doorstepped and berated for their antistate behaviour. Meanwhile, representative 'western' democracy was disparaged by the SED in favour of a restless brand of popular democracy, but more often mobilised by the media than the masses. Besides the parties, a centralised trade union, the Free German Trade Union Association (FDGB), as well as a series of mass organisations, ensured that East German citizens were captured somewhere within the system.

Denazification in the SBZ was sweeping but short-lived. Certain sectors, such as education, witnessed mass removals, but despite the Marxist–Leninist diagnosis of fascism as the final, brutal expression of monopoly capitalism, not all entrepreneurs disappeared in 1945, showing a certain SMAD pragmatism, which left many of the details to German committees.[11] In 1948 the general purge was declared to be over. Yet, the blanket terms 'Nazis', 'militarists' and 'war criminals' covered a multitude of sins. Much interest has focused on the role of the SBZ's special internment camps, many of them former concentration camps.[12] The death rate among inmates, some genuine Nazis or alleged Hitler Youth 'werewolves', but also oppositional Social Democrats, was particularly high – around one-third. Although few of the visiting school parties to the memorials erected at Buchenwald or Sachsenhausen in the 1950s learned of their more recent reappropriation,[13] their taboo existence was later to tarnish the antifascist founding myth of the GDR.[14] Meanwhile, the GDR press lambasted the FRG as a state which had swept its Nazi past under the carpet.

What of conscious Sovietisation? Marxist–Leninists were supposed to believe that by altering the relations of production they could also create the 'socialist human being'. In the long term, perhaps; in 1945, however, Germany was so war-ravaged and filling with eastern refugees[15] that radical social engineering plans had to remain on the drawing-board. Under the additional geo-political constraints mentioned below, Sovietisation in one leap was deemed out of the question. Agitators thus spoke of 'antifascist-democratic recirculation', rather than revolution. The land reform of September 1945, which broke up the Junker estates concentrated in the north of the SBZ, is a case in point. This was decided by the Soviets in the late summer of 1945, much to the KPD's surprise, which had been primed when leaving Moscow that conditions were not yet ripe. Nor were some activists entirely happy with the type of change envisaged. Rather than Soviet-style collectivisation, the SMAD proposed dividing up the larger estates only, hoping to create a rural clientèle among smallholders and destitute refugees. For some Marxists this appeared to be creating a property-holding obstacle to socialism. In the event, smallholders and landless labourers were reluctant to follow KPD exhortations simply to seize land. It is also clear that there was considerable corruption on the ground, as local elites allocated prime land to themselves and their families, while leaving less fertile plots for newcomers.[16] Thus, the failure rate among new farmers from the East was correspondingly high, as they struggled without proper equipment to eke out an existence. Deprived of the bread basket of the lost eastern territories, all Occupation Zones suffered severe food shortages into the late 1940s, but only in 1958 was rationing lifted in the GDR.

Stalin is reputed to have told the exiled Polish leader Mikołajczyk that Communism would fit Germany like a saddle on a cow.[17] A saddle on a tractor would perhaps be more accurate. The SBZ was in places already heavily industrialised. Saxony, in the south, was the cradle of early textile manufacture. Leipzig and Dresden had become centres of machine-tool engineering. Saxony-Anhalt housed the massive chemical plants of Leuna and Buna and many of Berlin's industrial districts, too, including electrical subsidiaries of AEG and Siemens, lay in the East. Until 1954, the largest of these were run as SMAD enterprises, effectively producing reparations from current production for the devastated Soviet economy. More destructively, Moscow engaged in a rapacious dismantling programme, removing approximately 30 per cent of plant in the SBZ.[18] From the later 1950s, however, the GDR received substantial aid from the Soviet Union, in the form of raw materials, and by the 1970s was dependent on subsidised oil imports. What is clear, in the early years at least, was that Soviet interests overrode considerations of proletarian internationalism. Many of the decisions taken within the SBZ were reached for pragmatic 'imperial' gain rather than ideological correctness.

There were no blanket expropriations of factory-owners, although many spontaneously fled west in 1945. In 1946 plebiscites were held in Saxony to decide whether to nationalise the property of 'Nazis and war criminals', which produced a resounding 'yes' from three-quarters of the population. Out of these arose the 'People's Own Factories' or VEBs. A two-track economy emerged of state-owned factories and a private sector, with the state gradually starving competing enterprises of raw materials and labour.

Introduction

As Corey Ross has shown, however, even VEB functionaries had to work with the relics of the capitalist system. Many of them were themselves former white-collar middle-managers.[19] In related areas, such as self-employed small businesses, where one might have expected more antagonism, the state showed tolerance. It had to, since artisans were vital in supplying nationalised industry. Artisans were encouraged into trade co-operatives only fitfully over this period, until self-employment was effectively wound up in 1972, with damaging effects for the service sector.

For some observers, to borrow Stalin's own words, the SBZ appeared to be taking a 'zig-zag' course to socialism.[20] In 1946 German Communists had announced the 'special German road to socialism', bypassing the need for revolutionary upheaval. Later, when such autonomy appeared to be breeding national deviationism, exemplified by Moscow's rift with Tito's Yugoslavia in 1948, there was a reversion to a more strictly Soviet path. Yet, SED hopes in June of that year that a green light would be given to 'people's democratisation' proved premature, despite the breakdown of Cold War relations over the Berlin blockade.[21] Only in October 1949, after the proclamation of the FRG in May, did the SBZ take tentative steps towards becoming a separate state.[22] This gradualism, enforced by political calculation, but also material circumstance, clearly frustrated the SED's main leader, Ulbricht, who was always keen to force the pace of transformation. The official 'construction of socialism' thus hung fire until 1952, when Stalin seems finally to have given up on a unification deal with the western Allies.

The subsequent emphasis on capital goods, as well as the burden of rearmament, had disastrous effects on the still fragile consumer sector; so much so that as tensions mounted in the spring of 1953, the new post-Stalinist leadership in Moscow intervened to slow the pace, instigating the so-called 'New Course'.[23] Too late, of course, to avert the uprising of June 1953, one of the traditionally key moments in GDR history, attracting its own new research.[24] However inchoate and chaotic this event was, when half a million workers struck across the GDR, it signalled the limits of SED control. Originating in discontent among workers at having to shoulder the main burden of the construction of socialism, as well as a general supply crisis, it soon took on political overtones as demonstrators demanded free elections and even the overthrow of the SED. In the West this became the symbolic cry for freedom of an oppressed people. Whether in the East it constituted the 'inner founding of the state', as Ilko-Sascha Kowalczuk claims, close study of events reveals extremely diffuse dissent, bound only by immense resentment of the SED, as Pritchard demonstrates in Chapter 7 of this volume in the case of Saxony. Thereafter, party and trade union functionaries approached the revision of work norms with the utmost trepidation, entering an unspoken social contract which fatally undermined later attempts at rationalisation.[25]

From 1955, when the Soviet Control Commission (successor to the SMAD) was wound up, Moscow monitored rather than dictated SED decision-making. Ulbricht had already effectively abandoned the New Course, but in 1958 he pledged the GDR to overtake West German *per capita* consumer production by 1961, a miniature version of Khrushchev's race with the USA. Much of this overoptimism was based on recent successes in space, but Moscow soon realised that the price of such grandiose schemes was unaffordable subsidies to the GDR. Considerable CPSU–SED tensions simmered beneath the surface, as Peter Grieder has demonstrated.[26] For superpower-political reasons, the USSR, after much sound and fury, often chose the path of least resistance. When Ulbricht took Khrushchev at his word following his 1958 ultimatum to the western powers to vacate West Berlin – while in fact the Kremlin leader was more interested in ulterior goals – the crisis threatened to get out of control. Rather than go over the brink, Moscow sanctioned a compromise solution: the Berlin Wall. With GDR labour resources stabilised, subsidies could be reduced, and rather than forcing the West to sign up to *de jure* GDR recognition, Khrushchev was right in thinking that this would occur gradually and *de facto*.[27]

These were the larger political and economic frameworks of change. The contours were, of course, already familiar before 1989, but subsequent research has filled in many gaps in individual case-studies of the so-called 'transmission belts' between state and society. What was not so well known was how these macro-political and economic developments affected 'ordinary' East Germans. Already in the 1980s there had been moves in West Germany to write an 'everyday history' (*Alltagsgeschichte*) of the Kaiserreich and Third Reich, as Fulbrook discusses in Chapter 16 of this volume. This was an attempt to break away from 'structural' social history and systems analysis, which had concentrated on secular trends and aggregate data, not wholly dissimilar to East German social scientists' statistical preoccupations. A more refined historical sociology has, of course, continued after 1989 and is important in gauging change over the whole 45–year period of the SBZ/GDR.[28] Models of hierarchy, as well as the creation of generational cohorts, based on representative interviews, are fundamental to this approach. The danger of some 'system-immanent' interpretations, however, is that while yielding extremely interesting insights into political intentions, they are often contradicted by the evidence of social reality – for instance, Sigrid Meuschel's model of a 'de-differentiating' GDR society.[29] The cleavages may have cut different ways, but as the contributions in this volume indicate, society was still riven by preferment and resentment. Yet, everyday history does not have to be history with the politics left out. In heavily politicised systems, such as the Third Reich and GDR, even the most banal actions, such as listening to popular music, could become ideological battlegrounds, as Michael Rauhut and Uta Poiger have shown for rock'n'roll and jazz, and Toby Thacker demonstrates for dance music in Chapter 13 of this volume.[30] The everyday Cold War was every bit as real as what went on in the Kremlin or the Pentagon. This is not a plea for a new unilateralism, but an integrated approach, history from above *and* below, which is beginning to emerge.[31]

For the former GDR we are in the fortunate position that the state itself was interested in gauging the public mood. This was partly a security matter, but also a didactic measure. The SED, like the bloc parties, collected so-called 'opinion reports' (*Stimmungsberichte*). Several contributors in the volume have used these; indeed, Mark Allinson has made a case-study of them in Erfurt and discusses their merits in Chapter 6 in this volume.[32] Controversies have arisen in subsequent source-readings by historians. Armin Mitter and Stefan Wolle's pioneering *Untergang auf Raten* made heavy use of them, but their teleological view of the road to 1989 perhaps obscured an otherwise valuable methodology.[33] Allinson's conclusions, on the other hand, emphasise the frequently ignored passive majority. The Ministry of State Security (MfS, or Stasi), also reported on the population. In 1953 its Central Evaluation and Information Group (ZAIG) was formed, covering first the factories, but then the population at large. Arguably its reports provided a less ideologically hedged view. So far, these non-operational Stasi sources have not been properly tapped, as research into the secret police has tended to focus on the Ministry itself,[34] or the more lurid espionage networks in the FRG. Given the close relationship between police and society, between case-officer and informant, this should prove a fertile area. In the present volume, we have contributions on both Volkspolizei and Stasi, from Richard Bessel and Jens Gieseke (Chapters 4 and 3 in this volume), who show that, as well as being instruments of control, the police viewed themselves as proactive 'social workers', improving the citizenry, while becoming unwittingly corrupted in the process.

Besides regular mood reports, from the 1960s the ideological commissions of the regional parties also produced 'consciousness analyses'. These served as progress reports along the road to socialism, but also revealed the petty gripes undermining the confidence of the public. Indeed, it is a truism of societies in the Eastern bloc that, while the general idea of socialism was usually held to be a 'good thing', it was constantly undermined by the rather more grimy reality. GDR citizens became adept at double-think, articulating support in public, but moaning in private. The state did offer some public channels for complaint, such as petitions (*Eingaben*), which have aroused interest as an index of long-term opinion in the GDR, but also as the nexus of citizen–functionary discourse.[35] Petitioners appropriated the language of the party to lend weight to entreaties, while the recipients often dispensed lessons in socialism. As well as these sources, from 1964 the SED sponsored its own demoscopic research by the Institut für Meinungsforschung.[36] Its founder, the former interior minister, Karl Maron, carefully distanced its tasks from those of commercial market research in the West. Yet, the party was keen to know the populace's thoughts on a number of issues, such as the German question, work-experience and leisure. Although questions were often skewed to elicit specific responses, and some respondents were clearly trying to please, a differentiation between certain groupings is possible. Women tended to remain more apolitical; youth and workers were often more outspoken; while the intelligentsia were most publicly conformist.[37]

In such a recently demised state there is also the possibility of interviewing its former citizens. Oral histories began even before the GDR's collapse, when a group of West German historians were unusually granted permission to interview East Germans in the industrial south.[38] Since then, surprisingly few oral histories have emerged, despite personal biography's evident importance in determining attitudes to socialism. After so much change in such rapid succession, the ghosts of the past still loomed large. Many could remember the Kaiserreich and Weimar, and most the Third Reich. The new regime complained constantly about 'bourgeois' carry-overs from capitalism. The antifascist experience had deeply marked those who had suffered Nazi persecution, but some of the 'Hitler Youth generation', too, were seeking a new vocation, while others had become permanently depoliticised.[39] Those expelled from the lost eastern territories, 23 per cent of the population by 1950, tended to be particularly anticommunist. It is also evident that personal circumstances, whether one had relatives in the West for instance, were important in determining who fled the GDR (see Patrick Major's Chapter 11 of this volume). For those born into the system, however, there was little against which to compare life under 'real existing socialism', especially once the Berlin Wall went up in 1961.

Despite attempts at a negative integration in the face of the West German 'other' beyond the Elbe, the cosy phrase 'hier bei uns' ('here with us'), regularly intoned by officials, always rang somewhat hollow. Equally doggedly, agitators tried to encourage the mental break from the individualist 'me' to the collectivist 'we'. Citizens certainly formed communities of interest, in the work-brigade, on the farm collective, in the school corridor, but often in spite, rather than because, of socialism. An identity arose by default of long-suffering resignation, in which GDR citizens became the butt of their own political jokes. The neo-absolutist state, as Fulbrook labels it in Chapter 16 of this volume, also generated its own Potemkin villages. When the state leadership visited the trawlermen of Rostock, for instance, the men, under pressure from local functionaries, worked around the clock to repaint their rusting vessels. When it became clear that they did not have enough time, or paint, to finish the job, a pragmatic but absurd solution was found – to paint them, but only on the landward side.[40] Out of public view, the ships, like their sailors, told a rather different story. If there is an ethos to the current volume, it is to present both halves of this history, from above and below, public and private.

The GDR authorities also liked to talk of the Workers' and Peasants' State. The initial state emblem of 1950 depicted a hammer-and-wheatsheaf symbol, uniting factory and countryside.[41] Considering that workers were the state's central reference-point, in theory if more than practice, research on them has been relatively slow to develop. Peter Hübner's was among the first systematic shopfloor examinations, tracing the simmering conflicts and standoffs over norms and premiums which continued under the planned economy.[42] Until the building of the Wall, another option for some 50,000 workers was to commute daily to 'enemy' West Berlin. But did such behaviour represent an anticommunist stand or a subconscious continuation of anticapitalist *Eigensinn* (loosely translated, 'self-interest'), which had always viewed job-changing or pilfering as legitimate? Considerable attention has been paid to the work-brigade, that militarised smallest unit of production of around a dozen workers. For some, the brigades were extensions of the rationalising goals of the state collective; for others they were an autonomous expression of worker voluntarism. Histories from below reveal that they could be both. The illegal, but regular strikes risked in this period often grew out of brigade solidarity, but then nor were selective status rewards – activist medals and citations – wholly unsuccessful. Yet, this currency was soon debased. Any visit to a flea market in the 1990s revealed trayfuls of unloved lapel pins and badges.

Initially, farmers were less tractable. Lindenberger's work on the rural Volkspolizei demonstrates how local communities could cold-shoulder village constables.[43] Bauerkämper also stresses the pre-1945 continuities on the land. Although peasants were a supposed ally in the 'anti-fascist–democratic recirculation', SED members were all too aware that in the 1930s the central German countryside had been an NSDAP (Nazi Party) bastion. Former Nazi officials still lived in their villages, sometimes as mayor. Change was on the horizon, however, as Jonathan Osmond shows in Chapter 8 of this volume.[44] Although the land reform had preserved private property, in 1952 the SED moved seriously towards collectivisation. In the first line-of-fire were so-called *Großbauern*, the kulaks of the GDR. The numbers fleeing to the West in 1952–53 convinced the authorities, nevertheless, to keep Agricultural Production Co-operatives (LPGs) voluntary. In the meantime the state attempted to popularise itself by establishing tractor stations and village launderettes, although Germany's long-term flight from the land continued unabated, as rural sons and daughters sought more remunerative employment in industry. Collectivisation took a quantum leap in 1960, however, when it was pushed through, on paper at least, during the so-called 'socialist spring in the countryside'. This was clearly unpopular among many farmers at the time, who complained of being railroaded by the SED, although it was nothing like the violent experiment of thirty years before in the USSR. Indeed, agrarian policy might be counted one of the few successes of the GDR.

In the countryside, but elsewhere too, adult GDR society was predominantly female, a demographic legacy of war. Women often had to keep farms going under the most difficult circumstances. A particularly taboo subject throughout the GDR was the mass rapes by Soviet troops, which persisted for years while commanding officers turned a blind eye.[45] The result was deep resentment and low SED support among women. Although abortion was permitted in the 1940s, a radical change from Nazi eugenics policy, in 1950 the GDR banned it in the interests of rebuilding the shrinking population. Not until 1972 was it relegalised, only to fall victim to reunification in 1990. As Harsch shows here, emancipation for East German women was a contradictory experience. Unlike their West German counterparts, they were expected to work. In the 1940s they had no choice, with 'rubble women' forced to pitch in, as everywhere in Germany. Especially in the 1960s, however, as the labour market shrank, women were encouraged into skilled jobs, incurring a dual burden of work and family. Women workers often had to knock off early to beat the ubiquitous queues for the shops, and despite the introduction of all-day creches and public awareness campaigns showing men changing nappies and performing household chores, a certain proletarian machismo persisted.

Although there will continue to be debate on how far upward mobility for women extended – one obstacle was the SED's insistence on military training for leading cadres – there is no doubt that the GDR did create new functional elites. Workers became party officials; students graduated from an expanded education sector, including 'worker and peasant faculties'. These new opportunities evidently created loyalties among those elevated. They also created tensions, as Weimar-vintage labour activists felt themselves being supplanted by better-educated youngsters, often without the passion or experience of antifascism. The so-called 'old intelligentsia', the professional caste of an educational bourgeoisie, also felt under threat from new cadres.[46] These fears proved unfounded, however, even among former Nazis. The GDR presented itself as the high-tech brains of the Eastern bloc.[47] When the state emblem was finalised in 1951, it included a pair of architect's dividers. Engineers became the metaphor for reconstruction society.[48] In the 1950s, however, the lure of the West was often stronger. With the open border it was relatively easy for professionals to find higher-paid employment in the FRG, a process repeated in 1989–90 during the GDR's collapse. The SED consequently got into the habit of concessionary policies, placating elites with high salaries and naturalia, even behind the Wall.[49] Meanwhile, in the face of such privilege, the term Workers' and Peasants' State rang ever more hollow for genuine manual labourers.

Another group which has attracted a level of research disproportionate to its size, are the churches. Gerhard Besier's revelations about Stasi infiltration initially led to a corruption debate.[50] Attempts to preserve its autonomy as a 'church within socialism', while also linked with West German institutions (before splitting in 1969), certainly led the Protestant church into a series of compromises with the state. Merrilyn Thomas shows in Chapter 12 of this volume the lengths to which the SED would go to manipulate the church

Introduction

from behind the scenes. However, grass-roots studies of local 'troublesome priests' counter too cosy an impression of church–state relations. One focus has been the miniature *Kulturkampf* following the introduction of a secular confirmation ceremony, the *Jugendweihe*, in 1954. The period witnessed liturgical experiments, as trendy vicars launched evangelist blues masses and from 1964 supported conscientious objection. Peace propaganda, although used as an SED lever to prise the churches away from the West in the 1950s, later rebounded, when widespread third-way pacifism spread behind church portals. By the 1980s the church hierarchy was fighting a war on two fronts between the regime and its own activist parishioners, who were instrumental in the revolution of 1989.

Society changed considerably in the 1960s, not simply because of the Wall. Considerable attention has been paid to the New Economic System (NÖS), adopted in 1963, but partly dismantled later in the 1960s, then fully repudiated by Ulbricht's successor, Honecker, in 1971.[51] Enterprises were encouraged to make profits and a limited decentralisation was countenanced. Ulbricht became a proselytiser for the technological revolution, and it was in the 1960s that the seeds were sown for the later, much-contested computerisation programme. These bold experiments were not without their problems. In 1970 the GDR economy experienced serious breakdowns, encouraging a faction around Honecker to depose Ulbricht in 1971. The new leader subsequently never departed from his more populist 'unity of economic and social policy', whose subsidies by the 1980s – when a tram ticket still cost what it had in 1945! – had turned the GDR into a western loan-junkie.[52]

On the consumer side there were conscious attempts at modernisation in the 1960s and life was perhaps not quite as gloomy as many westerners liked to believe, fixated as they were on externalities such as the Wall. An exhibition in 1996 revealed a system paying more attention to product design, experimenting with self-service supermarkets and fashion clothing.[53] After 1963, once the acute food shortages of the 1950s were over, the Ministry of Supply was keen to develop alternatives to beef and pork. Highstreets sprouted fish bars and the 'Goldbroiler', the GDR's answer to Kentucky Fried Chicken. Although the GDR was anticapitalist, it still advertised products, the results of which have been re-examined, not without a certain postmodern glee.[54] Nevertheless, many of these innovations were left in suspended animation. Packaging which would not have been out of place in the FRG in the early 1960s, looked distinctly antiquated by 1989.[55] Some of this interest in material culture has undoubtedly also been riding the wave of 'Ostalgie' – nostalgia for the East – which resulted in a retro-cult in the 1990s, including several tongue-in-cheek board-games, recreating the authentic 'Ost' experience. Yet, accusations that the everyday history of the GDR necessarily trivialises it are often misplaced. Katherine Pence's work on shopping reveals how retailing was used as a form of propaganda.

Shopwindows became miniature displays for socialism.[56] Yet Jonathan Zatlin's research on the Trabant car, *the* chronic shortage good, exposes the party's ultimately futile contortions in trying to square demand with socialist distributive justice.[57] Opinion reports show an abiding awareness of the comparative prices of products in the 'Golden West', as it was ironically referred to, which was to prove crucial in the dissolution of the GDR in 1990.[58]

Before the *Wende* or 'turn' of 1989 GDR studies were very much the preserve of literary and film scholars. 'Histories' were relatively few and far between.[59] As the limits of archive-only research become apparent, however, there has been renewed interest in combining previously hidden histories with the public culture of the GDR. Now it is possible to view the mechanisms of censorship alongside the texts which did make it through (and those which did not). Simone Barck, Martina Langermann and Siegfried Lokatis have been pioneering in this regard.[60] The Stasi was also heavily involved in monitoring the GDR's writers.[61] Christa Wolf, the staple of GDR reading-lists, cannot be read in quite the same light after the revelation of her conversations with the Stasi in the 1960s. Literary scholars would do well to contextualise their studies with the abundant material from the Academy of Arts and the Ministry of Culture archives. Likewise, historians are to be encouraged to re-examine the public texts of the GDR, as a number have already begun to do.[62] Stefan Berger and Heiko Feldner in Chapters 14 and 15 of this volume reassess SED historiography, arguing that even in this most heavily circumscribed area of official writing, historians were still writing within nationalist and rationalist traditions. The censor's blue pencil cannot explain all of the GDR's discourses.

Of course, high culture is not all culture. Although initially hostile to what it perceived as Americanised 'unculture', SED agitprop functionaries soon realised that popular music and comics could capture a mass audience. The homegrown comic *Mosaik* showed the antics of the Digedags as they travelled through history, helping to liberate Roman slaves, but also travelling to the distant world of Neos, which bore remarkable similarities to an idealised GDR.[63] Nevertheless, the constant runs-in with the censor showed that the authorities always felt they were playing with fire.[64] Besides the use of its state-sponsored cinema, DEFA,[65] the Ministry of Culture also tried to liven up television programmes. Although viewers could not vegetate in front of the same glitzy game-shows as in the West, there were talent contests and music programmes, clearly designed as entertainment. The insatiable German appetite for 'Krimis' was catered for by the detective drama 'Polizeiruf 110', in which Volkspolizisten reasoned with wrongdoers rather than just shooting them. Primitive consumer programmes also existed, although their function was as much to mask as to expose difficulties.[66] In the mid-1960s, as Mark Fenemore shows in Chapter 10 of this volume, there were also experiments with 'beat' music, with the state record label even issuing Beatles singles. By the early 1970s, it was acceptable to depict long hair and hedonism on the cinema screen. The 1973 film 'The Legend of Paul and Paula', including scenes of nudity, and a soundtrack by the country's most popular band, the Puhdys, became the GDR's all-time box-office hit.

Other areas of popular culture which the regime attempted to influence to its advantage were the space race and technology. Retrospectively, it is hard to think of the GDR as cutting-edge, but when Sputnik was launched in 1957, followed by Moon probes and a manned orbit in 1961, the East German media went into a frenzy of diagrams and dialectics to demonstrate socialist, and by extension military, superiority. Keen work-brigades launched 'rockets', cardboard cutouts paraded around the shopfloor, with 'stages' for colleagues to sign up to. In 1963 Gagarin and Tereshkova were feted in the GDR as stars, and astronomy became a fixed part of the school curriculum.[67] GDR science fiction also flourished. 'Utopian novels' were perfect vehicles for future scenarios, and in contrast to 'nihilistic' western science fiction, depicted a brighter future, although by the mid-1960s even this optimism began to disintegrate. Dystopian visions of environmental disaster emerged in the 1970s, as well as not-so-subtle allegories on 'Harmonopolis'.[68]

Sport was another area where state and society met and sometimes collided. Although official organisations such as the Free German Youth (FDJ) and Society for Sport and Technology hoped to use the sportsfield as a recruiting ground, it was into high-performance sport that the GDR channelled its resources. It is often forgotten that in the 1950s and early 1960s the two Germanies competed in the Olympics as a single team. Only in 1968, at Mexico, did the final rift occur.[69] Nevertheless, even before this the media would list medals in separate tables, east and west. Stars of track and field, such as racing cyclist Täve Schur or ice-skater Katarina Witt, became household GDR names. In spite, or perhaps because, of the doping scandals revealed after 1989, many have been appropriated by former West Germans, as victims of the Cold War, but also as winners. Adorning the cover of one Sydney Olympics 2000 companion was former GDR long-jumper and gold-medalist, Heike Drechsler. Only on the football pitch did the GDR fail to match up to the West, except for a rogue 1–0 victory over the FRG in the 1974 World Cup.[70]

Nevertheless, GDR citizens also developed their own leisure interests, independent of both western influences over the airwaves or official fare. Günter Gaus famously talked of the 'niche society', in which private spaces persisted.[71] Some recent anthropological studies have examined the popularity of naturism – during the 750th anniversary of Berlin a nudist float paraded past the party podium to Honecker's evident delight[72] – as well as the cultivation of the allotment garden. DIY became a major pastime, as homebuilders 'organised' material to improve their homes. Mushroom-picking and preserve-making became necessary skills, with endless magazine tips on how to do more with less. Possibly, this latter-day hunter-gathering bred slightly fewer couch potatoes than in the West; certainly, it created communities of interest. Word-of-mouth and personal connections became vital in acquiring 'stoop goods' (*Bückwaren*, so named because the shopkeeper had to stoop to fetch them from under the counter).[73] Nevertheless, the contingential nature of these networks was revealed by the rapidity with which they collapsed in 1990, at the onset of the cash culture.

As the various perspectives in this volume make plain, 'ordinary' East Germans were affected by the high politics of superpower conflict to a degree perhaps matched only in Cold War Korea or Vietnam. Likewise, the East German state was present in the everyday lives of its citizens to an extent inconceivable in postindustrial western societies retreating into the private sphere. Maier has spoken of the 'contaminatory state', which replicated relations of domination far down the social hierarchy.[74] Yet, besides a 'statification' of society, some commentators have pointed to a 'socialisation' of the state.[75] It was a relationship which worked both ways. Moreover, not all subcultural legacies were positive. Swastika graffiti were widespread in the 1950s and a skinhead scene was already developing in the 1980s which is now causing much alarm in the Berlin Republic of the early twenty-first century. A heavy drinking culture was also rife, and left a high incidence of eastern alcoholism after 1990.[76]

Mixing schnapps with beer might be seen as a Russian legacy; alternatively, it might simply be a north German proclivity. This is the dilemma for the historian of the GDR, trying to tease apart continuities and breaks, as well as deciding what was a genuine Soviet import, and what was 'made in Germany'. To fellow Eastern European states, the GDR appeared in some ways more Russian than the Russians. To western visitors, it seemed more authentically 'German' than the Americanised FRG. Quite clearly, some of the political structures, such as the internal make-up of the SED from 1949, were heavily borrowed from the CPSU. The Stasi, as Gieseke shows, was also a close copy of the KGB (Soviet secret police). Yet, this was not a formal one-party state. In the economy there were certainly five-year plans and work-to-norms, but as the reforms of the 1960s show, the GDR was prepared to show the way to its senior partner, much to Brezhnev's irritation. More problematic is the assessment of the Sovietisation of society at large.[77] This is a debate already familiar from the 'Americanisation' of western Germany, which was by no means America writ small. East Germans were undoubtedly even less receptive to Soviet influences, partly as a legacy of Nazi propaganda, but also because of real Stalinist violence. 'High' Russian culture, as exemplified by Pushkin or Dostoevsky, was only a minority interest. More populist cultural approaches, such as the epic war film, also failed to overcome the basic problem: that Russia had won and Germany lost. When the film 'Battle for Germany' was shown to sixth-formers in Meissen in 1963, it was disrupted by whistles, boos and even an alarm clock.[78]

By the 1950s the governmental face of Communism was German not Russian. The SED became the public voice, speaking a language attuned to German ears. As Corey Ross demonstrates in Chapter 5 in this volume, military terminology was widespread in public discourse. The Berlin Wall, or 'Antifascist Defence Rampart', was justified for maintaining order and keeping decadence at bay. In its sexual prudery, too, the party's petit-bourgeois moralising struck a chord with 1950s' reconstruction society, searching for security. Whether this is peculiarly German is open to debate, but it is instructive that officials felt the need to invoke secondary virtues such as cleanliness in defence of their 'big idea' of socialism. Even after the German question had effectively lapsed, SED leaders still appropriated traditional German values, while West Germany supposedly fell victim to American 'unculture'. In many cases it was as much about modernity as Americanism. In a famous 'storm in a coffee-cup', Ulbricht criticised the modernism of crockery from the GDR's design institute, arguing – probably correctly – that German workers preferred to drink from more Biedermeier ware.[79]

As the SED experimented with consumer socialism, however, society was afflicted by the same late-industrial problems as the West. Workers wanted a shorter working week; women juggled careers with families; youths, disenchanted with industrial routine, revelled in the electrified 'sound' of the 1960s or vandalised their neighbourhoods. Ulbricht himself was perhaps perceptive enough to realise these tendencies, attempting a 'flight forward' into the technological revolution, believing that socialism needed modernisation to win the Cold War. But, like the sorcerer's apprentice, the 'Great Magician', as one thinly-veiled allegory painted the SED leader, had unleashed forces which the Communist regime could scarcely control in the longer term.[80] The Workers' and Peasants' State increasingly lost touch with many of those who had been prepared to give it the benefit of the doubt in 1949. By the 1960s the Functionaries' State was firmly established. The antifascist founding myth struck ever fewer chords with the younger generation. Yet only gradually, in the 1980s, did the beginnings of a civil society evolve in the uncomfortable space between state and populace, which was able to challenge and ultimately to defeat Communism in the only genuinely mass movement of the GDR's history, the 'gentle revolution' of 1989.

Notes

1 For researchers and archives see Ulrich Mählert, *Vademekum der DDR-Forschung* (Bonn, 1999). Although there is no thirty-year rule for GDR material, most current research is on the 1950s and 1960s, hence our timespan. The only current overview of the 1970s and 1980s is: Stefan Wolle, *Die heile Welt der Diktatur: Alltag und Herrschaft in der DDR, 1971–1989* (Berlin, 1998).

2 Dietrich Staritz, *Geschichte der DDR* (2nd edn; Frankfurt/Main, 1996); Klaus

Schroeder, *Der SED-Staat: Geschichte und Strukturen der DDR* (Munich, 1998); Wolfgang Engler, *Die Ostdeutschen: Kunde von einem verlorenen Land* (Berlin, 1999).
3 Mary Fulbrook, *Anatomy of a Dictatorship: Inside the GDR 1949–1989* (Oxford, 1995).
4 Wilfried Loth, *Stalin's Unwanted Child: The Soviet Union, the German Question and the Founding of the GDR* (Basingstoke, 1998); Hope M. Harrison, 'The bargaining power of weaker allies in bipolarity and crisis: Soviet–East German relations, 1953–1961' (PhD, Columbia, 1993).
5 Norman M. Naimark, *The Russians in Germany: A History of the Soviet Zone of Occupation, 1945–1949* (Cambridge, Mass., 1995).
6 Stefan Creuzberger, *Die sowjetische Besatzungsmacht und das politische System der SBZ* (Weimar, 1996); Jan Foitzik, *Sowjetische Militäradministration in Deutschland (SMAD) 1945–1949* (Berlin, 1999).
7 G. P. Kynin and Jochen Laufer, *SSSR i germanskij vopros 1941–1949: dokumenty iz Archiva vnesnej politiki Rossijskoj Federacii* (Moscow, 1996 ff.).
8 Andreas Malycha, *Auf dem Weg zur SED: Die Sozialdemokratie und die Bildung einer Einheitspartei in den Ländern der SBZ* (Bonn, 1995); Norbert Podewin and Manfred Teresiak, *Brüder, in eins nun die Hände . . . : Das Für und Wider um die Einheitspartei in Berlin* (Berlin, 1996).
9 Gareth Pritchard, *The Making of the GDR, 1945–53: From Antifascism to Stalinism* (Manchester, 2000), Ch. 5.
10 Andreas Malycha, *Partei von Stalins Gnaden?: Die Entwicklung der SED zur Partei neuen Typs in den Jahren 1946 bis 1950* (Berlin, 1996); Andreas Malycha, *Die SED: Geschichte ihrer Stalinisierung 1946–1953* (Paderborn, 2000); Harold Hurwitz, *Die Stalinisierung der SED* (Opladen, 1997).
11 Helga Welsh, *Revolutionärer Wandel auf Befehl?: Entnazifizierungs- und Personalpolitik in Thüringen und Sachsen (1945–1948)* (Munich, 1989); Manfred Wille, *Entnazifizierung in der Sowjetischen Besatzungszone Deutschlands 1945 bis 1948* (Magdeburg, 1993); Olaf Kappelt, *Die Entnazifizierung in der SBZ* (Hamburg, 1997); Damian von Melis, *Entnazifizierung in Mecklenburg-Vorpommern: Herrschaft und Verwaltung 1945–1948* (Munich, 1999); Timothy Vogt, *Denazification in Soviet-Occupied Germany: Brandenburg, 1945–1948* (Cambridge, Mass., 2000).
12 Sergej Mironenko et al. (eds), *Sowjetische Speziallager in Deutschland 1945 bis 1950* (2 vols; Berlin, 1996); Peter Reif-Spirek and Bodo Ritscher (eds), *Speziallager in der SBZ: Gedenkstätten mit 'doppelter Vergangenheit'* (Berlin, 1999).
13 Manfred Overesch, *Buchenwald und die DDR* (Göttingen, 1995).
14 Raina Zimmering, *Mythen in der Politik der DDR* (Opladen, 2000).
15 Alexander von Plato and Wolfgang Meinicke, *Alte Heimat – neue Zeit: Flüchtlinge, Umgesiedelte, Vertriebene in der Sowjetischen Besatzungszone und in der DDR* (Berlin, 1991); Stefan Donth, *Vertriebene und Flüchtlinge in Sachsen 1945 bis 1952* (Cologne, 2000).
16 Arnd Bauerkämper (ed.), *Junkerland in Bauernhand?: Durchführung, Auswirkungen und Stellenwert der Bodenreform in der Sowjetischen Besatzungszone* (Stuttgart, 1996).
17 Anne McElvoy, *The Saddled Cow: East Germany's Life and Legacy* (London, 1992).
18 Rainer Karlsch, *Allein bezahlt?: Die Reparationsleistungen der SBZ/DDR 1945–1953* (Berlin, 1993).

19 Corey Ross, *Constructing Socialism at the Grass-Roots: The Transformation of East Germany, 1945–1965* (Basingstoke, 2000).
20 Rolf Badstübner and Wilfried Loth (eds), *Wilhelm Pieck: Aufzeichnungen zur Deutschlandpolitik 1945–1953* (Berlin, 1994), 260.
21 Thomas Friedrich (ed.), *Entscheidungen der SED 1948* (Berlin, 1997).
22 Elke Scherstjanoi (ed.), *Provisorium für längstens ein Jahr* (Berlin, 1993).
23 Christoph Kleßmann and Bernd Stöver (eds), *1953: Krisenjahr des Kalten Krieges in Europa* (Cologne, 1999).
24 Torsten Diedrich, *Der 17. Juni in der DDR* (Berlin, 1991); Manfred Hagen, *DDR – Juni '53: Die erste Volkserhebung im Stalinismus* (Stuttgart, 1992); Ilko-Sascha Kowalczuk et al. (eds), *Der Tag X: 17. Juni 1953* (Berlin, 1995); Heidi Roth, *Der 17. Juni in Sachsen* (Cologne, 1999).
25 Jeffrey Kopstein, *The Politics of Economic Decline in East Germany, 1945–1989* (Chapel Hill, 1997).
26 Peter Grieder, *The East German Leadership, 1946–1973* (Manchester, 1999).
27 Michael Lemke, *Die Berlinkrise 1958 bis 1963* (Berlin, 1995).
28 Johannes Huinink et al., *Kollektiv and Eigensinn: Lebensläufe in der DDR und danach* (Berlin, 1995); Rainer Zoll (ed.), *Ostdeutsche Biographien* (Frankfurt/Main, 1999).
29 Sigrid Meuschel, *Legitimation und Parteiherrschaft: Zum Paradox von Stabilität und Revolution in der DDR 1945–1989* (Frankfurt/Main, 1992).
30 Michael Rauhut, *Beat in der Grauzone: DDR-Rock 1964 bis 1972* (Berlin, 1993); Uta G. Poiger, *Jazz, Rock and Rebels: Cold War Politics and American Culture in a Divided Germany* (Berkeley, Cal., 2000).
31 Hartmut Kaelble et al. (eds), *Sozialgeschichte der DDR* (Stuttgart, 1994); Richard Bessel and Ralph Jessen (eds), *Die Grenzen der Diktatur: Staat und Gesellschaft in der DDR* (Göttingen, 1996); Thomas Lindenberger (ed.), *Herrschaft und Eigen-Sinn in der Diktatur: Studien zur Gesellschaftsgeschichte der DDR* (Cologne, 1999); Konrad Jarausch (ed.), *Dictatorship as Experience: Towards a Socio-Cultural History of the GDR* (New York, 1999).
32 Mark Allinson, *Politics and Popular Opinion in East Germany 1945–68* (Manchester, 2000).
33 Armin Mitter and Stefan Wolle, *Untergang auf Raten: Unbekannte Kapitel der DDR-Geschichte* (Munich, 1993).
34 Jens Gieseke, *Die hauptamtlichen Mitarbeiter der Staatssicherheit: Personalstruktur und Lebenswelt, 1950–1989/90* (Berlin, 2000).
35 Jonathan R. Zatlin, 'Ausgaben und Eingaben: Das Petitionsrecht und der Untergang der DDR', *Zeitschrift für Geschichtswissenschaft*, 45 (1997).
36 Heinz Niemann, *Meinungsforschung in der DDR* (Cologne, 1993); Heinz Niemann, *Hinterm Zaun: Politische Kultur und Meinungsforschung in der DDR* (Berlin, 1995).
37 Walter Friedrich et al., *Das Zentralinstitut für Jugendforschung Leipzig, 1966–1990* (Berlin, 1999).
38 Lutz Niethammer et al., *Die volkseigene Erfahrung: Eine Archäologie des Lebens in der Industrieprovinz der DDR* (Berlin, 1991).
39 Ulrich Mählert, *Die Freie Deutsche Jugend 1945–1949* (Paderborn, 1995).
40 Landolf Scherzer, *Fänger und Gefangene* (East Berlin, 1983), 46.
41 Harry D. Schurdel, 'Hoheitssymbole der Deutschen Demokratischen Republik', in Dieter Vorsteher (ed.), *Parteiauftrag – ein neues Deutschland: Bilder, Rituale und Symbole der frühen DDR* (Munich, 1997), 44–62.

42 Peter Hübner, *Konsens, Konflikt und Kompromiß: Soziale Arbeiterinteressen und Sozialpolitik in der SBZ/DDR 1945–1970* (Berlin, 1995); Peter Hübner and Klaus Tenfelde (eds), *Arbeiter in der SBZ/DDR* (Essen, 1999).
43 See Bessel's Chapter 4 in this volume for further references.
44 Antonia Maria Humm, *Auf dem Weg zum sozialistischen Dorf?: Zum Wandel der dörflichen Lebenswelt in der DDR von 1952 bis 1969* (Göttingen, 1999); Damian von Melis, *Sozialismus auf dem platten Land: Tradition und Transformation in Mecklenburg-Vorpommern von 1945 bis 1952* (Schwerin, 1999).
45 Helke Sander and Barbara Johr (eds), *BeFreier und Befreite: Krieg, Vergewaltigungen, Kinder* (Frankfurt/Main, 1995).
46 Ralph Jessen, *Akademische Elite und kommunistische Diktatur* (Göttingen, 1999).
47 Kristie Macrakis and Dieter Hoffmann (eds), *Science under Socialism* (Cambridge, Mass., 1999).
48 Raymond G. Stokes, *Constructing Socialism: Technology and Change in East Germany, 1945–1990* (Princeton, NJ, 2000).
49 Arnd Bauerkämper *et al.* (eds), *Gesellschaft ohne Eliten?: Führungsgruppen in der DDR* (Berlin, 1997).
50 See Merrilyn Thomas' Chapter 12 of this volume for further references.
51 André Steiner, *Die DDR-Wirtschaftsreform der sechziger Jahre* (Berlin, 1999).
52 Charles S. Maier, *Dissolution: The Crisis of Communism and the End of East Germany* (Princeton, NJ, 1997), Ch. 2.
53 Neue Gesellschaft für Bildende Kunst (ed.), *Wunderwirtschaft: DDR-Konsumkultur in den 60er Jahren* (Cologne, 1996).
54 Annette Kaminsky, *Kaufrausch: Die Geschichte der ostdeutschen Versandhäuser* (Berlin, 1998); Simone Tippach-Schneider, *Messemännchen und Minolpirol: Werbung in der DDR* (Berlin, 1999).
55 Georg Bertsch *et al.*, *SED: Schönes Einheitsdesign* (Cologne, 1990).
56 Katherine Pence, 'Schaufenster des sozialistischen Konsums', in Alf Lüdtke and Peter Becker (eds), *Akten, Eingaben, Schaufenster: Die DDR und ihre Texte* (Berlin, 1997), 91–118; Ina Merkel, *Utopie und Bedürfnis: Die Geschichte der Konsumkultur in der DDR* (Cologne, 1999).
57 Jonathan R. Zatlin, 'The vehicle of desire: the Trabant, the Wartburg, and the end of the GDR', *German History*, 15 (1997), 358–80.
58 Christian Härtel and Petra Kabus (eds), *Das Westpaket: Geschenksendung, keine Handelsware* (Berlin, 2000).
59 Martin McCauley, *The German Democratic Republic since 1945* (Houndmills, 1983); David Childs, *The GDR: Moscow's German Ally* (London, 1983).
60 Simone Barck *et al.*, *Jedes Buch ein Abenteuer: Zensur-System und literarische Öffentlichkeiten in der DDR bis Ende der sechziger Jahre* (Berlin, 1997).
61 Joachim Walther, *Sicherungsbereich Literatur: Schriftsteller und Staatssicherheit in der Deutschen Demokratischen Republik* (Berlin, 1996).
62 Lüdtke and Becker (eds), *Akten, Eingaben, Schaufenster*.
63 Gerd Lettkemann, *'Schuldig ist schließlich jeder ... der Comics besitzt, verbreitet oder nicht einziehen läßt': Comics in der DDR* (Berlin, 1994).
64 Simone Barck *et al.* (eds), *Zwischen 'Mosaik' und 'Einheit': Zeitschriften in der DDR* (Berlin, 1999).
65 Thomas Heimann, *DEFA, Künstler und SED-Kulturpolitik* (Berlin, 1994); Sean Alan and John Sandford (eds), *Defa: East German cinema, 1946–1992* (Oxford, 1999).

66 Ina Merkel (ed.), *Wir sind doch nicht die Mecker-Ecke der Nation: Briefe an das DDR-Fernsehen* (Cologne, 1998).
67 Horst Hoffmann, *Die Deutschen im Weltraum: Zur Geschichte der Kosmosforschung in der DDR* (Berlin, 1998).
68 Angela und Karlheinz Steinmüller, *Literatur as Prognostik: Das Zukunftsbild der utopischen Literatur der DDR in den fünfziger und sechziger Jahren* (Gelsenkirchen, 1994).
69 Grit Hartmann, *Goldkinder: Die DDR im Spiegel ihres Spitzensports* (Leipzig, 1997).
70 Elke Wittich, *Wo waren Sie, als das Sparwasser-Tor fiel?* (Munich, 2000).
71 Günter Gaus, *Wo Deutschland liegt: Eine Ortsbestimmung* (Hamburg, 1983).
72 'Die Nackten und die Roten: FKK in der DDR' (Spiegel-TV Extra broadcast on Vox, 4 January 2001).
73 Dokumentationszentrum Alltagskultur der DDR (ed.), *Tempolinsen und P2* (Berlin, 1996); Dokumentationszentrum Alltagskultur der DDR (ed.), *Fortschritt, Norm und Eigensinn: Erkundungen im Alltag der DDR* (Berlin, 1999); Evemaria Badstübner (ed.), *Befremdlich anders: Leben in der DDR* (Berlin, 2000).
74 Charles S. Maier, 'Geschichtswissenschaft und "Ansteckungsstaat"', *Geschichte und Gesellschaft*, 20 (1994), 616–24.
75 Ralph Jessen, 'Die Gesellschaft im Staatssozialismus: Probleme einer Sozialgeschichte der DDR', *Geschichte und Gesellschaft*, 21 (1995), 96–110: 109.
76 2.5 million East Germans were categorised as 'heavy drinkers': Hans-Joachim Maaz, *Der Gefühlsstau: Ein Psychogramm der DDR* (Berlin, 1990), 87.
77 Konrad Jarausch and Hannes Siegrist (eds), *Amerikanisierung und Sowjetisierung in Deutschland 1945–1970* (Frankfurt/Main, 1997).
78 SED-ZK (Abt. Parteiorgane to Sicherheitsfragen), 26 November 1963, SAPMO-BArch, DY 30/IV A2/12/140.
79 NGBK (ed.), *Wunderwirtschaft*, 96–103.
80 Johanna and Günter Braun, *Der Irrtum des Großen Zauberers* (Berlin, 1972).

I
State

2

The leadership of the Socialist Unity Party of Germany under Ulbricht

Peter Grieder

In April 1946 the German Communist and Social Democratic Parties in the Soviet Zone merged to form the Socialist Unity Party of Germany (SED). When it was founded it did not present itself as a Leninist party committed to Sovietisation but as a Marxist party committed to parliamentary democracy. After 1948, however, it was transformed into a highly centralised, hierarchical organisation based on the model of the CPSU and swearing allegiance to Marxist–Leninist ideology as interpreted by Stalin. The doctrine of 'democratic centralism' was adopted and power concentrated in a small Politbüro and central committee. Social democracy was vilified and the principle of parity between former Social Democrats and Communists abandoned. In this 'party of the new type', as the SED liked to call itself, party discipline (enforced by control commissions functioning as a kind of internal police force) became the main weapon of Stalinist power consolidation. Those suspected of deviating from the official line were purged. This 'revolution from above' entailed a return to the traditions of the KPD. Once again, the apparat was the fountain-head of power.

Not only did the SED undergo internal Stalinisation, it became a hegemonic elite dominating all other institutions. Like the CPSU, it attempted – although, as contributions elsewhere in this volume reveal, not always successfully – to control all areas of public life and society. Its 'leading role' was enshrined in the new East German constitution of 1968,[1] although it had exercised this hegemony since the foundation of the GDR in 1949. The SED saw itself as the political vanguard of the working class leading the way in the inevitable transition to socialism.

Contrary to the image it liked to present of itself, the SED leadership during the Ulbricht era was no monolith. During the late 1940s, there were disagreements over Stalinisation and the type of socialist system suitable for Germany. In February 1946, the KPD's chief of ideology, Anton Ackermann, asked whether the working class could, given the total collapse of 'bourgeois' state institutions in the wake of the Third Reich, attain power through peaceful and parliamentary means rather than through violent revolution. The question was answered in the affirmative, thus banishing an old KPD dogma.[2]

Enshrined in the SED's founding charter, the 'democratic way to socialism'[3] was interpreted in two divergent ways. Some (mainly former Communists) saw it as a special German road to Sovietisation, a tactical manoeuvre designed to persuade reluctant Social Democrats to join the new party. Others cherished a vision of a qualitatively different socio-political system to that existing in the Soviet Union (USSR). Walter Ulbricht, *de facto* SED leader after 1946, subscribed to the former view; Ackermann and his supporters to the latter. Ackermann argued that the lessons of the Russian revolution could not be mechanically applied to Germany. The SED needed to take account, not only of Lenin and Stalin, but of socialists such as Plekhanov, Bebel, Liebknecht, Kautsky and Hilferding. Unlike their Russian comrades, the German working class constituted a majority of the population and could therefore win power through the ballot box.[4] It was highly significant, he declared, that the party's statement of principles eschewed the term 'dictatorship of the proletariat'.[5]

> When we use the term 'political power of the working class' and not 'dictatorship of the proletariat', that means that we do not regard the same forms of working-class rule in Russia as necessary or possible ... In Germany the possibilities not only of coming to power but also of exercising that power through democratic means are incomparably better than they were in Russia.[6]

One of Ulbricht's key supporters, Paul Wandel, took issue with this, arguing that there could be no difference between German and Soviet perceptions of socialism:

> [T]he dictatorship of the proletariat in the Soviet Union is in essence rule by the working class, and here rule by the working class, whether the people like it or not ... will be a dictatorship ... in the sense that Marx and, after him Lenin and Stalin, essentially understood it ... The road in the Soviet Union is also democratic, because it is based on the will of the overwhelming majority of the people.[7]

From 1948, however, the party was forced to undergo Stalinisation and the 'special German way to socialism' was abandoned. In September of that year Ackermann reluctantly published a condemnation of his previous views.[8]

Stalinisation had a particularly devastating effect on ex-Social Democratic members of the SED. In September 1946, the former leader of the SPD in the Soviet Zone, Otto Grotewohl, conceded that the process of fusion had yet to be consummated. Striking cultural differences remained, for example the Social Democrats' use of the polite 'Sie' against the Communists' preference for the informal 'Du'. These diverging attitudes often led to factionalism.[9] Meanwhile, many former Social Democrats apparently dreamed of the day when they would be able to drop out of the new party. As Tiul'panov, head of the propaganda (later information) department of SMAD, put it: 'there is still a sense that two distinct groups exist... Both Social Democrats and Communists keep their cards. And when you talk to them, they pull out their old membership cards and say: "I am a former Communist and member of the SED."'[10]

The campaign against former Social Democrats was officially launched by Ulbricht in June 1948.[11] War was declared on so-called 'Schumacher agents' accused of infiltrating the party and sabotaging its operations (Kurt Schumacher was leader of the SPD in the western zones). Those with misgivings about Stalinisation were purged and sometimes given long prison sentences. In the leadership, only one of their number, Erich Gniffke, fled to the West. In his farewell letter to the SED, he wrote: 'Today I resign from the "party of the new type", or rather from Ulbricht's KPD of 1932.'[12] All the others capitulated. Weary from years of persecution under the Nazis, many former Social Democrats lacked the courage and will to withstand the assault of their false brothers in the SED. In the harsh climate of Stalinisation, opposition was hardly an option. They were left with a stark choice: defect or collaborate. Defection was not only dangerous, it meant conceding defeat, bowing out of politics, losing material privileges and parting with loved ones. Some felt guilty about the SPD's anticommunism during the Weimar years; others believed that the only way to protect their former comrades was to remain inside the ranks of the SED. There was also disapproval of the 'restoration' being carried out in the western zones and animosity towards the SPD of Kurt Schumacher. All these factors help explain why so many ex-Social Democrats converted to Marxist–Leninism after 1948.

The 'party of the new type' was to Communists what the medieval church was to Catholics – the source of all truth and redemption. To engage in 'factionalism' was to violate the first commandment of Stalinist politics: that 'the party was always right'. It was better to be wrong with the party than right against it. Any deviation from the official line was interpreted as an attack on party unity and a distraction from the fight against capitalism. 'Objectively', such people were 'counter-revolutionaries' who were giving succour to the class enemy. Demoted, ostracised and persecuted, they were required to recant in a public ritual known as 'self-criticism'. The ultimate sanction was excommunication, even execution. Conflict, then, was taboo for a Communist leadership which regarded the maintenance of party discipline as a fundamental article of faith. It is against this background that we must view SED high politics between 1948 and the overthrow of Ulbricht as first secretary in 1971.

The main source of conflict during the 1950s was Ulbricht's dictatorial leadership style. However, since it was impossible for a member of the

Politbüro to challenge the official party line without being branded an enemy of the people, this was sometimes used to camouflage more substantive disagreements over policy. Ulbricht's opponents in the leadership were particularly concerned about the forced tempo of socialist development, because it exacerbated the division of Germany, worsened the crisis inside the GDR and harmed the credibility of the party. They also criticised the lack of internal party democracy and sectarianism towards the bloc parties and mass organisations. The steady flight of refugees to the West persuaded them that a more moderate brand of politics was required. Consequently, they favoured more flexible policies towards the economy, churches, peasantry, bourgeoisie, working class and the intelligentsia. Despite their misgivings, however, they remained trapped within the Stalinist consensus of the period. It would be wrong, therefore, to see them as reform Communists in the sense of Dubček in Czechoslovakia or Gorbachev in the Soviet Union. Their differences were often of a tactical nature, although it is important to remember that changes in tactics often require changes in policy.

Latent conflicts in the SED Politbüro surfaced during the spring and summer of 1953 following the death of Stalin and the subsequent abandoning of the 'accelerated construction of socialism' in the GDR. Against a background of severe socio-economic crisis, Moscow decreed a New Course for the country. With regard to the economy, satisfaction of consumer needs replaced the emphasis on heavy industry, restrictions on private capital were lifted and the collectivisation of agriculture abandoned. In the political sphere, measures were announced to guarantee civil rights, restore the position of the middle classes and intelligentsia, correct abuses by the Soviet occupation authorities, strengthen the role of the bloc parties and mass organisations and end the campaign against the church. All propaganda about the necessity for socialism in the GDR was condemned as inappropriate. The creation of a 'united, democratic, peace-loving and independent Germany' was proclaimed as the ultimate goal. In the light of this it was deemed necessary to adopt a more conciliatory attitude towards the West German SPD and sign a peace treaty with the Allies.[13]

Initially supported by the majority of Politbüro members, Rudolf Herrnstadt, the chief editor of the party's daily newspaper, *Neues Deutschland*, and the minister for state security, Wilhelm Zaisser, sought to reduce Ulbricht's power, mitigate the worst excesses of his regime and implement the New Course in full.[14] But instead of leading the GDR out of its existential crisis and preparing the ground for German reunification, the sudden *volte-face* unleashed the popular uprising of 17 June 1953. Only Soviet tanks could quell the unrest and prevent the collapse of Communist rule. Ulbricht's invention of the Zaisser–Herrnstadt conspiracy enabled him to circumscribe the New Course, purge his opponents and consolidate his own embattled position.[15]

Opposition surfaced again following Khrushchev's denunciation of Stalin at the twentieth party congress of the CPSU in February 1956. Not only did the Soviet leader condemn Stalin's personality cult, he debunked his other doctrines too, for example the inevitability of war and the intensification of class struggle during the period of socialist development. The necessity for 'collective leadership' and policies attuned to the special needs of indigenous populations were also proclaimed. 'Coexistence' with the West became the guiding principle of Soviet foreign policy. Against this background, two members of the SED Politbüro, Karl Schirdewan (head of cadres) and Fred Oelßner (chief of ideology) attempted to rein in Ulbricht's personality cult and slow down the renewed attempt to 'construct socialism' in the GDR.[16] They were supported by prominent members of the central committee such as Ernst Wollweber, minister for state security, Gerhart Ziller, central committee economics secretary and Fritz Selbmann, deputy prime minister. The opposition was defeated in 1958 (Ziller having committed suicide) and its members expelled from the leadership.[17]

Different shades of opinion on the German Question must be placed in the context of Moscow's *Deutschlandpolitik* during this period. Controversy has raged for decades over whether Stalin aimed for a Germany united under communism, a democratic, capitalist but neutral Germany, or a separate communist GDR. In the long run, he had undoubtedly set his sights on the first objective. When Yugoslav and Bulgarian leaders visited Moscow in the spring of 1946, Stalin is reported as saying: 'All of Germany must be ours, that is, Soviet, communist.'[18] Interviewed in 1972, Stalin's foreign minister and loyal lieutenant, Molotov, testified that the aim had been to extend communism to the country as a whole, albeit in stages.[19] An indication of what would eventually be expected from the SED in a reunited German state was its conversion to Stalinism in 1948.

In the medium term, however, Stalin advocated the creation of a united, 'democratic', and 'peace-loving' German state on the basis of the Potsdam Agreement signed by the Allies on 1 August 1945. Stalin's vision seems to have been of a left-wing government for the country as a whole, radically implementing Potsdam's stipulations on demilitarisation, denazification and decartelisation of German industry. These were regarded by the communists as essential if the 'sources of war' in Germany – 'monopoly capitalism' and Junker landowners – were to be destroyed. Stalin and the SED initially believed that they would do well in free elections and that the days of capitalism were numbered.[20] The 'special German way to socialism' was based on this illusion and served as the link between Moscow's medium and long-term agendas. Following Ulbricht's return from a meeting with Stalin in February 1946, the future East German president, Wilhelm Pieck, noted: 'parliamentary traditions in the West – pursue a democratic road to workers' power – not dictatorship.'[21] If the SED could win a nationwide free election, Germany would be reunited by the communists and their allies. This was exactly what Stalin wanted. On 4 June 1945, he had instructed

Pieck and Ulbricht to 'secure the unity of Germany via a united KPD [and a] united central committee'.[22]

Given the draconian restrictions on monopoly capitalism, such a 'democratic' and 'peace-loving' Germany would not have been compatible with the western idea of democracy.[23] On the contrary, it would have acted as the springboard from which the SED could seize absolute power in future. In 1944 Stalin had dismissed any immediate prospect of a Soviet Germany, telling the exiled Polish leader Mikołajczyk: 'Communism fits Germany like a saddle on a cow.'[24] A cautious approach therefore had to be adopted. The USSR's immediate interests were served by obtaining a peace treaty, generous reparations, a stake in the heavy industry of the Ruhr and economic assistance from the West. Any precipitate action by Moscow to Stalinise the whole of Germany would have alienated the Western Allies and placed these things in jeopardy.

Because of these considerations, the USSR treated the SBZ as a special case among its satellites. In Moscow on 18 December 1948, Stalin chided the SED leadership for contemplating 'socialism' in a divided country, emphasising the need to pursue 'reunification', 'peace' and 'democracy'.[25] Indeed, he regarded the division of Germany as the least favourable scenario, even if he never ruled out the option of a separate GDR. During the meeting with Stalin on 4 June 1945, Pieck noted: 'Perspective – there will be two Germanies – despite the unity of the Allies.'[26] Yet the SBZ, ravished by war, impoverished by Soviet dismantling, bereft of raw materials and constituting only one-third of the German nation, hardly looked like a viable German state. It was therefore with great reluctance that Stalin agreed to the establishment of the GDR on 7 October 1949, five months after the foundation of the FRG in May. Even then, the SED received only associate membership of the Cominform. The GDR did not participate on an equal basis with the other eastern European states in major diplomatic initiatives, and the USSR did not establish full diplomatic relations with it until after Stalin's death.[27] Six days after the GDR was founded, Stalin sent a congratulation telegram which did not mention the word 'socialism', but instead referred to his goal of establishing a 'united, independent, democratic [and] peace-loving Germany'.[28] The Soviet leadership continued to pursue this medium-term agenda up to and beyond Stalin's death.

While Ulbricht's main priority during this period was to consolidate the GDR as a separate socialist state, others were concerned not to lose sight of the all-German perspective. These included Franz Dahlem (Ulbricht's main rival in the SED leadership until his expulsion in March 1953), Anton Ackermann, Rudolf Herrnstadt, Karl Schirdewan and the East German prime minister, Otto Grotewohl. Unlike Ulbricht and his close associates, they tended to emphasise Moscow's medium-term agenda and advocated a more active policy towards West Germany.[29] Ulbricht, however, rightly perceived that German reunification was unlikely and, in any case, a threat to socialism in the GDR. Britain, France and the USA – eagerly supported by the West German Chancellor Konrad Adenauer – quickly lost interest once it became clear that Germany could not be united as a democratic and capitalist state integrated into western security structures. Ulbricht's *Deutschlandpolitik* was therefore also *Realpolitik*. From the mid-1950s on, the Soviet Union came to accept the existence of two German states. With the building of the Berlin Wall in 1961, the division of the country was set in concrete.

Traditional assumptions about why Ulbricht was deposed in 1971 require revision. Until recently, he was viewed as an unreconstructed Stalinist determined to block moves towards détente. These were not, however, the reasons for his downfall. During the 1960s, he showed himself to be an innovative, creative but also extremely unrealistic leader prepared to adopt a high-risk strategy in pursuit of his goals. Both at home and abroad he revealed a remarkable ability to embrace new ideas and adapt to a changing environment. From the early 1960s, Ulbricht underwent a metamorphosis from incorrigible Stalinist to fanatical technocrat. He was the driving force behind Eastern Europe's first economic reform programme and mitigated the worst aspects of state repression. Contrary to previous interpretations,[30] he also worked for dialogue with the West German SPD and rapprochement with Bonn. However, his aim to 'overtake' the FRG by forcing the pace of the 'scientific–technological revolution' caused serious economic difficulties in 1970. An innovator in the ideological field, he propagated the GDR as a model for socialism and obstructed Allied negotiations over West Berlin. His determination to pursue this agenda without recourse to Moscow led to his being replaced by Erich Honecker in May 1971.[31]

Recognising the importance of the 'scientific–technological revolution', Ulbricht significantly modified the Stalinist model of centralised command management after 1963. His pioneering programme of economic reform inaugurated in that year attempted to combine plan and market by circumscribing the central planning bureaucracy and granting factory managements a degree of autonomy. Profit and limited forms of private and semi-private ownership were also legitimised.[32] Originally named the 'New Economic System of Planning and Management' (NÖS), it was relaunched on a more centralised model in December 1965 and rechristened the Economic System of Socialism in 1967.[33] According to a lengthy critique of Ulbricht's economic policy written shortly after his downfall and signed by Honecker, Ulbricht wanted to go much further in reducing central planning, even proposing its replacement with a system of 'self-regulatory' mechanisms.[34] Whether or not this is true, he certainly did favour enabling factories to claim compensation from agencies which imposed harmful decisions.[35] He also came close to endorsing the concept of bankruptcy.[36] But his fanciful aim of 'overtaking' the FRG led to serious economic problems which played into the hands of those in the leadership who wanted to jettison the reforms.[37]

In the late 1960s, Ulbricht propagated the idea of a 'socialist human community' which eschewed class conflict and offered the hope that different social groups could coexist in harmony. By 1971 he was being accused of encouraging the 'capitalist sector' and granting a special status to private and partly state-run businesses.[38] Ulbricht wanted to preserve these enterprises[39] and insisted that the new constitution drafted in 1968 include a clause giving them security of tenure.[40] When Honecker became first secretary, however, he had them all nationalised, deleting the heretical clause from a revised constitution of 1974.[41] The first secretary also initiated a less repressive style of government in the 1960s. Between 1963 and 1965 Ulbricht presided over a cultural thaw, an easing of restrictions on travel to West Germany and the beginnings of a dialogue between party and population. In 1963 important legislation on the family and educational reform was put to public debate. The party structure was decentralised according to the 'production principle' and a new statute promulgated, containing 'additional' safeguards against the violation of 'Leninist norms'. There was condemnation of 'dogmatism', 'heartless bureaucracy' and 'sectarianism' and greater emphasis on the role of the 'bourgeois' parties in the decision-making process.[42] A communiqué of 21 September granted East German youth a degree of independence and a 'workers' and peasants' inspectorate' was set up to oversee the proper implementation of party and state directives.[43] In 1964 Ulbricht announced a new electoral law enabling voters to choose between individual candidates (thus abolishing the system of *en bloc* voting). There was also less interference in the work of the churches.[44] The seventh party congress in April 1967 referred to the 'further development' of 'socialist democracy',[45] and later that year Ulbricht warned against confusing democratic centralism with 'bureaucracy' and 'sterility'.[46] The new constitution of 1968 was submitted first to public debate and then to a plebiscite.[47]

In September 1967 Ulbricht used the centenary celebrations of Karl Marx's *Das Kapital* to debunk the view (enunciated by Marx, Engels and Lenin) that the period of transition from socialism to communism was of relatively short historical duration. Instead, he proclaimed 'the developed social system of socialism', an autonomous socio-economic formation.[48] The concept enabled Ulbricht to present certain essential rudiments of his economic reforms (for example, profit) as positive features of the 'socialist' system rather than as discredited vestiges of an earlier capitalist era. Since the USSR had already announced the transition to communism, this did not go down well in the Kremlin.

Proposals drawn up by a working group of Ulbricht's advisers in preparation for the eighth party congress in June 1971 were conceived as contributions to the 'developed social system of socialism'. Among other things, they foresaw a greater role for the elected representatives and parliamentary committees. There were also attacks on 'heartless bureaucracy'[49] and heavy emphasis was placed on popular participation, consultation and accountability.[50] The declared aim was to 'enhance the effectiveness of socialist democracy'.[51] These proposals were based on the premise that, as society became more complex and the population more educated, the political system would evolve to a qualitatively higher level. The main manifestation of this would be the way in which the SED exercised its 'leading role'. In a speech to district leaders in Leipzig on 21 November 1971, Ulbricht said that the challenge for the party was to establish friendly relations with all sections of the East German population.[52] Lower echelons of the political hierarchy were to be granted greater autonomy so that decisions could be made at the 'appropriate' level.[53] As Ulbricht's personal adviser, Wolfgang Berger, put it, Ulbricht strove for 'a better division of labour within the system'.[54] Whether these proposals were practical or even meaningful must remain speculative. After all, Ulbricht remained an implacable opponent of political 'liberalisation'. In December 1965 he had poured scorn on the idea of an opposition party in the GDR.[55] His advisers always took special care to emphasise the irreconcilable conflict between 'liberalisation' and 'socialist democracy'.[56]

From the mid-1960s, without waiting for Moscow, Ulbricht tried to foster links with the West German Social Democrats and pursue rapprochement with Bonn. It was on his initiative that the SED tried to arrange an exchange of speakers with the SPD in the spring and early summer of 1966.[57] Three years later, Ulbricht welcomed the election of Willy Brandt as Chancellor of the FRG, believing it would now be possible to improve relations between the two German states. Initially, he was strongly opposed by both the Kremlin and his Politbüro comrades.[58] The full extent of Brezhnev's anger became clear when Honecker visited him in Moscow on 28 July 1970. In a private conversation, the Soviet leader expressed his displeasure at Ulbricht's determination to pursue rapprochement and reminded his visitor that the Soviet Union had troops stationed in the GDR.[59]

In January 1968 Ulbricht had apparently welcomed the coming to power of reform communist Alexander Dubček in Czechoslovakia. His aim seems to have been to encourage him to follow the East Germans in promoting economic reform. During a trip to Prague in February of that year, Ulbricht allegedly advised the new first secretary to purge the 'dogmatists' from his leadership and replace them with a younger generation of 'technocrats'.[60] But once Dubček began liberalising the political system, Ulbricht turned against him and supported the Warsaw Pact invasion of 20 August 1968. He does, however, seem to have been worried about the potential consequences of military intervention for his own policies in the GDR. Only this can explain his last-minute talks with Dubček at Karlovy Vary eight days beforehand. In an SED Politbüro meeting three years later, however, the former first secretary was blamed for 'damaging' the East German leadership on this issue.[61] In 1992, Berger claimed that Ulbricht had used every opportunity to render military invasion unnecessary.[62] The traditional view of Ulbricht as one of Dubček's most implacable enemies, Brezhnev's chief lackey and diehard proponent of military intervention, therefore requires qualification.

On 9 August, Ulbricht had called a special session of the East German parliament to propose that his government immediately exchange high-level representatives with Bonn with the aim of concluding a renunciation-of-force agreement.[63] The FRG was expected to relinquish the Hallstein Doctrine[64] and its claim to sole representation but, significantly, Ulbricht had not made full recognition of his regime a prerequisite. To the surprise of many listeners, Ulbricht also raised the possibility of trade talks with West Germany. This unexpected proposal was not linked to any of the above preconditions and was reaffirmed on 16 August when the GDR officially informed Bonn of its interest in beginning ministerial negotiations. Both initiatives were shelved as a result of the invasion of Czechoslovakia. Significantly, the joint communiqué released after the conclusion of the Karlovy Vary talks on 12 August welcomed Ulbricht's initiative 'to guarantee European security and normalise relations between the two German states'. At a press conference the next day, Ulbricht also lectured his hosts on the superiority of the East German economic system and reaffirmed the desirability of diplomatic relations between the GDR and Federal Republic.[65]

Contrary to previous assumptions, divisions of the GDR's National People's Army (NVA) do not seem to have been included in the force which crossed Czechoslovakia's borders on the night of 20 August.[66] According to top party functionaries, Ulbricht supported the invasion but opposed the deployment of GDR troops.[67] Shortly before he died in 1990, former Politbüro member Horst Sindermann explained the reasoning behind the decision. Direct participation would have evoked memories of Hitler's Wehrmacht invasion, unleashing a tidal wave of anti-German feeling: 'Blind as we were to many things, we at least saw that clearly at the time.'[68] The East Germans did, however, provide other forms of moral, technical and military assistance.

Once the Prague Spring had been crushed, reform projects across Eastern Europe were put on ice because of the risk they posed to political stability. The dilution and eventual abandonment of economic reform in the GDR must be seen in this context. As far as East–West relations were concerned, the invasion delayed the coming of détente and temporarily set back Ulbricht's plans for an accommodation with the Federal Republic. Yet despite his desire for co-operation with the new SPD–FDP (Freie Demokratische Partei, or Free Democratic Party) government in Bonn after 1969, he refused to recognise western occupation rights in Berlin, protesting that the whole city should be under East German control.[69] It was only after his removal as first secretary that the four-power negotiations over Berlin began to make progress, culminating in the Quadripartite Accord of 3

September 1971. Ulbricht also forged an independent policy towards China. By refusing to follow the other Warsaw Pact states in unequivocally condemning Beijing, he infuriated his Kremlin patrons and alienated Politbüro colleagues.[70]

Ulbricht's policies between 1963 and 1971 must be seen in the context of the new situation in East Germany after the building of the Berlin Wall. Once the escape route to the West had been sealed, the GDR achieved a degree of stability, and reform became a viable option. A combination of economic crisis, the need to placate an alienated population, the beginnings of a reform debate in the USSR and rising living standards in West Germany persuaded Ulbricht that a new economic strategy was required. His policy of rapprochement with the SPD was partly a response to the latter's *Ostpolitik*, partly an attempt to gain a foothold in the FRG. In the short term he hoped to split the SPD off from the CDU (Christian Democratic Union), Grand Coalition partners between 1966 and 1969, and gain international recognition for the GDR. He might also have wanted to buttress his economic reform programme by forging a new relationship with Bonn.[71] Moreover, the rise of the neo-Nazi National Democratic Party (NPD) in West Germany seems to have persuaded him that an alliance with the SPD was necessary.[72] Only in this way, he believed, could the 'forces of reaction' be held at bay. His longer-term goal was to achieve the speedy reunification of Germany as a socialist state.

After Ulbricht's overthrow in 1971, the economic reform programme was abandoned and plans for an immediate rapprochement with the FRG shelved. Thereafter, negotiations with Bonn were linked to a policy of 'demarcation' (*Abgrenzung*), designed to stress ideological, political, socio-economic and cultural differences between the two German states. References to the 'social system of socialism', 'economic system of socialism' and 'socialist human community' were removed from the 1974 constitution.[73] Furthermore, the GDR was no longer defined as 'a socialist state of the German nation'[74] but as 'a socialist state of workers and peasants'.[75] The clause pledging the 'gradual rapprochement of the two German states until their unification on the basis of democracy and socialism' was also deleted.[76]

Despite its reputation as Moscow's most reliable and dependent ally, the East German leadership enjoyed greater room for manoeuvre *vis-à-vis* the Kremlin than has generally been assumed. As we have seen, Ulbricht's policies in the SBZ did not always concur with Stalin's medium-term agenda for postwar Germany. In 1952, Ulbricht apparently persuaded a reluctant Soviet dictator to approve the 'accelerated construction of socialism' in the GDR. In March of that year, the SED Politbüro had approved an agenda for the second party conference which concentrated on 'the new tasks in the struggle for a peace treaty, German unification and national reconstruction'.[77] 'Socialism' was not even mentioned. This was because, on 10 March, Stalin had made his famous offer on German reunification to the western powers. But once the USA, Great Britain and France had rejected these overtures, Ulbricht took advantage of the situation to canvass his own programme. On 2 July 1952, with full Politbüro support, he wrote to Stalin saying that it was time to begin building 'socialism' in the GDR.[78] On 8 July, just one day before the SED party conference, Stalin consented.[79] Twenty-four hours later in Berlin, Ulbricht was given a rapturous reception when he announced the new agenda to astonished delegates. Stalin, however, eschewed the term 'socialism' altogether in his telegram to the conference and confined himself to wishing the party 'new successes' in the 'historical task of creating a united, independent, democratic and peace-loving Germany'.[80] Furthermore, Soviet officials broke with tradition and stayed away from the conference proceedings.[81]

In 1953, Ulbricht initially ignored the Kremlin's advice to moderate his domestic policies. At the end of 1952, he had appealed to the Soviets for financial and material aid. The request went unanswered. On 15 April, after another appeal, Moscow sent a negative reply and advised the SED to adopt a softer line.[82] At the same time, the Soviet deputy planning chief, Nikitin, arrived in the GDR with news that the Kremlin was planning a New Course.[83] He recommended that the party moderate its economic policies with a view to improving living standards. Ulbricht, however, decided to ignore these warnings. Already on 9 April he had authorised the council of ministers to withdraw food-rationing cards for 2 million people.[84] Two weeks later the central committee increased factory work norms by 10 per cent, stoking the fires of discontent still further.[85]

Ulbricht also appears to have instigated the purge of Dahlem in March 1953 and kept another of his rivals, Paul Merker, in prison long after the Soviets had lost any interest in his case.[86] Zaisser and Herrnstadt seemed unaware of the power struggle being waged in the Kremlin during the spring and early summer of 1953. Having circumscribed the New Course, Ulbricht went on to resist destalinisation. In 1958 he purged Schirdewan, disregarding Khrushchev's advice. In January of that year, a Politbüro delegation travelled to Moscow to obtain Khrushchev's permission to purge Schirdewan and Oelßner from the leadership. Yet Khrushchev was loath to oblige and even went so far as to defend Schirdewan.[87]

The NÖS seems to have been the brainchild of the SED and Ulbricht nurtured it throughout the 1960s in the face of Moscow's increasing scepticism. Observers sometimes assumed that Khrushchev was using the GDR as an experimentation ground for his own projects or that Ulbricht was following the prevailing line in Moscow. In the end, thoroughgoing economic reform failed to materialise in the USSR and Khrushchev seems to have had misgivings about the East German project.[88] If we are to believe the retrospective testimonies of those involved, the reforms owed more to the initiative of Ulbricht than hitherto believed. As Berger put it: 'before this important decision there was no prior checking or confirmation in

Moscow.'[89] This account was supported by Gerhard Schürer (chairman of the State Planning Commission after 1965) who, unlike Berger, never classified himself as a supporter of the reforms. According to him 'Khrushchev tolerated but did not support the NÖS'.[90]

In 1964 Khrushchev was overthrown and replaced by the more conservative Brezhnev. The tepid programme of economic reforms introduced in 1965 by the Soviet premier, Kosygin, failed to deliver. During a private conversation with Honecker in Moscow on 20 August 1970, the Soviet leader seemed to issue a warning: 'What is important is that the GDR has a structure like the S[oviet] U[nion] and other socialist countries, otherwise we will get into difficulties ... The GDR is not only your concern, she is the concern of us all.'[91] Although Ulbricht's political, economic and ideological schemes after 1963 – his 'developed social system of socialism', his 'socialist human community', his new *Deutschlandpolitik*, his stances on West Berlin, China and the Prague Spring – had all deviated from official Soviet policy, he remained SED first secretary until May 1971. In the end it was Erich Honecker (backed by a majority of Politbüro colleagues) who obtained Brezhnev's permission to depose him.[92]

This greater room for manoeuvre requires us to pay more attention to indigenous factors in explaining how and why the various oppositions were defeated. The 'Ulbricht factor' is particularly significant in this regard. Rejected by the majority of his Politbüro colleagues and still bereft of Kremlin backing three weeks after the June 1953 uprising, Ulbricht used all the weapons at his disposal to reverse the situation. Displaying the consummate skill of a shrewd political operator, he apparently persuaded the Soviets to back him. He then neutralised his opponents in the Politbüro before presenting the central committee with scapegoats for the debacle of 17 June. Between 1956 and 1958, Ulbricht intimidated the opposition, playing its different members off against each other and preventing the full rehabilitation of unjustly condemned leaders. This time, however, his critics were in a minority. During the 1960s, Ulbricht became the inflexible proponent of flexible policies. He overestimated his ability to defy Moscow and his Politbüro colleagues, thus paving the way for his own downfall.

Ulbricht's critics themselves must bear a heavy responsibility for the defeats inflicted on them between 1946 and 1958. Ultimately, they all proved willing to sacrifice their principles on the altar of party discipline. The maintenance of party unity was the first commandment of Stalinist politics. As one member of the central committee put it in 1953: 'For us, party discipline is the ultimate freedom!'[93] In July of that year, Zaisser and Herrnstadt refrained from going public with their criticisms on the grounds that this would have split the party and harmed the Soviet Union.[94] Five years later, Herrnstadt accused the leadership of taking advantage of his communist discipline to deny him rehabilitation. Nonetheless, he promised to die 'saluting the party' as Zaisser had done.[95] In 1958, Fritz Selbmann declared that he would 'chop himself into pieces' for the sake of the party.[96]

Loyalty to the SED, however, was only one side of the equation. Persecution, ostracism, imprisonment, perhaps even death awaited those who deviated from the official line. Rehabilitations, if they occurred at all, were half-hearted and there is no example of any purged SED leader being restored to his previous position. Herrnstadt cited fear as one of the reasons why he did not openly contest the decision to expel him from the party.[97] None of Ulbricht's critics engaged in opposition lightly – the potential consequences were too severe. By comparison with purged communists in other Soviet bloc countries, however, disgraced SED leaders were treated relatively leniently. Show trials and executions did not in the end materialise. Zaisser and Herrnstadt were only expelled from the party. Ackermann, Dahlem, Schirdewan, Wollweber, Oelßner, Selbmann and others all remained inside the ranks of the SED.

In the early 1950s, preparations were under way to stage an East German show trial similar to those of Rajk in Hungary, Kostov in Bulgaria and Slánský in Czechoslovakia. One of the prospective defendants, Leo Bauer, recalled being informed by Erich Mielke (state secretary in the ministry of state security) in August 1950, that it was scheduled for February 1951 at the latest. Some weeks later, another of Mielke's officials stressed the personal role of Ulbricht in the whole affair.[98] Bauer's testimony is supported by the deputy chairman of the KPD and member of the West German parliament, Kurt Müller, who was arrested in 1950.[99] That it did not in the end take place can probably be attributed to five factors. First, the special status of the GDR within the communist bloc: the country still had an open border with the West and German reunification had not yet been ruled out. Second, the marked relaxation in Soviet policy following the death of Stalin. Third, the proclamation of the New Course in the GDR at Moscow's behest in June 1953. Fourth, the overthrow and execution of Beria, the Soviet interior minister whose agents had organised the purges across East-Central Europe. Fifth, the refusal of Paul Merker and Franz Dahlem to co-operate with attempts to frame them as 'imperialist agents'.[100]

Although there is no evidence that Ulbricht helped prevent the trial and execution of his rivals in the SED leadership, a moderating influence may have been exerted by Grotewohl, who spoke up for Ackermann,[101] by Pieck, who intervened on behalf of Ackermann and Merker,[102] and Zaisser, who apparently expressed misgivings about the Dahlem case.[103] It is also important to remember that Soviet-style purges had never been part of the communist tradition in Germany. After 1953 there were no more show trials in eastern Europe. The twentieth party congress of the CPSU in 1956 ensured that they remained a thing of the past.

Despite the strait-jacket of communist politics, conflict was a salient feature of the East German leadership under Ulbricht. There were a number of reasons for this. In the period until 1961, the Stalinist system was in its formative years and the 'national question' still open. The GDR was in a state of continual crisis and this stimulated argument over the future direction of policy. Another factor was Ulbricht's style of leadership. During the 1940s and 1950s, he repeatedly provoked criticism with his sectarian and dictatorial approach to government. In the 1960s, it was his determination to pursue his own agenda in defiance of the Kremlin and his Politbüro colleagues that aroused controversy. SED high politics during the Ulbricht era can broadly be characterised as a struggle between hawks and doves, reformers and hardliners. In this unequal struggle, the hawks were always victorious.

From a post-1989 perspective one is bound to ask whether any of the defeated alternatives described above could have built a better East Germany. The question is, of course, unanswerable. Other communist states which did introduce reforms ultimately fared no better. For the SED, however, such attempts were especially fraught with dangers owing to the magnetism of the FRG. They might always have triggered a revolution from below and the collapse of communist rule. Paradoxically, then, Stalinism was both the lifeblood and the wasting disease of the GDR.

Notes

1 Article 1, *Verfassungen deutscher Länder und Staaten von 1816 bis zur Gegenwart* (Berlin, 1989), 495–518: 495.
2 Anton Ackermann, 'Gibt es einen besonderen deutschen Weg zum Sozialismus?', *Einheit*, 1 (February 1946), 22–32: 30.
3 'Grundsätze und Ziele der Sozialistischen Einheitspartei Deutschlands', *Einheit*, 2 (March 1946), 2–4: 4.
4 SAPMO-BArch, DY 30/IV 2/1/10, Ackermann at the sixth SED-PV, 24–25 October 1946.
5 'Grundsätze und Ziele', 4.
6 SAPMO-BArch, DY 30/IV 2/1/10.
7 *Ibid*.
8 'Über den einzig möglichen Weg zum Sozialismus', *Neues Deutschland*, 24 September 1948, 2.
9 SAPMO-BArch, DY 30/IV 2/1/8, Grotewohl at SED-PV, 18–19 September 1946.
10 From Tiul'panov's report to CPSU Central Committee Commission, 16 September 1946, cited in Norman Naimark, 'The Soviet occupation: Moscow's man in (East) Berlin', *Cold War International History Project Bulletin*, 4 (Fall 1994), 34, 45-48: 46.
11 SAPMO-BArch, DY 30/IV 2/1/48.
12 Erich W. Gniffke, *Jahre mit Ulbricht* (Cologne, 1990), 364–72: 369.
13 CPSU-PB resolution, 8 July 1952, cited in Rolf Stöckigt, 'Ein Dokument von großer historischer Bedeutung vom Mai 1953', *Beiträge zur Geschichte der Arbeiterbewegung (BzG)*, 5 (1990), 648-54.
14 Herrnstadt's draft resolution for SED-ZK: 'The New Course and the renewal of

the party', in Wilfriede Otto, 'Dokumente zur Auseinandersetzungen in der SED 1953', *BzG*, 5 (1990), 655–72: 659–67.

15 See Peter Grieder, *The East German Leadership, 1946–1973: Conflict and Crisis* (Manchester, 1999), Ch. 2. Also Helmut Müller-Enbergs, *Der Fall Rudolf Herrnstadt: Tauwetterpolitik vor dem 17. Juni* (Berlin, 1991); Nadia Stulz-Herrnstadt (ed.), *Das Herrnstadt-Dokument: Das Politbüro der SED und die Geschichte des 17. Juni 1953* (Reinbek bei Hamburg, 1990).

16 Schirdewan at SED-PB, January 1958, in G. Bretschneider *et al.*, 'Karl Schirdewan: Fraktionsmacherei oder gegen Ulbrichts Diktat? Eine Stellungnahme vom 1. Januar 1958', *BzG*, 4 (1990), 498–512; SAPMO-BArch, NY 4215/112, Oelßner at SED-PB, 5 January 1958.

17 See Grieder, *The East German Leadership*, Ch. 3.

18 Milovan Djilas, *Conversations with Stalin* (London, 1962), 139.

19 Interview by Felix Chuyev cited in 'Messengers from Moscow', BBC2 TV documentary, 19 February 1995.

20 Dirk Spilker, 'The Socialist Unity Party of Germany (SED) and the German Question, 1944–53' (DPhil, Oxford, 1998).

21 SAPMO-BArch, NY 4036/631.

22 SAPMO-BArch, NY 4036/629, Pieck's notes from conversation with Stalin on 4 June 1945 in Moscow.

23 Wilfried Loth, *Stalins ungeliebtes Kind: Warum Moskau die DDR nicht wollte* (Berlin, 1994).

24 Ann McElvoy, *The Saddled Cow. East Germany's Life and Legacy* (London, 1992), 2.

25 SAPMO-BArch, NY 4036/695, Pieck's notes of conversation between Stalin and SED leaders in Moscow, 18 December 1948.

26 SAPMO-BArch, NY 4036/629.

27 John Lewis Gaddis, *We Now Know: Rethinking Cold War History* (Oxford, 1997), 127.

28 Loth, *Stalins ungeliebtes Kind*, 161.

29 SAPMO-BArch, DY 30/IV 2/1/89, speeches to the third SED-ZK plenum, 26–27 October 1950; see also Grotewohl at the first SED conference, January 1949. Socialism, he said, could not be built until three main objectives had been achieved: reunification, a peace treaty and a 'democratic government' for the nation as a whole: *Protokoll der Verhandlungen der 1. Parteikonferenz der SED* (Berlin, 1949), 327–97: 356; see also Schirdewan's draft report to 29th SED-ZK in November 1956, prioritising German reunification: SAPMO-BArch, DY 30/J IV 2/2A-532.

30 Alfred Grosser, *Geschichte Deutschlands seit 1945* (Munich, 1977), 389; M. Sodaro, *Moscow, Germany and the West from Khrushchev to Gorbachev* (London, 1991), 165; Peter Pulzer, *German Politics, 1945–1995* (Oxford, 1995), 116; A. J. Nicholls, *The Bonn Republic* (London, 1997), 229, 231.

31 See Grieder, *The East German Leadership*, Ch. 4; Peter Grieder, 'The overthrow of Ulbricht in East Germany: a new interpretation', *Debatte*, 6 (May 1998), 8–45; Monika Kaiser, *Machtwechsel von Ulbricht zu Honecker: Funktionsmechanismen der SED-Diktatur in Konfliktsituationen 1962 bis 1972* (Berlin, 1997).

32 Ulbricht's speeches in: *Protokoll der Verhandlungen des VI. Parteitages der SED*, i (East Berlin, 1963), 28–250; SAPMO-BArch, DY 30/IV 2/1/337, eleventh SED-

ZK; *Protokoll der Verhandlungen des VII. Parteitages der SED*, i (East Berlin, 1967), 25–287.
33 For a path-breaking study of the reforms in practice, see Jeffrey Kopstein, *The Politics of Economic Decline in East Germany, 1945–1989* (Chapel Hill, 1997).
34 SAPMO-BArch, DY 30/J IV 2/2A/3196, 'Zur Korrektur der Wirtschaftspolitik Walter Ulbrichts auf der 14. Tagung des ZK der SED 1970'.
35 *Protokoll der Verhandlungen des VII. Parteitages der SED*, i, 158.
36 *Ibid.*, 161.
37 SAPMO-BArch, DY 30/J IV 2/2/1300, SED-PB resolution, 8 September 1970.
38 SAPMO-BArch, DY 30/J IV 2/2A/3196, 'Zur Korrektur'.
39 *Protokoll der Verhandlungen des VI. Parteitages der SED*, i, 115.
40 Article 14(2), 1968 constitution, *Verfassungen*, 501.
41 Article 14, revised 1974 constitution, *Verfassungen*, 519–40: 523.
42 *Protokoll der Verhandlungen des VI. Parteitages der SED*, i, 233–4, 240–5. The 'production principle' envisaged 'offices' at local, district and national level to supervise party organisations in industry and agriculture. Staffed by highly qualified professionals rather than SED apparatchiks, they limited the remit of the Politbüro and Honecker's central committee secretariat. In 1967–68, at Honecker's instigation, the 'production principle' was effectively disbanded.
43 *Protokoll der Verhandlungen des VI. Parteitages der SED*, i, 181.
44 David Childs, *The GDR: Moscow's German Ally* (2nd edn; London, 1988), 71, 92.
45 *Protokoll der Verhandlungen des VII. Parteitages der SED*, i, 95, 102.
46 *Neues Deutschland*, 13 September 1967, 3–6: 6.
47 The numbers withholding approval or boycotting were unusually high compared to parliamentary elections: 'only' 94.5 per cent of those entitled to vote supported the constitution (in East Berlin 90.9 per cent).
48 *Neues Deutschland*, 13 September 1967.
49 SAPMO-BArch, DY 30/J IV 2/202/402, 'Hauptprobleme ... im Prognosezeitraum 1971–1980'.
50 *Ibid.* See also SAPMO-BArch, DY 30/J IV 2/202/403, 'Gruppe Innenpolitik ... Stand: Februar 1971'.
51 *Ibid.*
52 SAPMO-BArch, J NL 2/32.
53 Interview with former deputy SPK chairman and close Ulbricht ally, Herbert Wolf, 13 October 1992.
54 Interview with Berger, 27 November 1992.
55 SAPMO-BArch, DY 30/IV 2/1/338. Ulbricht at eleventh SED-ZK, 18 December 1965.
56 SAPMO-BArch, DY 30/J IV 2/202/403. 'Gruppe Innenpolitik'.
57 SAPMO-BArch, DY 30/J IV 2/202/88/1, Ulbricht to Brandt, 7 February 1966; SAPMO-BArch, DY 30/IV 2/1/342, Ulbricht at twelfth SED-ZK, 27–28 April 1966; SAPMO-BArch, DY 30/J IV 2/2/1064, Ulbricht to Brandt, 22 June 1966.
58 SAPMO-BArch, DY 30/J IV 2/2A-1.403, SED-PB, 18 November 1969, draft of Ulbricht's speech to twelfth SED–ZK; SAPMO-BArch, DY 30/IV 2/202/346, xii, Ulbricht to Brezhnev, 20 November 1969.
59 SAPMO-BArch, DY 30/J IV 2/2A/3196, record of conversation between Honecker and Brezhnev, 28 July 1970.

60 SAPMO-BArch, DY 30/J IV 2/2 A/3196, 'Zur Korrektur'.
61 SAPMO-BArch, DY 30/J IV 2/2/1360, Axen at SED–PB, 26 October 1971.
62 Interview with Berger, 7 October 1992.
63 SAPMO-BArch, DY 30/IV 2/1/382, Ulbricht at seventh SED-ZK, 7 August 1968; *ibid.*, DY 30/IV 2/1/385, at eighth SED-ZK, 23 August 1968.
64 The doctrine proclaimed in December 1955 according to which the Federal Republic denied full diplomatic recognition to any state (apart from the Soviet Union) which recognised the GDR.
65 Ilse Spittmann, 'Die SED im Konflikt mit der CSSR', *Deutschland-Archiv (DA)*, 6 (September 1968), 668.
66 Rüdiger Wenzke, 'Zur Beteiligung der NVA an der militärischen Operation von Warschauer-Pakt-Streitkräften gegen die CSSR 1968', *DA*, 11 (1991), 1179–86: 1185.
67 Interviews with Kurt Hager (6 April 1994), Alfred Neumann (23 October 1992) and Gerhard Schürer (5 November 1992). Their testimony is supported by Ulbricht advisers Berger (7 October 1992) and Wolf (13 October 1992). See also Rüdiger Wenzke, *Prager Frühling – Prager Herbst: Zur Intervention der Warschauer-Pakt-Streitkräfte in der CSSR 1968* (Berlin, 1990).
68 W. Rehm, 'Neue Erkenntnisse über die Rolle der NVA bei der Besetzung der CSSR im August 1968', *DA*, 2 (1991), 173–85: 176.
69 SAPMO-BArch, DY 30/J IV 2/202/345, xi, Brezhnev to Ulbricht, 8 April 1967; SAPMO-BArch, DY 30/J IV 2/2A-1.481, i, SED-PB, 30 November 1970.
70 SAPMO-BArch, DY 30/J IV 2/2/1360, i. At a Politbüro meeting on 26 October 1971, Axen accused Ulbricht of 'underestimating' the danger of Maoism and 'overestimating' the SED's role as broker between China and the USSR.
71 Interview with Berger, 14 December 1992.
72 SAPMO-BArch, DY 30/J IV 2/202/88/1, Ulbricht to Brandt, 22 November 1966.
73 Cf. Articles 9 and 18 of 1968 and 1974 constitutions, *Verfassungen*, 495, 500–1, 520, 522–3.
74 Article 1, 1968 constitution, *Verfassungen*, 495.
75 Article 1, revised 1974 constitution, *Verfassungen*, 519.
76 Cf. Article 8 of 1968 and revised 1974 constitutions, *Verfassungen*, 499 and 521.
77 SAPMO-BArch, DY 30/IV 2/2/203, SED-PB, 18 March 1952.
78 SAPMO-BArch, DY 30/IV 2/2/218, SED-PB, 1 July 1952. Letter to Stalin of 2 July 1952 on preparations for second SED conference, 9–12 July 1952.
79 CPSU-PB resolution, 8 July 1952, cited in: Stöckigt, 'Ein Dokument', 652.
80 *Protokoll der Verhandlungen der II. Parteikonferenz der SED 9.–12. Juli 1952* (Berlin, 1952), 58.
81 Dietrich Staritz, *Die Gründung der DDR* (Munich, 1987), ii, 183–4.
82 *Der Neue Kurs und die Aufgaben der Partei* (East Berlin, 1953), 9. See also Arnulf Baring, *Uprising in East Germany: June 17, 1953* (London, 1972), 20.
83 Fritz Schenk, *Mein doppeltes Vaterland* (Würzburg, 1989), 99.
84 Loth, *Stalins ungeliebtes Kind*, 197.
85 SAPMO-BArch, DY 30/IV 2/1/115–16, 13th SED-ZK resolution, 14–15 May 1953.
86 Grieder, *The East German Leadership*, Chs 1 and 3.

87 SAPMO-BArch, NY 4090/699, Grotewohl's notes of Khrushchev's meeting with SED delegation in the Kremlin (29 January 1958); interview with Schirdewan, 12 October 1992: 'The Soviets defended me until the last moment.'
88 SAPMO-BArch, DY 30/J IV 2/2A/3196, Ulbricht to Rodenberg, 23 October 1971. Ulbricht admitted to fierce disagreements with Khrushchev over economic policy in the GDR.
89 Wolfgang Berger, 'Zu den Hauptursachen des Unterganges der DDR', *Weißenseer Blätter*, 4 (1992), 26-37: 31. Also interview with Wolf, 13 October 1992.
90 Interview with Schürer, 5 November 1992.
91 SAPMO-BArch, J NL 2/32, record of conversation between Honecker and Brezhnev in Moscow, 20 August 1970.
92 SAPMO-BArch, DY 30/J IV 2/2A/3196, letter to Brezhnev signed by thirteen SED–PB members appealing for support in Ulbricht's removal, 21 January 1971.
93 SAPMO-BArch, DY 30/IV 2/1/120, Johannes R. Becher at the fifteenth SED-ZK, 24–26 July 1953.
94 Stulz-Herrnstadt (ed.), *Herrnstadt-Dokument*, 158, 163.
95 SAPMO-BArch, DY 30/IV 2/4/392, Herrnstadt to Ulbricht, 28 November 1959.
96 SAPMO-BArch, DY 30/IV 2/1/193, Selbmann at the thirty-fifth SED-ZK, 3–6 February 1958.
97 Stulz-Herrnstadt (ed.), *Herrnstadt-Dokument*, 158.
98 Leo Bauer, '"Die Partei hat immer recht". Bemerkungen zum geplanten deutschen Rajkprozeß (1950)', *Aus Politik und Zeitgeschichte*, B27 (4 July 1956), 405-19: 409.
99 Hermann Weber, 'Kurt Müller: Ein historisches Dokument aus dem Jahre 1956', *Aus Politik und Zeitgeschichte*, B11 (9 March 1990), 16–29: 19.
100 SAPMO-BArch, NY 4102/27, Merker to Pieck, 14 April 1956; SAPMO-BArch, NY 4090/699, Grotewohl's notes of conversation with Dahlem.
101 SAPMO-BArch, DY 30/IV 2/1/52, Grotewohl's interjection during Oelßner's speech to SED–PV, September 1948.
102 *Ibid.*, Pieck's interjection during Oelßner's speech to SED–PV, September 1948; SAPMO-BArch, DY 30/IV 2/11/v 801, Pieck to Ulbricht, 26 April 1951; SAPMO-BArch, NY 4102/27, Pieck to Merker, 28 August 1952.
103 SAPMO-BArch, DY 30/IV 2/4/392, Else Zaisser to the fifth SED congress, July 1958.

3

Ulbricht's secret police: the Ministry of State Security[1]

Jens Gieseke

Translated from the German by Mary Carlene Forszt and Patrick Major

'A special organ of the dictatorship of the proletariat'

Officially dubbed the 'shield and sword of the Party', the Ministry of State Security (MfS) – or, more colloquially, 'Stasi' – was the 'most frightening and at the same time grotesque part' of the SED power apparatus and consequently a cornerstone of the GDR state.[2] By origin and design, the MfS was a secret organisation, monitoring and combatting real and perceived opponents of party dictatorship. It could arrest dissidents and hold them for trial at its own interrogation and detention facilities. More ambitiously, it strove to bring the whole of society under its control. It was also one of the world's most successful espionage and counter-espionage agencies. Over the decades the apparatus grew into a ramified bureaucracy with numerous ancillary tasks: providing bodyguards for leading GDR functionaries and operating the Politbüro settlement in Wandlitz; as passport inspectors at border crossings, monitoring traffic between East and West; trading in weapons and technology; even running its own sports club, FC Dynamo Berlin, which became GDR football champion many times.[3]

In the Cold War context, the MfS saw itself as part of the global conflict between socialism and 'imperialism', being waged on German soil between two separate states. As its then chief, Erich Mielke, rather lugubriously put it in 1975:

> In the MfS a special organ of the dictatorship of the proletariat arose with both the capability and means, under the leadership of the SED, together with the other state organs and armed forces and in close connection with the workers, to reliably defend the Workers'-and-Peasants'-Power and the revolutionary process against any counter-revolutionary activity by enemies both foreign and domestic, as well as to ensure universal internal security and order.[4]

So ran the security logic: inner social conflicts were viewed, on principle, as orchestrations of West German or other 'imperialistic' secret services and 'enemy' organisations. Accordingly, domestic counter-intelligence and external reconnaissance co-operated closely, blurring the boundaries between foreign intelligence gathering and internal repression.[5]

The MfS thereby saw itself engaged in a 'cold civil war' with the 'enemy', justifying any means.[6] Legal considerations or self-restraint seemed like betrayal of the duty to protect, to be employed only for political expediency, but not as a matter of principle. MfS members consciously identified themselves as 'Chekists' upholding the spirit of the revolutionary founder of the Russian Bolsheviks' secret police, Feliks E. Dzerzhinsky, whose motto was allegedly: 'Only a person with a cool head, warm heart and clean hands can be a Chekist.'[7] A revolutionary-cum-romantic legend was spun, with Stasi agents calling themselves not spies but *Kundschafter* – pseudo-military scouts – fighting on the 'invisible front', and even cultivating their own James Bond figure, Achim Detjen, star of the 1970s television series 'The Invisible Visor'.[8] Such rituals and bonding processes were designed to inculcate an elite consciousness among professional revolutionaries, 'first-class comrades' as the founding Minister described them.[9] This was meant to mould the psyche deeply. In one introductory session new recruits learned that:

> The combatting of the class enemy contributes firstly to forming and consolidating these Chekist personality traits. In the process of work MfS members acquire Marxist–Leninist, political-operative as well as political-specialist insights and experience for successful work against the enemy.[10]

This 'fighting' consciousness was most pronounced in the 1950s, springing from the Stalinist maxim of the 'permanent intensification of the class struggle', and reinforced by a tendentious antifascism appropriated for anti-imperialist purposes, positing an unbroken continuity of the American-inspired FRG with the Third Reich.

The dichotomous world view of friend and foe extended well beyond the political level, however, deep into everyday culture. Precisely those 'superficial' western influences on clothing, hairstyles, musical tastes and lifestyle were deemed to be especially refined forms of imperialist psychological warfare, known as 'political–ideological diversion' (PID) in MfS jargon. Anti-western values were combined with a petit-bourgeois, law-and-order mentality. This included a sexual hypocrisy which allowed MfS agents to come down hard on pornography, while at the same time circulating its hotly sought-after products within its own ranks. The voyeurism of the surveillance machinery itself encouraged sexist stereotypes, especially against oppositional women. Even the Marxian long hair and beards of male oppositionists in the 1970s and 1980s provoked disdain compared with the militarily correct, short back-and-sides ethos of the Chekists. Such attitudes evinced a mental continuity with the German 'political culture of an apolitical society' – what has been labelled a 'culture of fear ... of the main enemy of heterogeneity, of the chaos of civilisation, as western modernity was still perceived to be'.[11]

Despite its elitist tendencies, the Ministry was not a 'state within a state': it remained under the political leadership of the SED's First Secretary, which meant Walter Ulbricht until 1971, then Erich Honecker (and Egon Krenz briefly in autumn 1989). Although a 'Secretary for Security Affairs' represented the MfS in the Central Committee apparatus, the direct axis between minister and party chief was more crucial. Additionally, as an 'armed organ' the Ministry was part of the SED's Security Commission and, from 1960, of the National Defence Council, also under Ulbricht and Honecker. MfS headquarters were located in Berlin-Lichtenberg, from 1963 inside a large building complex in the Normannenstraße (now a museum), but the Stasi also maintained a local presence with fifteen regional administrations (*Bezirksverwaltungen*) and 209 district offices (*Kreisdienststellen*). As at the top, political control lay in the hands of the local first SED secretary. Within the MfS there were even party branches, run by a central office in Berlin attached to the Central Committee.[12] In addition, the Ministry ran so-called 'object offices' in important businesses and facilities, for example, at the VEB Carl Zeiss Jena optics works, as well as a 'site administration' from 1951–82 in the Soviet–German uranium mining enterprise, Wismut. The various MfS departments were also vertically linked according to the so-called 'line' principle; for example, the line 'Security of the National Economy' ran from the Main Department (*Hauptabteilung* or HA) at Normannenstraße down to the corresponding district departments, all following the same schematic numbering (HA XVIII).

Forerunners in the SBZ 1945–49

Unsurprisingly, the MfS role-model was the Soviet secret police. During the nearly five years before the official formation of the Ministry in 1950, the Soviet occupying power and the KPD/SED had, stage by stage, built up a secret police apparatus in the Soviet Zone.[13] The People's Commissariats of Internal Affairs and State Security (NKVD and NKGB, respectively), operating from Moscow, installed their own extensive networks, under Colonel-General Ivan A. Serov, then, after 1946, Nikolai K. Koval'chuk, both of whom later rose to head the Soviet State Security Service. In January 1946 some 2,200 NKVD and 400 NKGB personnel, as well as nine rifle regiments, numbering some 15,000 interior troops, were stationed in the SBZ. Among its other tasks, the NKVD ran ten so-called 'special internment camps', in which approximately 154,000 Germans and 35,000 foreigners were detained from 1945 to 1950, a third of whom died, mostly of hunger or disease.[14]

The Soviet security organs also began, directly after the Occupation, to set up commissariats for political crimes within local police departments, consisting of groups of German Communists, many from the former underground. These were formalised under the German Administration of the Interior (DVdI), established in August 1946, as the so-called 'K5' desks of each criminal investigation department. The future tasks of the MfS were already emerging: prosecution of cases involving assassination; sabotage; infractions of SMAD orders; economic crimes; weapons violations; investigation of former Nazi organisations and crimes against humanity; rumour-mongering, 'removal and besmirching of democratic propaganda' and other breaches of the new order.[15] The K5 units functioned primarily as auxiliary organs of the Soviet Ministry of State Security's operational groups, arresting actual or alleged Nazi activists, as well as anticommunist opponents, including Social Democrats. From 1947 both K5's staff and jurisdiction were extended to permit its own denazification investigations: in Saxony, for example, the number of employees increased from about 160 in 1946 to almost 700 in April 1948. More closely vetted than other sections of the Volkspolizei, all top K5 positions were filled by long-standing KPD members – either former concentration camp inmates or close associates of the Soviet power.

At SED insistence, Stalin, in a CPSU Politburo resolution, at last gave the green light for the establishment of an independent zonal secret police on 28 December 1948. Walter Ulbricht, Wilhelm Pieck and Otto Grotewohl had won through against the objections of the Soviet Minister of State Security, Viktor S. Abakumov that, because of the public effect on the western Allies as well as the lack of vetted German cadres, the 'fight against anti-Soviet elements and spies' in the SBZ should continue in Soviet hands. In May 1949, however, K5 was made separate from the other criminal investigation departments. Erich Mielke, who, as Vice-President of the DVdI had hitherto dealt with police personnel and political orientation, was entrusted with the establishment of the new apparatus. Known initially as the 'Directorate for the Protection of the National Economy' within the Ministry of the Interior, with corresponding directorates in the SBZ's *Länder*, it finally acquired ministerial status in 1950.

Foundation and consolidation 1950–53

On 8 February 1950 the GDR Volkskammer unanimously passed the 'Bill to Establish a Ministry of State Security',[16] following a secret SED Politbüro resolution at the end of January. A week later, in his capacity as deputy prime minister, Ulbricht appointed Wilhelm Zaisser as minister and Erich Mielke as permanent secretary. Zaisser was at the same time co-opted both onto the party executive and the Politbüro. Minister of the Interior, Karl Steinhoff (SED), proclaimed before the chamber that:

> the main tasks of this Ministry will be to protect national enterprises and factories, transportation and national property from attacks by criminal elements;

furthermore to combat activities of enemy agencies, subversives, saboteurs and spies, to wage energetic battle against bandits, to protect our democratic development and to safeguard our democratic, peaceful economy and the undisturbed fulfilment of our economic plans.[17]

Parliamentary or ministerial scrutiny was not envisaged; the Ministry acted, as deputy prime minister Otto Nuschke (CDUD) stated in 1952, as an 'authority with its own responsibility'.[18] In actuality, Soviet KGB officers held the MfS reins[19] – every head of a service unit had his own 'instructor' and in important cases the Soviet organs continued to conduct investigations themselves, such as the case of an employee of the anticommunist Investigative Committee of Free Jurists, Walter Linse, whom the MfS had violently abducted from West Berlin. In 1953 it was a Soviet military tribunal which condemned him to death.[20]

At the same time the MfS implemented the will of the SED party leadership. Its primary task was that of locating and arresting opponents of the GDR's transformation to a Soviet-style people's democracy, in all areas of society: in the economy and agriculture, state institutions, political parties and mass organisations, and even inside religious groups. Moreover, during the Stalinist purges of the early 1950s the MfS conducted, alongside the Central Party Control Commission, investigations against purported 'antiparty elements', as well as alleged Trotskyites and Titoists. Among the most prominent victims were the deputy chairman of the West German Communist Party, Kurt Müller, and the railways director, Wilhelm Kreikemeyer, who somewhat mysteriously died in MfS custody. Even the leading functionary Paul Merker, expelled from the SED in 1950, was arrested by the MfS in 1952, for an abortive show trial centred on the alleged American spy Noel H. Field, until his acquittal in 1956 following the destalinisation thaw.[21]

The main methods of the Stasi during this phase of 'terroristic-administrative attainment and securing of power'[22] consisted of arbitrary arrests and extortion of confessions using unremitting nightly interrogations and other torture methods. These aimed to 'prove' arrestees' espionage for western intelligence services and underground organisations such as the Task Force against Inhumanity, the League of German Youth or the eastern bureaux of West German political parties and trade unions. Nevertheless, even where agency seemed to be lacking, Stalinist conspiracy theories preferred to interpret 'objective' deficiencies, such as worn-out or overloaded machines, as hostile acts of sabotage. The MfS likewise considerably increased its activities at times of ideological conflict. After Ulbricht proclaimed the 'construction of socialism' in July 1952 and announced a renewed 'intensification of the class struggle', nearly 1,500 persons were arrested between August and December alone. Among the most prominent victims were Trade and Supply Minister Karl Hamann (LDPD), arrested in December 1952 for 'sabotage of the scheduled supply for the population', and Foreign Minister Georg Dertinger (CDUD), accused one month later of espionage. At the turn of the year persecution switched to Jewish communities, as a new, antisemitic purge was announced in the Soviet Union against the so-called 'doctors' conspiracy'. More than 400 Jews fled the GDR, among them SED Volkskammer deputy Julius Meyer, as well as five of the eight Jewish community leaders.

In the course of the GDR local government reform in 1952, the MfS dissolved its five provincial *Länder* administrations and set up fourteen regional administrations (*Bezirksverwaltungen*) in their place. The 'Greater Berlin Administration' and the 'object administration' in Wismut, founded in 1951, remained as they were. Staff and infrastructure were not yet sufficient to set up local offices in all the 217 new urban and rural districts and municipal boroughs of East Berlin, but by March 1953 192 local offices (*Kreisdienststellen*) existed. Finally, whereas the MfS had begun in February 1950 with only about 1,100 staff, mainly in the *Länder* administrations, with the 'intensification of the class struggle' the full-time apparatus was nearly doubled in 1952 from about 4,500 to about 8,800 employees.

The MfS leadership consisted almost entirely of long-standing Communists, among them experienced underground fighters such as minister Zaisser and his office head Heinrich Fomferra. But since the volatile developments of 1952, the MfS had taken on mainly young SED, Free German Youth and Volkspolizei cadres with no personal experience of the Communist labour movement before 1945. They came mainly from underprivileged, proletarian backgrounds and had only an elementary education, with equally limited police and secret service knowledge. Yet, in the view of senior officers their ideological spirit was more important:

> Comrade Köhler has said here that there are comrades who were hired who can't write. It seems to me that what is important is that this comrade, who perhaps can't write, knows how to win and what to do to destroy enemies. Let's check for once how many can write splendidly and how wonderfully they can blather on and then let's check to see how many enemies they've destroyed. That's why I don't think this line of questioning is quite right. That's why it's necessary to pound belief in victory into the people, so they know how to win ... And if he can't even sign his own name, that's not important, but if he knows who the enemy is, he's on the right path.[23]

By 1953 about 92 per cent of operatives were SED members; the others were regarded by Zaisser as 'party members without a membership card'.[24] The MfS took on personnel neither from the Gestapo nor the SS Security Service nor former police officers. In 1951, to improve the knowledge of its employees, the MfS founded its own centre for further training on the premises of the former Prussian Police Officers' Academy in Potsdam-Eiche. The bulk of employees, however, acquired their skills through practical work, know-how imparted mainly by the ubiquitous Soviet intelligence service officers and old KPD comrades experienced in underground fighting.

By 1955 the payroll had increased to almost 14,900 agents. Over the following two years Zaisser's successor, Wollweber, strove for a reduction of 10–20 per cent, but had to settle for seeing the numbers stagnate. (It cannot be conclusively clarified whether this recruitment freeze was related to liberalisation plans, as Ulbricht and Honecker later reproached him.) To raise the exceptionally low standard of education of MfS members the leadership improved the training system, but the internal upgrading of the Potsdam-Eiche academy to an 'Institute of Higher Studies' could not disguise the fact that the majority of employees still enjoyed only the lowest level of police or intelligence service training, a fact which encouraged the resort to primitive and brutal methods. A campaign in the same year specifically to recruit sixth-formers for MfS service brought a number of new cadres into the apparatus who, nevertheless, required even more intensive ideological training. Older colleagues had to drum into recruits the dangers and callousness of imperialism, and justify the cover stories and subterfuges required in MfS work. Yet these messages were not always internalised. By the 1970s, as one study recognised:

> The result is that some newly-recruited operational members claim: 'The first thing I learned in the State Security is to lie!' or: 'A State Security man must learn to lie without turning red' or: 'Working under operational cover stories contradicts my previous socialist education; it may be necessary, but I cannot lie!' Recruits are in danger of concluding that socialist morality does not apply to them – that they enjoy a special status in society – that they can apply conspiratorial means and methods for use against the enemy to life within the collective, thus withdrawing from the basis of trust and collective education.[25]

The Stasi also increasingly came to vouch for the external security of the state. In 1952 the SED, following Soviet example, put the MfS in charge of the German border and transport police, secretly monitoring their personnel. In addition, the MfS had its own militarily structured guard units, garrisoned from 1950 at Berlin-Adlershof, as well as at the seats of the regional administrations. With a total strength of 3,020 (154 officers, 537 non-commissioned officers and 2,329 troops) at the end of 1952, these troops resembled light infantry rather than plainclothes secret policemen.[26] During the 17 June 1953 uprising, such units had to protect party and government buildings from their own population, including the House of Ministries in Berlin. Demonstrators successfully stormed the district offices in Bitterfeld, Görlitz, Jena, Niesky and Merseburg, however, and shot an employee in front of one Magdeburg prison. In Rathenow an irate mob even lynched a well-known local former K5 member. Since Zaisser had forbidden shooting and guards had not been suitably trained, only Soviet troops saved the East German secret police from disaster.

From 17 June 1953 to destalinisation

After the suppression of the uprising, the MfS was substantially involved in the mass arrests of 'ringleaders' and alleged western organisers. By 22 June alone, together with the People's Police, it had arrested over 6,000 persons. More than fifty protestors were killed during the disturbances; at least twenty more were summarily executed. The Stasi, however, had not fulfilled its most important function: recognising harbingers and early signs of insurrection and nipping them in the bud. Accused of negligence, as well as having formed a 'faction' with party press chief Rudolf Herrnstadt, the SED discharged Zaisser as minister on 18 July 1953 and later expelled him from the Politbüro and Central Committee. A few months later, in January 1954, he was forced to leave the party. His successor was Ernst Wollweber, a former maritime sabotage specialist;[27] Mielke was reinstated as acting head of State Security, his service record vindicated. In order to demonstrate stronger control and subordination, however, the Ministry was converted, following Soviet precedent, into a permanent secretary's office within the Ministry of the Interior. Nevertheless the apparatus remained internally largely independent and on 24 November 1955 re-attained ministerial status. However, the SED leadership bound its state security service considerably more tightly to itself politically: Wollweber was made a Central Committee member in April 1955 (although a seat in the Politbüro continued to elude him), while Ulbricht personally took over responsibility for state security in the Politbüro.

Moreover, in 1953 the Stasi instigated independent information groups to combine their collective expertise into 'mood reports', in order to gain a clearer picture of the population. Owing to their small size and lack of qualified personnel, however, their usefulness initially remained limited. Only later did the MfS' so-called 'Central Evaluation and Information Group' (ZAIG) come to play a role comparable to that of the Nazis' *Sicherheitsdienst* (Security Service), gathering digests of intelligence on party and public opinion for strategic decision-making. Despite the continuing gulf between state and society, however, MfS operatives still liked to think of themselves fulfilling a duty of paternalistic welfare towards the people.[28] In this premodern view, tied to emotionalised family imagery, the Stasi was following in authoritarian traditions whose roots lay in Imperial Germany as well as Tsarist Russia. Such a positively accented caring image clearly played an important role in the recollections of former MfS personnel after 1989. As Maier discovered in his research on the final crisis: 'Stasi officials themselves ... envisaged their roles as much as social workers as policemen; they were the heirs to eighteenth-century *Polizeywissenschaft* and cameralism.'[29]

The basis of the 'friendly' self-image lay in the dialectical–materialist definition of the 'inevitable' historical role of the people, on whose behalf the MfS was fighting. Of course, in the MfS operative's everyday dealings this did not help much. As one assessment explained: 'Experience of practical induction teaches that a series of newly-appointed operative members who have not previously unofficially collaborated with the MfS, often come into a conflict situation when apprised of the unofficial means and methods of the MfS, requiring the help of experienced comrades.'[30] Entering the closed world of the Stasi was clearly a shock. Neither were the 'love' and 'respect', required to preserve the paternalistic identity, always forthcoming on the outside. The first Politbüro resolution on matters relating to MfS work in March 1952 spoke of the 'full trust of the whole progressive population', implicitly conceding the existence of 'non-progressive' sections of the populace.[31] Internally, assessments were even more cautious. In one study of the MfS' history in the early 1950s, it was admitted that: 'The work of the Ministry of State Security was very greatly impeded at this time by the mistrust of people who compared the MfS with the Gestapo and the SD. The mistrust accorded to the fascist power apparatus was applied to the MfS.'[32]

Whether so many really distrusted the National Socialist state is academic, yet the limits of the acceptance of the postfascist order were clearly marked. Later, after the 'victory of socialist relations of production' and the proclamation of the 'developed socialist society', such concessions were unthinkable. Yet the claim to be 'objectively' working on behalf of the 'people' stood in stark contrast to everyday experience. Certainly the hundreds of thousands of informants co-operated more or less committedly, and likewise the official partners in state, party and economy, yet it could not have escaped MfS personnel that precisely its idealised blue-collar workers were underrepresented in the informant network, and SED members and other regime officials correspondingly overrepresented. They were fully aware how widespread 'negative' opinions were in the population, since they had to deal with the consequences on a daily basis. If real signs of support were lacking, the avant-gardist didactic resorted to explanations of insufficient consciousness: people had 'not yet' recognised the superiority of socialism. Imagined popular support was predicated on the potential Stasi threat, which compelled a superficial loyalty.

Following the 1953 insurrection, the recruitment was intensified of 'unofficial collaborators' (*inoffizielle Mitarbeiter* or IMs), ordinary citizens already *in situ*, rather than full-time employees. Between 1953 and 1955 the number of these part-time agents ranged between 20,000 and 30,000.[33] The quality of informers, however, remained altogether low owing to uneven distribution and high fluctuation, so that the Stasi was dependent to a considerable degree on external tip-offs, for example, from party offices. In the short term, therefore, the MfS relied on demonstrative force. In November 1953, endeavouring to achieve quick success to find the 'organisers and people behind the fascist putsch attempt', as 17 June had come to be known, it launched Operation 'Fireworks', in which several hundred alleged agents were arrested amid considerable publicity. Further arrests followed, such as Operation 'Blitz' in March 1955, whose remit was:

> to ruthlessly expose the criminal role played by American espionage headquarters in Germany to the entire German public. This will be achieved with a concentrated operative blow aimed at the espionage headquarters in West Berlin and their agencies. In the first phase of the operation it is planned to strike at the following enemy offices in West Berlin: the East Bureau of the CDU (Christian Democratic Union Party), the VPO, the Organisation for Refugees from the East, the East Bureau of the FDP (Free Democratic Party), the UFJ (the Investigative Committee of Free Jurists), the so-called 'Task Force against Inhumanity', as well as hostile groupings created in West Berlin by the Americans which, under the camouflage of 'SED opposition', are directing all of their activity at our party machinery.[34]

According to available estimates, between 600 and 700 persons were abducted from the West to the communist sphere of influence, both during such arrest actions as well as in individual snatches, including 120 of the approximately 400 MfS members who fled west before 1961.[35]

In the course of the later very patchy destalinisation in the GDR, following Khrushchev's exposure of Stalin's crimes at the twentieth CPSU congress in February 1956, 25,000 political prisoners were released early. They included some 400 bloc party functionaries, nearly 700 Social Democrats, several hundred 'war criminals' sentenced by Soviet military tribunals and, not least of all, a group of Communists around Paul Merker and the former Minister of Justice Max Fechner, arrested after 17 June. At the same time the Stasi's practice of continuous interrogation and other torture techniques were called into question. Until the autumn of 1956 the MfS made substantially fewer new arrests. However, this phase of uncertainty and confusion ended abruptly with the suppression of the uprising in Hungary in November 1956. A new wave of repression followed in the GDR, the most prominent victims of which were the national Communist philosopher Wolfgang Harich and the head of the 'Aufbau' publishing house, Walter Janka, arrested on 6 December 1956 and sentenced to five years in prison for founding a 'counter-revolutionary group'.

Development into a state security bureaucracy 1957–71

The turn-around in Budapest also recemented Ulbricht's position. Wollweber, who had been pressing for the MfS' resources to be channelled outwards, against the FRG, was gradually deprived of power, and finally forced to step down on 1 November 1957.[36] In February 1958 he was excluded from the Central Committee for alleged 'factionalism' (along with the SED functionaries Karl Schirdewan and Gerhart Ziller) but, unlike Zaisser, was allowed to remain a party member. The vacant position fell to Erich Mielke, one he held until November 1989. While his predecessors could all count on Soviet protection, Mielke had distinguished himself as a member of Ulbricht's retinue. The MfS was now undisputedly subordinate to the political instructions of the First SED Secretary. In 1958 the Soviet KGB considerably reduced its presence in the MfS apparatus. Of the formerly ubiquitous Soviet 'advisers', only 32 remained as liaison officers in the Ministry. The subsequent relationship was characterised more by co-operation than subordination. However, until 1990 the KGB still ran its own network of residencies and agents in the GDR, monitored by a branch of its First Directorate (espionage) in Berlin-Karlshorst with 800–1,200 staff, as well as a military counter-espionage residency (Third KGB Directorate) assigned to the Group of Soviet Armed Forces in Germany (GSSD).[37]

After defeat on 17 June 1953 was averted only by Soviet army intervention, the SED leadership learned the lesson of preparing more intensively for military conflict or domestic unrest within the GDR. In 1954 it thus formed a Security Commission as well as district and local operational staffs (*Einsatzleitungen*), in which the Stasi was also represented. MfS guard units in the former provincial capitals (except for the Berlin Guards Regiment) were combined with standby police units, previously under the authority of the Ministry of the Interior, to form the 'domestic troops'. The disturbances in Poland and Hungary, combined with the accompanying revolt of party intellectuals and students in the GDR, gave Ulbricht cause for further changes, switching the main emphasis from direct actions against the western intelligence services and underground organisations to the internal opposition forces in the GDR, which, in the official jargon, had been 'softened up' and 'subverted' by imperialist ideology. In November 1956 the Politbüro approved a multi-stage plan to suppress civil unrest using armed GDR troops, as well as Soviet troops if necessary. According to the 'first stage', the People's Police, armed MfS units, as well as the Kampfgruppen militia, would suppress disturbances using 'simple police means' such as water-cannon and cordons. NVA units would be called into action only in exceptional circumstances.[38]

Mielke willingly took on this hard line, having demonstratively rejected the critique of Stalin at the twentieth CPSU congress. Nor did he later make any secret of his admiration for the 'great Soviet leader', in April 1957 telling MfS employees 'Don't retreat when fighting the enemy', and accusing the justice authorities of 'going soft', 'which has also led to faltering within our ranks'.[39] The MfS' quota of politically motivated conflicts both in times of crisis and stability in fact remained far lower than in the police and army. After the twentieth CPSU congress and after the crushing of the Prague Spring there were only isolated reform-communist auto-critiques. Indeed, when Ulbricht made his famous understatement in 1956 that Stalin no longer belonged to the 'classics of Marxism–Leninism', some MfS comrades complained that this was an antiparty position which they could not accept.[40] In 1957–58, following the new party line of the 35th Central

Committee plenum, Mielke further refined the MfS concept of the 'enemy' and its 'political–ideological subversion', tracing all forms of domestic opposition in socialist countries back to the influence, direct or indirect, of 'imperialistic enemy headquarters'. The Stasi trained its sights particularly on those using democratic socialism to criticise Stalinism, castigating them variously for 'social democratism [sic], opportunism, revisionism'.[41] The fight against allegedly omnipresent 'political–ideological subversion' even provided Mielke with a legitimate reason to build the State Security Service up into a 'government office authorised to exercise control over the rest of the apparatus of state', as the senior SED functionary Hermann Matern complained in 1962.[42]

In the wake of the building of the Berlin Wall in 1961, the hard line initially continued. The MfS arrested many GDR citizens who had protested against the construction of the Wall, but also other *personae non gratae* previously spared to avoid unrest (and by extension a further increase in the number of flights to the West – see Patrick Major's Chapter 11 in this volume). Direct compulsion therefore remained at the core of MfS practice, backed by the equally effective use of the unspoken threat. A test-case for the efficiency of the apparatus came with the Prague Spring in 1968 in neighbouring Czechoslovakia and its violent suppression by Warsaw Pact troops. This (historically final) attempt at reforming communism along humane, democratic lines corresponded in almost textbook fashion to the MfS' perception of the enemy and its political–ideological subversion. It took part with its own forces in turning the course of events in Czechoslovakia, and after the successful suppression helped the Czech secret police to purge its apparatus of reformers and reconsolidate. In the GDR itself there was a wave of over 2,100 protests and more than 500 investigative proceedings, mainly for 'propaganda hostile to the state', against GDR citizens who had publicly shown their solidarity with the cause of the Prague Spring. But the MfS could sum up: 'There was no serious discord or unrest, nor were there any occurrences involving larger population groups, which could have expanded into political actions against the GDR and the measures [taken by] the five Warsaw Pact states.'[43] In this respect the MfS had absolutely fulfilled its repressive function. Preventive surveillance, however, had been shown to have gaps: not even a quarter of all registered protest cases had been solved, and in those in which the MfS was successful, it turned out that most involved individuals who had not previously attracted negative attention.

Alternative surveillance techniques took on greater importance in the 1960s. Following the consolidation of political power after the 'secret founding day of the GDR'[44] in August 1961, and Moscow's new destalinising impulses in October 1961, the MfS' remit shifted. Investigators and prison warders less frequently committed open brutalities against prisoners; prison conditions, while still degrading, were eased. The repertoire of criminological and intelligence gathering techniques was expanded; the permanently increasing number of full-time employees and the quantitative and qualitative improvement of the informant network made it possible to extend secret police operations inside opposition groupings. Moreover, 'preventive reconnaissance' of potential trouble spots became as important as direct persecution. In short, the Stasi was becoming more modern.

Yet the long-term role of the MfS in the walled republic, with the 'enemy' supposedly held at bay by the 'Antifascist Defence Rampart', had by no means been decided by the party leadership: the KGB role-model was having to re-orientate itself during the thaw under Khrushchev; Ulbricht was propagating the 'socialist human community' and had initiated reforms; and the army and police had to accept budget cuts. But just as Honecker succeeded in mobilising the 'conservative' interests of the party against any spirit of reform in the arts and among youth (see Mark Fenemore's Chapter 10 in this volume), so did Mielke after 1963–64 with his ideas for the development of state security.

The economic reforms of the 'New Economic System' after 1963 provided one such avenue. Already the MfS had seized on the ambitious, but ultimately doomed, aviation programme in the GDR, riddled with purportedly 'unreliable' engineers, as its own pilot project.[45] Exposing hostile activities in the economy was, according to Mielke, the main task of the MfS in contributing to an increase in productivity. From 1964, it established a network of trouble-shooting 'security representatives' headed by the inspection division of the Council of Ministers. In the head offices of the economic bureaucracy of the centrally regulated organisations of the state-owned factories, as well as in the 459 most important combines, enterprises and institutions, the security representative positions were filled with Officers on Special Assignment (OibE). After 1968 the top economic OibE, Harry Möbis, was also head of the Inspection Department in the Council of Ministers.

The Stasi strove not only to infiltrate society at large, but also moved into labour-intensive police tasks which could hardly be considered 'secret', such as passport controls from 1962, and supervision of traffic across the inner-German border in 1963–64. The working groups formed for these purposes were united in 1970 in the Main Department VI. This additional area of responsibility arose from experience gained during 1963–66, when a limited border-pass agreement had been in force, enabling inhabitants of West Berlin to cross over to the eastern part of the city for the first time since the building of the Wall. The MfS set itself the task of surveilling the onslaught of approximately 1.2 million visitors during the Christmas season of 1963, seconding all its employees onto special task forces. Additionally, the reconnaissance units of the border police (already under an MfS OibE since 1959) were placed under MfS authority, while a division of labour was agreed with the NVA military intelligence. 'Personal protection' was another growth area. The MfS not only provided bodyguards but also the paternalistic 'total care' of functionaries and their families at the Wandlitz Politbüro settlement, right down to the sales personnel in the special supermarket supplying them with western products.

Thus, from 1964, the MfS was expanding its staff once again, and in 1968 went over to a policy of continuous expansion. Whereas at the beginning of the Mielke era in 1957 the MfS had had 17,400 employees, by the end of the Ulbricht leadership in 1971 it was 45,500. One of the most important internal beneficiaries was the central ministerial apparatus. By this point, at considerable expense, the MfS also operated training and further training programmes for its employees. The number of unofficial collaborators increased up to 100,000 in 1968. The MfS developed into a post-Stalinist, large-scale bureaucracy, a 'general enterprise for security, power-consolidation and oppression'.[46] By autumn 1989 its payroll had grown to 91,015 full-time employees, far outstripping the state security services of other socialist states. Thus, for every 1,000 GDR citizens there were approximately 5.5 MfS personnel, compared with 1.8 in the Soviet Union and 1.1 in Czechoslovakia. They were 84 per cent male and almost all SED members. The reason for the unprecedented size lay primarily in the uniquely dangerous position in which 'socialism in half a country'[47] perceived itself to be, on the frontline of the East–West conflict.

The ancillary apparatus became just as impressive. As its 'main weapon in the fight against the enemy'[48] the MfS, by the time it came to an end in 1989, had taken on approximately 175,000 unofficial collaborators. These kept their eyes and ears open in their daily lives, carried out assignments for their case-officers or opened their homes for meetings and surveillance. Overt chains of influence – via the party machinery, Volkspolizei, government administrations and economic apparatuses, cadre sections, army district defence commands and mass organisations – together with covert bugs and cameras, telephone, radio and postal monitoring, searches of flats and workplaces, and shadowing of suspects, all added up to a policy of 'total surveillance' (*flächendeckende Überwachung*).[49] In the event of war or domestic tension the MfS had contingency plans to detain 'hostile-negative' GDR citizens in isolation camps. It even secretly took odour samples of supposed dissidents or marked objects radioactively.

Moreover, Ulbricht's secret police managed to survive Ulbricht, when in May 1971 Erich Honecker overthrew his long-standing mentor and advanced to the position of First SED Secretary. Beforehand Mielke had in fact already entered into a loose 'coalition of interest' with the new party leader. He even had Ulbricht observed by his own bodyguards. The Minister of State Security was now one of the beneficiaries of the change in leadership.[50] At the eighth SED party congress in 1971, the Central Committee elected him as a candidate to the Politbüro. Five years later he became a voting member. However, this only incompletely describes the subsequent position of the MfS in the hierarchy of the SED state: Honecker discussed decisive issues regarding MfS activities with Mielke in weekly confidential chats. Thus the Minister belonged to the inner circle of leaders within the 'Politbureaucracy', thereby enlarging Mielke's political room for manoeuvre to pursue MfS sectional interests.[51]

While to the outside world the impression of unconditional subordination to the party leader prevailed, in the following two decades the Stasi became an 'army behind the scenes' of almost unlimited power. In the long term, the Ulbricht years were to prove the formative era for the MfS. In the 1950s it was moulded by its Stalinist image of the enemy and the world, which provided the key to its relationship with the civilian population. At the same time GDR citizens garnered their own, frequently painful experiences of the Communist security apparatus, which remained with them for the rest of their lives. After collectivisation and the building of the Wall the role of the Stasi changed, however: thenceforth it concerned more the consolidation of social power than establishing dominance. Everyday physical force receded, while, step by step, the MfS presence in all areas of society intensified. Yet in the long run even these experts in oppression and control did not manage to avert the GDR's final collapse.[52] The penetration of a society under 'total surveillance' had not prevented the growth of a reform movement. In his first and last speech to the Volkskammer, on 13 November 1989, when Mielke claimed to an increasingly restive audience that, 'We have, comrades and deputies, an extraordinarily close contact with all the working people', the irony was unintended. A note of uncertainty crept into his voice, however, and ripples of laughter spread around the chamber, at his now notorious claim that 'I love everybody, each and every one!'[53] If this was love, it was the tough love of an obsessive and ultimately self-destructive guardian, rejected by his children.

Notes

1 This is a condensed version of sections of an illustrated brochure of the Federal Commissioner for the Stasi Records: Jens Gieseke (with Doris Hubert), *The GDR State Security: Shield and Sword of the Party* (Berlin, forthcoming). Additional material can be found in: Jens Gieseke, '"Genossen erster Kategorie": Die hauptamtlichen Mitarbeiter des Ministeriums für Staatssicherheit als Elite', in Peter Hübner (ed.), *Eliten im Sozialismus: Beiträge zur Sozialgeschichte der DDR* (Cologne, 1999), 201–40; see also Jens Gieseke, *Die hauptamtlichen Mitarbeiter der Staatssicherheit: Personalstruktur und Lebenswelt 1950–1989/90* (Berlin, 2000).

2 Christoph Kleßmann, *Zeitgeschichte in Deutschland nach dem Ende des Ost-West-Konflikts* (Essen, 1998), 39.

3 For general information see Jens Gieseke, *Mielke-Konzern: Die Geschichte der Stasi 1945–1990* (Stuttgart and Munich, 2001); David Childs and Richard Popplewell, *The Stasi: The East German Intelligence and Security Service* (Basingstoke, 1996); Joachim Gauck, *Die Stasi-Akten* (Reinbek, 1991); David Gill and Ulrich Schröter, *Das Ministerium für Staatssicherheit: Anatomie des Mielke-*

Imperiums (Berlin, 1991); Mary Fulbrook, *Anatomy of a Dictatorship: Inside the GDR 1949–1989* (Oxford, 1995).
4 Erich Mielke, 'Mit hoher Verantwortung für den zuverlässigen Schutz des Sozialismus', *Einheit*, 30/1 (1975), 43 f.
5 A slight détente emerged in East–West relations in 1955. The eastern European secret services 'compensated' accordingly. Secret activity aimed at the West was to be substantially expanded, including both espionage and subversion in the opposing camp. The MfS district administrations formed their own espionage departments and the western assignments of the counter-intelligence lines were expanded. In line III (national economy), for example, working groups were set up for activities against western manufacturing concerns. Among other things, they were supposed to engage in industrial and military espionage. The work against 'inner enemies' was to take second place to this new main area of emphasis.
6 Mary Fulbrook, 'Herrschaft, Gehorsam und Verweigerung: Die DDR als Diktatur', in Jürgen Kocka and Martin Sabrow (eds), *Die DDR als Geschichte* (Berlin, 1994), 78.
7 Erich Mielke, *Sozialismus und Frieden – Sinn unseres Kampfes* (Berlin, 1987), 106. I have not been able to verify Dzerzhinsky's original.
8 Otto Bonhoff and Herbert Schauer, *Das unsichtbare Visier* (Berlin, n.d.).
9 Zaisser at the fifteenth SED-ZK plenum, 24–26 July 1953, SAPMO-BArch, DY 30, IV 2/1/119, fos 187–201: 190 f.
10 HA KuSch, Schulungsmaterial, 'Die Entwicklung tschekistischer Persönlichkeitseigenschaften', 4.
11 Sigrid Meuschel, *Legitimation und Parteiherrschaft in der DDR* (Frankfurt/Main, 1992), 19.
12 Walter Süß, 'Zum Verhältnis von SED und Staatssicherheit', in Andreas Herbst *et al.* (eds), *Die SED: Geschichte–Organisation–Politik: Ein Handbuch* (Berlin, 1997), 215–40; Siegfried Suckut and Walter Süß (eds), *Staatspartei und Staatssicherheit: Zum Verhältnis von SED und MfS* (Berlin, 1997); Silke Schumann, *Parteierziehung in der Geheimpolizei: Zur Rolle der SED im MfS der fünfziger Jahre* (Berlin, 1997).
13 Norman M. Naimark, *The Russians in Germany: A History of the Soviet Zone of Occupation, 1945–1949* (Cambridge, Mass. and London, 1995); Jan Foitzik, *Sowjetische Militäradministration in Deutschland (SMAD) 1945–1949* (Berlin, 1999).
14 Peter Reif-Spirek and Bodo Ritscher (eds), *Speziallager in der SBZ: Gedenkstätten mit 'doppelter Vergangenheit'* (Berlin, 1999).
15 Criminal offence class 5 of the Basic Classification of Criminal Offences, n.d. [1947]; BAB, DO-1/7/355, fos 210–19: here 219.
16 *Gesetzblatt der Deutschen Demokratischen Republik*, 15 (21 February 1950).
17 Provisorische Volkskammer, Protokoll der 10. Sitzung, 8 February 1950, 213.
18 'Die Volkskammer-Delegierten vor der Presse', *SBZ Archiv*, 3/18 (1952), 275.
19 Roger Engelmann, 'Diener zweier Herren: Das Verhältnis der Staatssicherheit zur SED und den sowjetischen Beratern 1950–1959', in Suckut and Süß (eds), *Staatspartei*, 51-72.
20 George Bailey *et al.*, *Battleground Berlin: CIA vs. KGB in the Cold War* (New Haven, 1997); for the death penalty see Richard J. Evans, *Rituals of Retribution: Capital Punishment in Germany, 1600–1987* (London, 1997), 805–71.

21 Wolfgang Kießling, *Partner im 'Narrenparadies': Der Freundeskreis um Noel Field und Paul Merker* (Berlin, 1994).
22 Jan Foitzik, 'Die stalinistischen "Säuberungen" in den ostmitteleuropäischen kommunistischen Parteien: Ein vergleichender Überblick', in Hermann Weber and Dietrich Staritz (eds), *Kommunisten verfolgen Kommunisten: Stalinistischer Terror und 'Säuberungen' in den kommunistischen Parteien Europas seit den dreißiger Jahren* (Berlin, 1993), 423.
23 Erich Mielke, Talk at the SED Party active conference in the MfS on 28 January 1953, BStU-ZA, KL-SED 570, fo. 24.
24 Wilhelm Zaisser at the SED Delegates' Conference in the MfS, 14–15 June 1952; BStU-ZA, KL-SED 572, fo. 504.
25 Horst Bischoff *et al.*, 'Zu den Angriffen der imperialistischen Geheimdienste gegen das MfS' (Diss. A JHS , 1977), BStU-ZA, HA KuSch AKG 4, Abschnitt 2.4, 2 f.
26 Torsten Diedrich *et al.* (eds), *Im Dienste der Partei: Handbuch der bewaffneten Organe der DDR* (Berlin, 1998).
27 Jan von Flocken and Michael F. Scholz, *Ernst Wollweber: Saboteur, Minister, Unperson* (Berlin, 1994).
28 On the concept of 'socialist paternalism', see Gerd Meyer, *Die DDR-Machtelite in der Ära Honecker* (Tübingen, 1991), 319–94: 339 f; also Konrad Jarausch, 'Realer Sozialismus als Fürsorgediktatur: Zur begrifflichen Einordnung der DDR', *Aus Politik und Zeitgeschichte*, B 20/98, 33–46.
29 Charles S. Maier, *Dissolution: The Crisis of Communism and the End of East Germany* (Princeton, NJ, 1997), 48. Herbert Reinke, 'Policing Politics in Germany from Weimar to the Stasi', in Mark Mazower (ed.), *The Policing of Politics in the Twentieth Century: Historical Perspectives* (Providence and Oxford: Berghahn, 1997), 91–106.
30 HA KuSch, Schulungsmaterial 'Die Entwicklung tschekistischer Persönlichkeitseigenschaften', 4.
31 SED-PB, 18 March 1952, SAPMO-BArch, DY 30, IV 2/2/202, fos 81–6: 81.
32 Cited in Georg Herbstritt, 'Volkspolizei und Staatssicherheit: "Operatives Zusammenwirken" gegen die evangelische Kirche in Mecklenburg', *Deutschland Archiv*, 31 (1988), 961–75: 962.
33 Helmut Müller-Enbergs (ed.), *Inoffizielle Mitarbeiter des Ministeriums für Staatssicherheit: Richtlinien und Durchführungsbestimmungen* (Berlin, 1996), 35–7.
34 Karl Wilhelm Fricke and Roger Engelmann, *'Konzentrierte Schläge': Staatssicherheitsaktionen und politische Prozesse in der DDR 1953–1956* (Berlin, 1998), 321 f.
35 Karl-Wilhelm Fricke, *Akten-Einsicht: Rekonstruktion einer politischen Verfolgung* (Berlin, 1995).
36 Roger Engelmann and Silke Schumann, 'Der Ausbau des Überwachungsstaates: Der Konflikt Ulbricht-Wollweber und die Neuausrichtung des Staatssicherheitsdienstes der DDR 1957', *Vierteljahrshefte für Zeitgeschichte*, 43 (1995), 341–78.
37 See Engelmann, 'Diener zweier Herren'.
38 Documented in Joachim Krüger, 'Votum für bewaffnete Gewalt: Ein Beschluß des SED-Politbüros vom November 1956', *Beiträge zur Geschichte der Arbeiterbewegung*, 34 (1992), 75–85.

39 Closing remarks of Comrade Mielke, minutes of the meeting of the SED District Administration, 18 April 1957; BStU-ZA, KL SED 91, fos 232–3 and 474–83: 482.
40 Speech by Szinda, Kreisdelegiertenkonferenz der SED-Parteiorganisation im MfS, 10–11 March 1956, BStU-ZA, KL-SED 572, fos 1200–3.
41 Deputy minister Bruno Beater to heads of the Bezirksverwaltungen, 21 November 1960; BStU-ZA, DSt 101156.
42 Hermann Matern at the second District Delegate Conference of the MfS, SAPMO-BArch, DY 30/IV A2/12/128, n.p. See also Siegfried Suckut, 'Generalkontrollbeauftragter der SED oder gewöhnliches Staatsorgan? Probleme der Funktionsbestimmung des MfS in den sechziger Jahren', in: Suckut and Süß (eds), *Staatspartei*, 151–67.
43 Quoted according to Monika Tantzscher, *'Maßnahme Donau und Einsatz Genesung': Die Niederschlagung des Prager Frühlings 1968/69 im Spiegel der MfS-Akten* (Berlin, 1994), 35 f, 122.
44 Dietrich Staritz, *Geschichte der DDR* (2nd edn; Frankfurt/Main, 1996), 196.
45 Gerhard Barkleit, *Die Rolle des MfS beim Aufbau der Luftfahrtindustrie der DDR* (Dresden, 1996).
46 Klaus Dietmar Henke, 'Staatssicherheit', in Werner Weidenfeld and Karl-Rudolf Körte (eds), *Handbuch zur deutschen Einheit* (new edn; Bonn, 1996), 646–53: 647.
47 Dietrich Staritz, *Sozialismus in einem halben Lande* (Berlin, 1975).
48 Müller-Enbergs (ed.), *Inoffizielle Mitarbeiter*, 305. Robert Gellately, 'Denunciations in twentieth-century Germany: aspects of self-policing in the Third Reich and the German Democratic Republic', in Sheila Fitzpatrick and Robert Gellately (eds), *Accusatory Practices: Denunciation in Modern European History, 1789–1989* (Chicago and London, 1997), 185–221; Barbara Miller, *Narratives of Guilt and Compliance in Unified Germany: Stasi Informers and their Impact on Society* (London and New York, 1999).
49 Timothy Garton Ash, *The File: A Personal History* (London, 1997).
50 John Schmeidel, 'Shield and sword of the party': internal repression, exterior espionage and support for international terrorism by the East German Ministry for State Security 1970–1989 (PhD thesis, University of Cambridge, 1995); Roger Woods, *Opposition in the GDR under Honecker, 1971–85* (Basingstoke, 1996).
51 H. Gordon Skilling and Franklyn Griffiths, *Interest Groups in Soviet Politics* (Princeton, NJ, 1971).
52 Walter Süß, *Staatssicherheit am Ende: Warum es den Mächtigen nicht gelang, 1989 eine Revolution zu verhindern* (Berlin, 1999); Roger Engelmann, 'Funktionswandel der Staatssicherheit', in Christoph Boyer and Peter Skyba (eds), *Repression und Wohlstandsversprechen: Zur Stabilisierung von Parteiherrschaft in der DDR und der CSSR* (Dresden, 1999), 89–97; Konrad Jarausch, *The Rush to German Unity* (New York, 1994).
53 *Deutschland Archiv*, 23 (1990), 121.

4

The people's police and the people in Ulbricht's Germany

Richard Bessel

The police in the new democratic state is in its essence and in its tasks something different than what it was in the Nazi state, which had to maintain its terror regime precisely through the police, especially the 'Secret State Police' [Gestapo]. Today the police really shall be the helper and protector of all sections of the people who are well-intentioned and willing to engage in rebuilding. It must become a People's Police [Volkspolizei] in the best sense of the word. (Georg König, Chief of Police in the Province of Saxony, May 1946)[1]

The establishment of the 'people's police'

The GDR was a postwar state, whose rise and fall coincided with the beginning and end of the postwar era in Europe. Far from being the expression of universal values and objective laws of historical development, as its leaders may have hoped and believed, this socialist experiment on German soil was the product of a specific conjuncture: the catastrophic end of Germany's Second World War. This fact frames the political, economic and social history of Ulbricht's Germany, including the establishment and early development of its new police force: the 'People's Police', the Volkspolizei. After the Second World War regimes across Europe faced the fundamental challenge of establishing order in the wake of the explosion of violence and destruction which had just occurred, and the effective policing of civil society was crucial to achieving this task. In the German territories which fell under Soviet control in 1945, this challenge was to prove particularly difficult.

Despite its importance, the policing of civil society in East Germany has tended to be somewhat overlooked by historians until fairly recently.[2] For perhaps understandable reasons, once the archive materials of the GDR became accessible to historians, investigation of the GDR's security apparatus – a security apparatus which grew to an astonishing size in what was, after all, quite a small country – first concentrated their attention on the secret police (the notorious 'State Security' organisation, MfS or the Stasi) and the military establishment in what became a highly militarised state. Accordingly, the main themes for historians who have looked at the development of the East German police have been first and foremost its organisational development, its politicisation and its relationship to the 'State

Security' and the 'National People's Army', both of which originally were offshoots of the Volkspolizei.[3] These certainly are important themes, and they cannot be disentangled from our subject here: how society was policed in a country as it emerged from Nazism and war and was subjected to a political and economic revolution.

In the aftermath of the Second World War, Germany's new rulers faced enormous problems of public order. The obligation to suppress any possible opposition to the occupying powers, the determination to impose a new political system upon a defeated population and the massive upsurge in crime and threats to public security in the chaotic postwar conditions combined to make policing a crucially important concern in postwar Germany. These concerns were present in all four Occupation Zones after 1945, but in the East – in the SBZ and in the GDR during its early years – they posed especially difficult problems. Not only was SMAD particularly rigorous and often brutal in enforcing its will, but the new political order being imposed in the East met with considerable and widespread popular hostility.

Soon after the Soviet military took control of what became the SBZ, Germans began bit by bit to be given responsibility for public order and security. Local officials – mayors and *Landräte* put in post by the Russians and usually veterans of the German labour movement or exiled Communists who had returned to Germany with the Red Army – were given the task of setting up local police forces.[4] The new police were drawn as far as was possible from among 'proven antifascists' – veterans of the labour movement, workers who had supported the Communists. Those known to have worked in police formations under the Nazi regime were removed, opening the police to people who never had been in police uniform before. Internal statistics compiled with almost obsessive energy on the composition of the police during the postwar years confirm that, as the German Administration of the Interior (or DVdI, set up under SMAD to operate the German internal security formations) asserted in its 'Annual Report for 1946–1947', 'over 90 per cent of the members of the police in the Soviet Occupation Zone are people from outside the profession'.[5]

The first East German police formations set up in the wake of the Nazi defeat had few resources at their disposal with which to deal with the huge problems they faced. The size of the new police initially was quite modest: in January 1946 the total personnel (both male and female, including clerical staff) of the German police in the SBZ was only 21,973 – or just over one police officer per 1,000 inhabitants.[6] Even in an orderly and peaceful society, this would have been a small number. What this meant on the ground may be illustrated by the case of the rural Pomeranian district of Demmin: there in August 1945 the police numbered only 85 people in a district containing roughly 90,000 inhabitants.[7] The new police members were almost completely inexperienced and untrained, having been chosen for political reliability rather than professional competence or previous service in police formations (something which usually served to disqualify people for employment in the newly formed Volkspolizei). They were relatively old, since trusted 'antifascists' tended to be either Social Democrats or Communists from the Weimar period or people who had had some experience of underground or trade union activity, and thus older than the sorts of men normally recruited into a police force. In any event, immediately after the war most of Germany's young men were either dead or in prisoner-of-war (POW) camps. As the head of the police in Bitterfeld explained in October 1946, 'many tested antifascists, who came from workshops and factories', initially had been taken into the new police; 'these were in many cases older comrades whose mental abilities were not sufficient to master service in the police'.[8] Many were underweight, and prone to illness.[9]

The new People's Police were also remarkably poorly equipped. Not until 1946 did the Soviet occupation authorities permit the bulk of the German police in their zone to be armed.[10] Even in late 1946 only 30 per cent of the personnel of many units had firearms, making it impossible for them effectively to confront armed criminals (at a time when there were many illegal arms in circulation) and breeding 'a passivity within the police which can have catastrophic consequences for public order and security'.[11] They possessed few if any motor vehicles, and even bicycles were a rarity (and bicycle tyres difficult to acquire), making the idea of police mobility little more than a joke.[12] They possessed little or nothing in the way of working telecommunications equipment, as the telephone network had been disrupted in large sections of the country owing to war damage and since the Soviet authorities initially did not permit the German police radio communication and allowed them to get their own telex network only in 1947.[13] The result was that in the first couple of years after the war it was virtually impossible for police stations to communicate quickly with one another or for local commanders to communicate with their superiors or subordinates. Almost none of the new police had had any police training; even after police training schools had been set up in all the East German *Länder*, following the opening of the first police training school in Saxony in March 1946, only a small proportion could be trained for their new profession quickly.[14] Many of the newly hired police recruits proved ill-disciplined and/or corrupt, as many had joined the force neither out of political conviction nor out of an altruistic desire to serve the public but primarily in order to gain food (ration cards), clothing (uniforms, boots) and shelter (police barracks); cases of drunkenness and theft among the Volkspolizei were not uncommon.[15]

Furthermore, huge problems stemmed from the Soviet military presence. During the period between the German surrender in May 1945 and the establishment of the GDR in October 1949, SMAD predictably took an active interest in matters concerning the police, keeping tight control over the activities of the Volkspolizei. At the same time, the Soviet presence constituted a fundamental problem for a police force caught between the concerns of the population which nominally it existed to protect and the demands and actions of the Soviet military. During the immediate postwar period, Soviet soldiers were a main source of violent crime, which began with the orgy of rape and other violence which accompanied their arrival in Germany in the winter and spring of 1945 and which continued to make the SBZ a very dangerous place after the German surrender.[16] Not just the civilian population but even members of the police could become victims of the violence of the occupier, and those German police who attempted to intervene in cases where Russian soldiers raped German women risked arrest or being shot.[17] Indeed, during the postwar years the rise and fall of violent crime, often by armed 'bandits' who frequently were Soviet soldiers or deserters, were mirrored in the numbers of casualties among the Volkspolizei: from May to December 1945 37 Volkspolizisten were killed in violent incidents; in 1946 the number rose to 87; and in 1947 the number dropped to 26 (although by this time the total number of German police in the SBZ had risen substantially).[18]

What is more, the Volkspolizei also had to take its orders from and to place a sizeable proportion of its personnel at the disposal of the Soviet military – to guard Soviet installations and to prevent theft and sabotage at reparations factories which had been taken over directly by the occupying power (the *Sowjetische Aktiengesellschaften*, or SAGs). For example, in the spring of 1947, SMAD ordered that 115 of the 130 regular constables (Schutzpolizei) in the city of Brandenburg be charged with 'guarding the bridges, reparations factories, shops and storage areas etc. of the Soviet occupation power', leaving only 15 (11.5 per cent of the total) for 'normal police work'; in Cottbus similar demands left only about a quarter of the city's Schutzpolizei available to plod the beat and staff police stations.[19] At the same time, the Volkspolizei – like all East German institutions – had constantly to maintain fawning allegiance to the USSR and its organs in Germany, and to refrain from taking action against Soviet soldiers no matter what the provocation. This latter point was driven home both privately and publicly; indeed, in 1948 in an article published in the new illustrated police journal, *Die Volkspolizei*, on 'The use of firearms', the members of the new German antifascist–democratic police force were told in no uncertain terms that 'use of weapons must never and under no circumstances be made against members of the occupation forces'.[20] This did not make life easy for an initially small and poorly equipped police force operating in one of the most severely disrupted societies Europe had ever seen.

Although its beginnings were modest, the new 'antifascist–democratic' Volkspolizei did not remain small and ill-equipped for very long. Already in 1946 a process of rapid expansion had begun: the total number of German police in the SBZ rose from 21,973 in January 1946 to 38,767 in July 1947, 54,729 in April 1948, 68,148 in September 1948 and to 83,178 (including

18,229 Border Police – Grenzpolizei – and paramilitary formations – Bereitschaften) in March 1949.[21] It would be mistaken to assume that this remarkable growth was primarily a response to rising crime. In fact it occurred as crime fell: the postwar crime wave peaked in late 1946–early 1947, and during 1947 and 1948 crime diminished in the SBZ.[22] Instead, the impetus was largely political and occurred at least partly at the insistence of SMAD, which was concerned to see the Germans take over security tasks – under Soviet supervision of course. For example, the Border Police had been created in November 1946 at the order of the Soviet authorities, who wanted the Germans to help patrol the border with the western occupation zones. This, of course, does not mean that German heads of the newly created DVdI lacked enthusiasm for the expansion of the Volkspolizei; it would be a strange police authority which sought anything other than an increase in the numbers of people under its command. Citing the high levels of crime in the SBZ and the considerable numerical strength of the police in the Weimar Republic, in late 1946 Erich Reschke and Willi Seifert, respectively President and Vice-President of the DVdI, attempted to convince SMAD to sanction a huge increase in the size of the Volkspolizei (to a level of four police per 1,000 inhabitants); their arguments, however, initially cut little ice, and the German proposals were dismissed by the Soviet military authorities on grounds of cost.[23] Nevertheless, by the time the GDR was established in October 1949, the manpower levels which Reschke and Seifert had proposed three years before had been reached and indeed, if one includes the Border Police and the special formations in barracks (kasernierte Bereitschaften) in the equation, had been exceeded. However, the stimulus here appears to have come less from concerns about the safety and security of the German civilian population than from a desire to impose political control as the Cold War came to dominate political life.

Policing for the regime; policing for the people

All police forces have a basic dichotomy in their function: between their responsibility to ensure the security of the civilian population and their duty to defend the state which employs them. To an extent this parallels the division in the function of the police on the beat (the Schutzpolizei, who were directly responsible for 'public security and order') and those involved in criminal investigation (the Kriminalpolizei, who were the 'investigative organ' of the public prosecuting service).[24] More generally, it reflects, on the one hand, the genuine concern to serve the people and, on the other, the necessity, when push comes to shove, to protect the state. Of course, just about all police forces will assert, in their public pronouncements, that this involves no fundamental contradiction, and this assertion usually is central to the self-perception and legitimation of the police, whether in pluralist or dictatorial regimes.

For an organisation which had been christened the 'People's Police', this contradiction and its denial necessarily assumed a heightened significance. Inherent in its name and in the ideology to which its leadership subscribed was the claim that the Volkspolizei existed to serve the people; inherent in its position, called into being ultimately to obey a foreign occupying power and to protect a new political system lacking broad support, was the fact that it served an unpopular regime. Both the claims of the Volkspolizei to be serving the true interests of the German people and the repeated insistence that its activity was explicitly political and that it existed to defend aggressively a particular political order against its enemies – alongside the insistence that this involved no contradiction – were particularly vehement. This reflected both the nature of the East German regime, whose leaders felt a deep distrust of a population (including the working class) which only a few years before had so enthusiastically supported Hitler,[25] and the intensity of the Cold War, which provided the necessary international context for the establishment and consolidation of the GDR. Indeed, with the deepening of the Cold War and the division of Germany, the security apparatus in the SBZ became increasingly politicised and important to the new regime. Control of a reliable and capable police force was crucial to efforts to impose a political and economic system which lacked the support of a sizeable proportion of the population and, later, to create a new East German military force.

This was reflected in the changes which the Volkspolizei underwent during the crucial year of 1948. Indeed, one may speak with some justification of 1948 as the year of the real establishment of the Volkspolizei. It was at that point that the intensification of the Cold War and the transformation of the SED into a 'new-type' party was reflected in a transformation of the police in the SBZ, which involved reorganisation and purges. In July Kurt Fischer replaced Erich Reschke as President of the DVdI and Chief of the Volkspolizei, and during the summer of 1948 'Political Culture' (Polit-Kultur, 'PK') sections were introduced into the Volkspolizei, mirroring developments elsewhere in the growing East German administration and following the model established in the Soviet military and police forces.[26] Fischer, who had been a member of the KPD's underground military organisation during the Weimar period, a student at the Soviet Military Academy between 1928 and 1932 and a Spanish Civil War veteran, spent the Second World War in the USSR, where he had been active in the secret services and served as an officer in the Red Army; in May 1945 he returned to Germany as a member of the KPD 'Initiative Group' sent to Saxony. After he had been named Saxon Interior Minister in 1946, the police under his command formed something of a model for the development of the Volkspolizei in the Soviet Zone.[27] Until his sudden death in June 1950, after which command of the Volkspolizei fell to Karl Maron, Fischer energetically and brusquely sought to turn the East German police into a thoroughly centralised, politicised and increasingly militarised force. Behind Fischer stood Walter

Ulbricht himself. It is clear that, among the German Communists setting up the new regime in the SBZ, Ulbricht was the driving force and possessed an authority far above that of his comrades, especially in decisions involving the all-important area of security and policing.

The 'PK-organs' were an essential element in adapting the Volkspolizei to the new, thoroughly politicised and dictatorial structures which were taking shape. Under the supervision of Erich Mielke, later the long-serving head of the Stasi, during the late summer and autumn of 1948 a PK officer was introduced at all levels of the police, to be 'responsible for the political and cultural activity of his area'.[28] Following a pattern whereby the nominal second in command was often more important than his superior, the PK officer was the 'First Deputy' to the commander of police units, and all orders required his counter-signature. The PK officers, to be chosen from among 'the best and most reliable sons of the working class', were responsible for the indoctrination and disciplining of the Volkspolizei members of their unit, and thus became the central figure in the repeated campaigns to purge the ranks of politically unreliable or suspect individuals during the late 1940s and early 1950s – campaigns which coincided with a slowdown in the numerical growth of the Volkspolizei in 1949. In addition, the PK-sections became responsible for the social, cultural and material interests of Volkspolizisten[29] – in effect assuming tasks which otherwise would have fallen to trade unions.

The Volkspolizei, as its leadership made clear time and again, was explicitly political. Criminality and the efforts to combat it, as well as the behaviour of individuals within the Volkspolizei, were to be measured against political criteria and from a 'class standpoint'. As an officer of the Thuringian Volkspolizei put it at a conference at the end of 1949: 'Police work is party work. One cannot separate these concepts.'[30] There was no sense of the new force being an impartial enforcer of the law: the 'People's Police' were expected explicitly to take sides in favour of the 'progressive' forces of the new antifascist–democratic, then socialist order. The point was made particularly forcefully by Karl Maron in a speech in Berlin in February 1953, delivered against the background of the development of the militarised 'People's police in barracks' (kasernierte Volkspolizei or KVP, the forerunner of the NVA) and shortly before the blow-up of June 1953:

> Its [the Volkspolizei's] essential task consists in breaking the resistance of the big capitalists and big landowners who have been overthrown and expropriated, in the liquidation of all attempts to restore the power of capital. That means that each individual Volkspolizist must lead an active struggle for the victory of democratic legality and the constant, unceasing strengthening of our popular power [Volksmacht], for the overpowering of enemies and enemy agents working from within ... The Volkspolizei can never be 'neutral' or 'unpolitical'.[31]

Published in *Die Volkspolizei*, this mission statement was meant as yet another clear signal to individual police officers as to how they were to behave and regard their profession. Obviously such an approach to policing was designed in the first instance to win the hearts and minds of a population largely sceptical and often hostile to the aims of the East German regime.

The police in Ulbricht's Germany

Despite its undoubted importance in helping to establish the East German state and despite the huge growth it had experienced during the late 1940s, the Volkspolizei did not become the most important element of the security apparatus of Ulbricht's Germany. That is to say, the relative importance of civilian policing clearly diminished as the GDR took shape and the huge postwar crime problem receded. The period of rapid numerical expansion of the Volkspolizei came to an end as the GDR's military establishment and its state security establishment began to grow parallel to the Volkspolizei, something which confirms that the main impetus for this expansion had not come from the requirements of policing civil society. Both the military and the state security apparatus – both of which were, in the later years of the GDR, to overshadow the Volkspolizei itself in terms of numbers, armament and importance – were, institutionally speaking, outgrowths of the People's Police. The origins of the notorious Staatssicherheit (Stasi) lay with the DVdI's 'Section for the Protection of the People's Economy' and with the notorious 'K5', the fifth department of the Criminal Police of the Volkspolizei. (The K5 had been charged with handling 'crimes of a special nature' – in other words war crimes, political crimes – and worked directly with the Soviet secret police from the outset; it became, as Norman Naimark has put it, 'the central organ for the political activities of police authorities in the zone'.)[32] These were joined together in May 1949 in the Volkspolizei's 'Main Administration for the Protection of the People's Economy', which in turn was transformed into the Ministry of State Security in February 1950. The origins of the NVA also lay with the Volkspolizei: its immediate predecessor was the 'People's police in barracks' (KVP), which had been set up in 1952 and which itself was the successor to the paramilitary formations (the kasernierte Bereitschaften) established at the insistence of the Soviet authorities during the second half of 1948.

During the early 1950s, civilian policing in the GDR underwent significant and far-reaching changes. Major catalysts for change came in 1952, when the administrative structure of the GDR was reformed, when Ulbricht committed the East German regime to building the 'foundations of socialism' on an inadequate resource base and when the Volkspolizei were charged with sealing the border to West Germany and enforcing the restricted zone (*Sperrzone*) which had been established abruptly and brutally at the end of May.[33] Speaking at the beginning of February 1953 to the assembled heads of the Volkspolizei on 'The Work of the Volkspolizei 1952 and the Perspectives for 1953', Karl Maron asserted that 'more has been changed and re-organised in the Volkspolizei in the last 4–5 months than in the entire period heretofore'.[34] Among the changes he listed were:

- The introduction of a 'special order' along the Demarcation Line (with West Germany).
- The re-organisation of the Volkspolizei in line with the administrative reform which abolished the five east German *Länder* and established fifteen new administrative regions (*Bezirke*) in their place. This meant not only a re-organisation of the top level of the Volkspolizei once Interior Ministries of the *Länder* (to which the police in the various *Länder* had nominally been responsible) were dissolved, but also an increase in the number of district police offices (VP-*Kreisämter*) from 127 to 199.
- The introduction of the system of 'Volunteer Auxiliaries' – *Freiwillige Helfer* – of the Volkspolizei.
- The appointment within the Volkspolizei of 'Section Plenipotentiaries' (*Abschnittsbevollmächtigte* or ABVs), which were to take over a large proportion of day-to-day policing. (In the case of both the *Freiwillige Helfer* and the ABVs, according to Karl Maron, the Volkspolizei benefited greatly from 'help and experience of the Soviet militia'.)
- The Kriminalpolizei were made a separate branch of the Volkspolizei and re-organised.
- A new internal disciplinary code was brought into force.
- 20,000 new members were recruited in connection with the transfer of police recruits to the militarised kasernierte Volkspolizei.
- The 'Main Administration of the German People's Police' (Hauptverwaltung der Deutschen Volkspolizei or HVDVP) took over running the prisons and youth detention centres.[35]

This amounted to a major restructuring of East German policing. Broadly it reflected the fact that the secret police and military functions had been or were being hived off, leaving the Volkspolizei with the (relatively) less important concerns of policing civil society. More specifically, the changes appear to have been prompted by two sets of concerns: on the one hand, the 'austerity regime' (Maron) required as the GDR was committed to the headlong rush to 'create the foundations of socialism' and the Volkspolizei had to divert resources to creating the KVP; and, on the other, the establishment of closer links with and closer control over the civilian population. Although the events of 1953 were to make many of the 'perspectives' outlined by Maron superfluous, the intention to bring the People's Police closer to the people through the *Freiwillige Helfer* and the ABV system should not be dismissed as mere window-dressing. As East German society became more law-abiding and easier to control than it had been during the immediate postwar years,[36] there developed scope for a more responsive model of civilian policing. In any event, as Maron pointed out, there was not the money available to increase the size of the Volkspolizei yet further.

Introduced by Maron, 'on the basis of the experiences of the Soviet Union', in the autumn of 1952 (first in Chemnitz/Karl-Marx-Stadt, then throughout the GDR),[37] the ABV system perhaps might be described best as the East German version of 'community policing'. Again and again it was stressed that the ABV had to develop a 'closer bond with the population'.[38] Its introduction in late 1952 fundamentally changed the organisation of everyday policing, giving all GDR citizens in effect their own local policeman on the beat; indeed, it was described by one leading police officer in 1956 as 'the most significant structural change of the German People's Police' since its creation after the Second World War.[39] The entire country was divided into mini-districts (*Abschnitte*) with roughly 3,500–4,000 inhabitants each, which gave the GDR roughly 4,700 ABVs altogether.[40] The ABVs, who were to be recruited from among 'only the most reliable and conscious Volkspolizisten with great experience of the most varied areas of police activity',[41] were made responsible for a wide variety of tasks in their own particular mini-district – for ensuring order, giving advice to local inhabitants, providing references (for example, if a resident applied for papers for travel to the West), keeping a watch on visitors especially if they came from the West, organising fire-prevention watches (something very important in rural districts) and preventing the 'sabotage' of production sites. He was expected to know all the residents in his area and visit them periodically, to live locally (which often proved a problem, as decent housing was difficult to find) and to be constantly on call. In short, he was responsible for just about everything in his district, and had to carry out his duties largely on his own.

The position of the ABV seems, therefore, to have been somewhat paradoxical: on the one hand, he was supposed to develop a 'close bond to the population'; on the other he was supposed to represent at all times the political imperatives dictated by the ruling SED.[42] Moreover, the ABV was the local face of a dictatorial and increasingly centrally controlled security apparatus;[43] yet, in practical terms he often was left to carry out day-to-day duties as he saw fit. As one former ABV (who after the 'Wende' took up working for a private security firm in Magdeburg) said, the ABV 'had to look for his work'.[44]

To help him with his tasks, the ABV was expected to rely on another major innovation introduced in 1952: the *Freiwillige Helfer*, the volunteer auxiliaries, of the Volkspolizei. The *Freiwillige Helfer* were supposed to be citizens who voluntarily signed up to help the Volkspolizei (and, particularly, to assist the ABV) with their tasks. They numbered roughly 27,000 in March 1953 and about 35,000 by the time of the June 1953 protests.[45] As their name implies, they were used to support the regular police: to assist on special occasions, such as when a police presence was required for events on state holidays, to act as a fire-prevention watch in rural areas during periods of dry weather, to guard factories and warehouses, to help with manhunts and to assist the police with their regular beats or patrol neighbourhoods to ensure that the streets were safe and that all was peaceful.[46] Although the volunteers sometimes complained about being required to put in too much time as police auxiliaries and sometimes failed to show up for duty,[47] roaming around with the red armband of the *Freiwillige Helfer* had its attractions. Some auxiliaries genuinely were motivated to help build the new socialist system; some quite liked the idea of being able to exert a measure of authority over their neighbours; some took advantage of their position to get free beer at the local inn; some had bowed to the pressure to join up which was applied by their local party organisation; and for some it offered the least onerous way to show their commitment to 'socialism' and thus fend off pressure to volunteer for something more demanding.[48]

Here the two aims of extending political control and coping with tight financial constraints appeared happily linked. The introduction of the *Freiwillige Helfer* and the ABVs was intended to enable the Volkspolizei to develop a model of policing which was close to the people, which exercised control over the population's everyday activities, and which was cheap to operate. Had not popular discontent boiled over as a result of political repression and severe economic difficulties and shortages (caused by the decision approved at the second SED Party Conference in July 1952 'to create the foundations of socialism in all areas of society') and had there not been an open border to the West, then perhaps this policing system would have functioned well.

With the 1953 uprising, however, visions of effective policing close to the people receded into the background. The events of June 1953 were a milestone in the history of policing in the GDR, as indeed they were for the history of Ulbricht's Germany as a whole. Although it was apparent that the headlong drive to create 'the foundations of socialism' had caused increasing hardship for the mass of the population and provoked widespread popular discontent, the East German ruling elite – including the heads of the Volkspolizei and of the secret police – were caught by surprise when unrest erupted first among the building workers on the Stalinallee in Berlin and then spread rapidly throughout the GDR. This was clearly worker protest: as the demonstrations spread on 17 June workers went out onto the streets to show their solidarity with the striking comrades on the building sites of the Stalinallee.[49] They therefore constituted a direct challenge to the ideological legitimation as well as to the physical survival of the regime. The protests also exposed the inadequacy not only of the secret policing regime (and cost the first Minister for State Security, Wilhelm Zaisser, his job), but also of public policing, including the innovations which had been put into place during the previous year. The attempt to bring the police closer to the people and thereby to cement loyalty to the new state and effectively to extend its control over the population had failed.

This was made evident by the events of June 1953 in three ways. First, although serious violent incidents had taken place between the Volkspolizei and workers during the previous years, most notably with Wismut miners in Saalfeld in August 1951,[50] the police failed to foresee trouble in 1953 or to make adequate preparations for possible serious unrest. Whatever its merits and successes in other regards and notwithstanding its importance in later years, the introduction of the ABVs and *Freiwillige Helfer* appears to have been irrelevant to the storm brewing in the GDR when Stalin died. Second, although they were able to hold the line in many places and although they subsequently were praised for their courage in upholding socialism against an alleged fascist coup attempt,[51] the Volkspolizei were not always able to maintain order or suppress the unrest on the day. Reports telexed from police stations from throughout the republic to Berlin testify to the fact that in a number of localities the police largely lost control of the situation.[52] It did not help that some members and officers were reluctant to shoot the people, and subsequently this was harshly criticised.[53] The most notable case was that of Herbert Paulsen, Chief of the Volkspolizei in the Magdeburg region, who was removed from his command and disciplined by the party in August 1953 for his 'capitulationist behaviour' in June (that is, his failure to order his men to shoot at the public), behaviour which allegedly had allowed demonstrators successfully to storm a number of public buildings including the Magdeburg police headquarters.[54] Third, in a number of towns (most notably Leipzig, Halle, Merseburg, Magdeburg, Potsdam and, of course, Berlin), the Volkspolizei themselves were the targets for popular hostility and were physically attacked, suffering a number of dead and seriously injured.[55] The anger and violence seems to have been directed at the police primarily in their role as gaolers, keeping behind bars people accused of political crimes; the most serious violence arose where crowds attempted to take over police prisons and free prisoners.

For the Volkspolizei, and for the Ulbricht regime as a whole, 1953 was a turning point.[56] As noted above, by that time 'state security' and the embryo of the future 'National People's Army' had already effectively been hived off from the Volkspolizei. The numbers of police, which had risen rapidly in the late 1940s and from which the kasernierte Volkspolizei had been recruited in the early 1950s, peaked at around the time of the 1953 uprising. Although the uprising taught the East German leadership the necessity of improving their internal security apparatus, this did not lead to a further growth in the Volkspolizei. Their numbers remained fairly steady, declining somewhat during the second half of the 1950s and again during the 1960s, before increasing thereafter.[57] It became a feature of Ulbricht's Germany that policing was by no means limited to the Volkspolizei, and it was the MfS and the NVA which grew substantially in the years which followed the uprising. In addition, after the 1953 rising the 'Factory Combat Groups'

(Betriebskampfgruppen), which had begun to be formed in a sporadic manner within factories in a number of industrial centres in 1952, were expanded rapidly throughout the GDR to become an important element of national defence. Although from 1955 these 'Combat Groups of the Working Class' (Kampfgruppen der Arbeiterklasse) were trained by the Volkspolizei and took their orders from the local Volkspolizei headquarters, after the establishment of the NVA the Kampfgruppen became explicitly part of the national defence establishment, and even participated in Warsaw Pact exercises in 1970.[58]

Although the Volkspolizei were relatively eclipsed after the 1953 rising, the experience of mass protest and the obvious inadequacies of the police response led it to improve its operational planning for the event of popular unrest. At the end of 1953 a comprehensive alarm plan was introduced with the aim of ensuring that the police could suppress quickly any sudden oppositional activity; on the first two anniversaries of the 17 June 1953 the entire Volkspolizei organisation was placed in a state of heightened readiness; and in November 1956, after the Hungarian uprising, a new two-stage plan for combatting internal unrest was decreed, which aimed to co-ordinate the activities of the police with those of the other armed forces at the disposal of the east German state (in the first instance with the Ministry of State Security, the Kampfgruppen, and – if these should prove inadequate – then the NVA, which would assume responsibility for the action).[59] In the wake of the events of June 1953 the Volkspolizei also saw its firepower increase, although the amount of weaponry given to the police continued to fall short of what was desired.[60] And in 1957 the names of officers' ranks were changed to military ones, reversing the decision in 1945 to introduce civilian terminology into the East German police formations.[61] As the Volkspolizei declined in relative importance as an organ of the security apparatus, it became increasingly militarised, reflecting the general militarisation of state and society in the GDR.

Concluding remarks

In March 1949, *Die Volkspolizei* published a poem by Police Oberkommissar Werner Ludwig. Entitled simply 'Die Volkspolizei', it went as follows:

Wir sind aus dem Volke geboren,	We are all the sons of the people,
dem Volke gehört unsre Kraft	to the people belongs all our strength
Im Kampfe vereint und verschworen	In struggle we swear our allegiance
mit jedem, der aufbaut und schafft.	to all those who build and create.
Drum auf die Reihen geschlossen,	Therefore let's close up our ranks,
dann sind wir einig und frei!	then we're united and free!
Wir sind eure Brüder und Schwestern,	We are your brothers and sisters,
wir Kämpfer der Volkspolizei!	we fighters of the People's Police!

Wir standen selbst in den Betrieben, am Schraubstock, am Pflug, im Büro.	We ourselves stand guard in the factories, at the workbench, at the plough, at the desk.
Wir schützen das Werk eurer Hände, daß nie mehr ein Feind es bedroh.	We're protecting the fruits of your labours that no foe might again cause them harm.
Drum auf die Reihen geschlossen, dann sind wir einig und frei! Wir sind eure Brüder und Schwestern, wir Kämpfer der Volkspolizei!	Therefore let's close up our ranks, then we're united and free! We are your brothers and sisters, we fighters of the People's Police!
Wir sind keine Söldner und Knechte, nicht Diener der Ausbeuterschicht. Den Aufbau des Landes zu sichern ist unsere Ehre und Pflicht.	We are not mercenaries nor vassals, not slaves of the exploiting class. It is both our honour and duty to ensure that our land is rebuilt.
Drum auf die Reihen geschlossen, dann sind wir einig und frei! Wir sind eure Brüder und Schwestern, wir Kämpfer der Volkspolizei!	Therefore let's close up our ranks, then we're united and free! We are your brothers and sisters, we fighters of the People's Police![62]

Ludwig may not have been one of the twentieth century's great literary figures, but his ode captures the way in which the Volkspolizei sought to present itself in public during its early years. The naive hopes and posturing, the simplistic reflection of the ideology of East German communism, and the unconscious parallels to the public language of the first German dictatorship were typical of the formative years of Ulbricht's Germany, as was the lack of any public acknowledgement of problems which contradicted this picture. In its later years, especially under Erich Honecker, the Volkspolizei increasingly tried to present itself as a technically competent and professional force thoroughly capable of protecting the public and upholding the security of the state. The best reflection of this is the two-volume official history of the Volkspolizei published shortly before the collapse of the GDR, which in its second volume (covering the period from 1961) gave much space to projecting the police as a modern and technically sophisticated force (complete with numerous photos illustrating the Volkspolizei using its new equipment).[63] Another – and for its effect upon popular perceptions probably far more important – example is the long-running East German television series 'Polizeiruf 110', which attempted to bring a note of social realism into popular entertainment in the GDR and showed a modern, competent and personally sympathetic police. Nevertheless, neither the Volkspolizei nor the GDR as a whole ever really freed itself of the stylised, politicised picture presented in the poem above: of a police force of the people, the 'brothers and sisters' of the Volk, 'fighters' serving the people in a political struggle. In this sense, neither the Volkspolizei nor the state and system which it served, ever really emerged from the postwar era in which it was born. When the postwar era ended, Ulbricht's Germany and its People's Police ended with it.

Notes

1 Landeshauptarchiv Sachsen-Anhalt (LHS S-A), MdI, Nr. 3021, fos 44–7: Chef der Polizei, 'Rundererlaß Nr. I', 21 May 1946.
2 Richard Bessel, 'Polizei zwischen Krieg und Sozialismus: Die Anfänge der Volkspolizei nach dem Zweiten Weltkrieg', in Christian Jansen *et al.* (eds), *Von der Aufgabe der Freiheit: Festschrift für Hans Mommsen* (Berlin, 1995), 516–31; Bessel, 'Grenzen des Polizeistaates: Polizei und Gesellschaft in der SBZ und der frühen DDR', in Richard Bessel and Ralph Jessen (eds), *Die Grenzen der Diktatur* (Göttingen, 1996), 224–52; Thomas Lindenberger, 'Die deutsche Volkspolizei (1945–1990)', in Torsten Dietrich *et al.* (eds), *Im Dienste der Partei: Handbuch der bewaffneten Organe der DDR* (Berlin, 1998), 97–152; Thomas Lindenberger, 'Der ABV im Text: Zur internen und öffentlichen Rede über die Deutsche Volkspolizei der 1950er Jahre', in Alf Lüdtke and Peter Becker (eds), *Akten, Eingaben, Schaufenster: Die DDR und ihre Texte* (Berlin, 1997), 136–66.
3 For the GDR perspective, see Ministerium des Innern (ed.), *Geschichte der Deutschen Volkspolizei* (Berlin, 1987). On the legal position and organisation, see Hartwig Lüers, *Das Polizeirecht in der DDR: Aufbau, Befugnisse und Organisation der Deutschen Volkspolizei* (Cologne, 1974). On the Volkspolizei in the development of the GDR's armed forces, see Rüdiger Wenzke, 'Auf dem Wege zur Kaderarmee. Aspekte der Rekrutierung, Sozialstruktur und personellen Entwicklung des entstehenden Militärs in der SBZ/DDR bis 1952/53', in Bruno Thoß (ed.), *Volksarmee schaffen – ohne Geschrei! Studien zu den Anfängen einer 'verdeckten Aufrüstung' in der SBZ/DDR 1947–1952* (Munich, 1994), 205–72; Joachim Schunke, 'Von der HVA über die KVP zur NVA', in Wolfgang Wünsche (ed.), *Rührt euch! Zur Geschichte der NVA* (Berlin, 1998), 39–74.
4 See, for example, the informative account by the II. Bürgermeister of Anklam, installed in office in May 1945. Mecklenburgisches Landeshauptarchiv (MLHA), KT/RdK Anklam, Nr. 39, fos 29–33: II. Bürgermeister, 'Tätigkeitsbericht für die Zeit vom 7. Mai bis zum 16. Juli 1945', 16 July 1945.
5 For example, statistics compiled by the DVdI for June 1947 show that of the 39,683 Volkspolizei members in the SBZ, 2101 (6.0 per cent) had worked in the police before 1945 and a further 940 (2.7 per cent) before 1933. BAB, DO-1/7/138, fo. 66: 'Personalstruktur. Monat: Juni 1947'. The highest percentage of those employed in the police before 1945, 15.2 per cent, was among the Administrative Police, which also employed by far the highest percentage of women (46.0 per cent, as compared with 12.1 per cent as a whole); it is possible, therefore, that a disproportionate number of Volkspolizei members who had worked for the police under the Nazis were female clerical staff.
6 Wenzke, 'Auf dem Wege zur Kaderarmee', 237.
7 MLHA, KT/RdK Demmin, Nr. 69, fos 70–1: Kreis- und Ortspolizeibehörde to Präsident des Landes Mecklenburg-Vorpommern, 31 August 1945.
8 LHS S-A, LBdVP, Nr. 27, fos 87–103 (fo. 96): 'Protokoll der Konferenz der Polizeiführer der Schutz- und Landpolizei des Bezirks Merseburg am 26.10.1946 10.00 Uhr in der Provinzialverwaltung, Halle'. According to internal statistics on the personnel structure of the Volkspolizei in the SBZ in June 1947, 31.8 per cent of the Schutzpolizei as a whole (and 30.5 per cent of the 'Mannschaften'!) were over 40. BAB, DO-1/7/138, fo. 66: 'Personalstruktur, Monat: Juni 1947'.

9 LHA S-A, LBdVP, Nr. 309, fo. 178: Kommando der Schutzpolizei, 'Einrichtungen und Maßnahmen zum Schutze der Gesundheit von Polizeiangehörigen', 3 March 1947.
10 For example, for the 950 Schutzpolizei members in Magdeburg in November 1945 there were only 13 7.65 pistols available – one for the Commander, eight for the Section Chiefs ('Reviervorsteher'), two for 'keeping watch on the bank', one for 'purposes of training' and one for prisoner transports. LHS S-A, LBdVP, Nr. 290, fo. 14–15: Polizeipräsident to Bezirkspräsidenten, 8 November 1945.
11 BAB, DO-1/7/364, fo. 23: Deutsche Verwaltung des Innern (DVdI - Reschke und Wagner) to SMAD, Abt. für innere Angelegenheiten, Oberstleutnant Smirnow, [?] November 1946.
12 As late as October 1948 the Landesbehörde der Volkspolizei in Sachsen-Anhalt complained that, because police lacked bicycles and bicycle tyres, they were unable to protect farmers' fields effectively from thieves on bicycles who therefore were 'far better equipped than the police officers chasing them'. LHA S-A, MdI, Nr. 4161, fo. 129: Landesbehörde to Minister des Innern, 4 October 1948.
13 The Volkspolizei were given permission to set up a telex network in January 1947, but this was not in place and functioning until August. BAB, DO-1/7/19, fos 42–117 (fo. 74): 'Jahresbericht. Deutsche Verwaltung des Innern in der sowjetischen Besatzungszone, 1946–1947'.
14 In April 1947 Walter Mickinn, Head of the DV(d)I's Personnel Section, reported that in Thuringia 'roughly 65%' of police still had not received training, in Brandenburg 70 per cent, and in Sachsen-Anhalt and Mecklenburg 94 per cent and 95 per cent, respectively. BAB, DO-1/7/138, fos. 76–86: Landespolizei Thüringen; *ibid.*, fos 89–94: Landespolizei Sachsen-Anhalt; *ibid.*, fos 99–109: Landespolizei Mecklenburg; *ibid.*, fos 112–15: Landespolizei Brandenburg.
15 Norman Naimark, '"To Know Everything and to Report Everything Worth Knowing": Building the East German Police State, 1945–1949' (Working Paper No. 10, Cold War International History Project, August 1994), 4–5; LHA S-A, LBdVP, Nr. 27, fos 87–103: 'Protokoll der Konferenz der Polizeiführer der Schutz-und Landespolizei des Bezirks Merseburg am 26.10.1946 10.00 Uhr, in der Provizialverwaltung, Halle' (comments by Colonel Stachanowsky, fos 87–8).
16 Norman Naimark, *The Russians in Germany* (Cambridge, Mass., 1995), 357.
17 *Ibid.*, 116.
18 BAB, DO-1/7/169, fo. 1: Abteilung P[ersonal], 'Todesfälle von Polizeiangehörigen', to Präsidenten [der DVdI] via Vizepräsidenten Mielke, 2 July 1948.
19 *Ibid.*, Nr. 138, fos. 112–25: Landespolizei Brandenburg.
20 Polizeikommissar Boettcher, 'Die Anwendung der Schußwaffe', *Die Volkspolizei*, 1/7 (September 1948), 6.
21 These figures are not exactly comparable; for example, the 5,000–6,000 members of the railway police are not included for 1946–48. However, the general trend is quite clear. Figures taken from statistics compiled by the DVdI are published in Wenzke, 'Auf dem Wege zur Kaderarmee', 237. See also Lindenberger, 'Die Deutsche Volkspolizei', 99.
22 See *Geschichte der Deutschen Volkspolizei*, i, 115-16.
23 BAB, DO-1/7/5, fos 2–3: 'Niederschrift über die am 19.11.1946 stattgefundene Besprechung zwischen Oberst Leutnant Smirnow, Vizepräsident Seifert und Dr.

Zeitz in Haushaltfragen für die Polizei'; BAB, DO-1/7/5, ff. 39: Willi Seifert, 'Besprechung zwischen Generalmajor Malkow und Präsident Reschke am 18.11.1946'; LHA S-A, LBdVP, Nr. 27, fos 42–52: 'Bericht über die am 22. und 23. November 1946 bei der Deutschen Verwaltung des Inneren in Berlin-Wilhelmsruh, Kurze Straße 5, stattgefundene Arbeitstagung'.

24 Thomas Lindenberger, 'Der ABV als Landwirt: Zur Mitwirkung der Deutschen Volkspolizei bei der Kollektivierung der Landwirtschaft', in Thomas Lindenberger (ed.), *Herrschaft und Eigen-Sinn in der Diktatur: Studien zur Gesellschaftsgeschichte der DDR* (Cologne, 1999), 167–8; Thomas Lindenberger, 'Öffentliche Polizei im Staatssozialismus: Die Deutsche Volkspolizei', in Hans-Jürgen Lange (ed.), *Kontinuitäten und Brüche: Staat, Demokratie und Innere Sicherheit in Deutschland* (Leverkusen, 1999).

25 See the suggestive remarks in Olaf Groehler, 'Antifaschismus – vom Umgang mit einem Begriff', in Ulrich Herbert and Olaf Groehler, *Zweierlei Bewältigung: Vier Beiträge über den Umgang mit der NS-Vergangenheit in den beiden deutschen Staaten* (Hamburg, 1992), 33.

26 Dieter Marc Schneider, 'Innere Verwaltung/Deutsche Verwaltung des Innern (DVdI)', in Martin Broszat and Hermann Weber (eds), *SBZ Handbuch* (2nd edn; Munich, 1993), 212–3.

27 *Geschichte der Deutschen Volkspolizei*, i, 115; Naimark, '"To Know Everything"', 16; Schneider, 'Innere Verwaltung/Deutsche Verwaltung des Innern', 212.

28 *Geschichte der Deutschen Volkspolizei*, i, 131; Naimark, *The Russians in Germany*, 366–8; Norman Naimark, 'Moskaus Suche nach Sicherheit und die sowjetische Besatzungszone 1945–1949', in Siegfried Suckut and Walter Süß (eds), *Staatspartei und Staatssicherheit: Zum Verhältnis von SED und MfS* (Berlin, 1997), 45.

29 This was explicitly underlined by Heinz Hoffmann, then Vice-President of the DVdI. BAB, DO-1/7/101, fo. 17: Hoffmann, 'Die Aufgaben der PK-Abteilung im Kampf um die ideologische Festigung der Volkspolizei', at the second PK-Leiter Konferenz in Berlin on 8–9 September 1949.

30 BAB, DO-1/7/266, fos 152–69 (fo. 157): Landesbehörde der Volkspolizei, Abteilung Schutzpolizei, 'Protokoll-Notiz über die am 28.12.1949 bei der LBdVP Thüringen stattgefundene Arbeitstagung der Leiter der S.', 28 December 1949.

31 Karl Maron, 'Auch die Volkspolizei muß von der Sowjetunion lernen', *Die Volkspolizei*, 6/4 (February 1953), 1, 3.

32 Naimark, *The Russians in Germany*, 360-4.

33 Inge Bennewitz and Rainer Potratz, *Zwangsaussiedlungen an der innerdeutschen Grenze* (Berlin, 1994).

34 BAB, DO-1/11/70, fos 1–21 (fo. 20): HVDVP, Sekretariat, 'Protokoll über die Chefbesprechung am 3. Februar 1953', 5 February 1953.

35 BAB, DO-1/11/70, fos 1–21 (fos 3–4).

36 In his report, Maron noted that the number of criminal offences in the GDR fell from 157,118 in 1951 to 103,241 in 1952. BAB, DO-1/11/70, fos 1–21 (fo. 8). Thus the GDR police state was approaching a situation where the number of police exceeded the annual number of criminal offences! However, Maron also noted that the number of criminal offences committed by Volkspolizei members had risen from 967 in 1951 to 1,259 in 1952! This meant that the civilian population was, on average, more law-abiding than the police!

37 Comments by Chefinspekteur Strieder, in BAB, DO-1/11/70, fos 58–74 (fos 58–9): 'Protokoll über die Chefbesprechung am 1.12.1953'.
38 Lindenberger, 'Der ABV im Text', 143.
39 Weidlich, 'Der Abschnittsbevollmächtigte bekämpft die kleine Kriminalität', in *Die Volkspolizei*, 9/13 (1956), 13. Quoted in *ibid.*, 140.
40 On 1 June 1953 the number of 'Abschnitte' stood at 4,768, and the number of ABV at 4,643. BAB, DO-1/11/415, fo. 97: 'Stand der Abschnittsbevollmächtigten am 1.6.1953'. Generally, see Lindenberger, 'Der ABV als Landwirt', 169–72.
41 Politbüro resolution of 29 July 1952 'on the improvement of the work of the Volkspolizei', quoted in Lindenberger, 'Der ABV im Text', 142.
42 Lindenberger, 'Der ABV als Landwirt', 201–3.
43 On the centralisation process, see Bessel, 'Polizei zwischen Krieg und Sozialismus', 517–31.
44 'Man mußte seine Arbeit suchen.' Interview with N.N. in Magdeburg, 23 August 1994.
45 Comments by Chefinspekteur Strieder, in BAB, DO-1/11/70, fos 58–74 (fo. 62): 'Protokoll über die Chefbesprechung am 1.12.1953'; BAB, DO-1/11/414, fos 254–5: 'Ausbau des System der freiwilligen Helfer der Volkspolizei'.
46 BAB, DO-1/11/414, fo. 212: Polit-Verwaltung der HVDVP, 'Bericht über die Freiwilligen Helfer-Gruppen', 28 August 1952.
47 Comments by Chefinspekteur König in BAB, DO-1/11/70, fos 22–57 (fos 24–5): HVDVP, 'Protokoll über die Chefbesprechung am Freitag, den 20. März 1953', 25 March 1953.
48 Interview with N.N. in Magdeburg, 23 August 1994.
49 See telex reports sent by various police stations around the GDR on 17, 18 and 19 June 1953 to the HVDVP in Berlin, in BAB, DO-1/11/44.
50 For the most serious outbreak, see Andrew Port, 'When workers rumbled: the Wismut upheaval of August 1951 in East Germany', *Social History*, 22/2 (1997), 139-73; Richard Bessel, 'Patterns of provocation: the "People's Police" and the miners of Saalfeld, August 1951', in Richard Bessel and Clive Emsley (eds), *Patterns of Provocation: Police and Public Disorder* (Oxford, 2000). See also Heide Roth and Torsten Diedrich, 'Wir sind Kumpel - uns kann keiner: Der 17. Juni 1953 in der SAG Wismut', in Rainer Karlsch and Harm Schröter (eds), *'Strahlende Vergangenheit': Studien zur Geschichte des Uranbergbaus der Wismut* (St Katharinen, 1996), 228–59.
51 Karl Maron, 'Bewährungsprobe', in *Die Volkspolizei*, 6/12 (June 1953), 6–7.
52 Telex reports to the HVDVP in BA, DO-1/11/44.
53 BAB, DO-1/11/305, fos 224–32: [BDVP Halle], Polit-Abteilung, 'Instructeur-Bericht anlässlich der Provokationen am 17.6.53 im VPK Eisleben', 26 June 1953.
54 BAB, DO-1/11/305, fos 343–4: 'Protokoll über die am 12. August 1953 stattgefundene erweiterte Parteileitungstagung', 14 August 1953; BAB, DO-1/11/305, fos 345–6: 'Beschluß der Mitgliederversammlung am Mittwoch, den 12.8.1953 der Grundorganisation der BDVP Magdeburg'; BAB, DO-1/11/305, fos 350–2: [HVDVP], Politische Verwaltung, 'Bericht über das Verhalten des Genossen Chefinspekteur Paulsen am 17.6.1953', 17 August 1953.
55 BAB, DO-1/11/45, fos 11–16: HVDVP Operativstab, 'Rapport Nr. 166.

Gesamtbericht über die Ereignisse am 17.6.1953', 18 June 1953.
56 For the best overview, see Lindenberger, 'Die Deutsche Volkspolizei', 97–152.
57 See the tables in Lindenberger, 'Die Deutsche Volkspolizei', 107, 132.
58 Andreas Herbst et al., *So funktionierte die DDR* (Reinbeck, 1994), i, 465–66.
59 Lindenberger, 'Die Deutsche Volkspolizei', 119–21.
60 *Ibid.*, 110–11.
61 *Ibid.*, 121.
62 *Die Volkspolizei*, 2/3 (March 1949), 17.
63 *Geschichte der Deutschen Volkspolizei*. This can be seen in the treatment of themes such as 'The Increase in the Operational Effectiveness of the Volkspolizei and the Fire Service' (66–89), 'The Development of the Schutzpolizei into the Main Operational Force of the Volkspolizei' (104–21), 'The Carrying Through of New Working Methods the Volkspolizei' (160–72), 'The Decisive Course towards the Strengthening of the Operational–Preventative Activities and the Societal Effectiveness of Police Work' (185–210), and the 'High Effectiveness of the Actions of the Volkspolizei and the Fire Service' (278–95).

5

'Protecting the accomplishments of socialism'? The (re)militarisation of life in the German Democratic Republic

Corey Ross

The GDR has long been considered a highly militarised police state. Measured in terms of size and population, the GDR seemed quite filled to the brim with military and paramilitary organisations and installations: the KVP, out of which grew the NVA; various armed police units such as the Border Police (Grenzpolizei) and Alert Police (Bereitschaftspolizei); the Workforce Combat Groups (Kampfgruppen der Arbeiterklasse); the paramilitary Society for Sport and Technology (Gesellschaft für Sport und Technik, or GST); and of course the Red Army, all of which took up a huge amount of the small state's territory including the minimum half-kilometre strip along the border to the FRG. By the time the GDR collapsed, it is estimated that around 10 per cent of the working population (750,000 people) were involved in the web of military and paramilitary organisations, whether on a voluntary basis or as a primary or secondary occupation.[1]

Even apart from this proliferation of armed fighting units, East Germany has also long been considered a highly militarised society in a more general sense. Military metaphors have often been used to describe the Soviet-style socialist states, with their clear lines of command, stress on obedience, demands for strict discipline, bellicose rhetoric and constant attempts to mobilise the populace for the great struggle. Military training in some form or another was an aspect of everyday life which few East Germans, especially youths, could escape entirely. Even former East German apologist historians have remarked after 1990 that there was a certain 'societal militarisation' in the GDR, from the 'strict structures of command in the SED and state apparatus to the command-system economy to role calls and rituals of command in the schools and classrooms'.[2] The dozens of entries under the term *Militarisierung* in the multi-volume report of the Enquete-Kommission,[3] the official parliamentary body charged with examining the GDR's history and legacy for a united Germany after 1990, show that this concept has informed a large part of the discussion. Without attempting to offer a comprehensive overview of these debates, this chapter will examine the broad outlines of the process of militarisation during the Ulbricht era, during which East Germany was transformed from a demobilised Occupation Zone resounding with calls for 'peace, bread and socialism' to a small state on the front lines of the Cold War armed to the teeth and organised largely according to military principles of command and discipline.

But before proceeding, a brief word on terms of reference seems necessary. It is useful to distinguish at the outset between, on the one hand, 'militarism', a rather ambiguous buzzword which carries a wide range of connotations, and, on the other, 'militarisation', for the extent to which the GDR can be regarded as a 'militarised society' is largely a matter of how one defines the term. Focusing on the problem of states and armed conflict, Michael Geyer distinguishes between 'militarisation' as a 'social process in which civil society organises itself for the production of violence', and 'militarism' as an older concept denoting either the predominance of military over civilian authority, or more generally the prevalence of warlike values in society.[4] Whereas militarisation in this definition was clearly under way in East Germany during the 1950s and 1960s (though hardly confined to it), 'militarism' did not really pertain to the GDR, governed as it was first and foremost by the party leadership, who exercised control over the police and military and who constantly stressed the need for peace. Gerhard Ritter has adopted a broader social and cultural view of 'militarism', which he defines twofold: as the 'elevation of the military necessity of clear, unambiguous chains of command to a political principle' and the 'predominance of militant, aggressive traits in the basic political position ... such that the primary task of the state is neglected: to establish a lasting order of law and peace among the people'[5] – something that few would disagree was a major deficit of the SED state. In a slightly different vein, Michael Mann has suggested that 'militarised socialism' can be taken to mean a system-specific ideology for disciplining and social control of the populace, with the ultimate goal of preventing societal changes.[6] In this view, 'militarisation' was as much about securing internal control as about outward civil defence – again, something that most would agree characterised the situation in East Germany. In terms of these various definitions, there were, broadly speaking, two distinct yet closely interrelated forms of 'militarisation' in the GDR: first, the build-up of armed forces for civil defence as well as for maintaining internal order; and second, the more general attempt at social and political control through strict military-like forms of organisation and public ritual. The following will address each of these strands in turn.

The armed forces and East German society

Despite governing one of the most heavily militarised states in the world, the SED nonetheless devoted much of its propaganda effort to denouncing militarism. According to Marxist–Leninist doctrine, militarism and war are integral elements of capitalism, which can thrive only through expansion. Just as capitalist states function to secure and advance the interests of the capitalist ruling class, so too do their military forces. As a consciously socialist state that functioned instead in the interests of the common people, the GDR was a primary target for capitalist aggression. It was only a matter of time, so the argument went, before the ruling classes in the West would attack the enemies of capitalist exploitation. When that war came the GDR had to be prepared to defend itself, and in order to do so it needed armed forces. In short, the SED argued that militarisation in the GDR was necessary to defeat militarism. The demand for *sozialistische Verteidigungsbereitschaft* ('socialist vigilance') was by no means seen as contradictory to the SED's much-vaunted *Friedenspolitik* ('peace policy'), but rather as its very basis.

The rearmament of the GDR under Ulbricht was largely carried out in three primary 'pushes'. Although the Soviets and SED had already established a sizeable 'police force' in the late 1940s numbering around 20,000 men whose arms, uniforms and organisation resembled more those of soldiers than police,[7] the first overt 'push' was the expansion of the KVP in spring 1952, following the confusion wrought by the famous 'Stalin Note' and western agreements on the European Defence Community (EDC). As Wilhelm Pieck recalled from talks with Soviet leaders in Moscow on 1 April 1952, the object for the GDR was to 'create a People's Army without a big fuss' by expanding its existing paramilitary forces.[8] Including the heavily armed police units, altogether the GDR had around 90,000 men in arms by December 1952 and 113,000 by summer 1953, at a cost already exceeding 2 billion marks.[9] The KVP comprised the bulk of the GDR's ground forces, including infantry, tank and artillery units. Complementing them were the People's Police Air and Marine units (Volkspolizei-See and -Luft), which in every way apart from their names resembled naval and air defence forces, as well as the Factory Combat Groups, or Betriebskampfgruppen (renamed Workforce Combat Units after 1959) which were initially intended as a paramilitary force for the protection of factories but which eventually took on broader functions of civil defence.[10]

The next push came with the KVP's conversion into the NVA in 1955–56. Although this move was presented as a reaction to West German moves towards creating the new Bundeswehr, in reality the GDR already had a sizeable army of some 120,000 men, and the change amounted to little more than removing the fig-leaf covering the KVP's actual nature and purpose. The Supreme Command of the KVP was basically renamed the Ministry for National Defence, and the Soviet-style uniforms were swapped for older Wehrmacht-style ones. There followed a general re-emphasis on the GDR's need to defend itself against its enemies, which was even given expression in a change to Article 5 of the East German constitution to the effect that military service was no longer merely an honour, but an 'honourable national duty' of the citizens of the GDR. Finally, in response to the dire problems in recruiting adequate numbers of 'volunteers' throughout the 1950s, there was a final recruitment push beginning in early 1961 and ending with the introduction of conscription in January 1962, which the SED leadership dared introduce only once there was no longer the possibility of would-be conscripts leaving *en masse* for the West.

The GDR was thus clearly a very well-armed state by the early 1950s, with a large percentage of its manpower and budget spent on defence. But what did this process of rearmament look like beneath the level of SED defence policy and the formal organisation of armed units, and how did ordinary East Germans respond to it? The internal reports of the regime make it abundantly clear that the carefully staged military parades lined with cheering crowds masked the broad disapproval and deep-seated misgivings among the ordinary populace about the existence of separate East German armed forces. While a small minority of East Germans actively supported the project – especially older people who thought the youth of the 1950s and 1960s could use some polishing up[11] – and a somewhat larger minority unenthusiastically accepted the argument that an East German military presence was necessary given developments in the West, what stands out most in the internal reports throughout the 1950s are three interrelated strands of criticism: the high costs, the widespread fear of war and the concern about deepening German division.

Much of the criticism referred back to the SED's own *contradictory* rhetoric. Given both the repeated promises of improving living standards and the constant criticism of military developments in the West, the SED's attempt to drum up support for the armed forces seemed rather hypocritical to most East Germans. During an assembly at the Houch factory in Berlin-Weißensee, workers even referred to Stalin to help prove this point: 'Stalin himself says it is impossible to strengthen armed forces and raise the living standard of the people simultaneously. Isn't then the strengthening of the KVP an attack on our living standard?'[12] Indeed, such sentiments appear to have been widespread even among the SED rank-and-file. At a party meeting in Prenzlauer Berg the district leadership was repeatedly confronted with angry comments from party functionaries who were now essentially being asked to contradict their own previous argumentation: 'For weeks now the party press has reported that the signing of the Atlantic pact and the re-militarisation in the West means a squandering of the people's wealth, etc. We can hardly talk ... Up to now we've preached "We shall not take up arms." It only costs money, pensions and wages.'[13]

Yet popular disapproval of East German armed forces in the GDR was not based solely or even predominantly on the deterioration of living standards that it caused. It is important to recognise that both Germanies of the 1950s were war-weary countries, still overcoming the material and emotional effects of the Second World War. The prospect of another war was also a constant source of concern throughout the 1950s, and any military build-up along the inner-German frontier was quite understandably viewed with great trepidation, as it was in the FRG.[14] These fears were expressed in innumerable reports and myriad different ways: occasional runs on savings accounts, periodic outbreaks of *Hamstern* (stocking up on food and other essentials), erecting bomb-proof shelters in gardens and the like. One 1952 SED report from Berlin even complains of an unwillingness among worker-activists to move into flats in the Stalinallee because the area might be a potential bombing target.[15] With all due caution regarding the prejudicial gender stereotypes of reporters within the party apparatus, it seems that such concerns were particularly widespread among women – or at least that women tended to be more vocal about them. In factories with a majority of female employees, political agitation on the question of the armed forces and recruitment often confronted outright hostility from working women, many of whom had already lost their menfolk in the last war.[16] A fairly typical illustration was the reaction by the predominantly female workforce at a clothing factory in Wusterwitz, where it was estimated that 90 per cent openly rejected the NVA during discussions: 'most of us don't have our husbands any more, and we are not going to send our children into a new war.'[17]

Moreover, this was a militarisation campaign – like that in West Germany – that ran against the grain of popular national sentiments. Although with hindsight it seems unlikely that German unification was ever achievable in the 1950s, to most contemporaries it still seemed a viable prospect, and a highly desirable one at that. In addition, hopes for unification were particularly high during the first two rearmament 'pushes': in 1952 they were raised by the immense publicity surrounding Stalin's note to the western powers in March, and in 1955 by the upcoming Geneva conference.[18] The expansion of the East German armed forces not only dampened these prospects, but also raised the spectre of German shooting on German in a future East–West conflict. Opinion reports about the establishment of the NVA in January 1956 are filled with such comments as 'We'll never shoot at our brothers in West Germany' and 'The West German workers won't shoot at our workers, but at the government'.[19] It appears that the SED's propagation of images of the western enemy met with little response during this period. No-one wanted war, and many still harboured hopes for German unification. The expansion of the armed forces seemed like a step in the wrong direction on both counts.

To a large extent, however, it did not really matter what the broader East German populace thought. A successful propaganda campaign was not absolutely necessary for establishing an effective fighting force; a successful recruitment campaign was. The organisational machinery enlisted for recruitment was immense, including a special recruitment agency (Verwaltung für Rekrutierung within the Interior Ministry), the police, the

SED and the mass organisations (especially the FDJ and the GST), which together allowed for an almost total coverage of all recruitment opportunities in the GDR – a saturation approach possible only in a modern dictatorial system like the GDR which few young people could possibly avoid.

Nonetheless, keeping the ranks filled was a constant problem before conscription. At some point the vast might of this organisational machinery had to confront young people as they were, with all their various interests and plans for the future. Not only were East German youths often less well-disposed and pliable than the party leadership would have wished; so, too, were many local functionaries asked to help recruit them. Pacifist refusals, whether self-serving or principled, were extremely common among recruitees. Although this was often blamed on the influence of the churches, it is clear that many young people objected on the basis of the SED's own prior teachings, seeing in the current calls for military vigilance and unquestioning discipline some of the very values they were taught to associate with the fascist past, not the socialist future. Indeed, the FDJ's new emphasis on 'military education' (*Wehrerziehung*) and its decidedly militaristic displays at its Fourth Parliament in Leipzig in May 1952, drove many otherwise well-disposed young people from its ranks.[20] In Loburg district youths even founded a clandestine group that called itself the 'FDJ Action Committee against the National Armed Forces'.[21] There were of course less constructive expressions of refusal, too. Graffiti and defacement of recruitment posters were rife throughout 1952–53 and 1955. Fairly typical were the slogans painted in Sangerhausen district: 'We'll tear up our draft papers, we don't want fratricide, not us (*ohne uns*)'.[22] Nor were all expressions of refusal strictly pacifist, as the apparent increase in the number of physical attacks on FDJ functionaries and police personnel during the recruitment pushes of 1952–53 and 1955 attests.

Probably the most common response to recruitment pitches was a Schwejkian reference to the regime's own previous 'peace and bread' rhetoric: 'What about the national hymn, that a mother will never again mourn her son? The national hymn has now become obsolete.'[23] Even among those who enlisted, it is clear that the majority were motivated less by political convictions than by the relatively good wages, the opportunity to obtain special technical training, or more banal concerns such as the ability to acquire a driving licence free of charge. Judging from the opinion and morale reports, it would seem that there was precious little difference in political outlook and opinion between rank-and-file soldiers and the general populace.[24] As Willi Stoph complained to the SED convention in April 1955: 'the pacifist attitudes that are common among a certain portion of the working-class have a negative effect on members of the KVP ... and we have discovered that when on vacation, young soldiers spread the widest range of hostile opinions.'[25]

Whatever parallels one might draw between the responses of would-be recruits in the GDR and the 'count me out' (*ohne mich*) movement in West Germany in the 1950s, it is important to recognise that in the GDR 'unwilling' youths faced far more pressure to join. Recruitment methods did not exclude forms of coercion, and especially from 1955 onwards recruitment appeared more and more like a thinly-veiled form of conscription: threatening someone with the loss of his job, hindering one's studies, or even, in a few cases, getting young men drunk and taking them to the NVA.[26] Yet while some functionaries were clearly a bit overzealous, most were far less than avid recruiters. It was a loathsome task given the pressure involved, and many could not be bothered to expend much effort. Among the SED district headquarters in the Potsdam region, for instance, there was 'moaning' about the extra work, as well as reports that the 'discipline and eagerness [to recruit] is none too strong'.[27]

Little wonder, since recruiters encountered all kinds of problems in their dealings with other functionaries. In one of its many complaints to the SED Central Committee about the lack of assistance from FDJ functionaries, the Ministry of National Defence quoted the comments of the FDJ secretary in Wanzleben district as typical: 'The main thing is that we have a lot of signatures, what comes after that is another matter.'[28] Even less helpful were local state officials and mayors. The mayor of Schnolde, near Pritzwalk, even took it upon himself to advise youths that 'whoever does not want to join the People's Army should leave the Republic, then when he returns he won't be called up' [for cadre-political reasons].[29]

Even more problematic than the apathy of local officials were the conflicts of interest and loyalty within the regime. Given the unceasing pressure to increase production and efficiency, many managers, union officials and factory-level party secretaries were quite understandably reluctant to forfeit their young, productive employees for military service which many of them deemed unnecessary in any case. The practice of giving the most lucrative jobs only to those who would not enlist appears to have become increasingly common as the shortage of labour grew more acute by the end of the 1950s,[30] and some economic functionaries even tried to change the minds of those who had already enlisted by offering them more money. As exasperated military recruiters in the Cottbus region complained in early 1961: 'The economic functionaries are a serious weakness. On repeated occasions and in a number of enterprises, youths who have pre-enlisted suddenly receive a considerable pay increase and then rescind their enlistment agreement'.[31] Even after the introduction of conscription in 1962, economic functionaries were still upbraided for their 'complete disregard' for military matters by applying for too many deferments and exemptions for their workers.[32]

Even when the ranks were filled, the armed units and paramilitaries were not deemed very effective during the early years – a view clearly borne out by the events of June 1953, which saw some armed units relinquish their weapons in the face of demonstrations. Rates of desertion were extremely high for the KVP during its first two years, and many of the Kampfgruppen members only occasionally showed up for training – 'today this one and tomorrow the other', as one report put it.[33] But despite these problems, the armed forces did make great strides from 1953 to 1961, when NVA soldiers and Kampfgruppen dutifully and efficiently sealed the border to West Berlin. However great the initial problems were and however little popular enthusiasm there was for East German armed forces, over time the SED was able to find enough soldiers and Kampfgruppen members willing to defend the GDR with force. Indeed, by the mid-1960s it was difficult to overlook the ubiquity of East German military and police forces, as western visitors commonly remarked.

A militarised society?

Of course, large defence forces were hardly uncommon in East or West during the 1950s and 1960s. In these terms, the USA and Britain (less so West Germany) could also quite justifiedly be regarded as 'militarised' societies in terms of the size of their armies and proportion of their budgets spent on defence. But western commentators long talked of the 'militarisation' of the GDR in a number of other ways. For one thing, the SED was inextricably entwined with the state's security forces; there was no clear separation between the two in practice. The NVA and police were formally under the control of the SED, and all of the leading positions in the army, police and paramilitary organisations were filled by party members, who saw themselves as 'party comrades in uniform'. Indeed, anyone who wanted to get ahead in the party hierarchy (and thus in the political system as a whole) had to possess significant military knowledge and training. After the shock of June 1953, the SED increasingly assumed the role of co-ordinator for the deployment of the various security forces. At the central level, this role was initially played by a special Security Commission of the SED Politbüro, later transformed into the National Defence Council in 1960, which consisted of representatives of the party, NVA, Stasi and police, but still under the chairmanship of Ulbricht as SED General Secretary. This basic structure was mirrored at lower levels, where the so-called 'regional and district operational commands' (Bezirks- and Kreiseinsatzleitungen) were likewise chaired by the first secretaries of the regional and district party organisations. In the event of a threat to state security, whether from within or without, these bodies co-ordinated all troop deployments, which placed a heavy burden of responsibility and know-how on party secretaries. Granted, party secretaries wore many hats. But this role of quasi-military officer was one of their most important functions at every level, which was also one of the main factors discriminating against women moving up the party hierarchy.[34]

Perhaps more importantly, this general emphasis on the military values of vigilance and discipline extended well beyond the regime apparatus. In contrast to the FRG, where the military played a rather low-key role in public life and military ceremonies took place mostly behind barracks gates, in the GDR militaristic ceremonies, rituals and forms of organisation were maintained and positively encouraged. Given the GDR's self-definition as all things counter to the Third Reich, the similarities of many of its rituals and organisational forms to those under the Nazis are striking indeed. The daily experiences of young people in particular who had grown up in the GDR of the 1950s and 1960s were not wholly dissimilar from the militaristic regimentation of life in the Third Reich: uniforms for the Young Pioneers and FDJ, frequent flag ceremonies at schools, 'military education' both during and after school, pre-military training in the GST, and all of this even before formal military service, which itself might be followed by further involvement in paramilitary organisations like the GST or Kampfgruppen. Although it was young men who faced the most pressure in terms of actual military service, young women and girls were also expected to play their part: to stand at attention at school flag ceremonies, to march in formation at FDJ parades and to acquire certain military knowledge and skills such as map-reading and survival techniques in the 'military education' curriculum and GST.

Military language was another integral cultural element of 'militarised socialism'. Ever since Lenin, the semantics of the socialist struggle tended to straddle the military and civilian spheres with such vocabulary as 'party soldiers' and the 'march of the battalions of the proletariat'. Metaphors taken from military life permeated official discourse on an everyday basis: from the constant news reports of the class struggle 'from all fronts' to the exploitation of the 'class enemy', sabotage by internal 'enemies', even the 'production- and harvest-battle'. It is little wonder that Victor Klemperer's famous book, *LTI: Notizbuch eines Philologen*, on the language of the Third Reich, was so popular among young East German intellectuals, because of its many parallels to the SED's ideological jargon.[35] Both languages moved in a dualistic universe of friend and foe, and both tended to conjure up the feeling of a state of emergency. As under the Nazis, the inflationary use of these bellicose terms far beyond periods of crisis and struggle eventually led to an impoverishment and devaluation of the language, such that it had become essentially meaningless by the latter years of the GDR.

The deliberate cultivation of images of the enemy worked along the same dualistic lines. It was not enough simply to overcome one's pacifism and view the world in terms of friends and foes. The SED also tried to teach East Germans to hate their foes as well – not just the capitalist system and states *per se*, but also particular individuals (mostly western politicians or industrialists) and groups, including enemy soldiers. As Defence Minister Hoffmann put it, it was not sufficient 'simply to reject and hate imperialism as a system; one must above all direct this hatred against everyone who acts under the orders of imperialist generals and officers'.[36] In this dualistic universe, hatred of the 'Bonn warmongers and revanchists' corresponded to love for the working class, as 'military education' textbooks made clear: 'The education of the pupils to love of the working class and its party, to esteem for the creative accomplishments of the working class and all working people and to trust in its political leadership must be accompanied by the education to hatred towards every kind of exploitation and repression',[37] which was of course equated with the capitalist system and its defenders.

As pervasive as such rituals, rhetoric and imagery were in the GDR, they by no means convinced everyone. Indeed, it was precisely their ubiquity and inescapability that turned many people off, especially young people who were most directly affected. Throughout the 1950s and 1960s, there were various forms of youth protest against the regimentation and militarisation of their lives. The popularity of western youth culture was probably the most obvious sign of this, and one cannot fully understand its mildly rebellious attractiveness to East German young people – the unkempt or 'schlampig' hair and clothing, the informal manner of speech and interaction – outside the context of the SED's efforts to rear the diligent, disciplined and markedly conventional species of youth embodied in official propaganda.[38] In the eyes of party leaders, this influence of 'western decadence' and 'American unculture' was no less than a kind of 'psychological warfare' and 'moral and spiritual poisoning of our youth',[39] a cultural struggle of capitalist depravity versus 'socialist morality'. But of course the very 'westernness' of this youth subculture was a sign that the 'education to hate' and propagation of images of a western enemy were, at the very least, failing to stamp out young people's interest in things western – and in fact were probably nourishing the fascination instead.

A far more direct instance of protest against the militarisation of life in the GDR was the church-led campaign for a form of alternative service after the promulgation of the Defence Law in September 1961 and subsequent introduction of conscription in January 1962. Although some churchmen actually found conscription preferable to the constant pestering and pressure that had characterised the recruitment effort up until 1961,[40] the vast majority were resolutely against any kind of mandatory military service, and spoke out vociferously against it. The overwhelming majority of youth pastors refused to vote in the September 1961 elections, and there were reports of 'provocations' at a few polling-stations by seminary students in Naumburg and Berlin.[41] Indeed, the six remaining theological faculties in the GDR and the Evangelical student groups featured as focal points of dissent against conscription. Not only did the students by and large refuse to perform armed service, they also reportedly tried to influence others in this direction.

These protests were broadly in line with the official position of the Protestant churches, which called for the government to recognise conscientious objection and declared their intention to support those who chose it. The Protestant churches continually stressed the inviolability of the First Commandment for Christians, even for those who decided to perform military service, which in the event the vast majority of active Christian youth did. As one report put it, the majority of religious youths unenthusiastically 'adapted themselves' to the idea of a stint in the armed forces, despite their concerns about being able to attend services while in the army and their misgivings about the incompatibility of the oath of allegiance and the First Commandment.[42] Although disapproval was clearly widespread, it took great courage actually to refuse armed service after 1962, and many of the individuals who did so faced prison sentences for their beliefs. Indeed, it took considerable courage to refuse even after the legalisation of conscientious objection and alternative service as 'construction soldiers' (*Bausoldaten*) in 1964. Given the detrimental effects on educational and career prospects, not to mention the especially humiliating and sometimes brutal treatment reserved for the 'construction soldiers', such refusals were clearly the exception. The success of the churches in gaining conscientious objectors this status was on behalf of only a handful of highly committed individuals – no more than 1–1.5 per cent of eligible conscripts after 1964 – many of whom were later involved in the dissident peace and human rights groups of the 1970s and 1980s.[43] Although exceptional, the open refusals of the 'construction soldiers' nonetheless represented the tip of an iceberg of popular misgivings and disapproval. The SED may have possessed the power to coerce the vast majority of young people, even active Christians, into military service, but not to convince them of the threat of the western 'warmongers and revanchists', of the necessity of compulsory military training, or of the need to hate.

All of this raises an obvious question: why was there such an obsessive fascination with armed forces, military forms of organisation and friend–foe indoctrination in a regime that defined itself as peace-loving and against all things militaristic? It is in some ways tempting to say that the Nazis had partially paved the way. Arguably, their prior division of the world into friends and foes made this easier for the SED, even though the particular friends and foes had to change somewhat. While it was difficult to sell the idea of 'German–Soviet friendship' to people who had experienced the raping and pillaging of Red Army soldiers in the closing stages of the war, for the older generation at least, the idea of western decadence and the insidious influence of inferior 'American unculture' could quite readily build upon National Socialist teachings as well as older German nationalist thinking. It is also tempting to say that there was something specifically German – or better, Prussian – about it. Extolling the virtues of military-style discipline was nothing new in Germany, especially Prussia, though one might question how unique this was in comparison to other countries. It seems that many NVA officers felt a certain military prestige and pride at being 'Red

Prussians'. As one former officer remarked in 1995: 'One felt that we had got one over on the West German side when the colour and cut of the NVA uniforms or the goose-step at parades and military ceremonies visibly linked up to times before and after the First World War, although one of course laid claim to completely different content and values.'[44] In terms of official memorialisation, the Neue Wache on East Berlin's main boulevard Unter den Linden, a remarkably curious memorial to the 'victims of fascism and militarism' guarded round-the-clock by goose-stepping soldiers in traditional German uniforms, was probably the clearest expression of how this state, officially the inheritor of all the best humanistic traditions of Germany and having broken with Prussia's reactionary past, demonstrated its power with all the insignia of the old Prussian military.

But 'militarised socialism' was hardly limited to the GDR, and surely the answer to where it came from lies more in the history of the communist movement and the very way in which the Soviet-style system functioned; that is, the roots lie as much in Russia's past as in Germany's. It should not be forgotten that the communist movement of the late nineteenth and early twentieth centuries had to work illegally and in secret in many countries. In Russia, the revolutionaries fought against a repressive regime amid great persecution, and under such conditions the movement simply could not have survived without strict discipline. Moreover, it was preparing for and eventually led a revolution that entailed armed conflict and even civil war, which also required military discipline. As the Third Comintern Congress resolved in July 1921, 'party members are obliged to act always as disciplined members of a militant organisation ... The entire party should be trained as a fighting organisation for the revolution'.[45] Once the revolution was over, civilian authority in the Soviet Union was taken over by persons accustomed to issuing and obeying orders. And while in exile, the German Communists such as Ulbricht who escaped Stalin's purges and were to hold sway in the SBZ/GDR were, insofar as they needed any convincing in the first place, reared on this militaristic brand of Soviet communism.[46]

It was Lenin who most vigorously 'militarised' the socialist idea. His concept of the vanguard party, the rigidly hierarchical organisation composed primarily of professional revolutionaries, was founded on military precepts of organisation, discipline and willing sacrifice. Under state socialism, the same traits were expected of non-party members too. Indeed, the building of socialism was likened to a long campaign in which all must do their duty. Anyone who did not (or was accused of not doing so) was branded a 'traitor' or 'deserter', as distinct from more 'civilian' terms such as 'dissident', 'critic' or simple 'malcontent'. It is no coincidence that both Lenin and Trotsky saw the Red Army from the very beginning as an important educational and disciplining instrument for the rural populace of the early Soviet Union.

In terms of societal structures, it is telling that Lenin's model for

Communism was actually the German war economy of 1914–18, in which he saw the fundamental precursors of state socialism. The introduction of mandatory work-service, which itself grew out of universal conscription, strict economic and political centralisation and the central administration of all important resources under the Supreme Command of generals Hindenburg and Ludendorff, were for him key changes that occurred during the war. The point was to utilise these very same instruments of reactionary power for new revolutionary tasks.[47] Modern bureaucratic mechanisms would prevail over all other forms of social and economic co-ordination. In another telling choice of metaphor, communist society was to be organised like the German postal system, a strictly hierarchical command bureaucracy largely run by former army officers who imported much of the Prussian military culture into the organisation, leaving little room for spontaneity, creativity, or individuality, which smacked of effeminate liberalism and capitalist 'decadence'. Yet the impetus was not all negative, as this rigid discipline was also accompanied by constant talk of friendship, solidarity and 'comradeship' – the 'in-group' in the friend–foe dichotomy.

But well after Lenin, and indeed well after the death of the self-styled 'generalissimo' Stalin too, the challenges confronting state socialism in the decades following the Second World War also gravitated towards a further expansion of military values and forms of organisation in the socialist states. For one thing, the problems of economic productivity in a system with relatively few material incentives led to ever-increasing demands for soldier-like work discipline in the factories. Such concerns were particularly acute in the GDR, which was constantly being compared to its immensely productive western counterpart. In addition, the failures of the system of 'democratic centralism' to resolve the problems of economic planning or indeed to keep a tight rein on political developments after Stalin's death in 1953, meant that the hierarchical 'command' element – centralism – continued to outweigh any embryonic 'democratic' aspects of the system, especially after the political purges following the Hungarian uprising of 1956, and perhaps most fatefully in the decision to scrap the NÖS in the later 1960s. And finally, there was also, of course, the heavily-armed Western Alliance bent on 'rolling back' Communism, which inevitably fed the emphasis on military vigilance in the Eastern bloc.

But despite these understandable concerns about the military rivalry of the West, it seems that the process of rearmament and the militarisation of public life in the GDR during the 1950s and 1960s was at least as much a response to concerns about maintaining inner security and public order as about external civil defence. This was true for internal order in both a narrow and a broad sense. After all, it took soldiers and tanks to restore order and uphold the domestic status quo in June 1953, and there was no shortage of armed units and tanks on the streets to deter organised protest against the building of the Berlin Wall in 1961. But at a more general level, the socialist leadership in the GDR, as in most of the other Soviet-style states of East–Central Europe, found itself incapable of responding effectively to signs of social and economic disintegration, which were often ritually blamed on western influence, holdovers from the capitalist past or the imperfect realisation of 'scientific socialist' policies, rarely on the socialist system itself. Although signs of disintegration were arguably much more visible under Honecker, this was already clearly a problem under Ulbricht as well. The response was the build-up of a vast machine of indoctrination and party-controlled organisations, what the Sovietologist William Odom has called the 'military–educational complex' (a word-play on the American 'military–industrial complex') whose purpose was essentially to compensate for these signs of disintegration with increased discipline and obedience on the part of both the regime apparatus and the populace at large.[48] It was above all the size and nature of this 'military–educational complex' and the elevation of military forms of organisation to a political principle – not so much the proliferation of the armed forces themselves – that set the GDR apart from the FRG and other liberal democratic polities and that (justifiedly, in my view) has prompted its characterisation as a highly militarised society.

Notes

1 Hans-Joachim Gießmann, *Das unliebsame Erbe: Die Auflösung der Militärstruktur der DDR* (Baden-Baden, 1992), 75.
2 Rolf Badstübner, 'Militär in der DDR. Frieden oder Unfrieden für Politik und Gesellschaft?', in Detlef Bald et al. (eds), *Nationale Volksarmee – Armee für den Frieden* (Baden-Baden, 1995), 162.
3 *Enquete-Kommission*, ix, 831.
4 Michael Geyer, 'The Militarization of Europe, 1914–1945', in John Gillis (ed.), *The Militarization of the Western World* (New Brunswick, 1989), 65–102: 79.
5 Gerhard Ritter, 'Das Problem des Militarismus in Deutschland', in Volker Berghahn, (ed.), *Militarismus* (Cologne, 1975), 197, 206.
6 Michael Mann, 'The Roots and Contradictions of Modern Militarism', in Michael Mann, *States, War and Capitalism. Studies in Political Sociology* (Oxford, 1988).
7 See generally, Bruno Thoß (ed.), *Volksarmee schaffen – ohne Geschrei! Studien zu den Anfängen einer 'verdeckten Aufrüstung' in der SBZ/DDR 1947–1952* (Munich, 1994).
8 Cited in Rüdiger Wenzke, 'Auf dem Weg zur Kaderarmee: Aspekte der Rekrutierung, Sozialstruktur und personellen Entwicklung des entstehenden Militärs in der SBZ/DDR 1947–1952', in Bruno Thoß (ed.), *Volksarmee*, 261; see also Rolf Stöckigt, 'Direktiven aus Moskau: Sowjetische Einflußnahme auf DDR-Politik 1952/1953', in Jochen Černý (ed.), *Brüche, Krisen, Wendepunkte. Neubefragung von DDR-Geschichte* (Leipzig, 1990), 81–7.
9 This figure is from Torsten Diedrich, 'Aufrüstungsvorbereitung und -finanzierung in der SBZ/DDR in den Jahren 1948 bis 1953 und deren Rückwirkungen auf die Wirtschaft', in Bruno Thoß, *Volksarmee*, 306.
10 Armin Wagner, 'Die Kampfgruppen der Arbeiterklasse (1953–1990)', in Torsten

Diedrich, Hans Ehlert and, Rüdiger Wenzke (eds), *Im Dienste der Partei. Handbuch der bewaffneten Organe der DDR* (Berlin, 1998), 281–338; also Volker Koop, *Armee oder Freizeitclub? Die Kampfgruppen der Arbeiterklasse in der DDR* (Bonn, 1997).

11 SAPMO-BArch, DY 30/IV 2/12/57, 'Information: Stimmung zum Gesetz über die allgemeine Wehrpflicht', 25 January 1962, fo. 8. Similar findings are reported in: BAB DO-1/11/1120, '1. Bericht über Stimmungen und Meinungen der Bevölkerung sowie der Tätigkeit des Gegners zum Gesetz der allgemeinen Wehrpflicht', 27 January 1962, fo. 4; SAPMO-BArch, DY 34/22233, 'Information', 25 January 1962.
12 SAPMO-BArch, DY 30/IV 2/5/319, 'Einige Diskussionen und Stellungnahmen zur Frage der Nationalen Streitkräfte', 26 June 1952, 5.
13 *Ibid.*, 7.
14 There were, of course, similar sentiments in the FRG during the mid-1950s, especially after the Paris agreements of 1954, when the intensity and scope of anti-militarisation were great indeed, ranging from trade unions to important sections of the church to youths who howled down government speakers in Cologne and pelted the Defence Minister in Augsburg with beer mugs.
15 SAPMO-BArch, DY 30/IV 2/5/303, report of 18 December 1952.
16 SAPMO-BArch, DY 30/IV 2/5/544, 'DFD Stimmungsbericht von den Ereignissen des 17.6. in Berlin', undated, 1.
17 SAPMO-BArch, DY 34/20780, report of 16 Febuary 1956, 7.
18 See generally SAPMO-BArch, DY 30/IV 2/5/573; also BLHA Ld. Br. Rep. 332, Nr. 395, 'Meinungen zur Note der Sowjetischen Union an die Westmächte', 12 March 1952, unpag.
19 SAPMO-BArch, DY 34/22083, report of 21 January 1956, 1.
20 Edeltraud Schulze (ed.), *DDR-Jugend: ein statistisches Handbuch* (Berlin, 1995).
21 SAPMO-BArch, DY 30/IV 2/16/84, 'Aktionsausschuss der FDJ gegen die Nationalen Streitkräfte', fos 173–4.
22 SAPMO-BArch, DY 30/IV 2/5/302, 'Kurzinformation über aufgetretene gegnerische Arbeit', 21 May 1952.
23 SAPMO-BArch, DY 30/IV 2/5/319, 'Einige Diskussionen', 5.
24 See the reports on inspections of individual KVP divisions in BA-MA, DVH3/2683. Also BAB, DO-1/11/351, reports of 31 July 1952, 23 December 1954.
25 Cited in Michael Buddrus, '"Kaderschmiede für den Führungsnachwuchs"? Die Kadettenschule der Nationalen Volksarmee in Naumburg 1956–1961', in Hartmut Mehringer (ed.), *Von der SBZ zur DDR: Studien zum Herrschaftssystem in der Sowjetischen Besatzungszone und in der Deutschen Demokratischen Republik* (Munich, 1995), 176.
26 Volker Ackermann, *Der 'echte' Flüchtling: Deutsche Vertriebene und Flüchtlinge aus der DDR 1945–1961* (Osnabrück, 1995), 198.
27 BLHA, Bez. Pdm. Rep. 530, Nr. 2052, 'Bericht über den politischen Zustand ... in den Fragen der Werbung für die KVP', undated, fos 77–81; Nr. 2035, 'Bericht über die Anleitung der KL Königs Wusterhausen', 14 October 1952.
28 SAPMO-BArch, DY 30/IV 2/12/55, Ministry for National Defence report of 19 April 1960, fos 125–9.
29 SAPMO-BArch, DY 30/IV 2/13/397 'Wie ist die gegenwärtige Lage in der Abwanderung nach Westdeutschland?', undated, 11.

30 SAPMO-BArch, DY 30/IV 2/12/55, 'Textbericht', 22 April 1959. See also BLHA, Bez. Ffo. Rep. 730, Nr. 1100, 'Einschätzung der Werbung zur NVA, 8 November 1960, unpag.; BAB, DO-1/11/967, fo. 78.
31 SAPMO-BArch, DY 30/IV 2/12/58, 'Kurzinformation über die Sitzung der Bezirkswerbekommission Cottbus mit den Vorsitzenden der Kreiswerbekommissionen am 9.8.1961', fos 212–13.
32 SAPMO-BArch, DY 30/IV 2/12/57, 'Information über die durchgeführte Musterung in der Zeit vom 3.9.62-26.9.62', fos 95–102; 'Abschlußbericht über die durchgeführte Musterung in der Zeit vom 15.-31.03.1962', fos 73–9.
33 Wagner, 'Kampfgruppen', 294.
34 See generally, Diedrich *et al.* (eds), *Im Dienste der Partei*.
35 Victor Klemperer, *The Language of the Third Reich: LTI, lingua tertii imperii, A Philologist's Notebook*, trans, Martin Brady (London, 2000).
36 *Einheit*, 6 (1971), 690–702.
37 Ministerium für Volksbildung (ed.), *Handreichung zur sozialistischen Wehrerziehung* (Berlin, 1974), 45.
38 Dorothee Wierling, 'Die Jugend als innerer Feind: Konflikte in der Erziehungsdiktatur der sechziger Jahre', in Hartmut Kaelble *et al.* (eds), *Sozialgeschichte der DDR* (Stuttgart, 1994), 404–25; Dorothee Wierling, 'Der Staat, die Jugend und der Westen: Texte zu Konflikten der 1960er Jahre', in Alf Lüdtke and Peter Becker (eds), *Akten, Eingaben, Schaufenster: Die DDR und ihre Texte* (Berlin, 1997), 223–40.
39 SAPMO-BArch, DY 30/IV 2/16/90, 'Bericht über die Jugendkriminalität und das Rowdytum', January 1960, fos 28–57.
40 SAPMO-BArch, DY 30/IV 2/14/36, fos 24–5.
41 SAPMO-BArch, DY 30/IV 2/14/24, 'Einschätzung der Situation unter der konfessionell gebundenen Jugend in der Deutschen Demokratischen Republik', 3 December 1961, fos 201 ff.
42 SAPMO-BArch, DY 30/IV 2/14/24, 'Information über die Arbeit der "Jungen Gemeinden" und der Arbeit unserer Bezirksorganisation mit den jungen Christen', 5 April 1963.
43 On conscientious objection in the GDR generally, see Uwe Koch and Stephan Eschler, *Zähne hoch, Kopf zusammenbeißen: Dokumente zur Wehrdienstverweigerung in der DDR von 1962–1990* (Kückenshagen, 1994). This statistic from Rüdiger Wenzke, 'Die Wehrpflicht im Spiegel der marxistisch-leninistischen Theorie in der DDR', in Roland Foerster (ed.), *Die Wehrpflicht* (Munich, 1994), 119–32.
44 Karl Nuß, 'Militarisierung der Gesellschaft der DDR?', in Günther Glaser and Werner Knoll (eds), *Landesverteidigung und/oder Militarisierung der Gesellschaft der DDR?* (Berlin, 1995), 70.
45 From Jane Degras (ed.), *The Communist International, 1919–1943: Documents*, i (London, 1971), 269–70.
46 For a first-hand account, see Wolfgang Leonhard's classic *Child of the Revolution* (London, 1957).
47 V. I. Lenin, *Staat und Revolution*, in *Werke* (Berlin, 1977), xxv, 355 ff.
48 William Odom, 'The militarization of Soviet society', *Problems of Communism*, 25/5 (September/October 1975).

II
Society

6

Popular opinion[1]

Mark Allinson

The postwar reconstruction of Germany represented a huge undertaking, not merely in physically rebuilding the housing and workplaces destroyed in bombing raids, but also in social and political engineering. The Allies had agreed in Potsdam that the Germans required re-education as part of the denazification programme deemed essential in both East and West. Yet while the political and economic systems introduced in the western Occupation Zones often harked back to the values of the pre-Nazi Weimar Republic, albeit with a rather greater deal of structural stability than had existed in the years after the First World War, the authorities in the SBZ, the later GDR, embarked on a much more ambitious programme of political, economic and social restructuring. It lay in the nature of the centralising Soviet political system that the parameters – and often the minute details – of this restructuring were dictated by the political and economic theories of central political forces (the SED's Politbüro and Walter Ulbricht, as First Secretary, often acting directly on instructions from the Kremlin). The centre hoped that the SBZ/GDR's population would live up to these political ambitions. Thus Ulbricht's announcement at the SED's second Party Conference in July 1952 that the time had come to build socialism, reflected the party's tactical political aims in relation to the strengthening FRG, rather than any tangible shift of political or economic circumstances in the GDR itself.

Though the Marxist–Leninist political system expected a revolutionary avant-garde party to lead the way by guiding towards the socialist goal those whose political awareness and determination was underdeveloped, this did not mean that the SED could afford to neglect the contours of public opinion while its leading functionaries put in place a new political, economic and social order. Indeed the reverse was the case, given that the party owed its leading role not to a popular revolution, but initially to the superior military firepower of the Red Army over the dying Third Reich, and subsequently to the tactical interests of the Soviet Union in the developing Cold War. The party was well aware of the potential need to counter opposition to its power and to its plans for eastern Germany's reconstruction, both from those among its population who still hankered after National Socialism and, more commonly, from those (many) who would have far preferred a united Germany to develop along the lines laid down in the more prosperous western zones, the later FRG. The opposition to the socialist project in the GDR was strengthened by Nazi propaganda against the 'subhuman' Russians and the rapes, thefts and other excesses of the Red Army in the early postwar period. Furthermore the SED wished not only to be tolerated by the East German population, but to be welcomed and actively supported.

Consequently, the party and government apparatus in the SBZ/GDR quickly developed a systematic process of collecting information on public opinion. Indeed, the task of gathering this information began almost immediately after Soviet troops arrived in 1945, as the first KPD officials and supporters filed reports on popular attitudes towards the emerging political structures. It is largely from the many such reports filed between 1945 and 1989 that we are able to reconstruct the attitudes of normal GDR citizens. This chapter discusses the broad contours of public opinion towards the SED and attitudes among the East German population about the legitimacy (or otherwise) of the GDR state in the Ulbricht years, but a few further considerations are necessary about the practice of gathering such data, and about the validity of such sources for historical study.

The practice of collecting data on the public's thinking quickly became an important function not only of the SED apparatus, but also of various branches of the GDR's state administration, including the MfS (Stasi). The bloc parties – alongside the SED, the CDUD, LDPD, Democratic Peasants' Party (DBD), and NDPD – the mass organisations (such as the FDJ and DSF, or Society for German–Soviet Friendship) and their umbrella body, the National Front, also played their part by reporting the views of their respective clientèles, enabling detailed information to be gathered about the opinions of women, young people, farmers, clergy, intellectuals and other groups. Reports were submitted by functionaries in local and factory party organisations, but also by propagandists, activists and officials dispatched into the field specifically for this task. Often reports were written in response to questions posed by the party apparatus, such as 'What is the population saying about Comrade Ulbricht's speech at the party congress?', or 'What response is there to the abolition of ration cards?' To some extent the purpose of the exercise was also to focus the attention of local functionaries on issues the central leadership considered important. A related set of sources are the reports on the internal situation of local and regional branches of the SED and the other parties and organisations. These reports give valuable insights into the attitudes of those whose political membership and functions theoretically underpinned the entire system. By 1968, 1.8 million people were members of the SED alone.

The enormous paperwork generated under the GDR reflects the importance the SED attached to these tasks and, arguably, the party's paranoid realisation that the socialist experiment was regarded by much of the GDR populace as an undesirable imposition, whose future was in doubt. The great effort expended on finding out what the man and woman in the street were thinking had an essentially negative motivation. The principal aim was to equip state and party to react to difficulties which arose, not to take account of popular demands in the policy-planning process. Clearly, the Stasi's investigations were carried out as a special case with the clear purpose of taking preventive measures, usually against specific dissident individuals, to protect the security of the state and the SED's role within it (for more on this, see Jens Gieseke's Chapter 3 in this volume). Otherwise, the reports collated by other bodies were put to relatively little use, beyond helping the SED to plan its generally unsuccessful propaganda effort by focusing on particular themes causing public disquiet.

To give two brief examples: however many reports indicated that the population was opposed to a revival of militarism, the SED nonetheless created the NVA in 1956, and in 1962 introduced male conscription, guided by the imperatives of Soviet foreign policy. Public opinion reports left the party in no doubt that many people saw clear comparisons between the NVA's uniform and that of its Nazi predecessor, the Wehrmacht,[2] but such information was merely employed to guide the presentation of policy in the GDR media, not to initiate a policy review. Equally, the party could have been in no doubt from many reports in the Ulbricht era about the population's urgent desire for better news reporting. Yet, up to October 1989 the country's newspapers, all directly or indirectly under party control, and the nightly television news programme, 'Aktuelle Kamera', remained one-sided and evasive on topics likely to embarrass the party, particularly where factual reality radically parted company with the party line.

Though reports very often ascribed comments, positive and negative, to named individuals, reports collated by branches of the party and state other than the Stasi and police were generally not used as the basis for actions against alleged dissidents, unless evidence was uncovered of some plot apparently designed to undermine the state order. Indeed, had the authorities acted against all of the SED's many critics exposed in the 'information reports' and 'situation reports' they would have found themselves arresting very large proportions of the population, including significant numbers of SED members, a development which would in itself have seriously undermined the stability of the political order.

The records of public opinion compiled by the SED, its functionaries in the state apparatus and its allies in the other parties and mass organisations, have perhaps been of more use to historians since the *Wende* of late 1989 than they ever were to the ruling party beforehand. Naturally, historians have to be cautious of taking them entirely at face value. These records were written for a particular audience, often by functionaries in the localities to present to their superiors in the regional and central hierarchy. Understandably, functionaries preferred to present a positive view of viewpoints and developments in their own locality or workplace, to avoid criticism that they were failing in their political work. Critical views among the population may therefore have been underrepresented. However, the incidence of what the SED regarded as 'negative opinion' in these reports in the Ulbricht years is in fact rather higher than one might expect, given such temptations to paint a rosy picture of an often difficult reality. Indeed, in the late 1940s it is hard to find much positive resonance towards the SED and its policies at all. Instead, reports revealed that much of the population perennially blamed the Communists rather than the defeated Nazi regime for material hardships, and branded the KPD and SED as Russian lackeys. These findings must have made very depressing reading for the enthusiastic, committed party officials, then still optimistic about the possibilities of building a new Germany along socialist lines.

Although reports suggested greater popular support and commitment as the 1950s and 1960s progressed, their overall tone increased in plausibility at times of potential crisis, such as 1956 (when Soviet troops entered Hungary to put down an attempt to overturn the existing socialist system); 1961 (the year in which the Berlin Wall was erected); and 1968 (when Warsaw Pact troops invaded Czechoslovakia to end an attempt at an alternative, more moderate road to socialism). During these periods of crisis in the socialist camp, the leadership wanted accurate information about the public mood rather than reassuring fairy tales from functionaries anxious to advance their own careers by reporting dubious successes, and generally this information was forthcoming.

The high incidence of reported negative opinion also suggests that we should reappraise – at least for the Ulbricht era – the prevailing view of the GDR as a state whose citizens did not dare to express their genuine opinions, or who did so only in trusted company. These reports suggest that GDR citizens could be quite vocal in expressing dissent, and that they did so in all manner of public settings: in public meetings, on public transport (where party and state reporters often lurked) and even in response to direct questioning. How else are we to explain the politically courageous comparisons made by a forester, asked to buy a trade union sticker in 1963 to support a workers' sports event: 'Last year, apart from our union dues, we had to buy solidarity stickers for 15 pfennigs; this year you want 25 pfennigs. You're just a bunch of beggars, even worse than the Nazis.'[3]

While negative comments on the GDR's development are more easily digested into the mainstream of GDR historiography, there remains the problem of dealing with reported positive responses. Indeed, it is tempting to disregard positive reactions altogether, both because they are often phrased in terms which might have been lifted directly from the official SED daily newspaper, *Neues Deutschland*, and because they are at odds with preconceptions, particularly in western and anticommunist accounts, that people generally rejected the SED and all its works. Equally, where positive attitudes are ascribed to party members or state functionaries, it is easy to dismiss them on the basis of these individuals' status in GDR society, and to forget that they were also entitled to a say in their country's development, and that their positive reactions are as valid as the negative opinions of other individuals. Positive responses may indicate either that the view expressed was genuinely held, or that the speaker understood the importance of expressing a conformist view. Either conclusion is informative about the forces which enabled SED structures to survive for more than forty years. Most reports also indicate the relative weighting of different points of view. Pro-SED views are commonly ascribed to named individuals, while dissenting attitudes are often reported to have been held by 'many' or sometimes 'most'.

In the light of the above comments, what are the essential contours of popular opinion in the GDR as revealed in these sources for the Ulbricht years? To what extent do they reveal the GDR's population to have been committed to official state dogma, and what connection was there between popular attitudes and the relatively peaceful longevity of SED rule, as compared to the more troubled history of socialist states such as Poland, Hungary and Czechoslovakia? The basic range of responses to KPD/SED rule was established fairly quickly and remained essentially constant. At the root of much public opinion, from practically the very beginning of the postwar period, was a sense of helplessness and political apathy. This was balanced on the one hand by those ideologically committed to the prospect of socialism, who optimistically welcomed the chance to build a new antifascist Germany, and on the other by those ideologically opposed to socialism, let alone communism and the Soviet Union, who railed against the new political order. Yet most people's political outlook was characterised by a sense of near indifference to a political system over which they felt they had no influence, given the unconditional surrender of Germany at the end of the Second World War, and the country's division in the ensuing Cold War.

In the very early years the general apoliticism of much of the population was dictated by the severe material hardships of the immediate postwar era. These distracted most people's attention away from political life, and enabled the KPD/SED to establish new power structures with little opposition from a populace preoccupied with the business of day-to-day survival. For instance, although the SBZ's media discussed little other than the unification of the two workers' parties during the spring of 1946, in practice most people not immediately involved were mainly uninterested in the event. In Ilmenau, for instance, the public prosecutor's office noted complete indifference amongst workers and all other groups. Even in Gotha, where the Thuringian KPD and SPD held their unification party congresses, older people were said to be 'collapsing under the weight of their cares and can see no other escape from the current hardships than suicide'.[4]

Even the creation of the new GDR state on 7 October 1949, a date marked with grandiose celebrations throughout the GDR's history and highlighted in the historiography as an important turning-point, was characterised by widespread confusion and indifference at the time, despite the SED's attempts to popularise it with torchlit processions and other impressive events. For most people the dawning of this new age was entirely overshadowed by a potato shortage. It was several months before a widespread consciousness emerged that a new state had been created, and longer still before the demarcation between the governments of the GDR and the western FRG was generally clear to the populace. Some even displayed a natural loyalty to the West German chancellor, Konrad Adenauer, a fierce opponent of the GDR, and continued to display pictures of the last Kaiser in their homes. The political events of October 1949, though later presented as a watershed, mattered little to those still anxious to secure the next day's meals. Scepticism and rejection prevailed until the new government achieved concrete successes, and in particular economic improvements.[5]

This indifference or political apathy helps to explain both the longevity of SED rule in the GDR and the seeds of the system's eventual collapse. Despite the SED's perpetual political campaigns, even though hardly a week seemed to pass without some important anniversary, political event, essential meeting or diplomatic initiative, and although in the Ulbricht years, in particular, life was dominated by an endless round of local political activities, it was quite often to the SED's advantage that most people remained apathetic and more concerned with their private affairs. Although widespread enthusiasm for the party line would have been welcome, the SED leadership was increasingly prepared to settle for lip-service to its political programme. When opinions were expressed, they demonstrated that most people did not welcome the SED's policies and were not convinced by the party's world view. This dissent generally mattered little in the Ulbricht years as it was experienced passively and mainly privately. Most citizens regarded political complaints as less pressing matters than rebuilding homes, careers and personal relationships amid often difficult material circumstances. For those whose aversion to the SED's political line or dissatisfaction with the slow pace of economic advances proved too much, there remained until 1961 the option of leaving for the apparently 'Golden West', a topic explored in Patrick Major's Chapter 11 in this volume. Though the emigration of almost 3 million East Germans between 1949 and 1961 created existential economic problems for the young GDR, the phenomenon also rid the SED of large numbers of potential political dissidents. For the majority who remained, however, the continuing distractions of day-to-day problems precluded active protest on political matters, and enabled the SED's structures to take root virtually by default. Meanwhile, however, underlying scepticism among the public grew, laying foundations for the eventual abandonment of the socialist ideal by increasing numbers of those who had remained either neutral or passive, or who had at least been prepared to give socialism a chance.

A growing scepticism with socialism in the colours of the SED was hardly surprising given the sometimes drastic contortions of the party line over the years. This was particularly true in the wake of Stalin's death in 1953. The years that followed saw a partial destalinisation in the Soviet Union which was given a significant boost in 1956 by Khrushchev's quickly leaked 'secret' speech to the twentieth congress of the CPSU. Apart from revealing the extent of Stalin's crimes and reversing the personality cult which had existed around the deceased leader, Khrushchev also conceded that there might be more than one road to socialism after all; this led to the rehabilitation of the Yugoslav leader, Tito, isolated in the camp of socialist countries since refusing to follow the Moscow line in 1948.

Such significant changes to official party teachings did not go unnoticed by the East German population. Indeed, to judge by party 'situation reports', the public seemed to have almost been waiting for the opportunity to catch out the SED and mock its claims to possess a monopoly on truth. Nor could the party hide contradictions such as the presentation of the Soviet Union's invasion of Hungary later in 1956 as fraternal assistance to roll back the counter-revolution, while the Suez crisis of the very same week was reported as a clear case of imperialism by Britain and France in Egypt. In 1968, too, the SED found it hard to make a convincing case for a substantial difference between the Warsaw Pact's intervention to prevent the perceived danger of a capitalist revival in Czechoslovakia and the USA's war against Communism in Vietnam, which the party roundly condemned.

1956 is a good example of a period when the population noticed contradictions within the SED's dogma, but reacted with little more than rhetoric. In late 1956, during the crisis in eastern Europe fuelled by challenges to the Communist order in Hungary and Poland, opponents of SED rule certainly made their presence felt. There were isolated calls for strikes like those in Hungary and Poland, and some disruption in factories like Carl Zeiss Jena; SED members and functionaries received written and verbal threats, encouraged in late October and early November by highly exaggerated reports that many Hungarian communist officials had been murdered. Workers were heard discussing who would be hanged from which tree, or threatening violence towards party members. Some former Nazi party members were among those hoping that the tide of history was turning against the SED. Despite a number of minor incidents, however, the protests aimed against party or state registered by the Erfurt police were not significantly more numerous or serious in the autumn of 1956 than in the comparable period of the supposedly more peaceful year of 1955.[6]

This suggests an ongoing rumble of discontent among a population which mainly preferred the quiet life and avoided politics whether the climate was fraught or relatively peaceful. Instead, most people directed their discontent at tangible, local shortcomings. In a state where everything was ultimately centrally controlled, criticism of the SED was therefore implied, but often not expressed in so many words. As one reporter dejectedly noted just as international tensions mounted over Hungary: 'In general we can say that apart from the continual discussions and disputes about production questions, material difficulties, housing problems and supply questions, the situation in the factories is normal.'[7]

Thus, the situation in late 1956 remained predominantly peaceful, and the threats unrealised – many of them were in any case made when those concerned were drunk. Yet the ideological doubts raised, and the discrepancies in the political line noted in all sections of the population, were clear signs that the SED was not winning the political argument. Events such as 1956 undermined the faith of some loyal socialists and SED supporters, confirmed the cynicism already present in many circles and were an opportunity for existing critics to speak out. Nonetheless, the difficult political situation of late 1956 did not develop into a more shattering blow against the whole system, partly because there was no clear alternative. Unification with West Germany did not seem a viable option as long as the Soviet Union's global power remained intact – partly because of memories, personal or collective, of the crackdown by Soviet troops which had ended the June 1953 uprising, but also from a general fear of war. This latter consideration was one of the major dimensions of popular opinion which pervaded the entire period. Though crises such as 1956 appeared to present an opportunity for change, in the charged atmosphere of the Cold War and with memories of the devastation and loss of the Second World War still very recent, much of the population was too wary of the potential consequences of upheaval to do much beyond carp privately and generally keep the peace within the existing political parameters. Even as late as 1968, as the Czechoslovak crisis mounted, fears were prevalent among older people, in particular, that war might be imminent. Following the invasion of Czechoslovakia in late August, a move which immediately prompted widespread parallels with Hitler's actions in 1938, one cynic commented: 'Wars always start in September.'[8] While comments like this were rather more unusual by this point than they had been in the 1950s, they echo the many comments from 1956 on the creation of the army, such as: 'It's just like Hitler: there'll be conscription and then war.'[9]

The general apathy and apoliticism of the Ulbricht era was further marked, both before and after the building of the Berlin Wall in August 1961, by an ongoing sense that the final word had not yet been spoken on the German question – that the division of Germany, and by extension the very existence of the GDR, was a temporary measure which might yet be reversed. This lack of faith in the GDR's future was particularly strong among those who stood to lose from the socialist realignment of society and the economy (private businessmen and farmers in particular), and among those in border districts cut off from friends and relatives in the West. The tides of opinion on this topic were particularly marked in Thuringia, and other areas along the border to West Germany, which had initially been occupied by American or British troops in the closing phase of the war before the Red Army arrived. Rumours that the Americans would one day return and replace the Russians could be heard in Thuringia well into the 1960s, fuelled by the widespread notion that the western powers had only been able to enter Berlin in 1945 in exchange for vacating western portions of the SBZ. If the superpowers could agree on a solution for the West Berlin question, Thuringians hoped that the Soviets might swap control of Thuringia for control over the whole of Berlin. More generally, any superpower summits during the 1950s or upheavals, such as 1956 or 1968, encouraged people to think that the era of SED rule might be ending and that it was therefore permissible to hang fire on implementing SED policies. This was, for instance, the case during 1960 when many farmers believed that they should await the outcome of the Paris summit meeting in May of that year, rather than accepting the SED's insistence on a comprehensive programme of agricultural collectivisation.[10]

Though SED membership continued to rise during the 1956 troubles, it also became clear that some potential comrades were hesitating with application forms.[11] Workers were well aware that although party membership could confer advantages and potential privileges while SED power persisted, they might face negative consequences if the system collapsed, rather as nominal Nazis had suffered political, economic and judicial sanctions in the not-so-distant past. Even as late as 1968, the liberalisation of the Prague Spring encouraged some NDPD members to wonder if they needed to have bothered merging their private small businesses in the new trade co-operatives (PGHs), as socialism's future seemed uncertain.[12]

The evidence that a significant proportion of the GDR's population was waiting for the state to collapse following a superpower settlement at first glance seems to contradict the notion that a sense of GDR national identity emerged, or at least to suggest that this did not occur until after the Ulbricht years. And yet, the sum of the many reports from the 1950s and 1960s indicates that relatively quickly – certainly by the late 1950s – a consciousness did emerge that East Germans formed a distinct community within the German nation. However, it seems likely that most East Germans felt bound by a 'community of fate' during these early years, rather than by a 'community of interest' or by a firmly cemented cultural identity. These were developments which came later, and which are present today in GDR nostalgia (*Ostalgie*), but whose roots were only forming in the Ulbricht years.

1968 is a further good example of a year in which the SED's general failure to win the ideological argument was particularly apparent, but in which the GDR also remained relatively stable. The year was marked by two key political events: a public debate (*Volksaussprache*) conducted in the early spring in open meetings and special events organised by the parties and mass organisations, before a new socialist constitution for the GDR was adopted by plebiscite; and the Prague Spring, an attempt by the Czechoslovak party leader, Alexander Dubček, to give socialism a 'human face', but ended by Warsaw Pact forces' intervention in August 1968.

Direct attacks on the GDR's political and constitutional arrangements, and in particular the SED's grip on power, were rare during the *Volksaussprache*, with very few members of the public questioning the legitimacy of the electoral system, for instance. We must conclude either that people accepted that these were unalterable characteristics of the state in the circumstances of the ongoing Cold War, or that they generally feared raising such topics. However, the latter explanation seems less likely given the extreme readiness with which GDR citizens tackled other themes which, while not direct attacks on the SED, certainly had the potential to undermine the parameters of the GDR state.[13] Chief among these were the issue of freedom of travel (effectively the Berlin Wall and the other closed borders to the West) and the perennial 'German question' of unification or continued national division. Clearly a solution to either of these would mean at the very least the end of the GDR in its present form, if not the end of the GDR altogether. However, these consequences were not specifically spelled out as desired outcomes by members of the public who spoke in meetings.

The debate on the German question was sparked by Article 8 of the draft reformed constitution, which made it clear that unification could effectively occur only if West Germany joined the socialist GDR. The very process of approving a new constitution itself generated the impression that the East German population was endorsing its state and therefore the continuing division of the nation. Thus the emotive question, 'Is there still a German nation?', was regularly put at the public meetings to discuss the constitutional draft, and many observed (correctly) that: 'The constitutional draft will deepen Germany's division.' Such comments were clearly not to be taken as complimentary, as the first steps towards better East–West relations being taken by the FRG, which would later develop into the *Ostpolitik* of Willy Brandt's chancellorship, were generally warmly greeted by East Germans. The many questions in these meetings about the reasons for Germany's division may well have been designed to embarrass party representatives.

Article 18(2) of the draft constitution guaranteed 'personal freedom', and led to lively debates in public meetings about how this was to be defined and what, in practice, it allowed. For the population at large, and for young people in particular, this was an opportunity to raise the question of the right to travel both to the West, and inside the closed areas along the border to the West. The SED's generally tight control on young people's leisure activities provoked some to insist that real freedom would only come if they were allowed 'beat music',[14] a sign that the SED, despite significant investment in education and youth work, had failed to raise this first entirely GDR generation to loyalty towards their workers' and peasants' state, or to immunise young people against western influences.

When Warsaw Pact troops entered Czechoslovakia in August that year, there was more open public unrest than usual, with gatherings of youths in some town centres, a spate of leaflets in favour of Dubček's reform policies and large slogans daubed in prominent public places, though few of them directly attacked the SED. The criticism was usually more implicit, with support for reforms on the Czechoslovak model rather than rejections of the GDR's own system. Though the situation remained peaceful on the whole, this did not imply that the population supported or was unconcerned by the crushing of the Prague Spring, or that no conclusions were drawn about the GDR's own future or the legitimacy of socialism and SED rule. The seeds of doubt were sown even among socialists, who could not understand how such developments had been possible either in Czechoslovakia or previously Hungary, as they ran counter to the Marxist theory of historical development propagated by the SED.

More generally the population saw quite clearly that the socialist camp was not the strong united force it claimed to be, as Romania had refused to participate in the invasion. Furthermore, as official explanations that Czechoslovak leaders had requested the Warsaw Pact armies to protect socialism were unconvincing, many citizens asked how it was possible that Czechoslovakia, an independent country, had been invaded. Did this mean that, despite the new constitution, the GDR was not really sovereign either? Time and again, reports cited questions which must have been posed to embarrass party propagandists: if Yugoslavia, Albania and China were allowed to go their own ways, independent of the Moscow line, why should Czechoslovakia be any different? Would the GDR or USSR also march into these countries, if asked to? Supposing an imperialist Czechoslovak government had called for help from the West? Was the USA equally entitled to occupy Cuba? Could a country leave the Warsaw Pact to pursue its own path to socialism?

Yet it did not take major events such as the end of the Dubček era in Czechoslovakia or the uprising in Hungary to bring such ideological uncertainties to the surface. They had been expressed throughout the 1950s and 1960s. Although the final sealing of the borders in 1961 largely, but not entirely, put an end to *Republikflucht* ('flight from the Republic') as a means of expressing dissatisfaction with the GDR, attitudes towards the state and its ruling party remained fairly constant across this historiographical dividing line (see also Patrick Major's Chapter 11 in this volume). The Berlin Wall simply placed a further barrier between rulers and ruled.

The fundamental questions posed by young people in the mid-1960s highlight the SED's failure to educate the new generation to loyalty, noted above. 'Why,' they asked, was 'the GDR the "fatherland of all Germans"'?; 'Why bother with elections if there is no choice between the parties?'; 'Why must we study the classics of Marxism–Leninism?'; and: 'Is there any hope of implementing the party congress's resolution to overtake West Germany?'.[15] Young people were not alone in their lack of conviction in the fundamental tenets of their state. Reports of 1963 noted that workers, farmers and the 'intelligentsia' – in other words, the bulk of the population – had still not accepted the reasons for the Berlin Wall and the impediments to East–West travel. Few supported the GDR's official stance on the German question. The SED's lengthy 'National Document' of 1962, which emphasised the importance of spreading the advances of the GDR's socialism to the capitalist and therefore backward FRG,[16] was greeted with apathy by most people, and many of those who did read it believed it would make no practical difference, as the West would not act on the GDR's proposals. In any case, some believed, 'the dangers of war and of West German imperialism and militarism aren't really so bad anyway'.

Well into the 1960s, public meetings held to discuss matters of high politics still often turned to practical economic difficulties. Such discussions fulfilled an alibi function by avoiding the need to express loyalty or direct opposition to SED rule, but also enabled the population to express indirect opposition. However, an emphasis on material problems also suggests that personal interests of housing, food supplies and the like weighed more heavily than abstruse political questions which would ultimately be decided by the governments of the superpowers, not by farmers' meetings in deepest Thuringia. A builder summed up this view in one discussion on 'What is the German fatherland?' when he commented: 'We don't care which flag is raised on our roofs. The main thing is that we're well-off and that there's no war.'[17]

It is worth emphasising that, throughout the Ulbricht period, many of the general reactions and attitudes to the GDR and to the SED's centrally ordained policies were to be found within the party membership as well as the population at large. This highlights the opportunism of many party members, but also indicates a need for differentiation when discussing the SED. The party was not a homogeneous mass of Ulbricht loyalists. In 1968, for instance, it was clear that many rank-and-file members of the SED, and other parties, were practically incapable of explaining the official position to questioners, let alone of ably defending it in front of critics. Members were at best confused by the reforms introduced by the Czechoslovak party, and at worst – at least from the Politbüro's point of view – sympathetic towards them. In one extreme case, a young engineer commented: 'Dubček's doing the only right thing, and it must be possible here too,' and continued: 'I have nothing in common with the SED, can't I resign?'[18] Despite many resolutions of support for the official line, the SED was clearly not united behind its leadership over the fundamental issues raised by the Prague Spring.

Yet these reports of divisions within the SED were also nothing new. Great confusion had developed in the aftermath of destalinisation in 1956. At that time, many of the former Social Democrats still in the SED had hoped that liberalisation would permit tolerance of their more moderate path to socialism, and were heartened by Khrushchev's assertion that there were, after all, despite years of virulent attacks on 'social democratism' within the party, various ways to socialism. The crackdown on such an alternative path in Hungary shortly afterwards did not help to clarify the ideological position, but did serve as a reminder of the practical limits of destalinisation. Conversely, diehard Stalin loyalists were troubled by the party's distancing from the personality they considered central to the success of the world socialist movement.

The invasions of both Hungary and Czechoslovakia produced widespread confusion and many instances of open opposition within the SED's ranks. In 1968, some local SED functionaries even expressed their dissent publicly. As at other times of crisis in the GDR's history, such as the revolt of 17 June 1953, numerous SED members temporarily removed membership badges from their lapels to avoid becoming targets of popular discontent. Such actions revealed a serious lack of commitment to the party cause across large swathes of the grass-roots, extending up at least into the district leaderships. During the crisis of 1956, for instance, party educators in Worbis district (theoretically the most loyal comrades) often admitted to doubts caused by western broadcasts they should not even have heard, had they followed the party's injunctions to spurn the western media.[19]

The quality of political work even among paid, full-time party functionaries is a further indication of lacking commitment to the SED's cause. In Erfurt, for instance, only around a quarter of the party's propagandists attended training courses in late 1963 and early 1964, and the regional headquarters estimated that few of them would perform effective work.[20] When higher party organs checked the work plans of the local and district groups, they often found them politically weak and amounting to little more than a routine list of poorly prepared meetings. Although the local or national elections held every two to three years acted as a spur to political activity in the SED and the other parties and organisations, the revived structures and good intentions quickly lapsed in most cases once the campaigns were over. Thus local party organisations essentially adopted the same tactic as most of the rest of the population – political apathy – and avoided controversy wherever possible.

However, uncertainties and contradictions within the party rank and file coexisted with the SED's leading role, and generally did not undermine it. The importance of SED membership and the maintenance of state and party structures were too important to many careers, and the alternatives too uncertain, to allow discontent and indifference within the party to create open tensions. The memory of the purges of former SPD members in the early

1950s must also have acted as a disincentive. Instead, most party groups tended to ignore theoretical positions if at all possible and to concentrate instead on tangible local matters such as increasing productivity in individual factories to meet and overfulfil the requirements of the state plan.

In any case, despite these shortcomings and basic weaknesses in certain local groups, the party leadership in Berlin did not repeat the widescale (if incomplete) purge of party members and functionaries undertaken in the early 1950s, when the aim had been to remove social democratic tendencies within the party. From the reports it received, the SED hierarchy could have been in no doubt that the GDR's political structures were not strong in some parts of the country. A thorough purge would have seriously undermined the SED's ability to fulfil the leading role ascribed to it in the 1968 constitution, by removing the many functionaries who administratively preserved the system without taking its goals too seriously, a situation not uncommon in many rural areas and even in some district centres. Rather, the party's control commissions contented themselves with removing only the most incompetent, politically unreliable and damaging local leaders, and otherwise merely ensured that the willing functionaries co-operated with their less committed colleagues to preserve the status quo.

In conclusion: while the GDR remained a relatively peaceful country apart from the events of June 1953, and occasional, relatively minor public demonstrations thereafter, popular opinion towards the SED was principally characterised by indifference or apathy. This was occasioned by a combination of two main factors during the Ulbricht years: a sense that the GDR and socialism were temporary inconveniences to be weathered as well as possible until the wider international situation changed; and increasing suspicions or convictions, even among those initially enthusiastic about socialism or prepared to give it a chance, that the allegedly scientifically based theories on historical and economic development did not in fact hold water. The absence of any realistic alternative – with the possible and frightening exception of a Third World War with heavy German losses – and the increasing dependence of large parts of the population on the existing order for careers and livelihoods, ensured that indifference won out over dissent. Making the best of things and building personal or local tangible achievements within the given framework further helped structures to solidify, as did the active involvement of the very many genuinely committed to the GDR as an antifascist alternative to both the Third Reich and the FRG, which was presented in the SED press as essentially a continuation of pre-1945 politics.

In this view, the theory advanced soon after the GDR's collapse by Armin Mitter and Stefan Wolle that the state's downfall began with the events of June 1953 appears essentially false,[21] since state and party structures, both formal and informal, continued to become entrenched well into the 1980s, while the socialisation of the East German population to GDR norms continued. Yet the sense that the GDR was somehow an abnormal state of affairs remained constant throughout the Ulbricht years and beyond. When the courageous opposition groups of 1989 began to protest, they could draw on the support of a population, including much of the SED membership itself, which had never been entirely convinced by the party leadership's arguments, preferring to concentrate on their local concerns and private lives rather than risk upsetting a rather precariously loaded applecart.

Notes

1 The examples in this chapter are drawn from reports in the Thuringian state archives in Weimar (hereafter ThHStAW), now housing the corresponding archives of the Party of Democratic Socialism (hereafter LPA Erfurt PDS). The themes are explored at further length in Mark Allinson, *Politics and Popular Opinion in East Germany 1945–1968* (Manchester, 2000).
2 See reports of early 1956 in LPA Erfurt PDS, BIV/2/5/25.
3 LPA Erfurt PDS, BIV/2/9.01/13, SED Heiligenstadt, opinion report, 6 June 1963, 5.
4 ThHStAW, ObLW 12, public prosecutor's office reports, 1945/46, especially Ilmenau, 9 April 1946, and Gotha, 8 April 1946.
5 ThHStAW, AfI 87, 'Deutsch-sowjetische Freundschaft', 7 October 1949.
6 SED reports of October–November 1956 in LPA Erfurt PDS, BIV/2/5/26–27, and police reports of 1955 and 1956 in ThHStAW, Vs/St 534 and 545.
7 LPA Erfurt PDS, BIV/2/5/26, Heiligenstadt and Eisenach reports, 22 October 1956.
8 Reports following the invasion of Czechoslovakia are collated in ThHStAW, Vs/St 917, 918, 919 and 1076.
9 LPA Erfurt PDS, BIV/2/5/25, 'Kurzinformation Nr. 2/56', 20 January 1956.
10 1960 reports in ThHStAW, OI 271, 272, 273 and Vs/St 335.
11 LPA Erfurt PDS, BIV/2/5/26, 'Stand der Realisierung des Beschlusses ...', undated, 5-6, and BIV/2/5/27, 'Bericht über die Durchführung des Beschlusses des ZK ...', 28 November 1956, 7.
12 ThHStAW, NF 836, fol. 31, NDPD report, 21 August 1968, 2–3.
13 Reports on the 1968 *Volksaussprache* in ThHStAW, NF 558, 559, 560.
14 ThHStAW, J 28, 'Bericht über Meinungen ...', 22 February 1968, 2.
15 LPA Erfurt PDS, BIV/2/16/737, 'Informationsbericht 31/63', 15 October 1963, and 'Einschätzung über die Durchsetzung der staatlichen Jugendpolitik ...', 21 March 1963; ThHStAW, V 223, 'Probleminformation...', 15 March 1967, 4.
16 The 'National Document' is partly cited in Ernst Deuerlein (ed.), *DDR 1945–1970: Geschichte und Bestandsaufnahme* (3rd edn; Munich, 1971), 251–2.
17 Drawn from SED election reports of 1963, 1965 and 1967 in LPA Erfurt PDS, BIV/2/13/725; reactions to 'National Document' (1962) in LPA Erfurt PDS, BIV/2/9.01/13.
18 LPA Erfurt PDS, IV/B/2/5/183, 'Information über Aufweichungserscheinungen ...', 13 June 1968, 2–3.
19 LPA Erfurt PDS, BIV/2/5/027, 'Informatorischer Bericht Nr. 49/56', 14 November 1956.
20 LPA Erfurt PDS, BIV/2/9.01/654, 'Einschätzung des gegenwärtigen Standes der

massenpolitischen Arbeit in den Wohngebieten der Stadt Erfurt', 22 January 1964.
21 Armin Mitter and Stefan Wolle, *Untergang auf Raten: Unbekannte Kapitel der DDR-Geschichte* (Munich, 1993).

7

Workers and the Socialist Unity Party of Germany in the summer of 1953

Gareth Pritchard

At the beginning of June 1953, Walter Ulbricht was summoned to Moscow where the new Soviet leadership, Stalin's successors, ordered him to abandon many of the hardline policies that he had hitherto been pursuing in the GDR. Upon his return to Berlin, Ulbricht obediently, if reluctantly, introduced the so-called 'New Course'. Many measures against the middle classes, farmers and Christians were to be rescinded. The rapid collectivisation of agriculture was to be halted, and there would be increased opportunities for tradesmen and craftsmen. On one crucial issue, however, the government decided to remain firm. A 10 per cent increase in work norms, announced the previous May, was under no circumstances to be cancelled.

In the afternoon of 16 June 1953, building workers on the Stalinallee in East Berlin downed tools and marched into the city centre to protest at this failure to make the same concessions to the workers that were being made to other sections of the population. On the morning of 17 June the protests spread throughout most of the GDR, and around half a million workers went on strike. In the afternoon of 17 June, approximately 400,000 people marched into the centres of towns and cities throughout East Germany, where they vented their fury on prisons, party buildings, and other obvious symbols of the regime.[1] With the SED and state apparatus paralysed by indecision, and by conflict at the very top between Ulbricht and his reformist opponents, it was only the timely intervention of Russian tanks that saved the regime from ignominious collapse.

The June uprising has been the subject of intense interest on the part of historians, who have reconstructed the events of 16 and 17 June in minute detail.[2] Broadly speaking, one can identify three schools of thought in the historiography. Historians working in the GDR always attempted to explain away the uprising by calling it an 'attempted counter-revolutionary putsch'. According to this interpretation, the strikes and demonstrations were part of an attempted coup that had been organised by the West German government and the western powers, and instigated by provocateurs and secret agents who had been smuggled across the border into the GDR.[3] Amongst anticommunist historians, by contrast, there has always been a strong tendency to regard 17 June as a 'people's uprising', the purpose of which was to win freedom, western-style democracy and national unity.[4] Armin Mitter and Stefan Wolle, for example, have depicted the uprising as a kind of unsuccessful forerunner of 1989 which, had it not been crushed by the Red Army, 'would inevitably have led to reunification' and an end to socialism in the GDR.[5] The third main school of thought comprises left-wing but anti-Stalinist historians such as Lutz Niethammer, Benno Sarel and Torsten Diedrich, who have depicted the uprising as first and foremost a workers' uprising, the goal of which was not to destroy socialism in East Germany, but to rid the GDR of its Stalinist distortions. In the words of Torsten Diedrich:

> the demand for the abolition of the GDR simply was not raised. The main reason for this is arguably that the majority of the workers in the GDR did not regard the political system in the Federal Republic ... as the alternative. The thrust of the workers' rising therefore aimed at the democratic transformation of the East German state.[6]

It is not the purpose of this chapter to engage directly with the debate about the nature and character of the June uprising, for the present author has already done that elsewhere.[7] Instead, we shall confine our attention to a subject that has received much less historical interest, namely, relations between the SED and the working class in the weeks and months that *followed* the uprising. There are a number of good reasons for this. One of the main problems in studying Ulbricht's East Germany is that the documents on which the historian must rely were thoroughly infected by Stalinist jargon. Official newspapers and SED archival documents usually tell us far more about the mindset of the apparatchiks who wrote them than about the real world on which they were reporting. If one were to believe what one reads in *Neues Deutschland*, or in the SED's internal reports, one would conclude that the regime enjoyed the whole-hearted support of the great majority of the working masses, and that the people, under the inspired leadership of Walter Ulbricht, were marching cheerfully and confidently towards the sunlit uplands of socialism.

There was, however, one brief period during the Ulbricht era when the grip of Stalinism was loosened somewhat, and when party and state documents became rather more revealing. In the immediate aftermath of the June uprising, the SED engaged in a great deal of soul-searching to explain to itself and the outside world how so many workers could turn so publicly and violently against what claimed to be a workers' state.[8] Moreover, given the temporary weakness of Ulbricht and other hardliners in the party leadership, it was possible for disgruntled members and functionaries to express their concerns far more openly than previously. The workers, too, despite the crushing of their uprising by Russian tanks, did not immediately lose the confidence they had gained on 17 June. As Wolfgang Venohr has pointed out: 'Afterwards as before, the mood in the GDR was explosive. The workers, above all, did not mince their words.'[9] Given the greater willingness of workers to express their grievances, and the greater propensity of SED functionaries to record and acknowledge these grievances, documents produced in the aftermath of the uprising provide the historian with a unique window on the state of relations between the SED and the working class that it claimed to represent.

Working-class unrest in the summer and autumn of 1953

One point that emerges very clearly from official documents produced in the aftermath of the uprising is that mass working-class unrest did not subside with the crushing of the uprising, but continued into the late summer and early autumn of 1953. At its mildest, working-class discontent took the form of verbal protests and disruptive behaviour. In the weeks that followed the uprising, for example, the SED arranged thousands of workplace meetings in which workers would be harangued by party apparatchiks about the 'lessons' of 17 June, and given the opportunity to reaffirm their loyalty to party and government. Employees, however, often proved decidedly reluctant to attend. At the Sächsisches Serumwerk in Leipzig, only twenty-one out of 180 staff turned up to hear how they had been led astray on 17 June. At the 'Deutsch-Sowjetische Freundschaft' tram depot, also in Leipzig, only eighty of the 500 workers turned up.[10] Even where employees allowed themselves to be corralled into these meetings, they often disrupted proceedings with cat-calls and interjections. Thus on 27 June, at the '7th October' railway repair shop in Zwickau, some 2,500 staff were convened to listen to the district SED secretary. According to the official report, the speech was interrupted for several minutes by 'fascist provocateurs', who managed to get several hundred to join in their anti-SED chants.[11] When Politbüro member Fred Oelßner visited the giant Buna works in Schkopau on 26 June, the meeting 'degenerated into a wild provocation'.[12] At the end of August, a meeting at one building-site in Leipzig was disrupted by a bricklayer, who argued vehemently that no discussion was possible until all political prisoners had been released: 'Thereupon he provoked such a tumult that the meeting was broken up.'[13] In one of Leipzig's book-binderies, even as late as September, 'agents were able to make every meeting in the workplace impossible'.[14]

A second manifestation of working-class unrest in the late summer and early autumn of 1953 was the frosty reception given to the 'brigades' of SED activists that were sent into factories to purge 'unreliable elements', make personnel changes in management and generally to bolster the party's authority. Such brigades were usually met with a solid wall of hostility, not just from ordinary workers, but even from SED members and shopfloor functionaries. At the ECW works in Eilenburg, it was reported that: 'The members of staff refuse to discuss with the instructors sent into the workplace by the district leadership.'[15] At the Lowa plant in Altenburg, a veteran Communist was expelled from the SED for arguing that the mass deployment of agitators in his factory was creating an 'artificial disturbance'. Worse still: 'His hostility to the party manifests itself in [the fact] that he threatened and described as informers those comrades who had contributed to the unmasking of enemy elements in the workplace.'[16] In Leipzig, meanwhile, attempts by SED activists to approach workers in their homes were confronted with 'closed doors and ears',[17] and at the Meuselwitz Maschinenfabrik the unofficial shopfloor motto was 'hold your tongue'.[18]

Workers also articulated their discontent by more traditional means such as absenteeism and go-slows. At the beginning of September, the sick-rate in the coal-mines around Stollberg was running at 22.5 per cent, against a norm of 3 per cent. One distraught SED functionary noted 'that in the hard coal [industry] the principle of the go-slow is catching on. The plan is no longer being fulfilled and the pit foremen no longer want to take responsibility.'[19] In its monthly report for September, the regional party control commission in Karl-Marx-Stadt also noted that, in all areas, an increase in 'enemy activity' had resulted in a fall in productivity and a worsening in the quality of manufactured items.[20]

The classic means by which workers have traditionally sought to defend their interests is, of course, the strike. Stoppages continued throughout the summer and early autumn of 1953, although they tended to be small-scale and of short duration. On 23 June, for instance, workers at the TEWA plant and the RFT Gerätewerk in Karl-Marx-Stadt turned off their machines for a few minutes 'in memory of the victims' of 17 June, suggesting some form of cross-plant co-operation.[21] Between 15 and 17 July, there was a major strike at the Buna chemical factory in Schkopau, which was broken only through the massive intervention of the security forces and the arrest of a number of workers.[22] As late as September, the authorities in Karl-Marx-Stadt were continuing to complain that: 'Again and again it appears that the class enemy is attempting to exploit the bad mood which exists in order to achieve strikes in the various enterprises.' At the IKA works in Annaberg, up to sixty workers had struck for two hours in protest at the failure of the authorities to give them more than a minimal pay increase.[23]

Where feelings ran particularly high, there were even incidents of workers physically attacking SED functionaries. In September, there was a vicious street brawl outside a public house in Falkenstein between party members and anti-SED workers, resulting in several hospitalisations.[24] During the same month, the FDJ headquarters in Mittweida was attacked with stones, while a number of unfortunate FDJ functionaries were assaulted with knives.[25] The *Bürgermeister* of Domsdorf, meanwhile, felt that his physical security was so threatened that he complained to the authorities 'that he was without any protection and absolutely demanded a weapon'.[26]

Despite subsequent official claims that 17 June had been a 'flash in the pan', from the examples above it is apparent that industrial relations throughout the whole of the summer of 1953 were turbulent and potentially explosive. The exact political significance of this anger is more difficult to interpret. Were the East German workers rejecting the whole experiment of socialism in the GDR, as Mitter and Wolle would have us believe? Or were they, as Torsten Diedrich alleges, simply expressing their anger at the bureaucratic distortions of Stalinism and the economic hardships that Ulbricht had inflicted upon them?

Over the years, historians of various political persuasions have debated this point vigorously, indeed vituperatively. The newly available documents shed some more light, although they too have their limitations. Few workers, in the aftermath of 17 June, raised the demand for the abolition of the GDR, the dismantlement of socialism, or reunification with West Germany. Much more common were demands for the resignation of Ulbricht or the government. Typically, however, workers were reported as exercised about specific economic or political issues, such as the raising of work norms or the lack of freedom of speech and information. Workers in the private textile factories of Plauen, for example, were reportedly angry that their counterparts in state-run factories received higher wages.[27] At the Vereinigte Trikotagenwerke in Crimmitschau, the 600 female workers resented the fact that the plant had only six toilets, two showers and no canteen.[28] Women textile workers at the Feinspinnerei in Burgstädt were vexed by an unpopular Sunday nightshift,[29] and autobahn workers by, amongst other things, bread shortages.[30] At the SAG Bleichert in Leipzig, the workforce even complained that their tea was being served from rusty urns.[31]

It is also worth mentioning that where such practical grievances were remedied, a noticeable improvement in labour relations was often noted by the SED authorities. At the SAG Bleichert, it was reported on 7 July that, although there were still oppositional elements at the plant, the 'visible improvements' introduced since 17 June had led to a partial restoration of workers' faith in the SED. 'A fragment of trust in the government', one report argued, 'is thus present'.[32] At the Zinkhütte building-site in Freiberg, where there had been a major strike on 18 June, the efforts of the authorities to install running water and lighting in the barracks supposedly had a positive impact.[33]

How do we interpret this evidence? On the one hand, one might argue that, given the confidence of the workers and relative openness of reporting after 17 June, the preponderance of local and economic grievances accurately reflected the workers' mood. It is conceivable that many workers with backgrounds in the labour movement were still ideologically committed to socialism, and that even among the majority of largely apolitical workers, there was a willingness to accept SED rule provided that their direct material problems were being addressed. On the other hand, it is equally possible that, while workers felt safe to express mundane grievances, they did not dare to go further. According to Mitter and Wolle: 'One of the most important reasons why workers in the factories talked solely about economic problems was the justified fear of arrests or other reprisals.'[34] Yet even the fiercely partisan Mitter and Wolle seem uncertain on this point, claiming simultaneously that: 'During this period, a large part of the population had lost its fear of the authorities. The vast majority of SED functionaries found themselves well and truly put in the dock when they led meetings.'[35]

Conflict and tension within the SED

That workers who had been driven off the streets by Soviet tanks on 17 June continued to feel angry, and continued to seek every opportunity to give vent to their anger, is hardly surprising. What *is* surprising is the wide variety of views amongst SED members regarding the causes and character of this working-class discontent. Broadly speaking, it is possible to identify three main types of response on the part of SED members to the turmoil that surrounded them.

First, a significant minority of party members remained true to the SED and refused to take any part in the disturbances of 17 June or in the general unrest that followed. In one district of Leipzig it was estimated that, of 2,772 members and candidates, approximately 25 per cent of party comrades fell into this category.[36] Some of these were veteran Communists who had enthusiastically implemented the Stalinist policies of the later 1940s and early 1950s. There were also a number of younger comrades, indoctrinated in party schools and enjoying a relatively cushioned existence in organisations such as the KVP, who simply could not understand the popular anger.[37]

Such hardliners displayed little or no sympathy for the strikes and demonstrations, and were genuinely convinced that 17 June was indeed no more than a fascist putsch attempt.[38] According to Fritz Schenk, who at the time was a leading SED functionary in Berlin:

> The old Communists criticised the leniency which had been shown towards the strikers, and stressed again and again that one could only proceed against the 'hooligans' with brutality. 'The rogues who are standing outside cannot be convinced by words, but only by the truncheon, and, if that doesn't help, then by powder and lead', railed an old SED man.[39]

However, just because such members were hostile to the strikes and demonstrations did not mean that they were enthusiastic supporters of all the policies of the Ulbricht government. In the surviving archival records, we find numerous examples of hardline Stalinists for whom the so-called 'New Course', announced by the government on 11 June 1953, had made too many concessions to traditional enemies such as the churches and farmers.[40] Far from correcting the mistakes of the past, the New Course constituted a deviation from the principles of Marxism–Leninism. Indeed, when first introduced, many Communist functionaries could not accept that their leadership should have taken such a step, and forbade any discussion of the New Course on the assumption that it was western propaganda.[41] A number of hardliners even went so far as to hand in their party cards on the grounds that the SED had abandoned socialism and capitulated to capitalism.[42] According to a teacher of social sciences at the Lehrkombinat Deutsche Post in Gornsdorf, the Central Committee had 'deviated from the line of Marxism–Leninism', and he 'could not purvey the policies of the government, since before he had spoken differently'.[43] As late as August 1953, a member of the Rochwitz district leadership was still arguing 'that he is no longer in agreement with the politics of our party. He is and remains a Communist. If Comrade Stalin were still alive, there would be no New Course in the party.'[44]

A second, much more common response among SED members and functionaries was to voice criticisms of the Ulbricht regime and its policies, while refraining from taking any more concrete actions such as dropping out of party life or handing in party cards. On 17 June itself, such individuals had often acted indecisively. At the SAG Bleichert in Leipzig, for instance, it was estimated that about 70 per cent of the company's 575 SED members had behaved passively during the strike of 17 June: 'They stood to one side, dithered to and fro, a good number were even pleased when we few functionaries squabbled and scuffled with the provocateurs.'[45]

In the wake of 17 June, such individuals found it hard to accept the official explanation that the disturbances were part of a fascist putsch, organised in advance and precipitated by provocateurs who had slipped across the border from West Germany.[46] In reports on the mood of the party membership compiled during July and August 1953, one repeatedly encounters comments such as: 'The colleagues and comrades have not yet understood that the provocateurs in our enterprise were guided by fascism,' or: 'The character of 17 June is not clear even amongst the comrades.'[47] Even where it was conceded that agents might have been involved, disgruntled party members asked how so few provocateurs could have led the workers astray so easily.[48]

What comes over very strongly is that, among this section of the SED, there was a profound exasperation with the sudden changes of tack which had left ordinary members and functionaries bewildered and exposed to popular discontent. It was, after all, the party rank-and-file who had been expected to implement the ultra-left policies announced by Ulbricht at the party conference of July 1952. They had had to explain to workers, often more out of discipline than conviction, why work norms were being raised under an ever-harsher work regime, while living standards fell. With the advent of the New Course, all their efforts over the previous months 'appeared to have been flung to the winds in an abrupt and unexpected political *volte-face* at the top'.[49]

Unsurprisingly, being placed in such an uncomfortable position by the party leadership resulted in much confusion and resentment at the grassroots. According to Wolfgang Venohr, recording his own experiences in Berlin: 'The small and middle functionaries were thoroughly embittered [by the fact] that the "big shots" had made the most serious mistakes which they should now answer for to the population.'[50] A typical SED member from Flöha was reported to have exclaimed: 'At first the construction of socialism was proclaimed by the Central Committee, to which end several measures were taken, then everything was changed again and the whole thing reversed. He no longer has any idea what to argue.'[51] In Annaberg, it was still being noted some six weeks after the uprising that:

> The New Course required a great adjustment in both the party and state apparatus, necessitated by the fact that what was being propagandised yesterday became invalid the following day ... Put starkly, this has flung quite a few functionaries and members of the party into confusion, manifested in the view – I can't go along with this, it's a 180-degree turn-about.[52]

Such anger focused above all on the person of Walter Ulbricht, who was held personally responsible for the mess in which the party found itself, and was regarded with particular loathing by a significant section of the rank-and-file. Several comrades at VEB Herkules in Aue argued in public that: 'Walter Ulbricht must be dismissed on the grounds of the mistakes which have been made. If Ulbricht is consistent, he will resign.'[53] For a comrade at the Audi works in Zwickau, Ulbricht was 'the most dangerous man in the government'.[54] According to a comrade teacher from Oelsnitz: 'In Berlin there is a state of emergency. All this is on Ulbricht's conscience. The goat-beard must be made a head shorter.'[55] At an abattoir in Karl-Marx-Stadt, one SED worker, as he dispatched a goat, remarked that: 'If this were Walter Ulbricht, I would slaughter him in just the same way.'[56] Nor were such anti-Ulbricht feelings confined to the rank-and-file. Even so exalted a person as Paul Fröhlich, party secretary in Leipzig, could argue on 25 June that the Central Committee 'should also begin to get rid of the exaggerated cult of personality'.[57]

In addition to this general discontent, there were a number of specific issues vexing reformist-minded members which, in the weeks following the uprising, were brought up repeatedly in meetings and discussions. The privileges of the so-called 'technical intelligentsia', for example, were bitterly resented by members who clung to the belief that socialism meant equality. According to one SED member from Auerbach: 'It would be quite in order if the shops for the intelligentsia were burnt down.'[58] Likewise, a forthright comrade from Zschopau who wanted to see these outlets 'smashed', argued that the 'preferential treatment of the intelligentsia is a load of bullshit'.[59] As late as October 1953, it was noted that in Eilenburg and Delitzsch districts there had been numerous discussions among party members about the privileges granted to engineers, specialists and others. At Kulkwitz powerstation, several members had argued that, in view of the general poverty of the population, it was wrong to pay such high salaries to the technical intelligentsia.[60]

Another specific grievance that cropped up time and again was 'white-washing' (*Schönfarberei*). In the view of many members, the SED had lost contact with the masses partly because the authorities had turned a deaf ear to bad news. According to one high-ranking SED functionary in Leipzig, the provocateurs had chosen 17 June because their network of agents was better-informed of the mood on the shopfloor than the party apparatus.[61] Another Leipzig functionary maintained that the party had been taken by surprise because misleading information had been passed up from below. In his experience, functionaries were far too prone to tell superiors what they wanted to hear, while: 'Negativity was rejected as undesirable.'[62] At a meeting of the Leipzig regional leadership on 25 June, it was argued forcibly by one functionary that comrades in the city administration were reluctant to deliver critical reports to the district secretariat for fear of being 'thrashed to pieces'.[63] Again and again, the message percolated up that, rather than living in a fantasy world, the party leadership should at last confront the serious material problems facing the GDR.

By far the most pressing single complaint made by SED members and functionaries in the summer of 1953 was that the party had failed to do enough to address the material problems of the workers. There were repeated complaints that union functionaries were so preoccupied with their bureaucratic tasks that they had entirely forgotten that their primary function was to represent members' interests.[64] The *Bürgermeister* of Zaulsdorf, for example, exclaimed that: 'We can look where we want, everywhere only hunger ... Now we have the mess which the powers-that-be have landed us in, but for which we have to carry the can.'[65] At a Leipzig regional leadership session, one functionary argued that the basic reason for workers' discontent was poor trade union work: 80 per cent of demands, he claimed, were basically economistic in character. The trade unions, however, 'have simply ignored the cares of the people'.[66] At the same meeting, a functionary from the MS-Kirow-Werk argued that, before 17 June, workers had voiced a whole series of legitimate grievances, but these had been brushed aside by officials with the argument that sacrifices were necessary for the construction of socialism.[67]

If hardline SED members responded to the crisis by condemning the strikes and demonstrations, while more reformist members confined themselves to criticising certain aspects of SED policy, a third response, on the part of those who were most disillusioned, was to drop out of party life or, more dramatically, to quit the party altogether. Many of these anti-Stalinists had long been discontented with the hardline policies of Ulbricht, and regarded 17 June as the final straw. On the day of the uprising itself, such members had often sided unambiguously with the workers and against the party. At the MIKAS factory in Leipzig, it was noted that, on 17 June, 'a number of comrades joined in the clamour during the disturbances'.[68] At another Leipzig factory, one SED functionary was actually elected by the strikers to lead the delegation which presented demands to the management.[69] In Werdau district, an SED investigation concluded that, where there had been strikes, it had often been party members, and sometimes even leading members, who had acted as ringleaders.[70] According to one report from Leipzig, in large enterprises where there had been strikes on 17 June, no fewer than three-quarters of SED members on the shop floor had participated.[71]

In the aftermath of the uprising, it was not unusual for such members to register their disillusionment by dropping out of party life. Numerous SED members, such as six workers at the Bahnbetriebswerk in Leipzig, refused to pay subscriptions on the grounds 'that it should not have got to the point where Soviet tanks made their appearance'.[72] In Leipzig, the number of comrades attending evening classes fell from 40 to 25 per cent between April and the end of June, whilst in Delitzsch the figure fell from 59.6 to just 20 per cent.[73] Between May and August, subscriptions to the party paper *Neues Deutschland* in Leipzig fell by 9 per cent, whilst subscriptions to *Tägliche Rundschau* fell by a more substantial 23 per cent, most probably because of the paper's strong Russian connection.[74]

A good example of how the internal life of the SED following the uprising was withering on the vine is furnished by the Maschinenfabrik Meuselwitz 'John Schehr'. At the beginning of September, the factory was visited by an SED activist brigade which discovered that 'party groups and their organisers exist only on paper'. Of the thirteen members of the party leadership, only two were at all active, while participation in party meetings had shrunk to just 33 per cent. Moreover, in the members' meetings it was 'always the same comrades who make contributions, while the majority adopt a passive and reserved attitude'. Worse still, those comrades who did venture to speak up were almost invariably officials and managers rather than ordinary workers. Since 17 June no agitational work of any kind had been carried out in the plant, and some twenty SED members were refusing to pay subscriptions.[75]

The most extreme step that disenchanted SED members could take was to resign from the party altogether. The number doing so was not large, probably because leaving the party stigmatised resignees as dissidents and could upset career prospects or home life. Nonetheless, between 17 June and

3 August, some 218 party members had left the SED in Karl-Marx-Stadt region.[76] The great majority were workers, while a considerable number were labour veterans organised in the SPD or KPD before 1933.[77] In Leipzig region, some 306 comrades had handed in their cards by 10 August, including 211 workers and 25 veterans who had been politically active before 1933.[78] In particular localities and workplaces there were even a number of mass resignations. At VEB Textima in Altenburg, for example, 54 members abandoned the party in the two days following the uprising. All were workers, including 23 veteran members of the SPD.[79] By 25 June, no fewer than 200 members, or 54 per cent of the entire SED membership at Textima, had handed in their party documents.[80]

Those who quit the party on principle often wrote letters of resignation that provide a fascinating insight into the motives of those whose consciences no longer allowed them to remain. In Leipzig, for example, one SED member wrote that:

> A whole series of mistakes has been made on the part of the SED. These mistakes, however, were not made by myself as a former member of the party. Yet, when I argued against them ... I was ideologically unclear. In view of the rapidly changing course of the party, I have come to the decision to resign in order to avoid once again being or becoming ideologically unclear.[81]

At the University of Leipzig, one comrade academic wrote in his letter of resignation that, after 'mature reflection', he had come to the conclusion:

> that it is no longer possible to comply with the changing and contradictory decisions of the party. The rigid party discipline and dictatorial arrogance of our party leaders have, in the past, not allowed even a single word of sensible criticism to be uttered ... Now the attempt is being made to transfer the question of guilt for the mistakes which have been made onto those who, through the suppression of criticism, were not in a position to express their opinion without being exposed to some reprisal or other.[82]

Analysis of diverse responses on the part of SED members

It is easier to describe the variety of responses on the part of SED members than to explain them. However, two factors would seem to have been of considerable significance, both of which relate to the evolution of the East German labour movement since its liberation from Nazism in 1945.

First, as a result of its particular path of development, the SED by 1953 had become a rather fragile assortment of factions, each of which had come to the party by a different route and for differing reasons. The core of the party was made up of veteran Communists, who in 1945 had energetically set about rebuilding their party, and had soon found their way into functionary positions in the party, in industry, and in the reviving state apparatus.[83] Another important faction within the SED comprised former Social Democrats, who in April 1946 had accepted merger with the Communists with a greater or lesser degree of enthusiasm, but who, since the later 1940s, had found themselves coming under pressure as a result of Stalinisation.[84] In the later 1940s another faction had emerged in the party, made up of young and ambitious apparatchiks, who had little background in the traditions of the labour movement, but who had been thoroughly indoctrinated in the ways of Stalinism.[85] Finally, as a result of the efforts of the SED to become a truly mass party, many tens of thousands of quite ordinary people had been admitted to party membership, most of whom had a relatively low level of political consciousness and commitment.[86]

It is worth pointing out that often there was little love lost between these various factions within the SED. Former Social Democrats and Communists, of course, had a history of mutual conflict and suspicion stretching back to the First World War. There was also a discernible tension between veterans and the younger, ambitious Stalinists who were playing an ever-more prominent role inside the party. From the point of view of the regime, the new generation of bureaucrats being hatched out in the party schools were more reliable, more competent, and better educated than the veterans, and for this reason the younger apparatchiks were systematically fostered within the nomenklatura. Many veterans, by contrast, viewed the neophyte Stalinists who were displacing them in the party and state apparatus as 'conformists, subservient grovellers, crawlers, obsequious yes-men'.[87]

The second factor that was instrumental in producing diversity of opinion within the SED was the organic link that still, even in 1953, connected the party and the working class. Many rank-and-file SED members were ordinary people who happened to have a party card, and who were quite indistinguishable from the mass of the population among whom they lived and worked. It was only natural that the grievances of the working class as a whole – about work norms, the privileges of the technical intelligentsia, the role of Ulbricht – should have been reflected in the ranks of lowly SED members. Higher up the party apparatus, many functionaries, despite the years of Stalinisation, still adhered to the traditional view that the primary function of party and trade union officials was to represent the interests of their members, rather than those of the state and the employers.[88] In the summer of 1953, such functionaries found themselves having to choose whether to side with the party and the state, which they had done so much to build up, or with the working class from whose ranks they had come. As one SED functionary from Leipzig put it: 'Now I must decide either for the party or for the masses.'[89] It was an agonising decision, and functionaries could go one way or the other, or waver unhappily in the middle, depending on local circumstances and personal inclinations.

Taken together, the factional nature of the SED in 1953 and the overlap between the party and the working class go a long way to explaining, not just why different factions responded to the crisis in different ways, but why there were also significant differences *within* the various factions. If we look, for example, at how former Social Democrats behaved in the summer of 1953, we find that some at least still felt that their primary loyalty was to their party. In Stalinstadt, one veteran Social Democrat and founding member of the local SED, despite having been pushed out of the district leadership by Communists, prevented demonstrators from tearing down SED posters by threatening to unleash his dogs.[90] Elsewhere, former Social Democrats vacillated between party and class, unable to make a clear decision between the two. In Marienberg, it was reported that many old Social Democrats had 'lost their heads', arguing that the SED had been pursuing 'too severe a line'.[91]

In many other localities, former SPD members sided unambiguously with the protesting workers and against the party.[92] In Altenburg district, one of the centres of unrest was the giant Textima plant, an old SPD stronghold.[93] In Karl-Marx-Stadt region, one of the hotbeds of protest was Werdau district, where there had been short strikes at the Trikotagen-Werke and the Wärmegerätewerk in Crimmitschau and the Wälzlagerwerk in Frauereuth. It was no accident that, during the Weimar period, Werdau had been an SPD bastion, with six times more members than the local KPD. In 1946, the area had been a centre of opposition to the SPD/KPD merger, and, ever since, the SED authorities had complained about continued Social Democratic tendencies.[94]

Social Democratic hankerings continued for many weeks after the crushing of the uprising. A report of 20 June from Leipzig complained that many party comrades were making comments such as: 'We are not members of the SED but of the SPD.'[95] On 27 June, at an SED meeting at the VEB Nickelhütte in Aue, the majority of former SPD members argued in favour of refounding their old party.[96] In Leipzig on 8 August, it was reported that 25 workers at the Teeverarbeitungswerk were refusing to pay their SED subscriptions on the grounds that they wanted to rebuild the SPD.[97] In August 1953, the Karl-Marx-Stadt party control commission noted frequent Social Democratic sentiments, including the union leader in Freiberg who publicly argued that, in free elections, the SPD would crush the SED, or the comrade at the Formulardruck plant who predicted that, given the choice, 90 per cent of SED members would join a newly refounded SPD.[98]

Former Communists, by contrast, seem to have been much less likely than their Social Democratic counterparts to take the part of the workers. In Karl-Marx-Stadt region, the previous party affiliations of ninety-six of those who had left the party by 23 August are recorded. Of these ninety-six, ten had been members of the SPD before 1933, whereas only two had been members of the pre-1933 KPD.[99] Of the 116 comrades who had been expelled from the SED in Altenburg by the end of 1953, ten were former KPD members whereas seventeen were former Social Democrats.[100] Between July and

September in Leipzig region, some twenty-seven old Social Democrats were expelled from the SED as opposed to just four former Communists.[101]

As we have already seen, many of these old KPD men were hard-bitten Stalinists who, in the summer of 1953, sided uncompromisingly with the party against the working class. But even among the veteran Communists, there were many individuals whose sense of proletarian solidarity was still sufficiently strong to override their sense of party discipline. In the aftermath of 17 June, old Communists, too, could turn against the regime. According to one report from Zschopau: 'In this district, it has been above all a large portion of the older comrades (VVN [the antifascist veterans' association] – organised before 1933) who have stood up energetically, and who have expressed the opinion that there is no longer any trust in the authorities.'[102]

Precisely because such Communist veterans possessed long political experience, their critiques of the party leadership were often the most coherent and insightful. At the VEB Nickelhütte in Aue, a 61-year-old veteran Communist, who had joined the KPD back in 1920, cast doubt upon the official line that the disturbances had been the work of enemy agents. Some infiltrators, no doubt, had been at work, but the informant network in the GDR was so extensive that large-scale subversion from outside was inconceivable. He also attacked the current party line that, while the SED had made specific mistakes before 17 June, the general political approach had been correct. In his view, the only mistake had been to overestimate workers' patience:

> These are not mistakes which have been made, but an attempt, using every means possible, to squeeze the lemons to such an extent an explosion resulted. ... If we think back to when Social Democratic ministers allowed striking workers to be fired upon, then the KPD, which today is in power, raised a hue and cry and demanded that these labour leaders must clear off. The [People's Police] has fired on the workers and caused workers' blood to flow.[103]

Conclusion

Documents produced in the aftermath of the June uprising provide the historian with a unique window on the state of relations between the SED and the working class in Ulbricht's GDR. What the window reveals is a picture of confusion and seething discontent within the ranks of both the party and the working class. Though the evidence is sometimes difficult to interpret, at least three points can be made with some degree of certitude.

First, although the SED by the summer of 1953 had travelled a long way down the road to Sovietising, it was still not the CPSU. A great many SED members and functionaries clung to the traditional belief that the purpose of a socialist party was to represent workers' interests rather than those of the state. At lower levels, but in the middle echelons too, there was a powerful sense that the leadership had let down, even betrayed the working class, and that the SED should return to its roots, following a specifically German road to socialism.

Secondly, precisely because the process of Stalinisation was incomplete, the SED was still deeply fissured between hardliners and reformers, between former Social Democrats and former Communists, between veterans of the labour movement and younger apparatchiks. Each faction tended to respond differently to the crisis, though within factions there could also be significant variations. Faced with the awful decision of siding with the workers' party, which they had done so much to build up, or the workers, from whose ranks they had originally come, even functionaries and members from similar backgrounds could choose differently.

Thirdly, although the working class and the SED in 1953 were clearly heading separate ways, the divorce was not yet finalised. Many SED members were ordinary workers, and even many functionaries still felt bound by traditional class loyalties. In the weeks after the uprising, grievances, concerns and aspirations were often mutually shared by workers, SED members and functionaries alike. Had the reformers in the SED leadership emerged victorious from the power struggle with Ulbricht, they might have used such elements to construct a more popular, reform-Communism, as Gomułka did in Poland and Dubček in Czechoslovakia. Once Ulbricht had re-established his position, however, it became more and more difficult for SED members and functionaries to express reformist sentiments. By the early 1960s, the party had been disciplined and transformed into a reliable tool of the state. As the SED gradually lost any representative function, so the organic link between party and working class was irretrievably broken.

Notes

1 Figures taken from Torsten Diedrich, *Der 17. Juni 1953 in der DDR* (Berlin, 1991), Appendix 4.
2 See *ibid.*; Arnulf Baring, *Uprising in East Germany* (New York, 1972); Armin Mitter and Stefan Wolle, *Untergang auf Raten* (Munich, 1993); Ilse Spittmann and Karl Wilhelm Fricke (eds), *17. Juni 1953: Arbeiteraufstand in der DDR* (Cologne, 1982); Heidi Roth, *Der 17. Juni 1953 in Sachsen* (Cologne, 1999).
3 Rolf Badstübner *et al.*, *DDR: Wachsen und Werden* (East Berlin, 1974), 231–42; Joachim Heise and Jürgen Hofmann, *Fragen an die Geschichte der DDR* (East Berlin, 1988), 111–18; Ernst Diehl *et al.* (eds), *Geschichte der SED: Abriß* (East Berlin, 1978), 288–98.
4 Ullrich Rühmland, *Mitteldeutschland* (Stuttgart, 1959), 44; Wolfgang Venohr, *Die roten Preußen* (Frankfurt/Main, 1992), 85–105; Terence Prittie, *Germany Divided* (London, 1961), 143.
5 Mitter and Wolle, *Untergang*, 160.
6 Diedrich, *Der 17. Juni*, 152–3.
7 Gareth Pritchard, *The Making of the GDR* (Manchester, 2000), Ch. 8.

8 Roth, *Der 17. Juni*, 433.
9 Venohr, *Die rote Preußen*, 109.
10 Sächsisches Staatsarchiv Leipzig (SStAL), Bezirksparteiarchiv (BPA) Leipzig, IV/2/1/28, fo. 34.
11 Sächsisches Staatsarchiv Chemnitz (SStAC), BPA Karl-Marx-Stadt (KMS), IV/2/4/62, fo. 247.
12 Mitter and Wolle, *Untergang*, 111–12.
13 SStAL, BPA Leipzig, IV/2/3/147, fo. 99.
14 *Ibid.*, fo. 11.
15 *Ibid.*, fo. 13.
16 SStAL, BPA Leipzig, IV/2/3/148, fo. 87.
17 SStAL, BPA Leipzig, IV/2/3/147, fo. 12
18 *Ibid.*, fo. 20.
19 SStAC, BPA KMS, IV/2/4/30, fo. 125.
20 SStAC, BPA KMS, IV/2/4/46, fo. 288.
21 SStAC, BPA KMS, IV/2/4/62, fo. 126.
22 Mitter and Wolle, *Untergang*, 132–7.
23 SStAC, BPA KMS, IV/2/4/46, fo. 291.
24 *Ibid.*, fo. 292.
25 *Ibid.*, fo. 292.
26 SStAC, BPA KMS, IV/2/4/62, fo. 154.
27 SStAC, BPA KMS, IV/2/4/46, fo. 203.
28 *Ibid.*, fo. 221.
29 SStAC, BPA KMS, IV/2/4/62, fo. 126.
30 *Ibid.*, fo. 135.
31 SStAL, BPA Leipzig, IV/2/1/28, fo. 34.
32 *Ibid.*, fo. 74.
33 SStAC, BPA KMS, IV/2/4/62, fos 128–30.
34 Mitter and Wolle, *Untergang*, 132.
35 *Ibid.*, 129.
36 Roth, *Der 17. Juni*, 437–8.
37 See, e.g., Fritz Schenk, *Im Vorzimmer der Diktatur* (Cologne, 1963), 86–8; Pritchard, *The Making of the GDR*, 153–5; Diedrich, *Der 17. Juni*, 21–2, 171–4.
38 *Ibid.*, 171–4.
39 Schenk, *Im Vorzimmer*, 204.
40 SStAC, BPA KMS, IV/2/4/62, fo. 157; Mitter Wolle, *Untergang*, 116–17.
41 Diedrich, *Der 17. Juni*, 49.
42 Mitter and Wolle, *Untergang*, 66–7.
43 SStAC, BPA KMS, IV/2/4/62, fo. 154.
44 SStAC, BPA KMS, IV/2/4/46, fo. 263.
45 SStAL, BPA Leipzig, IV/2/1/28, fo. 71.
46 Roth, *Der 17. Juni*, 395–6.
47 SStAL, BPA Leipzig, IV/2/1/29, fo. 94; IV/2/3/147, fo. 28; IV/2/3/148, fo. 149; SStAC, BPA KMS, IV/2/4/62, fos 194–8.
48 Mitter and Wolle, *Untergang*, 115.
49 Mary Fulbrook, *Anatomy of a Dictatorship* (Oxford, 1995), 181.
50 Venohr, *Die roten Preußen*, 87.
51 SStAC, BPA KMS, IV/2/4/62, fo. 157.

52 *Ibid.*, fo. 168.
53 *Ibid.*, fos 136–7.
54 *Ibid.*, fo. 141.
55 *Ibid.*, fo. 138.
56 SStAC, BPA KMS, IV/2/4/46, fo. 261.
57 SStAL, BPA Leipzig, IV/2/3/144, fo. 239–40.
58 SStAC, BPA KMS, IV/2/4/62, fo. 144.
59 SStAC, BPA KMS, IV/2/4/46, fo. 226.
60 SStAL, BPA Leipzig, IV/2/3/148, fo. 149.
61 SStAL, BPA Leipzig, IV/2/1/28, fo. 85.
62 *Ibid.*, fo. 59.
63 SStAL, BPA Leipzig, IV/2/3/144, fo. 223.
64 SStAL, BPA Leipzig, IV/2/3/144, fo. 223 and 231.
65 SStAC, BPA KMS, IV/2/4/62, fo. 138.
66 SStAL, BPA Leipzig, IV/2/1/28, fo. 72.
67 *Ibid.*, fo. 46.
68 SStAL, BPA Leipzig, IV/2/3/144, fo. 231.
69 SStAL, BPA Leipzig, IV/2/3/147, fo. 226.
70 SStAC, BPA KMS, IV/2/4/46, fo. 246.
71 Roth, *Der 17. Juni*, 434–5.
72 SStAL, BPA Leipzig, IV/2/3/147, fo. 13.
73 SStAL, BPA Leipzig, IV/2/3/146, fo. 50.
74 SStAL, BPA Leipzig, IV/2/3/148, fo. 7–10.
75 SStAL, BPA Leipzig, IV/2/3/147, fo. 19–20.
76 SStAC, BPA KMS, IV/2/4/46, fo. 263.
77 SStAC, BPA KMS, IV/2/4/62, fo. 145.
78 SStAL, BPA Leipzig, IV/2/1/29, fo. 25.
79 SStAL, BPA Leipzig, IV/2/3/147, fo. 27.
80 SStAL, BPA Leipzig, IV/2/3/144, fo. 236.
81 SStAL, BPA Leipzig, IV/2/1/28, fo. 67.
82 *Ibid.*, fo. 86.
83 Pritchard, *The Making of the GDR*, Chs 3 and 4.
84 Andreas Malycha, *Partei von Stalins Gnaden?* (Berlin, 1996), Chs 4, 5.
85 Schenk, *Im Vorzimmer*, 86–8; Pritchard, *The Making of the GDR*, 153–5.
86 *Ibid.*, 67, 153–4, 169–70.
87 Andreas Herbst *et al.*, *So funkionierte die DDR*, Band 2 (Reinbek bei Hamburg, 1994), 1129.
88 Pritchard, *The Making of the GDR*, 182–3, 204–5.
89 SStAL, BPA Leipzig, IV/2/1/30, fo. 71.
90 Lutz Niethammer, 'Where Were You on 17 June?', *International Yearbook of Oral History and Life Stories* (Vol.1, 1992), 58.
91 SStAC, BPA KMS, IV/2/4/62, fo. 154.
92 Roth, *Der 17. Juni*, 447–51.
93 SStAL, BPA Leipzig, IV/2/3/146, fo. 2–10.
94 SStAC, BPA KMS, IV/2/4/46, fo. 220 and IV/2/4/62, fo. 124.
95 Fulbrook, *Anatomy*, 186.
96 SStAC, BPA KMS, IV/2/4/62, fo. 194.
97 SStAL, BPA Leipzig, IV/2/3/146, fo. 9.

98 SStAC, BPA KMS, IV/2/4/46, fo. 261.
99 Roth, *Der 17. Juni*, 440–1.
100 *Ibid.*, 454.
101 *Ibid.*, 460.
102 SStAC, BPA KMS, IV/2/4/62, fo. 143. The VVN was an organisation of former anti-Nazi resisters, most of whom had been Communists.
103 *Ibid.*, fos 194–95.

8

From *Junker* estate to co-operative farm: East German agrarian society 1945–61

Jonathan Osmond

A pocketful of rye and a sack of potatoes

The *Junker* landlords of East Elbian Germany loom large in German history up to 1945.[1] That year marked the end of their power at least on their home ground, as their estates were confiscated by the Soviet, Polish and Soviet Zonal German authorities.[2] So in one respect a rural social history of what was to become the GDR is that of a territory suddenly deprived of or – alternatively – liberated from its traditional ruling class. The 'democratic land reform' of 1945 marked a caesura in German history, a point when the personnel changed once and for all. The landlords were dispossessed and expelled; their fields and forests divided up, their possessions seized and their houses knocked down.[3]

This was not an autonomous German development. Agricultural reshaping, first in redistribution of land to individual owners, then in a process of collectivisation, was characteristic of the communist regimes of Eastern and Central Europe. At one extreme was the brutal Stalinist collectivisation in the Soviet Union from 1929. At the other was the return to widespread private farming in Poland in the mid-1950s. The experience of the SBZ/GDR lay in between.[4]

The social upheaval is not to be underestimated. In a little over fifteen years rural societies which had been characterised by a powerful landed gentry, poor rural labourers and a small peasant class were subjected to the depredations of war, economic and political collapse and foreign occupation, then to mass immigration by refugees from the east, to the seizure and redistribution of over one-third of the agricultural land in a matter of months, to incipient collectivisation from 1952, and to what amounted to forced, if not quite Soviet-style, collectivisation in 1960. In the process large numbers of farmers and their families left their homes, sometimes destroying them before they went. Thereafter the changes were less dramatic but no less far-reaching. The 1960s and 1970s saw the co-operative farms amalgamate into ever larger units and become overspecialised in their production, and in October 1990 German unification set in train a further agricultural upheaval, based on political and judicial reference back to the events of the earlier decades.[5]

These changes were almost entirely – but perhaps not entirely – instigated from above. The pattern for communist agricultural policy had been set by Lenin and then refined or debased by Stalin. Within Germany the Communists and Social Democrats of the Weimar Republic already had their own policies on land reform, so from both Soviet and German directions came the measures of 1945 and beyond.[6] First the large landowners were expropriated and their land divided up among the peasantry, refugees and rural proletariat (1945–47), then the larger peasant farmers were challenged (1948–53), and in the process collectivisation set as the pattern for the future (1952 onwards). The final stage of collectivisation (1960), bringing in the remaining independent farmers, was officially voluntary (even Stalin had maintained this fiction), but in practice a high degree of coercion was employed.

This chapter is not so much about the perpetrators of these policies (though they appear), but rather about the recipients – the *Junker* themselves, their tenant farmers, independent peasants, farmworkers and destitute incomers from the east – and the ways in which rural societies in eastern Germany were affected. The use of the plural here is to indicate the considerable regional agricultural variation in the GDR: from the middling peasantry of Saxony and Thuringia, through the tenant farmers of Saxony-Anhalt, to the large estates of Brandenburg and Mecklenburg. Although the end result of collectivisation was eventually similar in most instances, the local social impact varied enormously. Sensitivity to earlier social gradation for decades permeated the ostensibly uniform collectivist system, and is present even today.

The people affected did not know from month to month or year to year what the next turn in official policy was to be, though they might have their suspicions. Particularly in the years up to 1961 their lives were beset by economic and social uncertainty and by the additional question whether the state in which they lived would survive or be united with the rest of Germany. From the authorities' perspective there was never any question that the transformation of the countryside was a difficult process, part of a real 'class struggle in the village'.[7] There were attitudes from the past with which to contend; there was non-co-operation, opposition, protest and sabotage.

The archival source base has improved dramatically since 1989, but methodological problems remain.[8] Because of the political control inherent in the system and the paucity of written sources from a plurality of interests, when an attempt is made to go beyond the development of official policy there are serious questions. Do the reports on public opinion, party activity, economic performance and the development of new agrarian structures allow us to take their content as typical, or have a relatively few problem cases been highlighted? These difficulties are familiar to those who have worked on the documentation of the Third Reich, although the ever-advancing political jargon of the GDR makes the files more impenetrable than those of the National Socialist authorities. Quantification is a related problem, for although the GDR produced vast amounts of statistics, not all bogus, the dimensions of opposition are not easy to ascertain. True, the People's Police and party-brigades sought out problems, but their presentation was also coloured by a determination to support declared policy and to find support for it among the population. Another difficulty is that personal and class interests and attitudes were used as reified examples, without context for the historian. A prominent local figure would be characterised as a 'reactionary force', 'a large peasant element', or 'a progressive personality'.[9] In other words, the judgement has already been made and extraneous comment excised before the historian can make an assessment. Similarly, overheard comments, derogatory and otherwise, were cited out of context as examples of class attitudes or of 'lack of clarity' (a euphemism for social or political variance), without any indication of the numbers holding such opinions, who they were, or where they lived.[10]

In the early years the reporting language was only marginally affected by party gibberish. There is also the advantage of numerous letters sent by individuals to the parties and mass organisations. Here is another essential perspective, but it too must be treated with circumspection. Most, but not all, of the letters from farmers, labourers and refugees were complaints or denunciations, and one must be careful not to assume as typical those relatively few who objected or who shopped their neighbours. Nevertheless, the existence of such material gives an added dimension to the picture derived from the official reports and intra-party correspondence, not least because letters to party chairman and later president Wilhelm Pieck came from women as well as men.[11]

Class struggle in the village

The emphasis here is on identities, personal continuity and change, and the conflict and convergence of interests in the development of agricultural policy in the SBZ and GDR from the end of the war to the aftermath of the building of the Berlin Wall.[12] The argument is not that everything positive in the officially sanctioned historiography of the GDR must now be rejected in the light of new evidence, nor is it that collectivisation was solely a disaster marked by peasant uproar. That would make an exciting story, and some of the documentary evidence would tempt in that direction, but it would not be true. The purpose here is rather to explore the complex processes of social change, without resorting to teleological assumptions. If this is the corrective to the GDR literature there is also, however, a challenge to common western prejudices. Hard though times were, this was not a uniform, grey society. There was variety and conflict, and a certain space for traditional practice and for the social expression of individual character and purpose.

Categorisation and identity overlap but do not coincide. The former derives from the ways in which individuals and groups were described by the authorities, stripped as far as possible here of their ideological connotations; the latter refers to a more variegated bundle of self-perception, gender, generation, family history, language, religion and relations with others. We may deal with the simpler first. *Großgrundbesitzer* (large estate owners) were those who before 1945 owned land totalling 100 hectares or more, a group of so-called *Junker* conflating seriously landed gentry families with hectares by the thousand and, by international standards, moderately propertied working farmers employing primarily family labour and small numbers of outside workers. Many of these farmers thought of themselves rather as *Großbauern* (large peasants), though the original official classification referred only to owners or tenants of 50–100 hectares. *Mittelbauern* (middling peasants) and *Kleinbauern* (small peasants) were then, respectively, those who worked 5–50 hectares and 5 hectares or less. *Landarbeiter* (farmworkers) might live in with a peasant family, might have a small plot for their own use, might have nothing, or – before 1939 at least – they might be migrant and seasonal workers from Poland. Not to be forgotten were the *Verwalter* (administrators) of larger estates, who were classed in the minds of the Communists with their *Junker* employers.

A new categorisation came with the land reform of 1945. Those who were already in the peasant classes cited, whether or not they gained land under the redistribution, were *Altbauern* (old peasants), while those who had fled from the eastern territories or who had previously held little or no land and now received a parcel were *Neubauern* (new peasants). With the onset of collectivisation from 1952 another category appeared, *LPG-Bauern* (co-operative peasants). Increasing political reference was also made to *werktätige Einzelbauern* (working individual peasants) in order to divide those who used primarily family labour from *Großbauern* employing others.

These terms were part of a class-based analysis of the East German countryside, and they corresponded in certain obvious ways with reality. They are, however, a far from perfect definition of the social mix. The category of *Altbauern* did not hint at the difference of experience between, say, a substantial group of long-established middling farming families in a Thuringian village and a few remaining independent small peasants in formerly *Junker*-dominated Mecklenburg. Similarly, *Neubauern* might be former farmworkers reluctant to take on a holding themselves and willing to work for others; or refugees from a non-agricultural background in Königsberg (Kaliningrad), Danzig (Gdańsk) or Breslau (Wrocław); or industrial workers brought in to pave the way for collectivisation.

As for self-perception, the Communists were only too well aware of the legacy of the past. They recognised that deference to the gentry, peasant conceptions of land and property, religious belief and patriarchal relations all threatened to hamper the development of a co-operative economy.[13] Where they had an advantage was in the influx of refugees. These uprooted people posed enormous organisational, social and economic problems, but they might serve as a way of loosening the previous bonds of rural society, acting as a focus of class tension and providing a committed but socially weak core of rural support. For the *Neubauern* themselves the land reform was for some an exciting opportunity, for others the start of an unfamiliar, tough existence.

Dividing the earth

The 'democratic land reform' of 1945 was initiated not in the whole of the SBZ, but in the Prussian Province of Saxony. This implied a local decision, but the policy was actually conceived in Moscow and followed by almost identical measures in the other *Länder* and *Provinzen*. The decree of 3 September announced the 'liquidation of feudal–*Junker* large landed property and of the lordship of the *Junker* and large estate owners in the village', and specified the terms of expropriation.[14] All land and property was to be confiscated without compensation from those possessing 100 hectares or more, from war criminals and 'war guilty', from National Socialist leaders and from active proponents of the NSDAP. An explicit link was made between the class interests of the landed owners, the Prusso-German military tradition and the aggression of fascist 'Hitler-Germany'. The land reform was intended to put an end once and for all to the alleged dangerous influence of the *Junker*.

The land was to be distributed to land-impoverished peasants (those with under 5 hectares), landless labourers, 'resettlers' (*Umsiedler*) and refugees (*Flüchtlinge*) from the east, municipal authorities and urban workers and employees. There was provision for the maintenance of larger estates for livestock breeding, seed culture, forestry and agricultural experiment (the later *Volkseigene Güter* (VEG) or People's Own Estates), but otherwise parcels were to be kept small. They were generally to be no more than 5 hectares, but there was scope for permission for up to 10 hectares where soil quality was poor. This leeway, plus the fact that local conditions were to be taken into account when dividing up the land, meant that there were opportunities for individuals and families to advance their own interests, a consequence which was to plague the authorities in the coming years.

The mechanism to carve out the holdings was the Commission for the Implementation of the Land Reform, established at community (*Gemeinde*), area (*Kreis*) and district (*Bezirk*) level. In each community the Commission of five–seven persons was to be elected by those who stood to be recipients of land. This provision emphasised the 'democratic' nature of the reform, and linked it to the alleged popular upsurge in favour of reform in the months since the German defeat. How far it is legitimate to speak here of popular, democratic or revolutionary action is a matter for debate. The official depiction by the Communists then and subsequently was of a spontaneous rural movement in favour of reform, taken up and led by the Communists and their allies.[15] This propagandist slant should not, though, be taken as proof that there *were* no examples of local action. After May 1945 legal, administrative and economic breakdown and intense social pressures did create demand for rural reform, if not revolution. The strains of National Socialist agricultural control had engendered discontent. The absence at the front or early flight westward of larger landowners, their agents and National Socialist officials meant an absence of control not immediately filled by the advancing Soviet forces.

Certainly when the Commissions began their work, they were not entirely under the control of the Communists, who could not yet rely upon a developed network in the countryside. Representatives of the other parties permitted in the SBZ spoke out in favour of land reform, although the CDU and Liberal Democrats (LDP) sought compensation for those expropriated and the SPD differed from the KPD in proposing immediate collectivisation rather than parcelisation. Even the stipulation in the September decree that no former members of the NSDAP join the Commissions could not be enforced in all cases. The work of the Commissions – though increasingly controlled by the Communists and their Soviet mentors – was a confusion of political perspectives, desire for retribution and individual ambition.

The Commissions set to work immediately, visiting those whose land and property were to be seized. Backed by the Soviet military, instructions were given for evacuation of manor houses and estates within 24 or 48 hours. Male family heads faced arrest and transportation to the Baltic island of Rügen, where an unknown number perished.[16] Many had fallen or been interned in the Soviet Union, and others were already in the West. Therefore it was often the female family members who faced on the doorstep their former employees and tenants, or those drafted in on their behalf.[17]

Village meetings were then held to allocate the land parcels, by lot or decree. Sometimes these were accompanied by celebrations:

> The share-out took place on 23.9.45. Three hundred peasants took part, some from the surrounding villages. The candidates for land came up as families to the table, where the *Landrat* ceremonially handed over the title deeds. At the end of the meeting the Catholic priest made a ceremonial speech. Many were moved, some women wept. The peasants had decorated the village street.[18]

Alternatively – where residual deference for and sympathy with local landowners prevailed – the mood was more sombre. The author Erich Loest, for a short time in 1945 a farmworker in Saxony, described the expropriation of two elderly aristocratic sisters, whose predicament aroused the sympathy of the local women. Besides, the Silesian refugees holed up in the fine house wanted to go home, not take land in Saxony: 'No choir sang, no brass band played. It occurred to no-one to hang garlands. It was completely different from what painters painted later in their commissioned works or scribes inscribed.'[19] Whether there was enthusiasm or not, after the land division Commission members would go out to the fields and hammer in fence posts along the new boundaries – a favourite motif in the photographic record.[20]

Some landowners managed to hold out beyond September 1945, but most of the land earmarked for confiscation was redistributed in the autumn and early winter. The effects of this massive transfer varied. In regions where there had been a mix of large estates and middling-to-large peasant holdings, the larger peasants were able to take advantage of the land made available and bolster their own positions. This was not the outcome intended in the land reform and in many instances flouted the detailed prescriptions. Indeed, the documentation of 1945-48 is dominated by complaints sent in to the party authorities by small farmers and local officials, who saw the land reform being exploited by precisely those who should have been dispossessed or by those middling and larger farmers who sought to build up their holdings and benefit their own families. In May 1947 the SED mayor of Eichstädt in the Osthavelland wrote in characteristically aggressive tone to Pieck that: 'In large part reactionaries and timeservers of the worst kind have already re-established themselves on the partitioned land of the estates and other possessions.'[21] More specific examples abound, of which this loaded description from 1948 is one:

> The former estate Schönigsche Foundation in Kattkow, Cottbus area, 400 acres in size, came under the land reform. The former steward of the estate, Herr H., undertook in the course of the land reform the partitioning of the estate. The share-out went solely to members of his family, namely to the son, daughter, mother-in-law, brother-in-law and sister-in-law. Each individual family member received ten hectares of land ... The son and the brother-in-law were members of the SS. This estate is being maintained in its entirety and unity by the family members. The former steward H., now a *Neubauer*, has a masterly understanding of how to preserve the old character of the estate. This former estate steward brings in 25–30 labourers from the town of Cottbus as harvesters, sowers and drovers. He then plays the estate steward just as before ... Herr H. ... has the best official support. S., chair of the area council and a member of the SED, takes his holidays on this estate.[22]

Many small farmers complained that those who had acquired or consolidated new holdings conducted themselves far worse than the previous owners and managers. Bolstered by freshly adopted membership of the KPD/SED, the new owners paraded around the villages, preferably on horseback, with instructions for those whom they saw as their subordinates. In the Brandenburg village of Batzlow in 1948 the SED mayor and his wife behaved as 'dictators' who threatened the local population with the Red Army or with being locked up.[23] Not much had changed; Nazi bullies had been replaced by Communist bullies. Sometimes they were the same people.

At the end of the war male losses and absences meant that women and children were a significant majority of the population, and in October 1946 women made up about 57 per cent of those engaged in agriculture. The land reform therefore affected large numbers of women, both through expropriation of *Junker* families and through the allocation of smallholdings to single female refugees. The latter were among those facing the most difficult circumstances: sexual violation by the Soviet troops; disputes over property with the party authorities, male relatives and returning husbands; inadequate labour for heavy work; frequently inexperience and poor childcare facilities. Living conditions were dismal, crowded into farm dwellings and outhouses or into the confiscated grand houses. There were a few official voices who spoke out not only for the needs of women and children, but also took a pro-active line on women's legal, political and social rights. Frieda Haas, an SED member in the Association for Mutual Peasant Aid (VdgB, founded as a central organisation in 1947), sought to combine improvement of women's lot with the development of facilities of a kind which became reality only during the 1950s: communal childcare, laundries, bakeries and health provision. With the Stalinisation of the SED from 1947–48, however, her feminist perspective was silenced.[24]

The land reform did not suddenly produce a uniform agrarian society in the SBZ.[25] The dispossession of the large landowners was a step in that direction, but it engendered new stratification in rural areas. The remaining large peasants were in social and economic terms the dominant figures now not just in Thuringia but throughout the SBZ. Despite the war damage and dislocation which affected them too, and the rigorous demands of SED agricultural delivery policy, they were in an incomparably better position than the small *Neubauern*. The latter faced desperate housing conditions and shortages of equipment, livestock, feed, fertiliser and seed. Villages throughout the SBZ, but particularly in the north and east, were riven by conflict between established peasant families and the newcomers. The former, many of whom had benefited from the land reform, blamed the newcomers for being dirty, lazy and incompetent, while the smallholders, who found it hard to scrape a living from inadequate resources, claimed they were being maltreated by their more prosperous neighbours. The desperate conditions meant that agricultural production could not fulfil the needs of impoverished urban dwellers. The party response was to find scapegoats, and this against a background of Stalinisation, accelerated economic centralisation and planning and the rebranding of the SED as a 'party of a new type'.

Onto the tractors!

From a Marxist–Leninist standpoint the next logical step was to engineer the homogenisation of the rural population by attacking the large peasants, who were accused of furthering their own class interest and sabotaging the development of socialism. Walter Ulbricht led the way. In a speech to the German Economic Commission in September 1948 he inveighed 'Against the saboteurs of the people's food supply'.[26] He accused the large peasants of being inspired by western monopoly capitalism, and – albeit unwittingly in some cases – hindering the plan and sabotaging the food supply. He cited several specific cases, linking them with the remnants of fascism. This was a classic example of the conflation of economic and political class categorisation, which put the large peasants in the wrong whatever they did. By the nature of their economic class, their actions were political measures to damage agricultural development. Ulbricht insisted that the small and middling peasants must be supported through the development of the VdgB and the Machine Lending Stations (MAS). He did not mention it, but earlier that year the Democratic Peasants' Party of Germany (DBD) had been founded by the SED to organise the rural population. The party definition of 'large peasant' was now extended to include farmers with between 20 and 50 hectares of land, at variance with the self-perception of such people but with a degree of relative logic in the light of the social consequences of the land reform. By 1952 an even greater leeway of definition allowed Ulbricht to widen his range of fire: large peasants were those who owned more than 20 hectares of medium-quality land, plus an indefinite number with smaller areas of high-quality land which should also be counted as capitalist concerns.[27]

Splenetic speeches and press articles against saboteurs and capitalists were no doubt frightening and demoralising for those targeted, and there was more tangible impact. Some farmers found themselves in court on charges of sabotage and malpractice, many more faced petty harassment from party officials, while most experienced discriminatory treatment by the VdgB and the MAS in the allocation of machinery and delivery quotas. The result was an exodus: on 31 October 1953 (by which time the aftermath of the June Uprising had confirmed Ulbricht's political survival) the number of those who had given up and fled westward stood at some 14,000.[28]

The campaign against the large peasants was one component of the SED's promotion of co-operative, though not yet fully collective, production. While the position of the larger farmers was being eroded, the VdgB and the MAS extended their control of the weaker smallholders under the auspices of the first Five-Year Plan (1951–55). Ulbricht not only encouraged the elaboration of local 'village economic plans', but also set out his view of the past and the future of the co-operatives. Originally, he said, they had been peasant self-help organisations, which had then been turned into exploitative instruments by the large landowners and finance capital. Now with the creation of unitary village co-operatives under the aegis of the VdgB the peasants could return to the original character of self-help. By claiming that what was to take place was 'not a new idea', Ulbricht was trying to allay suspicions about collective work.[29] Indeed, in October 1951, less than a year before the first major promotion of collectivisation, Ulbricht was still saying that the fulfilment of the Plan depended on 'the full development of the the private initiative of the working peasants', albeit in conjunction with the growth of the MAS and the VEG.[30]

By the second SED Party Conference in July 1952, however, the stage was set for an acceleration of policy. Ulbricht characteristically framed it as the party responding to the local formation of co-operatives and to 'questions' from farmers about state support. He spoke highly of these initiatives and further insisted: 'I explicitly underline the absolute voluntary principle in the organisation of such co-operatives and point out that the use of any compulsion for the peasants in this question is impermissible. Comrade Lenin himself pointed out that one cannot introduce communal working of the land through decrees and laws.'[31] Though Ulbricht was later to ignore Lenin's advice and incline to Stalin's impatience, there was a kernel of truth in what he said. The encouragement of 'communal working' for the rest of the decade, assisted by any number of decrees and laws, proved a frustrating experience for the SED.

The founding of the LPGs (*Landwirtschaftliche Produktionsgenossenschaften* or 'agricultural production co-operatives') in the 1950s was multiple in meaning and effect. This was a feature unrecorded in official publicity about the growth of LPG numbers in the 1950s, but it was recognised and reported inside the parties. Put simply, peasants did not found or join LPGs just because they were forced to or because they sought socialism. In joining they were also technically not surrendering their land, just the use of it. There were complex personal, economic and local motivations, not the least of which – perverse though it may sound – was to avoid collectivisation. There are many examples of larger peasants combining in an LPG Type I (the lowest level of collective organisation, where arable land was farmed co-operatively) as a strategy to minimise outside interference. Poorer peasants, hoping to offset the local domination of the larger peasants and to benefit from pooled machinery and labour, tended to choose LPG Type II, requiring the surrender of machinery and draught animals, or more usually Type III, specified as a socialist large agricultural concern, where arable and livestock were collective.[32] An example of these different strategies was reported from the Erfurt district as late as 1959:

> In some of these places there are two LPGs ... The mass of the peasants of the village – the former farmworkers and *Neubauern* – work in the LPG founded first. They have already taken the step to Type II or III. The strong middling peasants are in the second LPG, which in both villages comprises only a few large concerns. In this case a few almost landless peasants are continuing to

work more or less as farmworkers for these strong middling peasants and thereby also belong to the LPG.[33]

Not surprisingly, the family dimension played a crucial role in the decision to join or not to join an LPG. The official view was that collective facilities – for childcare, laundry, cooking, purchasing, etc. – would be of particular benefit to rural women, and there is evidence that many did come to appreciate these daily advantages. However, it is clear from the documentary record that in the initial stages women tended to act as a brake on collectivisation. The stereotype of the farmer's wife scolding her husband for coming home from the tavern having promised the family holding to the co-operative and sending him out the next morning to retract was reflected in reality. This probably applied most to established farming families, but even among the *Neubauern* there was reportedly a tendency for the women to shy away from collective agricultural work.[34] Generational interests were also a determinant. Sons and daughters might intervene to prevent their parents surrendering what was seen as the family inheritance. Alternatively, parents might refuse to pass on the family farm to the next generation, fearing it would be handed over for the use of the co-operative.[35] One demographic feature apparently alarmed but possibly helped the authorities in the longer run. As opportunities for urban and industrial employment grew in the mid-1950s, it proved difficult to retain young people in the countryside.[36] This was a challenge in terms of replenishing the agricultural labour force, but it did possibly help to loosen family attachment to the land and thereby facilitate collectivisation.

Unsurprisingly, the majority of LPG members in the 1950s were *Neubauern* and farmworkers, whose economic situation was most precarious. In 1956 some 74 per cent of LPG members and their families across the GDR were from these backgrounds, and a further 10 per cent were former industrial workers. In areas formerly dominated by the large estates the proportion of these categories combined was even higher.[37] The relative reluctance of established farmers to join co-operatives was perceived by the authorities as both a political and an economic problem. For all the public rhetoric about the superior efficiency of the collective, production figures in the mid-1950s stubbornly showed the greater productivity of the independent peasants. In trying to persuade them to throw in their lot with the LPGs, there was a delicate balance to be struck between stressing the economic value of their skills and resources and admitting that they were better farmers than the LPGs. The rhetoric and the iconography of thriving co-operative enterprise were also belied by local disputes and by the hard realities of rural life in the 1950s.

A vivid impression of the bad atmosphere which could develop in a village under pressure in the early phase of collectivisation is conveyed in the furious submission of the master joiner D. in a village in the Potsdam district to Minister President Otto Grotewohl in 1955.[38] It indicates how local personalities could use collectivisation to their own advantage and antagonise others in the process, and how – for the accused and for the accuser – the personal and the political intermingled. The LPG, named after Grotewohl himself, had been founded in July 1952 by the farmer P. and a number of 'heavily indebted settlers'. P. had already attracted attention by fixing up a holding for one of his sons, who was not currently in the village, and by accommodating a second son in the house attached to it. The new LPG attracted funding from the Potsdam authorities and increased its membership from the local *Neubauern*. Early in 1953 there was an exodus from the GDR of neighbouring *Altbauern*, and their land, property, equipment and livestock were seized by the LPG. P. made much of his success, featuring in the local press and setting up placards on the incoming roads, declaring the 'first socialist model village'. However, his behaviour became arrogant, and he absented himself from the locality for months at a time. In May 1953 he had to be summoned back by telegram, and on his return gave way to alcohol and was seen stumbling along the village street by members of the co-operative. Not content with the village hostelry, he set up a tap-room in his own home and dismissed neighbours' complaints about the noise. He left all work to others and did nothing about repairing the harvester, which stood in the village street for four weeks. In July the first anniversary of the LPG was celebrated in excessive manner, and a hundred police officers arrived the following morning to sort things out. According to Grotewohl's correspondent, the harvests were brought in late, chickens and pigs were dying from neglect, and cows were left wallowing in their own excrement.

The joiner D. had complained about poor potato deliveries and P. responded with a postcard depriving him of all work for the LPG and the community council. This presumably represented a harsh blow to someone dependent on the local economy. Dignitaries from the district held an arbitration meeting and restored D.'s contracts, but P. jumped up saying 'I am the Chairman and I am the one who decides who does the work of the LPG'.

The offensive drunken antics continued. After a binge financed by the milk proceeds, P. had outraged local opinion by hitting his wife in the face on the village street. According to D., nobody wanted to work with the former LPG Chairman any more, because he was always trying to drag his co-workers with him into the public house. P. and his deputy were removed in late 1954, but by then the finances of the LPG had plunged into deficit (approximately 800,000 marks), so that wages were being withheld. In the village nothing was being done about the housing shortage, while four shops stood empty and two homes had been turned into drinking establishments.

The dismal picture painted vindictively by D. was not simply about the conduct of an individual. He was suggesting that the hold on local power by a few individuals was destructive of socialist ideals and of social solidarity:

> A few functionaries occupy all the positions. J. is deputy mayor and arbitrator. He was also party secretary, but was then removed from his post because of

constant drunkenness. The fact that he is not very particular about marital fidelity is not consistent with the post of arbitrator. The mayor T. is a former non-commissioned officer and still often adopts a sergeant-major tone. He promises everything to everybody and cannot keep his promises. The bar-keeper F. is making as much as he can, to give himself a comfortable life. On one acre of orchard he is feeding six pigs. His wife is in charge of the *Konsum* shop, and his daughter of the kindergarten ... Because of all these circumstances the workers are losing all desire to work ... What is happening in our village will in the end lead to catastrophe.

Another example from 1955 deals with the role of prominent local individuals, but adds to it the assimilation problems persisting ten years after the war. In this instance the members of an LPG in the west of Halle district had alerted President Pieck to the problems of establishing co-operative life and work.[39] A subsequent investigation blamed not only the bogeyman of the 'class enemy', but also overdiligent party members and the attitudes of immigrant *Neubauern*. The land reform had divided the estate into 203 holdings, and during the following decade all but thirty of the *Altbauern* had left the district. Of these, three joined the early co-operative in 1952, along with 26 *Neubauern*. The difficulty now was to expand the LPG. It was caused in part by the alleged 'sectarian' policy of the LPG, in particular that of the SED party secretary H. He was described as an alcoholic who pursued 'sledgehammer tactics' against the farmers who were outside the co-operative. This, it was said, made it easy for the 'antiprogressive elements' in the village to take the *Neubauern* in the 'wrong direction'. There was now a gulf between the party organisations inside and outside the co-operative, and the conflict had resulted in two serious cases of arson against LPG property: a large feed barn and a new cattle-shed both destroyed in early 1955.

Leader of those resisting the co-operative was one W., a settler who had acquired a holding on the site of the manor house itself. This property had already been the object of a tussle between W. and the LPG, which claimed it as its headquarters. W., supported by other immigrant *Neubauern*, was refusing to move and now – six years ahead of a more famous construction – the LPG was planning to build a wall partitioning W.'s holding from the LPG premises. A major part of the problem was that so many of the recalcitrant farmers from the east had not been integrated into village life. The mayor described them as 'sitting on their suitcases and waiting to return to their former homes'. An additional social problem was that of persuading former industrial workers (of whom 150 had settled locally) into agricultural labour.

If in this instance the immigrant *Neubauern* and workers were the problem, the authorities were concerned elsewhere with the attitudes of established *Altbauern*. The south-western districts of Gera and Halle had before 1945 been characterised by middling and larger peasants. Many of them had been drawn into co-operatives from 1952, but there were signs by the spring of 1955 that the LPGs were collapsing again.[40] In Gera district 104 *Altbauern* plus their families had withdrawn from the LPG, with dissatisfaction strongest in two areas: Stadtroda and Zeulenroda. Immediately before the foundation of the LPG in Stadtroda three farmers had been arrested, one of them a farmer and sawmill-owner, who was a figure of some local popularity and respect. The arrests created a depressed atmosphere and apprehension about further arrests, so all the farmers of the village joined the co-operative, without – as it was reported – 'the will to work co-operatively'. Until early 1954 the authorities scarcely intervened in the affairs of the LPG, but then an SED brigade was despatched. The result was a disaster, since its six members apparently sat in their quarters all day, observing the peasants at work through the window. This, plus the threats of economic reprisal issued by an agricultural official of the DBD caused 'justified aggravation'.

Near Zeulenroda the larger farmers (with only about 20 hectares each) were accused of dominating the LPG, acting only in their own self-interest and exploiting the smallholders. At the instigation of the local SED the LPG was forcibly dissolved, and a new one founded to accommodate the interests of the small farmers. This solution did not suit all, however, and one smallholder was prevented from joining by his wife, who had a 'disapproving, almost hostile stance'. To add to the confusion, she was herself a member of the SED.

In Halle district there was a link with recent political developments. Here thirty-nine *Altbauern* and seventy-six family members had left the co-operatives, mostly in the aftermath of 17 June 1953. They were complaining about increased delivery quotas and the great pressure placed upon the co-operatives by having to take over holdings abandoned by their former owners.

These detailed accounts are not adduced here as 'typical'. Allowance must be made for personal and political spite, and some of the more riproaring stories were reported precisely because they were unusual challenges for the authorities. The strains and stresses, however, were undoubtedly enormous. Gradually every aspect of personal and communal life came to be affected by political intervention and the promotion of co-operative farming. Antonia Maria Humm has charted closely the experience of the village of Niederzimmern (Erfurt district), and shown how living conditions were affected by the policy of allocating the homeless rooms in private dwellings, how sport, music and youth associations were brought under the aegis of the state and transmuted into tools of propaganda, and how religious observance was gradually eroded by SED policy.[41] In all these areas and in the development of the LPGs, however, there was a complicated local interaction of personal, familial, social, economic and political motivation, which militated against uniformity.

The socialist reorganisation of agriculture

The haphazard nature of collectivisation in the 1950s, SED scepticism about the effectiveness of the DBD and VdgB, concerns about agricultural production levels, and a haemorrhaging of the rural population through the inter-German border all contributed to the decision to press ahead with full collectivisation. Ulbricht had been encouraging co-operative farming through the late 1950s, for example in December 1957 in his exhortation of the young to play their part in the Machine Tractor Stations (MTSs) and the LPGs. He was obviously concerned that socialisation was stalling and indeed that young people were deserting the countryside. At the meeting of the Central Committee in February 1958 he reprimanded *Politbüro* member Fred Oelßner for allegedly suggesting that the weaker LPGs be disbanded in order to attract the so-far reluctant middling peasants. The VdgB also came under his fire for proposing the sale of tractors to individual farmers. Ulbricht made it clear that the correct party line was to press ahead with collectivisation.[42] This intention was reinforced in December 1959 and January 1960, when the go-ahead was given for a rapid campaign from 15 January until 1 May. Accompanied by vehicles, loudspeakers and floodlights, it began in the northern districts and more or less made its way southwards into the middling peasant regions of Thuringia and Saxony.[43]

Back in 1945 it had been the wealthier landowners who had awoken to find ardent deputations outside their windows. Now it was the turn of thousands of peasants. On their doorsteps or in their farmyards stood groups of neighbours, rivals, urban workers or unknown party officials seeking to persuade them voluntarily to join the LPG. They might decide to yield quickly under the pressure, they might argue or take evasive action. One farmer hid in the woods all day, hoping to avoid a decision, but then gave himself and his farm up. In despair at the agitators who harangued her from morning till night on her own farm, one woman threatened to kill herself, but not before she set her dog on the local party secretary. She gave way in the end too. The outcome was sadder in another case, where an innkeeper did commit suicide. The report of the incident implausibly suggested that this had nothing to do with collectivisation; the man had joined the LPG the week before and he had been completely inebriated when he took his life. A less drastic form of exit – flight – was chosen by many. In one instance a peasant member of the CDU assured the agitators of the date when he would join the LPG, but said that first he had to speak with his father-in-law, who was taking a cure elsewhere. He was not seen in the GDR again.[44]

It was not only the flight of farmers that compromised the future of agriculture. There had also been a steady drain of trained veterinary and medical personnel. The authorities collected reports on the departure of vets in the period before the Berlin Wall, noting complaints about poor career prospects under socialism and about the treatment of the farmers. As the area vet from

Bad Salzungen (Suhl district) put it, 'My conscience will not let me work in a state apparatus which has driven the peasants into the LPG with threats'. Doctors and other health professionals were also leaving in numbers sufficient to impair a rural provision which was still far from satisfactory. There were many individual motives, but a response to collectivisation was amongst them. According to the Rector of the Medical Academy in Magdeburg, 'Some doctors are very depressed, because amongst their patients are many co-operative farmers who cannot adjust to their new conditions of life and work and are quite desperate. They expect from the doctors help and support which the doctors are not in a position to provide.' This was a common experience for the clergy too, who at rural funerals were indicating that the deceased had not succumbed to clinical illness but 'have been spiritually broken by measures carried out recently'.[45]

In this collectivisation spring the Volkspolizei reported numerous examples of alleged attempts by peasants to prevent the foundation or functioning of LPGs. In Drewitz (Cottbus district), the founding meeting of an LPG in mid-March was interrupted by 'unknown persons' shorting the lighting circuits. On a similar occasion in Lastau (Karl-Marx-Stadt district), two intoxicated men rampaged around, damaging the car of the Area Prosecutor and attacking him and another official. In Helpt (Neubrandenburg district), a group of peasants repeatedly concerted to thwart the holding of LPG foundations, and, what was more, their spokesman was a member of the SED. In Schlieffenberg (Schwerin district), a middling peasant had used his economic hold – achieved, it was alleged, by 'speculation' – on almost all the local independent farmers in order to dissuade them from joining the LPG. On an evening in April the roads between two villages in the Gera district were blockaded with tree trunks and shrubs at the very time when an LPG was to be founded in one of the villages. At a general meeting in Doberburg (Frankfurt/Oder district) all the LPG peasants left the room in order to render the session inquorate. The official depiction of the collectivisation as voluntary was frequently contested. Even where the founding of an LPG was achieved, there were protestations about using the words 'voluntary' or 'free peasants'. Indeed disruption of meetings – particularly of the VdgB and of LPGs – was commonplace. A VdgB election meeting in Nottleben (Erfurt district) in May 1960 had to be abandoned at midnight because a heated evening had ended with a large number of participants suffering from overrefreshment.

Other forms of protest included the defacing or tearing down of posters, the daubing of slogans and swastikas and violence and threats of violence. Examples included the erection of a gallows and the placing of a noose on a car in order to intimidate officials, and the smashing of the windows of the home of a member of a socialisation brigade. In the night of 31 March six ammunition cartridges were left outside the local council of a fully collectivised village in the Suhl district, with the inscription on them: 'We are still here.' And as late as July the last independent farmer in a village in the Dresden district resorted to direct action when he was visited by the socialisation brigade: 'In the course of the discussion the peasant punched the party secretary of the Machine Tractor Station in the face.'[46]

Loss of production through tears

The official declaration on 14 April 1960 that collectivisation had now been completed masked a tumult in the rural GDR which did not completely subside even with the building of the Berlin Wall. Amongst the rural population there was rumour, uncertainty and panic, while the authorities' obsessions about the poisoning of animals, arson and the sabotage of machinery went beyond political cynicism into class paranoia. Even after August 1961 there were outbreaks of dissent, difficulties for co-operatives which had been founded at short notice and under duress and problems for the authorities in controlling developments in the way they wished. Well into 1962 there were critical reports of protest, violence, arson, dissolution of co-operatives, flight from the GDR and – by implication – of suicides.

As in the 1950s, the establishment of an LPG in 1960 did not automatically mean that the step into collective agriculture had taken place. Once again, there were examples of the larger peasants in a district clubbing together in a new LPG Type I to protect their individual interests, while their poorer neighbours tried to develop an LPG Type III. Even where there was only one co-operative in a village, it was as likely as not that existing social status was recognised openly or tacitly. The police observed in one instance that: 'On the occasion of the general meeting in the community of Doberburg/Beeskow it appeared that the co-operative farmers took separate seating according to whether they had earlier been large, small or middling peasants.' It was also of annoyance to the authorities that those elected to leading positions in the new co-operatives were often the very same large and middling owners who had previously held sway in their communities. In one case cited from the Frankfurt/Oder district there was additional criticism that former NSDAP and SS members were once again in positions of authority. Elsewhere, the chairman of an LPG in the Dresden district had reportedly been a National Socialist Local Peasant Leader [*Ortsbauernführer*] and was now trying to re-establish the old hierarchy and working practices of the pre-1945 period.

Once founded, not all LPGs proved robust. In the spring and summer of 1960 several thousand peasants revoked their membership, and these were in addition to those who had fled the GDR altogether. Working conditions, organisation and productive capacity were often problems, not least because of the bitterness of those who had been forced to comply. According to the police: 'At a meeting in Kritzowberg [Rostock district] some co-operative farmers compared the LPG stamp on their insurance documents to the fascist marking out of the Jews.'[47]

The months before August 1961 were particularly tense, especially in rural areas near the border with the FRG. The DBD reported damage to property, distribution of propaganda, outbreaks of graffiti, threats of violence and encouragement of flight from the republic, all of which were blamed on the West and on the (former) large peasants. The escape routes were finally sealed on 13 August, but the alleged occurrences of 'provocations', arson, poisoning and sabotage resurfaced. Now, though, the malcontents had nowhere else to go, and they were gradually drawn into line by ugly types of peer pressure, reinforced by the powers of the state. In the Plauen area open meetings were held under the slogan 'Who in the village is hindering co-operative work?'. Absentees were identified and fetched along to the next such gathering.[48]

The path of East German agriculture from 1945 to the early 1960s was marked by many contradictory indicators. During both land reform and collectivisation there was idealism, enthusiasm and a genuine attempt to break with a disastrous recent past and build anew. Mechanisation, construction and the provision of an educational and social infrastructure gradually began to have an effect on living and working conditions. But all this was accompanied by opportunism, petty retribution, attempts to maintain the status quo and the increasingly heavy hand of the party bureaucracy.

The archival accounts of rural dispute are vivid enough, but finally for a consummate picture of village life in the years leading up to full collectivisation, nothing matches Erwin Strittmatter's controversial novel *Ole Bienkopp* from 1963. The hapless rural equivalent of Franz Bieberkopf in Döblin's *Berlin Alexanderplatz*, Ole experiences tussles over collective work, tractors and open cowsheds as a battle of personalities in a politicised setting. He takes up the cause of the co-operative primarily as a consequence of the suspicious death of a friend and of his wife's adultery, but then falls foul of the dogmatically party-line woman mayor. Strittmatter, who had personal experience of life in the rural GDR, successfully communicated a crucial feature of his society under the pressure of collectivisation: the stormy blend of the normal petty competition, jealousies and desires of ordinary people with imposition from above of major structural change. The departure of the *Junker* and the influx of refugees opened up new tensions, which were then compounded by the direct intervention in village politics, whether for ideological or opportunist purposes, of representatives of state authority. The party jargon of agricultural modernisation is only one side of the story; the other is the murky atmosphere of mutual suspicion in the village inn:

> In the blue clouds of pipe and cigar fug hides a goblin. He hops from table to table, whispers something into the ear of one peasant and tweaks another on the nose. Ole raises his glass to drink. The goblin leaps onto the base of the glass and helps to tip it. The goblin's name is peasant dispute. He is getting pushier.[49]

Notes

1 Shelley Baranowski, *The Sanctity of Rural Life: Nobility, Protestantism, and Nazism in Weimar Prussia* (Oxford, 1995); Robert M. Berdahl, *The Politics of the Prussian Nobility: The Development of a Conservative Ideal 1770–1848* (Princeton, NJ, 1988); Francis L. Carsten, *A History of the Prussian Junkers* (Aldershot, 1989); Ralph Gibson and Martin Blinkhorn (eds), *Landownership and Power in Modern Europe* (London, 1991); Robert G. Moeller (ed.), *Peasants and Lords in Modern Germany* (Boston, Mass., 1986).
2 Arnd Bauerkämper (ed.), *'Junkerland in Bauernhand'? Durchführung, Auswirkungen und Stellenwert der Bodenreform in der Sowjetischen Besatzungszone* (Stuttgart, 1996); Norman M. Naimark, *The Russians in Germany: A History of the Soviet Zone of Occupation, 1945–1949* (Cambridge, Mass., 1995), 142–62; Jonathan Osmond, 'Kontinuität und Konflikt in der Landwirtschaft der SBZ/DDR zur Zeit der Bodenreform und der Vergenossenschaftlichung 1945–1961', in: Richard Bessel and Ralph Jessen (eds), *Die Grenzen der Diktatur: Staat und Gesellschaft in der DDR* (Göttingen, 1996), 137–69.
3 Large numbers of country houses were demolished in the late 1940s, though some were retained as administrative buildings, social facilities or tourist attractions. For dispute over demolition see SAPMO-BArch, DY 30/IV 2/7/238, SED-LV Mecklenburg to Zentraler Bauernverlag, 22 December 1947, and Haas to SED-Abt. Landwirtschaft, 14 February 1948, fos 92–3.
4 Athar Hussain and Keith Tribe, *Marxism and the Agrarian Question* (2nd edn; London, 1983); Sheila Fitzpatrick, *Stalin's Peasants: Resistance and Survival in the Russian Village after Collectivisation* (Oxford, 1994); Lynne Viola, *Peasant Rebels under Stalin: Collectivisation and the Culture of Peasant Resistance* (Oxford, 1996); Karl-Eugen Wädekin, *Agrarian Policies in Communist Europe: A Critical Introduction* (Totowa, NJ, 1982).
5 Hans Immler, *Agrarpolitik in der DDR* (Cologne, 1971); Hans Bichler, *Landwirtschaft in der DDR* (Berlin, 1981); Karl Eckart, *Die Landwirtschaft der DDR im Wandel* (Paderborn, 1981); Arnd Bauerkämper, 'Der Kampf um den Boden in den neuen Bundesländern: Die Debatte über die Restitution des Bodenreformlandes und die Privatisierung der Agrarwirtschaft seit 1989/90', *Revue d'Allemagne*, 31/1 (1999), 57–73.
6 The main proponent of agrarian reform in the Weimar Republic and the SBZ is portrayed in Nathan Steinberger et al., *Edwin Hoernle: Ein Leben für die Bauernbefreiung*, with a foreword by Walter Ulbricht (Berlin, 1965). Characteristic GDR treatments are Joachim Piskol et al., *Antifaschistisch-demokratische Umwälzung auf dem Lande 1945–49* (Berlin, 1984); Christel Nehrig and Lothar Noziczka, 'Die Weiterentwicklung der Agrarpolitik der SED 1956/57: Zur Situation in der Landwirtschaft der DDR vor Abschluß der Übergangsperiode zum Sozialismus', *Zeitschrift für Geschichtswissenschaft*, 33 (1985), 1082–96.
7 This is the term employed by the SED. See, for example, SAPMO-BArch, DY 30/IV 2/7/240, 'Klassenkampf auf dem Dorfe 1947–1949'.
8 The main sources used here are the records of the SED-ZK in SAPMO-BArch, DY 30/IV 2/7, Bereich Landwirtschaft 1946–1962, Teilbestand Abteilung Landwirtschaft; DY 30/IV 2/13, Abteilung Staat und Recht 1946–1962; DY

30/IV 2/15, Befreundete Organisationen; DY 30/IV 2/17, Abteilung Frauen 1945–1962; and DY 30/IV 2/19, Gesundheitspolitik.
9 For discussion of class and political stereotypes, see Viola, *Peasant Rebels*, 33-6.
10 For examples, see: SAPMO-BArch, DY 30/IV 2/15/5, Instrukteurberichte 1952–62; DY 30/IV 2/15/53, Entwicklung der DBD 1955–62.
11 SAPMO-BArch, DY 30/IV 2/7/230, Ausarbeitungen, Eingaben, Vorschläge zur Durchführung der demokratischen Bodenreform 1945–49; DY 30/IV 2/7/231, Eingaben zur Durchführung der demokratischen Bodenreform 1945–49; Nachlaß Otto Grotewohl NL 90/324, Einsprüche gegen die Sequestrierung und Enteignung von Betrieben der Naziaktivisten und Kriegsverbrecher August 1946 – Juli 1948.
12 Jonathan Osmond, 'Geschlechtsspezifische Folgen der Bodenreform in der Sowjetischen Besatzungszone: Gutsbesitzerinnen, Bäuerinnen und Landarbeiterinnen nach 1945', in Bauerkämper, *'Junkerland in Bauernhand'?*, 153-68; Osmond, 'Kontinuität und Konflikt'; and most recently, Antonia Maria Humm, *Auf dem Weg zum sozialistischen Dorf? Zum Wandel der dörflichen Lebenswelt in der DDR von 1952 bis 1969 mit vergleichenden Aspekten zur Bundesrepublik Deutschland* (Göttingen, 1999).
13 For example, Otto Rühle, *Vom Untertan zum Staatsbürger* (Berlin, 1958), 19, 25.
14 *Bündnis der Arbeiter und Bauern: Dokumente und Materialien zum 30. Jahrestag der demokratischen Bodenreform* (Berlin, 1975), 36–42.
15 For example, Rolf Stöckigt, *Der Kampf der KPD um die demokratische Bodenreform Mai 1945 bis April 1946* (Berlin, 1964).
16 Naimark, *The Russians in Germany*, 153, n. 44, 511–12; also *Weißbuch über die 'Demokratische Bodenreform' in der Sowjetischen Besatzungszone Deutschlands: Dokumente und Berichte* (Munich/Stamsried, 1988). For the experience of a family further east in now Polish Pomerania, see Christian von Krockow, *Hour of the Women* (New York, 1991).
17 Osmond, 'Geschlechtsspezifische Folgen', 156–9.
18 SAPMO-BArch, DY 30/IV 2/7/229, 'Bericht über den Gang der Bodenreform, 26 Sept. 1945', fos 1–2.
19 Erich Loest, *Durch die Erde ein Riß: Ein Lebenslauf* (Munich, 1992), 105–8.
20 For example, *Bündnis der Arbeiter und Bauern*, 59, 61, 65.
21 SAPMO-BArch, DY 30/IV 2/7/230, Bürgermeister der Gemeinde Eichstädt to Pieck, 30 May 1947, fo. 25.
22 SAPMO-BArch, DY 30/IV 2/7/231, 'Bericht über einige Zustände im Landkreis Cottbus', 16 November 1948, fos 152–3.
23 SAPMO-BArch, DY 30/IV 2/7/240, Bericht A. Jahnke, Batzlow, Kreis Freienwalde, 23 January 1948, fos 39–40.
24 Osmond, 'Geschlechtsspezifische Folgen', 163-7.
25 Arnd Bauerkämper, 'Neue und traditionale Führungsgruppen auf dem Lande: Politische Herrschaft und Gesellschaft in der Sowjetischen Besatzungszone', *Berliner Debatte INITIAL*, 4/5 (1995), 79–92.
26 Walter Ulbricht, *Die Bauernbefreiung in der Deutschen Demokratischen Republik*, i (Berlin, 1961), 'Gegen die Saboteure der Volksernährung', 23 September 1948, 169–73.
27 *Ibid.*, 'Die Bildung landwirtschaftlicher Produktionsgenossenschaften – ein großer Fortschritt', 9 July 1952, 287–8.

28 Bernhard Wernet-Tietz, *Bauernverband und Bauernpartei in der DDR: Die VdgB und die DBD 1945–1952* (Cologne, 1984), 160, 219.
29 Ulbricht, *Die Bauernbefreiung*, 'Über die Bedeutung der gemeinsamen Arbeit', 26 October 1950, 247–9.
30 Ibid., 'Der Fünfjahrplan erfordert die Initiative aller werktätigen Bauern', 31 October 1951, 260.
31 Ibid., 'Bildung landwirtschaftlicher Produktionsgenossenschaften', 291.
32 For full definitions see: Walter Schmidt, *Das Statut der LPG: Ziele und Aufgaben* (5th edn, Berlin, 1960), 36–42.
33 SAPMO-BArch, DY 30/IV 2/15/5, 'Bericht über den Einsatz im Bezirk Erfurt', 8 April 1959, fo. 2.
34 Rühle, *Vom Untertan zum Staatsbürger*, 228.
35 SAPMO-BArch, DY 30/IV 2/15/54, 'Bericht über die LPG Niederwürschnitz, Kreis Stolberg', 17 March 1958, fo. 6.
36 SAPMO-BArch, DY 30/IV 2/7/367, Mückenberger to Sekretäre für Landwirtschaft, 24 May 1957.
37 SAPMO-BArch, DY 30/IV 2/7/364, Mellentin to Schirdewan, 7 September 1956; Rühle, *Vom Untertan zum Staatsbürger*, 227.
38 BAB, DK 1/1216, Tischlermeister to Otto Grotewohl, 10 February 1955, fos 76–80.
39 Ibid., 'Bericht über die Überprüfung der Beschwerde der LPG', 7 April 1955, fos 86–90.
40 Ibid., 'Bericht über starke Austrittserscheinungen von Altbauern in den Bezirken Gera und Halle', 23 May 1955, fos 71–5.
41 Humm, *Auf dem Weg zum sozialistischen Dorf?*, 203–6, 248–68, 294–302.
42 Ulbricht, *Die Bauernbefreiung*, 'Miteinander arbeiten ist besser als gegeneinander', 644; 'Es ging um zwei Linien der Landwirtschaftspolitik', 663–4.
43 *Keesing's Record of World Events 1960–94*, xii (1960) April: Eastern Germany: Completion of Farm Collectivisation.
44 SAPMO-BArch, DY 30/IV 2/15/46, CDU-Parteileitung, 31 March 1960, fo. 7.
45 BAB, DK 1/4238, 'Ungesetzliches Verlassen der DDR durch Tierärzte 1960', fo. 6; DY 30/IV 2/19/97, 'Entwicklung des Gesundheitswesens auf dem Lande 1955-62'; DY 30/IV 2/19/20, Abt. Agitation und Propaganda, 1 October 1960; DY 30/IV 2/13/367, Bericht der Deutschen Volkspolizei, 2 June 1960.
46 SAPMO-BArch, DY 30/IV 2/13/367, Berichte des Operativstabes der Hauptverwaltung der Deutschen Volkspolizei über die sozialistische Umgestaltung der Landwirtschaft, 1960; DY 30/IV 2/13/368, Informationsbericht, 25 March 1960.
47 SAPMO-BArch, DY 30/IV 2/13/367, Berichte der Deutschen Volkspolizei, 15 and 21 April, 28 May, 5 August 1960.
48 SAPMO-BArch, DY 30/IV 2/15/53, DBD-Abt. Organisation, 29 August 1961, fo. 2.
49 Erwin Strittmatter, *Ole Bienkopp* (Gütersloh, 1963), 24.

9

Squaring the circle: the dilemmas and evolution of women's policy

Donna Harsch

The equality of women is rooted in their place in production. Where a woman is kept away from production or seeks to realise an ideal that keeps her out of production, she remains dependent on man, her so-called provider.[1] (Herbert Warnke, Chairman of the Free German Trade Union Federation, 1952)

[T] he most important lesson we can draw from the course of woman's emancipation is that her position in socialism is determined, above all, by her role in the process of social reproduction.[2] (Renate Credo, Chief Manager, Photochemical Works (East) Berlin, 1967)

The GDR became famous or, in some quarters, infamous for its extraordinarily high level of female employment. The employment rate represented the most striking social fact about East German women in the 1960s, a time when the 'working mother' was relatively uncommon in the West. In 1966, women in the GDR worked outside the home at the highest rate in the industrialised world: 49.1 per cent of the total workforce. By 1970, 66.1 per cent of all women worked for wages. Their workforce participation altered not only their physical relationship to the 'productive sphere', but their self-conception. The majority of women, including young mothers, saw waged labour as a central feature of their identity. The majority of husbands accepted that their wives worked for wages.

The GDR regime proudly trumpeted this tale of progress made possible by a socialist state's unwavering commitment to women's integration into the labour force. This was, however, a claim requiring some qualification. In emphasising changes in women's workforce participation, it ignored, first, continuities in the kinds of jobs women performed, their place in the workplace hierarchy and their wages relative to men's. Second, in focusing on change in the public sphere, this version veiled the SED's constant pronatalism on the one hand, and the barely modified family division of labour on the other. Third, in attributing causal agency to the state, it obscured the process of negotiation between state and society that here tripped up, there sped up, women's apparently steady march into the labour force. Women did not always embrace the party's plan. Men resisted women's integration into the workforce and balked at the very idea of redistributing domestic duties. SED local officials, union representatives, state bureaucrats and factory managers mediated between the party/state and the masses. In their case, too, official ideology often succumbed to the realities of gender identity: male administrators tended to favour the man's viewpoint, while female functionaries pressed for the advance of women.

The authorised version masked, finally, a gradual re-evaluation of the relative significance of production and social reproduction to women's emancipation. This conceptual evolution was driven, above all, by the dilemmas the SED encountered as it moved from quantitative mobilisation of women's labour power in the 1950s to forging a skilled female labour force in the 1960s. The party could no longer discount the weight of women's double burden. There also emerged a new sensitivity to the family as a central site of social and cultural reproduction and, thus, a new appreciation of women's work in the family. Moreover, the SED became friendlier to private consumption and, therefore, to woman as the family shopper.

This rethinking remained incomplete. It challenged neither the SED's production-centred ideology nor the assumption that women nurtured the family. Even this limited reinterpretation of the 'woman question' occurred only owing to the greater influence in the 1960s of leading women in the SED. Joined by experts in medicine and psychology, women Communists pressed the Politbüro for policies that made it easier to combine a profession with child-rearing and housework. They also urged the party leadership to grant women control over their reproductive lives.

Women in the SBZ 1945–49

As the European war ground to its bloody finale, chaos engulfed eastern Germany. Millions of civilians, mainly women and children, clogged the roads and manoeuvered around the last-ditch efforts of the German army. Refugees fled the dreaded 'Russian hordes' whom Goebbels' propaganda machine had painted as sexually rapacious barbarians. Unfortunately, for women, fear became reality. Soviet soldiers (without orders from above) wielded rape as a weapon of revenge against a nation whose legions had devastated the Soviet homeland. The waves of rape began in East Prussia in early 1945 and culminated in Berlin in the final week of fighting (24 April–3 May). Violence by undisciplined troops continued sporadically until experienced Soviet administrators replaced field commanders in the SBZ. Estimates of the numbers raped range from hundreds of thousands up to 2 million. Mass recourse to abortion followed. Although illegal, abortions were performed quite readily by doctors and midwives during the postwar emergency, especially if a woman claimed she had been impregnated by a Russian soldier.[3]

The influx of refugees created the most serious social problem. In 1946, refugees comprised 20.8 per cent of the SBZ population. The ratio of women was 142 to 100 men (among native Germans: 133 to 100). Impoverished refugees were thrown onto the charity of an indigenous population that was most adamantly not in a giving mood. A severe economic and food crisis gripped Germany, east and west. Malnutrition stalked the land, fuel was extremely scarce and people, especially women, spent their days foraging the countryside for food and trading what they owned, found, or stole on the ubiquitous black market. Though desperate for their husbands, many a woman discovered that the material benefits of a spouse's return came at the cost of psychological turmoil. Many husbands adjusted badly to independent wives and cheeky children. The divorce rate climbed. Prostitution and venereal disease (VD) also became much more common as thousands of women sold their bodies to occupying soldiers.

As much as they welcomed efforts to impose order on this bleak situation, women confronted the re-emergent political parties and government structures with suspicion. In the SBZ, several factors fed women's irritation. Soviet regulations assigned 'non-working housewives' a paltry ration, although, in fact, they laboured hard for their families. The slow return of prisoners-of-war (POWs) from the Soviet Union and, especially, the memory of rape also blighted relations between Russians and women. Women and German Communists, meanwhile, eyed each other with distrust. Relatively few working-class women had supported the pre-1933 KPD, put off by its radical actions, hostility to religion and claims on husbands' time. Although party ideology propagated women's emancipation, many Communist men disliked women's family orientation and church ties. The Nazi regime had widened the divide by bombarding Germans with anticommunist propaganda on the one hand, and images of traditional womanhood on the other. Communists did not speak the political language of women. Yet they were eager to learn it for, at least initially, the road to power ran through competitive elections and women composed 60 per cent of the electorate. In regional elections in 1946 and 1947, over 90 per cent of women voted but, to the SED's dismay, lopsidedly for the bourgeois parties, especially the CDU, whose female membership in 1946 was 44 per cent, while the SED's was 24 per cent.[4]

To bridge the gender gap, Soviet advisers and women in the SED exhorted its male leadership to experiment with democratic, non-partisan, and 'separatist' rhetoric and forms of organisation. Thus, although Walter Ulbricht was morally opposed to abortion, the SED called for the liberalisation, though not complete repeal, of Paragraph 218, Germany's antiabortion law. In 1947, SED legislators convinced provincial parliaments to enact an 'indications solution' that permitted abortion on medical, social and ethical grounds (for instance, rape). The issue that most preoccupied women was the supply and distribution of food. At the insistence of Elli Schmidt, the SED's highest body, the Executive, reluctantly asked the Soviets to revise their rationing policies. From autumn 1947, housewives were allotted higher rations. The SED also created a Woman's Section headed by Schmidt and Käthe Kern (a former Social Democrat), both members of the Executive.

Communist women cooperated with Social, Christian and Liberal Democrats in the Antifascist Women's Committees (AFA), grass-roots groups with tens of thousands of members who organised soup kitchens, child care centres, medical clinics and cultural activities for women. Many male party members and functionaries held the apolitical activities of the AFA in contempt. Historically, Communists had abhorred 'bourgeois feminism' which, allegedly, substituted gender war for class struggle. Under pressure, again from Schmidt and Kern, backed by the Soviets, the party leadership created, nonetheless, a non-partisan, centrally organised women's association, the Democratic Women's League (DFD). Over the next year, the DFD and the Women's Section moved in a strikingly proto-feminist direction. To the intense irritation of some male comrades, Kern and Schmidt introduced gender-segregated courses in Marxist theory, working-class history *and* the history of the international women's movement. The DFD also angered male trade unionists. Under the protection of Soviet administrators, it organised women workers in shopfloor committees, pressuring management and the unions to promote women, train them and provide child care in the factory.

As the SED consolidated its political hold and retooled itself into a Leninist party, women's electoral support lost its significance, room for experimentation contracted and traditional antagonism towards women's separatism reasserted itself. The Politbüro quashed the DFD's autonomous tendencies and workplace activism and turned it into a housewives' organisation, demoting the Woman's Section to a Department, attached to the Central Committee, not the Politbüro. Castigated for feminist 'deviations', Kern and Schmidt were not taken into the Politbüro, falling into line as did other women in the SED. In 1950, its female membership slipped to under 20 per cent and stagnated there for ten years. The party turned away from the 'woman question' to focus on industrialisation of the economy and political domination of German society.[5]

By 1949, the economic crisis had passed. Though food and consumer goods remained scarce in the newly founded GDR, the black market was suppressed and inflation brought under control. Unemployment declined and daily life was no longer a struggle for sheer survival. The signs of social stress also stopped flashing. The VD epidemic subsided, divorce levelled off, then declined and the family reconstituted itself along pre-1945 lines. If, however, women interpreted the ebbing of the crisis as a return to prewar conditions, they were deceived. A torrent of economic change was about to descend.

Forging a modern female workforce

The first Five-Year Plan (1951–55) projected a doubling of industrial production requiring 890,000 more workers. Because the working-age population was heavily female (6,461,000 women to 5,185,000 men), the plan projected a jump from 37 to 42 per cent in the number of working women over 18.[6] To reach this aim, the SED had to transform society's understanding of women's labour. In 1949, an internal memorandum acknowledged, the typical wife did not see that a job would 'make her independent, allow her to develop all her capabilities, and give her life meaning'.[7] Most men believed women 'belonged at home'.[8] In peacetime, no previous German regime had encouraged women's employment. In contrast, the GDR press profiled women in 'male jobs' with dozens of photographs of smiling women and their faithful machines.

Communists genuinely believed that women's emancipation depended on their participation in production. The campaign of the 1950s, however, was not about women or men but about labour. A female unionist complained: 'Nothing's being said about the social position of women, everything's single-mindedly concentrated on getting women to work because there are not enough men.'[9] As she recognised, women were the *secondary* object of the SED's campaign. The central economic goal was to construct an autarkic East German industrial base with the heavy physical labour and existing skills of male workers. In these years of frantic industrial build-up, training programmes for women, labour-saving services, child care and consumer production lay far down the list of priorities.

The sheer quantitative mobilisation of female labour was impressive. By 1955, hundreds of thousands of women had entered the workforce. Simultaneously, their employment profile lurched towards a modern structure. Family-based employment declined precipitously: by 1960, 76.7 per cent of all employed women were workers/employees. Simultaneously, they moved out of agriculture into industry, commerce and services. In 1950, the East German workforce was 39.6 per cent female (the primary sector 49.1 per cent). By 1960, both ratios were 45 per cent. In commerce and services, women's percentage among all employees, already high, increased impressively (to 65.6 per cent and 62 per cent, respectively, by 1960). The post-1945 shift of women into industry also continued a prewar trend, but considerably deepened it. In 1950, women composed two-fifths of the industrial workforce but were heavily concentrated in textile manufacturing. After 1950, relative to the western economies, women infiltrated some classically masculine areas, such as chemical production, and redefined a few occupations as 'female', such as crane operator. They remained, however, underrepresented in 'production' and continued to dominate textiles.[10]

Women began work in the industrial sector as unskilled workers. In 1945, even in the garment trades, only 21.3 per cent of women were skilled, and in the chemical industry, a tiny 1.5 per cent. By the late 1950s, huge numbers of women had attained some training, though the vast majority had been trained on the job and only moved into semi-skilled occupations. Their lack of skills meant that, the GDR's law for equal pay notwithstanding, women were bunched at the lower levels of the eight-step wage scale in every sector. Wage disparity was compounded by the fact that women tended to work in the worst-paid sectors. Women also worked disproportionately in light industry whose labour force earned much less than heavy industrial workers. Women benefited absolutely from pay raises that aimed to protect the worst-paid workers when rationing was finally ended in 1958–59. Still, they remained highly overrepresented on the lower half of the earnings scale.

The SED initially expanded the pool of women who had to work by eliminating pensions to able-bodied widows under 60 and drastically limiting access to public assistance. The gradual abolition of alimony forced divorced women into employment. By the mid-1950s, virtually all women 'standing alone' worked for wages, even if they had small children. Wives entered the workforce more slowly. In 1960, 56.7 per cent of wives of employed husbands worked for wages.[11] The proportion of married *mothers*' employment increased across the decade, though unevenly. In 1956, Minister of Justice Hilde Benjamin lamented that only 18.6 per cent of married mothers with young children worked for wages. The paltry data suggest that most married mothers dropped out of the workforce after childbirth but usually returned to employment when their children entered kindergarten. Still, in 1958, 2,207,700 women of working age were not employed, in contrast to fewer than 400,000 men.[12]

Women's experiences on the job varied tremendously. I will concentrate here on the industrial sector. In the early 1950s, all GDR workers laboured under intense pressure to increase production. Like men, female workers resisted the various forms of speed-up, though they did so less frequently and following more individualistic strategies, both because they had less experience with organised protest and had to juggle the demands of housework and waged labour. Thus, they were more likely to quit a job than organise a shopfloor protest. They dodged the pressure to produce under the excuse of carrying out household responsibilities. East German women became infamous for their tendency to take off time from work to get their shopping done. Yet, they too adopted collective tactics. In 1951–52, in dozens of textile factories, women workers refused to sign imposed wage contracts that introduced piece rates and high quotas. The FDGB and SED had to conduct individual shopfloor meetings to break resistance.[13] In June 1953, strikes swept through textile mills in Saxony and women joined walk-outs led by male workers. They participated, however, at a lower rate than men. Garment workers' strike meetings began in an 'extremely dangerous mood' but managers were often able to convince workers to return to work.[14]

Women played a small role on the rebellion's central industrial stages. Militant male workers did little to involve them in the struggle. Quite the contrary: at the huge chemical plant at Leuna, they hung a banner that denounced the SED's 'plan to promote women'.[15]

The issue that elicited protests from women workers throughout the entire Ulbricht era was the 'housework day' (HAT). This monthly paid day off was available to all *married* women, with or without children, but to single women only with children under 16 (and not to men). In the late 1940s, men claimed the HAT was unfair, provoking women to defend it as their right. In the 1950s, it was single women who complained about its unjust terms, demanding equality of rights with other women.[16] The FDGB and SED tried constantly to limit and even eliminate this expensive perk. Yet any attempt to tinker with it only raised more protest. In 1966, the SED took the HAT away from married women without dependent children, only to restore its original terms after hundreds of letters of complaint. The importance of the HAT to East German women says much about the regime's failure to address their double burden.[17]

Tensions between women of different marital status did not constitute the major dividing line on the shopfloor. Gender conflict held that place of honour. Throughout the 1950s, men resisted women's integration into the industrial workforce. Resentment took many forms: ridicule, lewd remarks and sexual advances; complaints about the incompetence and frivolity of women workers; the claim that men should earn more than women; refusal to promote qualified women to skilled or supervisory jobs. Opposition to women often united male workers, union officials, SED plant-based functionaries, foremen and plant directors, as a few examples will illustrate. An FDGB official sent in from central headquarters to gauge workers' mood at a precision machines plant found them 'largely satisfied with [piece] wages' but 'very tense' about gender relations because management paid many men at Level IV (out of eight) for a job that women did at Level II. Confronted with evidence of wage discrimination against skilled women workers in the Zeiss optics factory, a member of its trade union leadership retorted that he and his colleagues had 'more important problems to solve than deal with women', although they comprised 40 per cent of the workforce.[18] At the Leuna chemical concern, the SED factory organisation refused to train a woman who wanted to become a norm-setter because 'a woman can't perform that function.'[19]

The more intrepid women workers protested to FDGB representatives about wage discrimination and shopfloor harassment, but to little avail. SED women took up their cause, though more discreetly than in the 1940s. In 1952, the party revived the 'factory women's committees', placing them under control of neither the FDGB nor the DFD nor the plant-based SED, but of the local SED leadership. These committees published wall-newspapers for women workers, provided them with a safe place to complain, organised women's conferences and redressed individual cases of discrimination. Rather than fight systematically for women's rights on the shopfloor, however, they evolved, on the one hand, into social committees that pressed for childcare facilities and, on the other, into the female arm of the campaign for higher production.[20]

By the late 1950s, it became clear that new policies were necessary if, first, the GDR's 2 million non-employed women were to be drawn into a workplace whose labour shortage was ever more acute. The SED needed, second, to convince women that it was to their advantage to become well-trained, professional workers. In 1961, investigations conducted by the Women's Working Group of the Central Committee revealed the occupational attitudes of young textile workers to be sorely lacking. Certainly, many of them were active in the new 'socialist production brigades' that competed with each other to increase output. They were also more prosperous than earlier, arriving at work in stiletto heels and petticoats. Yet turnover was high and only 24 per cent of all female textile workers had a skilled worker's diploma. The majority of young women expressed little interest in qualification, in part *because* of improved wages. Young women, investigators concluded after a discussion with cotton spinners, had mixed-up priorities: 'The role of work is unclear, especially among young girls. They say: we want to put something by, so we don't go naked into marriage ... once we're married, we'll see if we want to continue working.'[21]

These investigators linked lacking job commitment to the continuing failure of male supervisors to encourage women to qualify and to assign them to appropriate positions once they did. By the early 1960s, the crude misogyny of the 1950s shopfloor had dissipated, replaced by benign neglect. In a labour-starved economy that allowed considerable social mobility, male workers no longer saw women as competitors, though they did not want them as bosses. The new locus of resistance to women's advance was the 'economic functionary', the fellow who figured out how each plant would meet its production quotas. These men defended their recalcitrance with various arguments. 'Many leading functionaries in chemical concerns', for example, believed that 'women will leave production when socialist reconstruction is complete'.[22] Other managers pointed to women's lack of interest in training and argued that, anyway, it was a waste of money to qualify women who constantly turned up pregnant.[23]

The building of the 'Antifascist Defence Rampart' created the context for renewed interest in women workers. The intensified isolation of the East Germany economy demanded that it modernise and diversify rather than rest on its basic-industrial laurels. The 'scientific–technological revolution' became the regime's new mantra. Realisation of this grand vision required the qualification of women workers, thrusting the 'woman question' into the centre of state policy and prompting the regime to devote new methods, a new language and more resources to women's policy. In December 1961, the Politbüro opened an unprecedented campaign for women's training and promotion. In a much-publicised 'Communiqué' entitled 'Women – Peace and Socialism,' the GDR's ruling body bluntly criticised the underrepresentation of women in leading functions and technical professions and called for a 'major discussion' of women's place at work.[24] The communiqué was heavily propagated in factories and offices. In 1962, a new Women's Commission, headed by Inge Lange, was attached, significantly, to the Politbüro. Lange and her fellow commissioners investigated the situation of women in every sector and level of the economy and government. The Commission not only kept women's qualification at the centre of public discourse throughout the early 1960s but also monitored the results of their agitation.[25]

Training programmes were reorganised to be 'woman-friendly'. Courses were specialised, shortened and divided into parts so workers could interrupt their studies. Factories offered 'special women's classes' during working hours. Women's professional training was also addressed. The gender ratio of higher education was already good but became even better as the university system admitted more students to make up for the pre-1961 flight of professionals, especially doctors. By 1966, women comprised 34.3 per cent of physicians and a gigantic 86.4 per cent of 'middle-level' health professionals. They constituted 53 per cent of district judges and not only 53.2 per cent of all teachers but 22.6 per cent of teachers and researchers at post-secondary level. Female students tended, however, to cluster in the humanities and health professions and to shy away from technical fields with often unwelcoming professors. In 1965, the GDR introduced affirmative action measures that increased the proportion of female engineering students from 6 to 35 per cent by 1975.[26]

Buoyed by the labour shortage and support from women in the SED, many women successfully rode the wave of qualification that washed over East German society in the 1960s. Still, their occupational structure and earnings changed much more slowly than the SED wished. By 1965, only 17 per cent of women had pulled themselves up to the higher steps of the GDR's eight-level wage scale, a mere 1 per cent increase over 1960! In 1965, in contrast, 73 per cent of men earned at Levels V–VIII (1960: 68.3 per cent).[27] Even more disturbing was evidence of a decline in women's commitment to career-employment. To tap into the reserves of non-employed women, in 1959 the regime allowed housewives to enter the workforce as part-time employees working approximately 30 hours a week instead of 45. This tactic drew thousands of housewives into waged labour but also motivated other women, already at work, to threaten to switch to another factory or office if their employer denied them this option. Many plant directors succumbed to their pressure. Soon, the dam broke. In 1960, 14.9 per cent of all women workers and employees worked part-time; by 1964, 24.2 per cent did; by 1969, 31 per cent had managed to reduce their hours. Part-time employment was especially widespread in the retail, postal and clerical branches but also invaded industry. Asked why they worked part-time, women said they felt a 'need' to work but, due to better material conditions, no longer 'had' to work full-time. The 45–hour week placed intolerable stress on them and their families, they explained, while part-time work was 'comfortable and pleasant'.[28] Just as the SED began seriously to implement programmes that enhanced the ability of women workers to move into skilled occupations and supervision, its investment in their training and education was threatened by a retreat into part-time work. Pointing to the stress of their double burden, women workers and employees forced the regime to shift its attention to the home front.

Raising the birth rate

Reproduction ran a close second to production when it came to policy towards women. In contrast to women's labour policy, however, pronatalism continued an established state tradition and did not offend popular beliefs about women's role. The press propagated higher fertility much less noisily than higher productivity. Nonetheless, the weekly of the Women's League, *Die Frau von heute*, communicated the state's interest in reproduction with photos of laughing children in the creche or mother's arms, and with stories about the joys of combining a job and three or four children.

Policy backed up propaganda. The Law for the Protection of Mother and Child and the Rights of Women (1950) included many programmes intended to encourage maternity and decrease infant and maternal mortality. Pregnant workers and employees received a paid five-week leave before delivery and six weeks afterward (increased to 11 weeks in 1956). All deliveries were covered by insurance. To encourage large families, a woman was given a 100 DM lump sum for her third, 250 DM for her fourth and 500 DM for her fifth child. Mothers received modest monthly allowances for the fourth and subsequent children. Single mothers received the same benefits. The Ministry of Health dramatically extended the existing network of maternity clinics to improve delivery and prenatal and postnatal care. By 1958, medical personnel examined 100 per cent of pregnant women at least once.[29]

Initially, however, the GDR relied more on cheap negative measures than expensive positive incentives. It never banned the sale of contraceptives but effectively discouraged their use through uneven availability and a *de facto* quarantine on public discussion of contraception. More significant was the strict regulation of abortion. Having reformed abortion law in the 1940s, the SED suddenly reversed its position in 1950. Article 11 of the Law for the Protection of Mother and Child authorised a termination only if a pregnancy 'seriously threatened the life or health of the pregnant woman' or if one parent suffered from a grave inherited condition. Replicating the abortion regulation of the Soviet Union, Article 11 recognised neither a social indication nor ethical grounds. Those who performed or underwent unauthorised abortions were liable to imprisonment. Medical boards vetted all requests for an abortion. Under the direction of Käthe Kern, once an outspoken supporter of legalisation, the Mother and Child Department of the Health Ministry closely monitored the rulings of the 'termination boards' and, up to 1962, held the GDR to one of the lowest incidences of legal abortion in the industrialised world. The state was unable, however, to repress illegal abortion. From 40,000 to 100,000 women a year turned to willing physicians and midwives in the GDR as well as to illicit West Berlin abortionists.[30]

Whether influenced by pronatalist measures or not, the fertility rate recovered from its mid-1940s plunge and then levelled off. State policy certainly enticed women to have their children younger and soon after marriage. Their average age at first delivery fell from 23 to 22 years between 1950 to 1970. Almost 70 per cent of women bore a child within a year of marriage.[31] Nonetheless, in 1957 the regime became concerned by the stagnation of the birth rate. It enacted a huge increase in child allowances in 1958, the same year that the regime began in earnest to try to increase the employment rate of married women. Every mother now received 500 DM at the birth of each of her first two children, 700 DM for the third, 850 DM for the fourth and 1,000 DM for the fifth. Immediately, fertility rose from 76.6 births per 1,000 women (15–44 years old) in 1958 to 84 in 1959.

Gratification over the solid birth rate was tempered by difficulties encountered in the campaign to increase women's qualification. It dawned on some members of the Central Committee that the majority of working women could not commit themselves to attaining skills, much less meet professional demands, if they could not plan their reproductive lives. At their suggestion, the abortion question was quietly reopened. In 1963, a 'working group on problems concerning abortion', composed of health officials, gynaecologists and SED representatives, including Women's Commissioner Inge Lange, began to consider ways to relax Article 11.[32] Besides gathering sociological data on abortion, the group read letters of protest to the Health Ministry from frustrated applicants for abortion that detailed the physical and psychic costs of too many pregnancies in rapid succession, high prices, low wages and cramped apartments. The working group also collected evidence on illegal abortion and its price in women's mortality. In their deliberations, group members showed considerable interest in the *social* roots of abortion but were told by Lange that their revision dare not refer to a 'social indication' because 'then we'd have to devise a new law'. Rather, they recommended that abortion be permitted if a woman was over 40 or under 16, had five children, became pregnant soon after the birth of her third child, or had been raped. The Ministry of Health adopted the new regulations in 1965 but did not publicise them. Simultaneously, it also quietly made methods of contraception, including the 'pill', available to more 'at risk' women, though, again, not on demand.[33]

Inge Lange's warnings against an explicit social indication, reminders that the consultations were confidential and admonitions against 'public dialogue' reflected the SED's fear that open discussion of abortion regulation would lead to demands for 'complete legalisation.' Legalisation, Lange argued, would cause the birth rate to plummet. In fact, calls for the repeal of Article 11 were circulating within the SED itself – at least among its women activists. A female gynaecologist warned the working group that SED and DFD speakers would denounce Article 11 at a women's congress scheduled for June 1964, if 'something [did] not happen' before it convened.[34]

Unfortunately for the SED, the silent relaxation of abortion did not satisfy the very people whom the Communiqué of 1961 aimed to encourage: young women who aspired to a profession. The number of complaints against rejected applications rose in the late 1960s. In contrast to earlier, desperate petitioners based their claim for an abortion less on their poor material situation than on their commitment to their studies, occupations, or 'political activity'. Many insisted that they had the 'right' to control the number of children they bore.[35] Like the pressure for part-time work, these letters made two things clear: the unbearable strain of combining career, studies, children and housework; and women's readiness to petition the authorities for the remedies that they, not the SED, wanted.

Between socialisation and private consumption

The SED approached consumption and its organisation with uncharacteristic uncertainty. It wanted to raise workers' standard of living but not to encourage greed and individualism. Ambivalence about consumption could not but spill over into the SED's relationship with women. In a poorly developed consumer economy, housewives devoted phenomenal energy and time to obtaining food, making it edible, hauling fuel, organising an overcrowded space, repairing clothes and, dreadful task, hand-washing the laundry. On top of all this, they had to tend their children. The SED aimed to move work out of the home by 'socialising' it in the form of child care facilities, canteens, laundries and repair shops. Yet, simultaneously, socialist planners envisioned a 'rationalisation model' via the electrification of housework. DFD activists knew that this second dream also entranced its housewife members. Eager to win readers, *Die Frau von heute* fed their appetites for household appliances with articles on the latest gadgets. Thus, even as it dreamed of a socialised future and looked askance at women's alleged consumer frivolities, the SED nourished the very desires that were also stimulated by glimpses of West German prosperity.

SED policies were as contradictory as its rhetoric. Before the rebellion of 1953, planners starved consumer production, disrupted trade and distribution patterns and unintentionally jeopardised the satisfaction of even basic nutritional, clothing and housing needs. The press treated West German consumerism with contempt. Yet the regime also invested little in the socialisation of services and, instead, relied heavily on the unpaid and onerous domestic labour of women to get the family through the prolonged scarcity. Compared to what existed before 1945, institutionalised child care was considerably expanded but remained woefully inadequate relative to mothers' increased employment rate. By 1958, 36.2 per cent of children (aged 3–6) attended kindergarten but a tiny 8.3 per cent had a place in a creche. The vast majority of working mothers had to find private providers, often their own mothers. The second best way to relieve women workers, planners reasoned, was to clean the family wash in central laundries located at the workplace. Again, the gap between intent and practice was wide. In the chemical concerns around Dessau, 17,000 women workers could wash their clothes in a laundry only twice a year. Even where availability was better, workers often did not get their items back for eight to nine weeks![36] Factories also served hot meals, as did schools. Working women complained bitterly that local stores were empty or closed by the time they went shopping, so the bigger factories opened shops and repair centres.

None of this made an appreciable dent on women's burden of housework. Wives performed the overwhelming majority of household tasks, spending an average of six hours more a day on housework than did men.[37] Though it occasionally called for men to pitch in at home, the SED did not see the redistribution of labour as a socialist solution to the drudgery and isolation of housework and loathed any whiff of war between the sexes. Instead, the factory women's committees called for services, especially child care. Indeed, in their effort to find a lever of influence within male-dominated power structures, women functionaries in the SED and FDGB exploited the child care issue for all it was worth. In a blistering account of gender discrimination in a coal-processing plant, for example, a woman instructor contrasted its club hall, sports centre and other facilities used mainly by men to its utter lack of childcare for the 300 mothers in its workforce.[38]

If the SED did not confront the division of domestic labour, neither did most East German women. Raised to see the home as woman's domain, they took pride in their ability to run a well-organised home under difficult conditions.[39] Though working women called for better child care and services, they seemed, above all, to yearn for all the things that would make their homes modern, efficient and easier to maintain. In the mid-1950s, with more money to spend, they flocked to demonstrations of new appliances, made suggestions about product design, and complained about the scarcity of washing machines, vacuum cleaners, mixers, waxers and bread slicers. Far from denigrating such materialistic concerns, SED and DFD activists relayed to economic planners the private consumer desires of women and insisted that these be satisfied.[40]

As filtered and even magnified by DFD and SED women, women's domestic wishes were increasingly acknowledged from above. In a typically grandiose gesture, the regime published a communiqué on 'the production of 1,000 little things' in January 1960. Ulbricht promised women increased manufacture of housewares, on the one hand, and higher investment in the socialised service economy, on the other. By 1970, there were places in creches for 26.5 per cent of infants and toddlers and 61.1 per cent of 3–6-year-olds attended kindergarten. Though the organisation, availability, and quality of consumer services remained problematic, they were expanded and improved. More striking, both in magnitude and novelty, was a leap in consumer production. In 1960, only 6.1 per cent of households owned a refrigerator and only 6.2 per cent a washing machine; by 1970, these percentages had jumped to 56.4 and 53.6, respectively. Television – beamed in 1960 into 17 of 100 homes – by 1970 could be watched in 69 per cent of them.[41] Thus, the SED set its state firmly on the road of competition with capitalist consumerism, a contest it could only lose.

In sum, privatisation and socialisation coexisted but with the effect that the family lost none of its significance as a central site of social reproduction, much less of emotional intensity. It continued to impose a burden of labour. Indeed, as in the West, the multiplication of 'time-saving' devices raised standards of cleanliness and cookery. In 1970, housework claimed 47.5 hours per week in a four-person household. Women performed 90 per cent of this work, thus spending as many hours at housework as at their paid jobs.[42] Tossed with much fanfare into production, the 'woman question' had tumbled unintentionally into reproduction, rolled willy-nilly into consumption and landed, like it or not, in the family nest.

Nurturing the socialist family

The SED never intended to erode the foundations of the nuclear family. It aimed, certainly, to shape the political beliefs of family members and to bring many aspects of family life into the public sphere, but neither planned to take children away from their parents, tolerated 'free love', nor entertained experiments in group living. In fact, its policies had the effect of increasing the marriage rate among East Germans and encouraging them to marry ever younger. By 1970, women's age at first marriage had declined to 21.9 years. In so far as the SED was interested in the family as an institution, it hoped to modernise the family by creating legal equality between husbands and wives, liberalising the terms of divorce, providing wives with financial independence via paid labour and recognising the equal rights of single mothers and their children. In the 1950s, even these modest goals encountered considerable resistance among East Germans, especially older couples in rural areas and small towns. Many farmer-husbands refused to let their wives join the SED's rural production co-operatives, while village wives listened attentively to the traditional message preached by the still active Protestant women's league. Urban spouses, too, and, indeed, many dedicated Communist couples functioned, if not on a patriarchal basis, similarly to the western family of the era. They consulted each other about their children's upbringing and jointly made family decisions. Nonetheless, the husband's career generally took precedence. His education and political activity filled evening and Sunday hours that his wife spent with their children.[43]

The Ministry of Justice discovered just how attached the populace was to such customs when, in 1954, it presented a draft family law for public discussion. People accepted its elimination of the patriarchal division of property, income and family decision-making. Yet, disrupting the Ministry's carefully orchestrated meetings, they spoke out angrily against its assumption that wives should work and, especially, its new regulation of divorce which replaced the guilt clause with a no-fault 'irretrievable breakdown' rule. Both the Protestant and Catholic churches agitated heavily against the draft. Older wives, many of whom had never worked for wages and had no skills, led the popular outcry. Just as single women resented the unfair terms of the housework day, so older wives feared that liberalisation of divorce would hurt them and benefit men and single women. Stunned by the vehemence of older wives' attack on the revisions, the Justice Ministry pulled the draft and silenced any talk of family law reform for a decade. It introduced the divorce regulations by decree. Nonetheless, family-court judges, most of whom were women, tended to rule to uphold older marriages whose husband had filed for divorce.[44]

Over time, the two-earner couple became the model, thus corresponding to the plan. The state, however, partially adjusted its social vision to fit popular mores. In 1965, the Justice Ministry presented a new family law that described the family as the 'most basic cell of society' and credited it with 'determining the personality in socialist society'. This formulation offered a concession to the common complaint that the regime overemphasised the work collective and underemphasised the family as the main agent of socialisation.[45] Communists themselves had come increasingly to recognise that economic change – women's rising employment – did not automatically transform family norms.

Not that wives' employment had left family relations untouched. Financially independent women could more readily leave intolerable marriages. Not only did the divorce rate rise in the 1960s but wives were ever likelier to file the complaint (1958: 53.4 per cent; 1970: 63.4 per cent).[46] Communists found it disturbing, however, that the only obvious familial impact of women's economic independence was more divorce! Studies showed that, especially in rural districts, working mothers filed for divorce because household tasks and child rearing were 'almost completely loaded' on them. Happily, in industrial districts there had developed 'a new relationship of men to women'. Yet, even in big cities such as Dresden, the ideal of the egalitarian socialist marriage had not materialised.[47] In fact, investigators for the Women's Commission found that many functionaries in the party, unions, government bureaucracy and economy did not want their wives to 'develop beyond them'. Even worse, these men avoided any workplace discussion of women's domestic burdens 'because the obvious consequences would reach into their own families'.[48] Confronted with such views, influential women in the SED and FDGB began to rethink the causal relationship between women's public and domestic roles. 'From my own experience, but also from interviews with women colleagues', wrote a woman in the FDGB's Women's Department, 'I believe that a woman can fulfil a responsible administrative function only when she finds support in the family – that is, has equality [in it]'.[49]

A final reason for the new attention to the family was a growing interest in the cognitive and emotional development of children. Influenced by Western psychology, the Soviet example, and the worried observations of East German mothers, the DFD conducted studies that showed that creches offered good basic care but neglected 'pedagogical matters'. Creche children entered kindergarten 'verbally and emotionally behind' those raised solely in the family and suffered from having less physical contact with their parents.[50] Though experts disagreed about whether such evidence meant that babies should stay at home with their mothers or that creche care should be improved, the debate highlighted the maternal role in child-rearing. Similarly, the academic problems of older, especially proletarian, children were attributed to inadequate domestic supervision. When queried about their preference for part-time employment, mothers reported that, according to teachers, they needed to spend more time with their kids.[51] Attention to their development benefited children. Ironically, however, in reinterpreting the family's contribution to moral and intellectual growth, representatives of the state refurbished the maternal role in nurture and pedagogy and, thus, undermined its campaign for the qualification and promotion of female workers, employees and professionals.

The more things change ...

SED women's policy was torn between its absent vision of a transformed family, pronatalism and commitment to women's employment. These basic contradictions never changed. Within each area, however, significant modifications occurred as economic and social priorities changed. Thus, women workers benefited as the quantitative mania of the 1950s gave way to the qualitative concerns of the 1960s. This transition also stimulated internal debate about social questions of great importance to women, including reproductive rights, household needs and family relationships. Under Ulbricht, however, the regime recoiled from social innovations, even as it introduced risky economic reforms. In contrast, Erich Honecker retreated from economic experimentation but implemented bold social reforms.[52]

Notably many of his reforms addressed women's issues: legalisation of abortion, generous maternal subsidies, dramatic expansion and improvement of daycare facilities, extension of the housework day to all workers who ran a household with dependants and, last but not least, the 'baby year' (extended maternal leave). Honecker fulfilled many of the demands raised by women workers, mothers, female Communists, psychologists and physicians in the 1960s, creating a society that was decidedly friendlier to women than before. Viewing the transition from Ulbricht to Honecker from a different perspective, feminist historians have argued that Honecker lost interest in regendering the labour force. Women consolidated their position in the workforce and performed increasingly qualified jobs, but did so in a segmented labour market. Sub-sectors such as chemical production, health services and commerce became totally feminised, while women's relative employment in metallurgy and heavy industry declined.[53] Women's labour policy was replaced with a maternalist family policy that reified women's biological and social reproductive roles, even as it also recognised the crucial contribution of the family to society. In a state that monopolised political discourse and suppressed civil society, the angry discussions of the 1960s among women, both outside and inside the SED, could not evolve into an independent women's movement that might have developed a fundamental critique of the gendered foundations of SED ideology, popular attitudes, spousal relations and economic structures.

Notes

1 SAPMO-BA, DY 34/21507, IG Bergbau, Konferenz zur Verbesserung unter den Frauen am 22.11.52 in Halle, 7. (Unless otherwise stated, archival references are to Stiftung Archiv der Parteien und Massenorganisationen der DDR im Bundesarchiv Berlin.)
2 DY 30/IV A2/17/8, Welche Faktoren hemmen den Einsatz von Frauen in mittleren und leitenden Funktionen . . .?, 5 September 1967, 1.
3 Norman Naimark, *The Russians in Germany* (Cambridge, Mass., 1995), 68–70, 72–4, 104–5, 117; Ingrid Schmidt-Harzbach, 'Eine Woche im April, Berlin 1945: Vergewaltigung als Massenschicksal', *Feministische Studien*, 2 (1984); Atina Grossmann, *Reforming Sex: The German Movement for Birth Control and Abortion Reform, 1920–1950* (Oxford/New York, 1995), 194.
4 Donna Harsch, 'Approach/avoidance: Communists and women in East Germany, 1945–1949', *Social History* (May 2000), 156–82.
5 *Ibid.*
6 Wolfgang Zank, *Wirtschaft und Arbeit in Ostdeutschland 1945–49* (Munich, 1987), 35; Gesine Obertreis, *Familienpolitik in der DDR, 1945–1980* (Opladen, 1985), 33, 57–58; Jörg Roesler, 'East German industry, 1945 to the present', in Erik Aerts *et al.* (eds), *Women in the Labour Force* (Leuven, 1990).
7 DY 30/IV 2/17/30, Bevölkerung, 30 June 1949, fo. 1.
8 Landesarchiv Merseburg, IV L-2/602/70, SED-Halle (Arbeit and Sozialfürsorge), Überprüfung einiger Betriebe um Einsatzmöglichkeiten für Frauen zu schaffen,

24 October 1949.
9 FDGB-BuVo, 2/a/422, Bericht von der Arbeitsausschusssitzung zur Förderung der Frauen.
10 Dietrich Storbeck, *Arbeitskraft und Beschäftigung in Mitteldeutschland* (Cologne/Opladen, 1961), 92; DY 30/IV 2/17/43, Arbeiter und Angestellte, darunter weiblich, fo. 82; *Statistisches Jahrbuch der DDR*: 1955, 32; 1956, 256–7; 1960/61, 192–3; Roesler, 'East German industry', 101.
11 *Statistisches Jahrbuch*: 1966, 452.
12 Hilde Benjamin, 'Wer bestimmt in der Familie', *Neues Deutschland*, 1 February 1958.
13 DY 49/16/35/1572, IG TBL, Bericht über den Instrukteureinsatz vom 27.6 u. 28.6.51 in Flöha und Leipzig; *ibid.*, 39/54/2613, IG TBL, Bericht über den Instrukteureinsatz am 17. und 18.3.53 beim Bezirksvorstand IG Te-Be-Le in Malchow, 2–3.
14 DY 49/39/54/2613, Protokoll über das BGL-Seminar am 12.6.53 in Glauchau; IG TBL, Bericht über die Belegschaftsversammlung im Textilwerk Einheit I, Glauchau am 8.7.53, 4; *ibid.*, 39/49/2610, IG Chemie-Zentralvorstand (Frauen), Niederschrift über eine Arbeitstagung ... am 16.9.53, 2.
15 Karin Zachmann, 'Frauen für die technische Revolution: Studentinnen und Absolventinnen Technischer Hochschulen in der SBZ/DDR', in Gunilla-Friederike Budde (ed.), *Frauen arbeiten: Weibliche Erwerbstätigkeit in Ost- und Westdeutschland nach 1945* (Göttingen, 1997), 132–3.
16 DY 30/IV 2/5/273, SED-KL Rathenow to SED-BL Potsdam, 7 August 1953, fo. 57; DY 46/11/559/2105, VEB Waggonbau Bautzen (Zentraler Frauenausschuß) to Bezirksvorstand, 14 May 1956.
17 Carola Sachse, 'Ein "heißes Eisen": Ost- und westdeutsche Debatten um den Hausarbeitstag', in Budde (ed.), *Frauen arbeiten*, 253–5.
18 DY 34/A 347, Untersuchung ... im Betrieb Feinmesszeugfabrik, Suhl, 10 November 1951; DY 30/IV 2/17/7, Protokoll der Sitzung mit den Abteilungsleiterinnen ... vom 8.12.50, fos 101–4.
19 DY 34/39/134/6009, Arbeitsbesprechung der Frauenkommission des Zentralvorstands der IG Chemie am 25.10.57, 3.
20 DY 46/11/310/1890, IG Metall (BV), Bericht über die Arbeit der Frauenkommission im Bezirk Potsdam, 11 Nov. 1953; DY 30/IV 2/17/65, Untersuchung des Standes der Arbeit unter den Arbeiterinnen ... im VEB Chemische Werke Buna, 12 November 1960, fo. 221.
21 DY 30/IV 2/17/37, Einschätzung zu einigen Problemen der Lage der jungen Arbeiterinnen in der Textilindustrie, fos 104–111; IV 2/17/70, Bericht über den Einsatz in Leipziger Baumwollspinnereien vom 28.11–2.12.61, fo. 99.
22 Landesarchiv Merseburg, IV 2/5/1441, SED-BL Halle, Beispiele für das Referat der Frauenkonferenz [1959], 2.
23 DY 34/Tribüne Nachmittage, 9th TN in Gera, 7 June 1961; DY 34/1503, Arbeitsgremium Frauen, Einsatz im VEB Mineralölwerke Lützkendorf vom 28.1–5.2.64; IV A2/6.04/368, SED-ZK (Maschinenbau and Metallurgie), [Z]ur stärkeren Einbeziehung der Frauen und Mädchen in dem politischen und ökonomischen Leben im Stahl, 27 May 1964.
24 'Hand und Herz der Frauen für das große Ziel', *Neues Deutschland*, 24 December 1961.

25 Susanne Kreutzer, '"Sozialismus braucht gebildete Frauen": Die Kampagne um das Kommuniqué "Die Frauen – der Frieden und der Sozialismus" in der DDR 1961/62', *Zeitschrift für Geschichtswissenschaft*, 47 (1999), 23–37.
26 DY 30/IV A2/17/23, Zu einigen Fragen der Arbeitskräftesituation in der DDR, [1966]; Karin Zachmann, 'Mobilizing for Marx: women in the engineering professions and the "scientific-technological revolution" in the GDR during the 1960s', unpublished manuscript. See also Gunilla-Friederike Budde, 'Paradefrauen: Akademikerinnen in Ost- und Westdeutschland,' in Budde (ed.), *Frauen arbeiten*.
27 DY 34/5471, Probleme der komplex-sozialistischen Rationalisierung und die weitere Förderung der Frauen und Mädchen, 7 January 1967.
28 DY 34/11873, Einschätzung einiger Ursachen für den zunehmenden Übergang der Frauen von der Voll- zur Teilbeschäftigung in Betrieben der Elektrotechnik/elektronik und Textilindustrie (Zeitraum 1968 bis 1969), 1–2; DY 30/IV 2/2.042/20, Entwicklung der Beschäftigung der Frauen in der Produktion, 24 November 1971, fos 245, 247.
29 BAB, DQ-1/5331, Bericht zum Ministerialratsbeschluss von 8.7.54, Gesundheitsschutz für Mütter, 29 May 1957.
30 Donna Harsch, 'Society, the state, and abortion in East Germany, 1950–1972', *American Historical Review*, 102 (1997), 59–61.
31 Wagner, *Scheidung in Ost-und Westdeutschland: Zum Verhältnis von Ehestabilität und Sozialstruktur seit den 30er Jahren* (Frankfurt/Main, 1997), 186–7, Heike Trappe, *Emanzipation oder Zwang? Frauen in der DDR zwischen Beruf, Familie und Sozialpolitik* (Berlin, 1995), 107.
32 DY 30/IV A2/19/22, Stellungnahme und Empfehlungen der Kommission zu Problemen der Schwangerschaftsunterbrechung in der DDR, [1963]. See also DY 30/IV A2/17/83.
33 DY 30/IV A2/19/22, Notizen während der Beratung am 21.4.64 mit führenden Gynäkologen, 9–10.
34 *Ibid*.
35 Harsch, 'Society', 74–9.
36 DY 34/39/94/5571, Protokoll über die Lage der werktätigen Frauen im Bezirk Halle der IG Chemie, 18 October 1956; A 1544, RdB Halle (Arbeit), Arbeitskreis der Arbeitskraftsreserven (Chemieprogramm), 20 April 1959, 28–9.
37 Helga Ulbricht *et al.*, *Probleme der Frauenarbeit* (Berlin, 1963), 28.
38 DY 30/IV 2/17/87, 299–302, Lierse, Die Lage der Frauen in den Braunkohle- und Eisengiessereibetrieben im Geiseltal Kreis, 30 June 1951.
39 Interview with Frau CD, Stanford, Cal, 30 October 1997.
40 DY 31/Folder 338, DFD (Frau und Staat), Auswertung der Handelskonferenz der Zentralkomitee der SED, [1960?], 5–6; Katherine Pence, 'Schaufenster des sozial-istischen Konsums: Texte der ostdeutschen "consumer culture"', in Alf Lüdtke and Peter Becker (eds), *Akten, Eingaben, Schaufenster* (Berlin, 1997), 114.
41 Harry G. Shaffer, *Women in the Two Germanies: A Comparative Study of a Socialist and a Non-Socialist Society* (New York, 1981), 106; Peter Hübner, *Konsens, Konflikt und Kompromiß* (Berlin, 1995), 170.
42 DY 34/9137, Studie zur Begründung des langfristigen Planes der Frauenarbeit im Kombinat, 25 June 1970, 17.
43 'Wir wollen darüber offen sprechen', *Die Frau von heute*, 2 January, 13 February,

6 March 1953; interview with Frau CT, Bernau, 27 July 1997.
44 BAB, DP-1/VA 243, DFD-Jena (Land), Aufstellung über die negativen Diskussionen in Justizausspracheabenden, 15 September 1954; DY 30/IV 2/13/99, Bericht über die Ergebnisse der Diskussion zum Entwurf des FGB ... 9.10.54, fo. 469.
45 In 1961, a sociological investigation (in itself, a sign of the new era) revealed this belief to the regime. See Herbert Zerle, *Sozialistisch Leben* (Berlin, 1964), 16–17.
46 Lothar Mertens, *Wider die sozialistische Familiennorm: Ehescheidungen in der DDR, 1950–1989* (Opladen, 1998), 36, 66.
47 DY 34/4290, Büro MM, Zusammenarbeit mit dem Ministerium der Justiz, 1966/67, 23–4.
48 BAB, DP-1/VA 1445, vol. 2, Information über den Verlauf der öffentlichen Diskussionen zum Entwurf des FGB, 25 July 1965, fo. 23; Bericht über die Diskussion zum Entwurf FGB, 6 October 1965, fo. 56; DY 30/IV 2/17/71, Bericht über den Einsatz Karl-Marx-Stadt vom 28.8.–7.9.62, fo. 117; IV 2/17/20, Abschlussbericht über den Einsatz der Arbeitsgruppe in Bezirk Halle, 5 April 1962, fo. 412.
49 DY 34/7763, Wenzel at Kolloquium 'Die Rolle der Frau und die politischen Funktionen der Gewerkschaften', 1968.
50 BAB, DQ-1/2963, DFD (Frau und Staat), Einschätzung des Standes der Realisierung der vom Bundesvorstand getroffenen Vereinbarungen mit dem Ministerium für Gesundheitswesen, 31 October 1960, 4.
51 DY 34/9820, Arbeitsökonomie und industriesoziologische Aspekte der Teilzeitarbeit, 1970; DY 34/11873, Analyse über die Teilbeschäftigung in VEB Schuhkombinat Banner des Friedens, [1970]; Obertreis, *Familienpolitik*, 157, 205.
52 Hübner, *Konsens*, 177.
53 Obertreis, *Familienpolitik*, 47, 205; Irene Dölling, 'Gespaltenes Bewußtsein – Frauen- und Männerbilder in der DDR', in Gisela Helwig und Hildegard Maria Nickel (eds), *Frauen in Deutschland 1945–1992* (Berlin, 1993), 23–52.

10

The limits of repression and reform: youth policy in the early 1960s[1]

Mark Fenemore

In picking over the bones left behind by the GDR's demise, researchers have tended to focus either on attempts by the regime to win young people's support or on the persistence, in the face of such efforts, of youthful protest and opposition. The first approach examines official strategies to integrate, indoctrinate and control young people through school and the official youth organisation, the FDJ.[2] The second explores ways in which young people could protest, ignore or resist official attempts to influence them. At one end of the spectrum of dissenting behaviour, a very small number of young people formed opposition groups such as the 'Eisenberger Kreis', operating conspiratorially with the aim of ultimately toppling the regime.[3] At the other extreme, much larger groups of young people withdrew from official incorporation strategies by submerging themselves into their own separate worlds of hobbies, youth-specific interests and sub-cultures.[4] While it is difficult to ignore the fact that the GDR was a dictatorship bent on (re)forming young people in its own image, it is just as important to recognise the extent to which political and social actors, young and old, were able – consciously or unconsciously – to impede, subvert and in some cases even transform official policy.[5]

This contribution focuses on the period 1961–65 because it is highly revealing of the contradictions between the regime's blueprint for societal development and the frustrating persistence of unwanted societal realities. It was during the four short years between the building of the Wall in August 1961 and the eleventh party plenum in December 1965, that the contradictions and ambiguities in official youth policy (and the ambivalent self-image which lay behind it) came closest to the surface.

Confronted by the fact that many young people fell far short of official expectations and remained stubbornly indifferent to the Workers' and Peasants' State, Ulbricht and the Politbüro moved from a policy of unmitigated repression to one of partial relaxation, only to revert to a hard line.

Although, in principle, the party accepted no limitations on its power, there was briefly under Ulbricht's leadership a recognition that, in practice, there were real limits to an educational dictatorship. In spite of the persistent urge among SED leaders to label young people who failed to conform 'traitors' and 'agents of western imperialism', Cold War stereotypes did briefly relent. There was, albeit temporarily, a recognition by Ulbricht's regime that young people growing up in the early 1960s had different experiences and expectations from the cohort encountered in the immediate aftermath of the war. 'The younger generation which lives in the German Democratic Republic today', an official report stated, 'is a new younger generation, one which has grown up in a new epoch, which has different problems from those young people had in 1945 and which must be influenced in a different fashion'. Devoid of direct experience of 'fascism, war, exploitation and privation', young persons were deaf to political warnings about the dangers of imperialism and militarism.[6]

In the event, however, the change of policy ushered in by the new 'Youth Communiqué' of 1963 failed to have the impact intended. The official hopes riding on reform were too ambitious, particularly as the expectations generated among young people pushed them in directions other than those envisaged by the regime. In her micro-study of the experiences of young people born in 1949, the year in which the GDR was founded, Dorothee Wierling also emphasises the great hopes the regime had placed in co-opting those born and raised in the GDR. She shows, however, that contrary to the regime's expectations, as they grew older, more sceptical and rebellious, those 'born into socialism' proved much less tractable than the 'Hitler Youth generation' of their parents and teachers, brought up and socialised in the Third Reich.[7] The brash confidence and naive optimism the regime had once seen exhibited in young people came into conflict with, and eventually gave way to, a deep-seated cultural pessimism. As the generation supposed to provide the foundations of a fully developed socialist society, young people came instead to be seen as dangerous 'enemies within'.

The building of the Wall

The period immediately following the building of the Wall on 13 August 1961 witnessed a generally harsher line towards the population, including measures to 'liquidate' gangs and 're-educate the workshy'.[8] In a speech to the Politbüro on 22 August, Ulbricht called for special measures against 'hostile elements'. 'Young people who don't want to work will learn how to in work camps.' A special resolution was duly passed on 24 August permitting internment of 'slackers (*Arbeitsbummelanten*)'. Ulbricht also announced a new show trial against members of the young Christian *Junge Gemeinde*. They were, he said, 'even worse than the young Social Democrats. They work in the houses of the church. They are the source of Christian

Democratic propaganda. They are followers of NATO [the North Atlantic Treaty Alliance] and clericalism. Social Democratic functionaries are often cowardly, but those of the *Junge Gemeinde* are fanatics. They are ready to die for God and Adenauer and are prepared to break the law.'[9]

The harshness of Ulbricht's stance resulted from years of impotent rage. Towards the end of the 1950s, members of youth gangs had become increasingly bold in flouting the regime's authority. A significant minority of young people who had grown up in the GDR seemed to believe that they could challenge the regime and get away with it. They were joined by a small, but conspicuous (and so easily scapegoated) number of young 'rowdies' and criminals from West Germany, who sought to take advantage of the relative 'safe haven' offered by the GDR from prison sentences and military service in the West. Although the East German authorities tended to exaggerate the role played by these new arrivals from West Germany, East Germans who had left the GDR only subsequently to come back – so-called returnees – were seen to pose an equally serious problem.[10] Indeed, the East German authorities believed that the reception camps in West Berlin for young migrants from East Germany were actually recruitment centres for western intelligence.

However much the authorities tried to ascribe nonconformity to direct or indirect western subversion, it was clear that official education policies were failing to prevent young people from migrating – both physically and mentally – between the two systems. The building of the Wall was designed not only to keep the population in, but to teach the lesson that from now on it would be impossible to escape the party's influence. As Ulbricht said in a speech on East German television, 'these measures also had a pedagogical function'.[11]

The act of walling young people in caused enormous resentment which expressed itself particularly in drink-fuelled provocations and attacks on party functionaries and policemen. Attempts to generate a cult of personality for Ulbricht by forcing FDJ members to buy pictures of him only succeeded in causing a spate of incidents in which he was burnt in effigy.[12] In a series of school incidents, pupils who expressed opposition or even indifference to the 'security measures' were marked out for exemplary punishment.[13] When, for instance, one group of sixth-formers from Leipzig and Jüterbog had met on the island of Rügen in the summer of 1961, they found no shortage of ways of amusing themselves. Having hoisted a jolly roger flag, they proceeded to bury a bottle containing the names of Eastern bloc leaders torn from a newspaper. They then erected a memorial to the 'fallen' and tended it each day with scraps of mouldy and half-eaten food. Mock flag ceremonies were held during which one of the group stomped about imitating Ulbricht, who was referred to with mock affection as 'Uncle Walter U'. When, after 13 August 1961, the police came to investigate these activities, the pupils involved were arrested, charged with 'organised counter-revolutionary subversion' and sentenced to up to two-and-a-half years in prison. Even the crime of 'spreading enemy propaganda' during break-time was deemed sufficiently serious to warrant a year in prison. To counter the harmful effects of their activities a special flag ceremony was held at their school (this time under official auspices), and although the pupils concerned were still under arrest awaiting trial, it was decided to set a symbolic example by ceremoniously expelling them from 'all secondary schools of the Republic forever'.[14]

The regime hoped that, with the Wall, it would finally be possible to shut out the harmful influences which it believed were behind such 'outrages'. It moved to bring young people under control by imposing tests of loyalty and punishing the most blatant signs of non-compliance. In order to stay in the education system, young people had to sign declarations pledging support for the measures of 13 August, wholehearted willingness to undertake military service, as well as promises not to receive western radio and television. In a campaign reminiscent of Nazi humiliation tactics, Thälmann Pioneers enacted a 'Blitz on enemy broadcasts' by denouncing people whose aerials pointed toward the West and in some cases even pinning donkey's ears on their doors. Far from ensuring the exclusion of western influences, however, surveys show that the popularity of western music and youth culture actually increased during the 1960s. Such was their appeal that even ideologically committed young people were not immune.[15] In 1963 an education official estimated that 40–50 per cent of pupils were still watching western television. Children were already tainted by the time they reached primary school age, as one report lamented: 'As interesting and lively as the children's drawings are, western cars etc. predominate.'[16]

The party's monopoly over educational and career opportunities taught that if young people wanted to succeed in life, they had to conform. However, it could not disguise the fact that outward conformity was often only given reluctantly and frequently belied a remoteness from the regime's claims. Scepticism was greatest in the *Oberschulen*, the former grammar schools, which had born the brunt of attempts to ensure smoother cadre production by purging and excluding middle-class and Christian children. But in spite of attempts to increase the proportion of working-class pupils and teachers, the former elite schools continued to exhibit, according to SED inspectors, 'reactionary and outdated modes of thinking'. There were complaints that when *Neulehrer* (the teachers hastily recruited after 1945) worked alongside 'old' teachers, they often developed a 'false' respect for the latter's abilities and subject knowledge and in some cases even sought to emulate them. Although widely perceived as ill-educated fanatics, there were *Neulehrer* who had joined the profession out of a genuine commitment to teaching and to the humanistic goals of socialism. It was teachers like these who found themselves particularly prone to ideological 'derailment', or even flight, following the events of 1953 and 1956. For instance, in May 1959 four of Leipzig's best *Neulehrer*, who had been awarded prizes for exemplary achievement on several occasions, were put on trial for 'propaganda and hatred threatening to the state'.[17]

The strict supervision of education proved much less effective in reality than on paper. Although it is important not to underestimate the degree to which the SED attempted total control, there were real limits to the implementation of an educational dictatorship. Not only were teachers often as disinclined to believe the party message as pupils, but they also proved highly resistant to change. In spite of repeated pressure from above to adopt a 'partisan attitude' and become mouthpieces of the party, a significant number remained stubbornly wedded to the notion that the teacher's function was to teach. While inspectors bemoaned continued objectivistic and liberalistic tendencies, teachers complained that constant political interference and repeated syllabus changes only hampered their pedagogical duties. Even ideologically committed teachers could become disheartened by the overemphasis on politics at the expense of education. Refusing to turn his maths lesson into a discussion of the National Document, one party secretary remarked: 'It's a case of either I teach OR I do politics.'[18]

Although, compared to other institutions, schools were relatively successful in obtaining conformity, this proved highly fragile. So fragile in fact that as inspectors noted, the behaviour of a particular class could change from hour to hour, depending on which teacher they had.[19] It was much easier for the regime to force young people to observe rituals of obedience than it was to convince them of its message. The attempt to enforce rigid boundaries between acceptable and unacceptable behaviour in many ways served to increase the possibilities of transgression. Attempts at total control turned all sorts of otherwise harmless hobbies (such as writing letters to foreign penfriends and even collecting stamps) into semi-illicit, potentially subversive and hence highly popular activities. Even when they did not engage in verbal opposition, pupils had subtle and not so subtle ways of making their scepticism felt. One headmaster reported that pupils had disrupted discussion of party policy by deliberately and maliciously grinning. Another reported that pupils had made the atmosphere in their class unteachable by chewing garlic during break.[20]

Skill in parroting the responses desired by the regime often belied inner detachment. Party leaders were alarmed by reports which showed the ease with which even apparently progressive pupils could slip into nonconformity. One young FDJ secretary reacted to the news that Stalin's body had been removed from the mausoleum in Red Square by asking if it would be permissible for Stalin's photograph to be removed from the classroom's 'pioneer corner'. During break the recently de-sanctified photograph was desecrated, mutilated and burned.[21]

The overpoliticisation of subjects like history, civics and modern languages did not make them more interesting for pupils and boredom was frequently a cause of mischief. Although they might have been able to give the right answers in 'exam conditions', when taken out of their normal routine, particularly to see Russian propaganda films, pupils were much more prone to rebel. From the 1950s to the 1970s, films depicting SS men brutally murdering, raping and pillaging innocent Russian civilians were liable to elicit whistles and cheers as well as cat-calls and roars of encouragement. The process of growing up was so full of contradictions, and young people were subject to so many restrictions and taboos, that some rule-breaking was inevitable.

Although a sizeable number of teenagers were by this time members of the FDJ, the youth organisation was not yet in a position to control their leisure activities. A report by Leipzig's regional council stated in 1958 that: 'As far as co-ordination of extra-curricular education and the FDJ is concerned, it must be said that little success has been achieved ... Where homework rooms do exist ... they do not enjoy a great deal of popularity ... The children just stream straight out of school. Besides, it is difficult to find suitable voluntary helpers for these tasks.'[22] In 1964, the FDJ leadership admitted that as many as 40 per cent of all local units did not hold meetings for months at a time.[23] As soon as school ended, pupils found themselves left to their own devices with the result that their lifeworlds were barely penetrated, let alone colonised.

Both police and teachers were forced to recognise the existence of 'hopeless cases', young people (nearly always boys) for whom ordinary methods of disciplining, shaming and punishing did not work. Restrictions on access to higher education did not have much effect on low achievers. Their value-system with its emphasis on physical strength and attaining a reputation as brutal fighters had little in common with the rather dour and anally retentive qualities expected of 'socialist personalities'. Their attention-seeking (positive or negative) was such that they often deliberately adopted aspects of the hostile stereotypes propagated by the regime, telling the police that they had been recruited by western intelligence or that 'Tag X' – the day planned for a fascist putsch – was nigh.

By deliberately provoking the regime, young nonconformists not only undermined its authority, but contradicted its claims to be in control of long-term social development. The hard-line emphasis on conscription, work camps and gang-busting failed to recognise, let alone deal with, the causes of deviance and nonconformity. Young people's thirst for experience, excitement and adventure frequently brought them into conflict with the regime. Damaged family relations, peer pressure, lack of attention and a search for recognition were persistent causes of nonconformity, particularly among boys. Once young men had embarked on deviant careers, it was very difficult to re-educate them, however 'tough' the measures used. One young offender showed what little 'deterrent effect' prison was having on him by getting one of his fellow inmates to tattoo a caricature of Ulbricht on his right buttock.[24] Open defiance on the part of girls was rare. This may in part have been because girls were subjected to significantly greater social control. Adult surveillance and parental restrictions governing 'unchaste behaviour' were far more insidious than the attention paid to them by the regime. They had much less scope for independent action before risking getting into trouble, and the recriminations when they did were more serious and unpleasant. Where girls did overtly rebel, it tended to be against the moral restrictions on appearance and behaviour.

The 1963 Youth Communiqué – an attempt at 'system-immanent liberalisation'?

With the Politbüro's publication in September 1963 of its Youth Communiqué, entitled 'Young People: Trust and Responsibility', the hard line gave way to a more moderate and optimistic policy emphasising the positive contribution of young people to the building of socialism.[25] Still, it was liberalisation within limits. The tone was markedly paternalistic and 'enemy' imagery was still to be found in among the more open-minded passages. But it represented the most radical and innovative attempt the regime had yet made to deal with young people. The exact reasons why Ulbricht opted for a partial liberalisation remain ambiguous. On the one hand, it can be seen as an attempt to take the wind out of the sails of more radical reformers. On the other, given the return to repression only two years later, the relaxation of 1963 can be seen as a disingenuous measure to trick young people into hanging themselves with their own rope. The private comments Ulbricht had made in August 1961 could certainly give that impression: 'We must discuss things openly, even with the gangs. We mustn't give the impression that we're going to lock them up straight away, there's still time for that. We must let them loose in order to identify where the enemy hides. You don't know that yet.'[26]

For all his conspiratorial rhetoric, there does seem to have been at least an implicit realisation by Ulbricht that a fundamental change was needed if problems in economy and society were to be overcome. Although inconsistent and at times highly reactionary, Ulbricht was nevertheless prepared to embark on bold and ambitious reforms. He was frustrated by the tendency of administrative hierarchies not only to block criticisms and opinions from below, but also reforms from above. In early 1962 the prerequisite for a more effective youth policy had been a change in working methods: 'That goes for all organs of the National Front, the parties, unions, FDJ and all the ministries.' The focus needed to be on local organs as it was impossible 'to direct youth policy from Berlin out'. According to Ulbricht, the aim was to 'clear the path for young people'.[27] Through a controlled release of pressure and ventilation of grievances, he hoped to overcome stagnation and stimulate greater activity among individual functionaries.

While efforts were made, particularly within the National Front, to ascertain the situation on the ground, the FDJ hierarchy remained stubbornly inactive. When presented with an FDJ draft for a new youth law, Ulbricht realised that a more radical shake-up would be needed. Legal niceties had obscured the problems actually confronting young people in their everyday lives. He criticised the draft's stilted and pedantic tone which showed 'how bureaucratised this apparatus of ours is', before making plain that such an approach would no longer be acceptable.[28]

The man Ulbricht picked to oversee the new policy was not a system-player.[29] The SED leader was impressed, however, by Kurt Turba's editorship of *Forum* magazine: '*Forum* poses genuine questions and makes a real effort to have an educational influence on young people.'[30] Through his emphasis on the need to tackle the 'psychological and intellectual problems' experienced by young people Turba had succeeded in boosting the magazine's sales as well as annoying the conservative FDJ leadership. Ulbricht encouraged Turba to be bold and innovative and gave him carte blanche in picking experts to form a new youth commission.[31]

Turba was later to take most of the blame for the 'false orientation' given by the Youth Communiqué. It was with Ulbricht's encouragement, however, that the document incorporated Turba's concept of 'impertinent socialism',[32] emphasising how young people's criticisms could be used to transform the GDR into a more open society capable of reform. Teenagers were encouraged to criticise failings in youth policy and to put pressure on local authority figures to be more active and open-minded. The communiqué not only proclaimed youngsters to be the 'masters of tomorrow', but declared that the hour of young people had already arrived.

Although sections of the communiqué continued to describe Beat music as 'American unculture' there was at least an attempt to alter the lens used to view young people. It stressed that if official youth policy were implemented more thoughtfully and effectively, the Enemy's ability to influence young people would be greatly reduced. The document was met with a mixture of jubilation in some quarters, express opposition in others and a large degree of apathy in between. For writers, songsters and film-makers it was like a breath of fresh air. They took it as a sign that the old shackles of Stalinism were gradually being removed and began experimenting with free expression by tackling previously taboo subjects. If Ulbricht had intended merely to take the wind out of reformers' sails, then he may have overestimated the degree to which large numbers of people (old and young) longed for reform. The expectation that critics would eventually talk themselves out proved wrong. Once the cork had been taken out, it was very difficult to put it back in again. Airing grievances tended to fan the flames rather than extinguish them.

In the educational sphere, the communiqué criticised overly-formalistic teaching styles which were leading to feigned allegiance. Instead it called for more attention to individual personalities and problems. The passages emphasising the need for adults to change their attitudes to (and prejudices against) young people naturally proved popular. Schoolgirls, in particular, expressed appreciation of the sections dealing with 'young love'. It was not right, they agreed, that adults should mock and tease a young person simply for having a boyfriend. On the whole, school pupils also welcomed suggestions that they be allowed more room for independent discussion. But as they all too readily pointed out, the communiqué did not actually change the situation. By freely expressing their opinions, they still risked personal disadvantage. As one schoolgirl complained: 'There's clearly too much discipline. That needs to be changed, but the question is how?'[33] For their part, teachers argued that young people should only be allowed to express their opinions when they were mature and disciplined enough to be trusted, suggesting that the likelihood of change was not all that great.

In the economic sphere, young people were presented as having innovative qualities which would help overcome lagging productivity. As part of the NÖS (Ulbricht's drive to modernise the economy), they were encouraged to pursue further qualifications and to offer suggestions on how to transform outdated work practices. Beneath talk of allowing young people greater responsibility and opportunity lay cool calculations about the ability of the socialist system to survive: 'when all is said and done, higher work productivity is decisive for the victory of the socialist societal order, for the superiority of socialism over capitalism.'[34] In essence, young people were being offered a trade-off between more autonomy in their free time and an active contribution to the building of socialism.

On the shopfloors, far from providing the 'intelligent and sensitive steering and leadership' Ulbricht had envisaged, the discussions which followed the communiqué not only revealed, but did much to exacerbate, hitherto hidden generation conflicts. Differences of experience and socialisation produced clashes over expectations and values. The younger generation proved more critical, more demanding and less easily satisfied. In contrast to older workers for whom work was an important source of identity and pride, young people tended to experience work more as an imposition than a privilege. While in their free time they could make their own decisions, work involved adapting to pre-determined rules and norms. Deprived of its ideological ballast, labour was perceived merely as a necessary evil for acquiring money, which got in the way of pursuing more enjoyable activities.[35]

The experience of work and the identity it conferred did, it is true, give members of youth sub-cultures the self-confidence that they were doing something 'real', that they were 'grown men' and that they were earning 'real money'. But the apparent lack of work discipline and pride in craftsmanship exhibited by young people, together with their 'wild' leisure behaviour frequently proved incomprehensible to older workers. 'Youth subcultures were not just straightforward reproductions of their proletarian culture of origin, but added new and often frictional elements which reflected the experiences specific to the younger generation.'[36] Contrary to adult expectations, young people regarded their autonomy as an inalienable right rather than as a reward for good behaviour. Gangs and sub-cultures provided a safety-valve and antidote to the cramping and belittling conditions experienced at work, and an opportunity to challenge the adult authorities which held sway over them during the day. Sub-cultures turned the fact of being under surveillance into the pleasure of being watched.[37]

If this type of generational conflict and its sub-cultural expression was a fairly typical development in modern industrial societies, in Germany it received an extra political cultural dimension as a result of older generations' experiences of growing up in and adapting to dictatorship. Lutz Niethammer argues that the experiences of the 'Hitler Youth generation' – raised under National Socialism, suffering defeat and occupation, only then to enjoy unexpected postwar social mobility – tended, retrospectively, to increase their allegiance to the regime.[38] But while this is particularly true of those who went on to take posts within the regime, lower down the social chain ordinary workers' attitudes remained highly ambivalent.

The obstinacy or *Eigensinn* of older workers was not just a means of preserving independence and autonomy from the regime. It also involved disciplining and controlling those underneath – in other words young people. Older generations found it difficult to understand and tolerate behaviour which deviated from norms that (in principle at least) they themselves observed. But while they were apt to complain about young people's lack of discipline and the length of their hair, they preferred to deal with young people themselves, using their own, often draconian methods rather than handing them over to the regime.[39]

While the older generation focused their criticism on drop-outs (*Gammler*), it was upwardly mobile young cadres they really feared. Older workers felt threatened by the emphasis in the communiqué and the NÖS on pay being related to qualification not experience. The issue of more qualified youngsters taking over positions currently occupied by older workers was a 'hot potato'. Not only did ambitious young 'go-getters' threaten to usurp positions already held by older workers, but they were perceived to lack the 'protective layers' older workers had built up against the regime. While they prided themselves in their work ethic, older workers were at the same time highly sceptical about schemes which involved doing more work for less pay.[40] There were even reports of older workers deliberately sabotaging youth projects in order to show that young people could not complete basic tasks without supervision.[41]

The discussions sparked by the communiqué revealed the generally low priority assigned to youth policy and its implementation at local level. Frustration with the failure of local party secretaries and work management to take young people seriously does seem to have led youth functionaries to invoke Turba's 'impertinent socialism'. A few days after publication of the communiqué, an article was published in the FDJ journal *Junge Welt*, criticising the mayor and functionaries of Delitzsch under the headline 'Have the town fathers of Delitzsch lost their heart for young people?'. They were accused of losing suggestions for improvements amid bureaucratic procrastination and incompetence and then blaming the FDJ and its functionaries for lacklustre cultural and leisure provision.[42]

To overstretched party secretaries, youth represented just another 'administrative headache'. All young people supposedly wanted were dances, but even this desire was difficult for the authorities to fulfil. The number of rooms available to young people had actually decreased by more than half between 1954 and 1960. In a third of all local communities there were no suitable facilities.[43] In rural areas, halls had often been commandeered for storing the harvest. In the towns, youth clubs tended to get taken over by rowdier elements. Arguing that such places were 'dens of iniquity', teachers frequently forbade female pupils from going anywhere near them. The fact that cola and soft drinks were much harder to come by than alcohol in the 'planned' economy of the GDR explained many of the problems that youth club leaders had in maintaining discipline. The ruling that only 40 per cent of songs played could be of western origin inevitably caused frustration when the quota was reached – in many cases often before the evening had even got started.

It was difficult to persuade young people to accept restrictions on music. 'Music is just music' was the widely held view. Describing officially produced East German popular music as 'corny', young people argued that pasteurised versions tended to take the fun out of Beat music. They resented continued interference in what they perceived as *their* sphere and described talk about 'American unculture' as nonsense.[44] In recognition of the popularity of Beat, the central FDJ leadership attempted to overcome its stuffy image by ensuring that the 1964 *Deutschland-Treffen*, an international youth jamboree, would be truly popular with young people. A special radio station, DT64, was created to cater specially for their interests and proved so popular that it not only outlived the festival, but survived the subsequent reaction against such 'distortions of youth policy'.[45]

The crackdown

Having encouraged a more open discussion of youth issues, the regime could not prevent expectations from expanding beyond the somewhat meagre improvements in work and study opportunities offered by the communiqué. Teenagers began not only to demand better leisure opportunities, but to engage in discussions about the way in which society was developing in both German states and to articulate hopes of travelling beyond the confines of the 'socialist world'.[46] Yet it was above all with the onset of Beatlemania that the attempt to institute a controlled release of pressure began to appear increasingly flawed. 1964 saw an exponential growth in the GDR of Beat groups with English names, performing cover versions of Beatles songs. While some youth functionaries tried to mediate between pressure from below and prescriptions from above, others took advantage of the increased room for manoeuvre by organising 'hot' Beat concerts under the cover of the FDJ.[47]

Peter Wicke argues that the sheer range and jumble of youth-related organisations meant that it was impossible for the authorities to exercise all-encompassing surveillance and control. In the game of 'cat and mouse' played between young people and the authorities, it was always possible to find a work canteen or somewhere on the edge of town, where the exercise of political control was more lax.[48] The speed with which Beat swept through East German youth during the course of 1964 contributed to the feeling that the situation was by no means under control. Not only could the party not compete with the extraordinary attraction of the Beatles and Rolling Stones, but there were signs that even upstanding young comrades were not immune.

The Youth Communiqué had not just awakened general expectations and grievances. It had also set in motion factions within the administration both for and against reform. Already at the beginning of 1965, the Politbüro's Ideological Commission, led by Kurt Hager, had stated that 'the personal interests of young people still stand in the foreground [while] contacts with the FDJ become ever more superficial, and the influence of the school ... and the teacher is [no longer] the most important factor'.[49] If Ulbricht had originally envisaged the communiqué as a means of overcoming young people's scepticism and indifference, Hager now argued that the communiqué was itself the cause of such attitudes.

In the power struggle which ensued between those in favour of continued modernisation and reform and those who wanted to revert to an emphasis wholly on ideology and control, the rapid upsurge of Beat seemed to offer an incontrovertible argument that reform was misguided. In order to make sure that Ulbricht shared this viewpoint, Erich Honecker began collecting evidence for a special report designed to show the dangerously high levels to which youth criminality had risen as a result of the influence of Beat music, in spite of an actual fall shown by the statistics.[50]

For journalists and members of Beat groups, the situation became highly confused. The Butlers, the most popular and successful of the Leipzig groups, had found themselves subject to continual petty harassment ever since their first public performance. But in April 1965, they suddenly found support from an unexpected quarter. *Neues Deutschland*, the official organ of the SED, published an article by Heinz Stern entitled 'Butlers' Boogie' about a concert held by the group at a youth club in Leipzig. Stern described 'the unbelievable love' the Butlers showed for their music, noting that they practised almost every day, 'often until two in the morning'. When called to a special meeting held by the SED regional authorities both Stern and the cultural editor of *Neues Deutschland* defended the Butlers against charges that they were work-shy. The Butlers worked so hard to please their public that they should be allowed to sleep once in a while, they joked. Stern was accused of committing ideological heresy by denying that it was possible to divide dance music into socialist and capitalist categories. He retorted that the music played by the Butlers was the same as that which had accompanied the civil rights marchers from Selma to Montgomery in Alabama (a reference which seems to have done little to appease the Leipzig authorities). Stern even described the harassment to which the group had been subjected as 'terror'. For their part, the Leipzig authorities interpreted the invitation for the Butlers to play at *Neues Deutschland*'s press festival as 'a deliberate provocation'.[51]

On 11 October 1965, the report prepared by Erich Honecker bore fruit in the form of a carefully orchestrated return to repression. Under Honecker's chairmanship a resolution was passed in the Secretariat of the Central Committee introducing measures forcing members of amateur groups to register with the authorities.[52] As before, the main charges against them were that they were not properly employed and were under the negative influence of western decadence, which manifested itself in English lyrics and band names. It was decided in advance that in the absence of any other charges, accusations of tax fraud would be used to brand amateur musicians criminals and thereby prevent them from playing in public.[53]

In Leipzig, the previous emphasis on the need for understanding was replaced by a strategy of defamation. In a carefully orchestrated campaign, articles were printed in the local press designed to whip up public opinion against youth excesses. An article in the *Leipziger Volkszeitung* of 20 October 1965 set the tone. Under the headline 'No room for the misuse of youth', it argued that the musicians and their fans were ill-educated, unsuitably employed, unwashed, unrestrained and 'whipped into a frenzy'. As far as young Beat fans were concerned, the campaign represented a deliberate misinterpretation of youth culture and an attempt to demonise their behaviour. 'It's like a sensationalist report by one of Springer's hirelings in the "Bild"-Zeitung [West Germany's leading tabloid]', one reader complained. 'Facts are mixed with lies and slanders in such an unbelievable way that the reader is presented with a distorted and untrue picture.'[54] While party editorials argued that the Enemy had used Beat music to turn young people against their state, members of Beat groups criticised the FDJ's sudden lurch to the right.[55]

When Beat fans in Leipzig planned a not particularly secret demonstration against the ban in October 1965, the regime moved to crush what it saw as signs of anarchy and 'Beat fanaticism'. Under Honecker's supervision, the police and Stasi staged a counter-demonstration of force. The town centre was flooded with policemen both in uniform and plain clothes. Patrols with dogs rounded up suspicious-looking individuals. Groups of demonstrators were broken up with water cannon and baton-charges, resulting in 267 arrests; dozens of those detained were sent straight for re-education in the coal mines in unhygienic and highly demeaning conditions.[56]

Isolated voices, from youth club leaders in particular, expressed concern at the official overreaction and argued that destroying young people's idols would prove counter-productive.[57] The authorities reacted to criticisms that such measures represented a restriction on personal freedom by having those who voiced them dismissed. The *Leipziger Volkszeitung* even justified the measures by publishing a picture of the Beatles holding armalite rifles, thereby implicitly linking Beat excesses to militarism:

> For those of you who don't recognise it, this is the Beatles, carrying not guitars but guns, responsible for the waging of war and genocide. An unsurprising fact given that the English government supports the crimes of its US allies in Vietnam! Today Beat – tomorrow sub-machine-guns and helmets. Today brutalisation – tomorrow war against peace-loving peoples. This is the imperialists' policy, driving the feelings of young people in false and dangerous directions, manipulating them for their class aims. The imperialist powers use the Beatles to propagate their psychological warfare, by holding up the Texas Ranger ethos as a role model for young people. It is no accident that this picture was found in the possession of young Leipzigers. This picture shows the absurdity of the oft-repeated claims about the 'peaceful' and 'harmless' nature of the western way of life.[58]

If the exacerbation of generational conflicts by the Youth Communiqué was unintentional, the massive overreaction to the demonstration by Beat fans can be seen as a conscious campaign of negative integration. The regime deliberately manufactured a symbolic showdown in order to have a scapegoat to divert attention away from problems inherent in the socialist project. Existing political stereotypes made it all too easy for the regime to project past fascism onto the contemporary West and then back onto young people in East Germany. Beat music made youngsters 'agents of fascist imperialism'. While even after the arrests and internments young people continued to protest their innocence, the 'moral panic' whipped up over Beat also served to forge a cultural consensus between officialdom and the older generation. In re-embracing the notion that the preservation of social order necessitated cultural purity, regime hardliners began unconsciously aping Nazi rhetoric. As an antidote to the disease caused by pernicious foreign influences, they prescribed a large dose of 'clean' German culture, or *Volkstümlichkeit*.

For the older generation the attack on Beat served to confirm the prejudices which – intentionally or unintentionally – had been fostered by the Youth Communiqué. In spite (or perhaps because) of their more direct and complicit experiences of war and Nazism, older East Germans were all too eager to point an accusatory finger at young people. The conclusions and lessons they drew from the incident were applied not just to Beat fans, but to young people as a whole. Deliberate misattribution in the press ensured that stigma was attached not only to young people who performed particular delinquent acts or who wore certain clothes, but to a particular social status, that of the adolescent. There was no longer any attempt to differentiate between 'young Turks' who were active members of the FDJ and the music fans and delinquents who were not. Young people as a whole were deemed to be irresponsible, immature, arrogant and lacking in respect for authority, however individually qualified, committed or engaged they happened to be.

The conflicts brought to a head by the communiqué were resolved with a purge of pro-reformers within the administration. Following the swing to repression instigated by Honecker and his allies in the summer of 1965, the youth commissions were wound up at central and local level. Those who had proved overeager in embracing what was now described as a 'false orientation', were removed. Wolf Biermann, the singer-songwriter whose father had been murdered by the Nazis at Auschwitz, was branded a 'rowdy'. The voices calling for reform since the late 1950s were effectively silenced. The FDJ hierarchy created by Honecker was firmly back in control. As Minister for Education, his wife, Margot, was able to dictate education policy. The suggestion that there was an alternative to a firm party line was no longer permissible. The Minister for State Security, Erich Mielke, drew up a new set of guidelines for dealing 'systematically' with nonconformist groups, noting that: 'The imperialist threat, in particular the measures of the West German imperialists for the preparation of a concealed war against the GDR, forces us to be more energetic in putting an end to the occurrence of such groups and above all to ensure that such herds do not arise in future. This is all the more urgently necessary because the appearance of such groups can easily be used by the Enemy as a means of feigning "resistance."'[59]

Conclusion

The repressive policy implemented in 1961 attacked the symptoms of nonconformity without dealing with the causes. The more liberal policy embodied in the 1963 Communiqué identified problems, without following through with solutions. While this represented a partial recognition of the problems inherent in the education system and the failures of official youth policy, it did not lead to fundamental changes. The Communiqué focused criticism on the inactivity of local functionaries and overformal and ineffective education in schools, but the figures of authority criticised remained the same ones responsible for overseeing its implementation.

Although the regime occasionally showed itself willing to sweeten its youth policy with attempts to recognise some of the problems affecting young people, such efforts were not accompanied by a recognition of interests which diverged from those of the state. Although the party had briefly encouraged young people's independence, initiative and creativity, it very quickly showed that it could not tolerate any developments beyond its rigid control.

In a period of social transformation the attempt to reduce conflicts and preserve the ideal of a conflict-free society often leads to renewed emphasis on supervising, educating and controlling youth as a result of its symbolic role as harbinger of the future. Whether intentional or not, by placing young people on a pedestal, the regime made it easier to knock them down. By making them responsible for solving societal problems as the 'masters of tomorrow', it was easier to scapegoat them for the failures of its own current policies.

Notes

1 Research for this chapter was supported by grants from the British Academy and the German Historical Institute, London. For their helpful criticism I would like to thank Josie McLellan and Frank Schulz.
2 Ulrich Mählert and Gerd-Rüdiger Stephan, *Blaue Hemden – Rote Fahnen: Die Geschichte der Freien Deutschen Jugend* (Opladen, 1996); Ulrich Mählert, *Die Freie Deutsche Jugend 1945–1949: Von den 'Antifaschistischen Jugendauschüssen' zur SED-Massenorganisation* (Paderborn, 1995); Leonore Ansorg, '"Für Frieden und Sozialismus - seid bereit!": Zur politischen Instrumentalisierung der Jungen Pioniere von Beginn ihrer Gründung bis Ende der 1950er Jahre', in Jürgen Kocka (ed.), *Historische DDR-Forschung: Aufsätze und Studien* (Berlin, 1993), 169–90; Sonja Häder, 'Von der "demokratischen Schulreform" zur Stalinisierung des Bildungswesens', in Jürgen Kocka (ed.) *Historische DDR-Forschung*, 191–214.
3 Patrick von zur Mühlen, *Der 'Eisenberger Kreis': Jugendwiderstand und Verfolgung in der DDR 1953–1958* (Bonn, 1995).
4 Michael Rauhut, 'DDR-Beatmusik zwischen Engagement und Repression', in Günter Agde (ed.), *Kahlschlag: Das 11. Plenum der SED 1965* (Berlin, 1991), 52–63; Michael Rauhut, *Beat in der Grauzone: DDR-Rock 1964 bis 1972 – Politik und Alltag* (Berlin, 1993); Peter Wicke, 'Rock around socialism: Jugend und ihre Musik in einer gescheiterten Gesellschaft', in D. Baacke (ed.), *Handuch Jugend und Musik* (Opladen, 1998), 293–305.
5 On the unofficial ways in which functionaries transformed policy, see Kerstin Thöns, 'Jugendpolitik in der DDR zwischen staatlichem Erziehungsanspruch und Selbstgestaltungsinteresse', in Helga Gotschlich (ed.), *'Links und links und Schritt gehalten...': Die FDJ: Konzepte–Abläufe–Grenzen* (Berlin, 1994), 227–41; Monika Kaiser, *Machtwechsel von Ulbricht zu Honecker: Funktionsmechanismen der SED-Diktatur in Konfliktsituationen 1962 bis 1972* (Berlin, 1997).
6 SAPMO-BArch, DY 6/3940, 'Analyse über die Lage unter der Jugend', 1–4.
7 Dorothee Wierling, 'Die Jugend als innerer Feind: Konflikte in der Erziehungsdiktatur der sechziger Jahre', in Hartmut Kaelbe *et al.* (eds), *Sozialgeschichte der DDR* (Stuttgart, 1994), 404–25, esp. 420–1; Dorothee Wierling, 'The Hitler youth generation in the GDR: insecurities, ambitions and dilemmas', in Konrad H. Jarausch (ed.), *Dictatorship as Experience: Towards a*

Socio-Cultural History of the GDR (New York and Oxford, 1999), 307–24.
8 The terms for combating nonconformity – 'reconnaissance, subversion, liquidation' – deliberately evoked guerrilla warfare. By the end of August 1961, a total of 77 'notorious work-shy, alcoholic and asocial elements' in Leipzig had been interned in work camps: Sächsisches Staatsarchiv Leipzig (SStAL), BDVP 24.1/201, 'Ergebnisse im Zusammenhang der Regierungsmaßnahmen v. 13.8.61'.
9 SAPMO-BArch, DY 24/3727, 'Rede des Genossen Walter Ulbricht im Politbüro am 22.8.1961'.
10 43,658 people aged 15–25 fled from January–September 1960, the majority young men. 10,546 people returned to the GDR in the same period: Wierling, 'Die Jugend', 406.
11 Ulbricht radio address in Hartwig Bögelholz, *Deutsch-deutsche Zeiten – Eine Chronik: Deutschland von 1945 bis 1995* (Munich, 1996).
12 SAPMO-BArch, DY 24/3726, Abt. Org.-Instrukteure, 'Information über Feindtätigkeit... vom 23.11.1961'.
13 For an account of the Anklam incident, see Mary Fulbrook, *Anatomy of a Dictatorship: Inside the GDR 1949–1989* (Oxford, 1995), 1–3.
14 Bundesarchiv Berlin (BAB), DR-2/6956, Abt. Oberschulen, 'Arbeit der Volksbildungsorgane in den Bezirken und Kreisen (Jan. 1960–Dez. 1961) – Informations- und Situationsberichte'.
15 Zentralinstitut für Jugendforschung, *Umfrage 69* (Leipzig, 1970), 25.
16 SStAL, IV A2/9.02/353, 'Bemerkungen zu den Fragen der Disziplin und Ordnung', 21 March 1964, fo. 64.
17 BAB, DR-2/4672, Freyer, 'Informationsbericht', 27 May 1959, fos 145–9.
18 BAB, DR-2/6298, 'Vertraulich! Sektor Örtliche Organe: Argumente zum Nationalen Dokument', 5 June 1962.
19 SAPMO-BArch, IV A2/9.02/353, 'Bemerkungen zu den Fragen der Disziplin und Ordnung'.
20 BAB, DR-2/6298, 'Argumente zum Nationalen Dokument'; StAL, IV A2/9.02/353, fo. 63.
21 Leipzig Stadtarchiv, StVuRdS, Nr. 2311, 'Informationsbericht zweite Hälfte November 1961', 4 December 1961.
22 SStAL, RdB Bildung, Kultur und Sport: 1723, 'Auswertung der Jahresanalyse der Kreise (1957) auf dem Gebiete des Jugendschutzes', 27 January 1958.
23 Thöns, 'Jugendpolitik', 238, n. 36.
24 SStAL, BDVP 24.1/348.
25 'Der Jugend Vertrauen und Verantwortung', *Neues Deutschland*, 21 September 1963, 1–3.
26 SAPMO-BArch, DY 24/3727, 'Rede des Genossen Walter Ulbricht im Politbüro am 22.8.1961'.
27 Thöns, 'Jugendpolitik', 235.
28 Rauhut, *Beat in der Grauzone*, 61–2.
29 Turba had been expelled from the party in 1953: Ulrike Schuster, '"Seine Intelligenz führte zu einer für ihn ungesunden Entwicklung": Bemerkungen anhand einer DDR-Biographie', in Gotschlich (ed.), *Links und links*, 242–50; See also Ulrike Schuster, *Wissen ist Macht: FDJ, Studenten und die Zeitung Forum in der SBZ/DDR* (Berlin, 1997), Ch. 5.

30 Rauhut, *Beat in der Grauzone*, 62.
31 Kaiser, *Machtwechsel*, 146–7.
32 Rauhut, *Beat in der Grauzone*, 60.
33 SStAL, IV A2/16/454, 'Einschätzung und Berichte zur Durchsetzung des Jugendkommuniqués, 1963–1966'.
34 SAPMO-BArch, DY 6/3940, 'Die arbeitende Jugend und ihre sozialistische Erziehung, Förderung und Entwicklung', fo. 10.
35 Hans-Jürgen Wensierski, '"Die anderen nannten uns Halbstarke": Jugendsubkultur in den 50er Jahren', in Heinz-Hermann Krüger (ed.), *'Die Elvis-Tolle, die hatte ich mir unauffällig wachsen lassen': Lebensgeschichte und jugendliche Alltagskultur in den fünfziger Jahren* (Opladen, 1985), 103–28.
36 This was also true for the reactions of older workers to youth sub-culture during the Third Reich. See Detlef Peukert, *Inside Nazi Germany: Conformity, Opposition and Racism in Everyday Life* (London, 1993), 171–2.
37 Wensierski, '"Die anderen nannten uns Halbstarke"', 118.
38 Lutz Niethammer, 'Zeroing in on change: in search of popular experience in the industrial province of the German Democratic Republic', in Alf Lüdtke (ed.), *The History of Everyday life: Reconstructing Historical Experiences and Ways of Life* (Princeton, NJ, 1995), 252–311.
39 Michael Hofmann, 'Die Leipziger Metallarbeiter: Etappen sozialer Erfahrungsgeschichte: Milieubiographie eines Arbeitermilieus in Leipzig', in Michael Vester *et al.* (eds), *Soziale Milieus in Ostdeutschland* (Cologne, 1995), 136–92, esp. 174.
40 Members of a youth brigade at a power plant in Lübbenau making enormous efforts to implement the six-day week were described by other workmates as 'class traitors': SAPMO-BArch, DY 24/3726, Abt. Org.-Instrukteure, 'Information über Feindtätigkeit . . . vom 23.11.1961'.
41 SStAL, IV A2/16/454, SED-Leipzig, 'Analyse zum Stand der Jugendpolitik der Partei . . .', 26 February 1964.
42 *Ibid.*, 'Inhaltliche und organisatorische Probleme und Maßnahmen zur Vorbereitung des Jugendforums . . .', 23 September 1963; 'Haben die Stadtväter von Delitzsch das Herz für die Jugend verloren', *Junge Welt*, 23 September 1963.
43 SAPMO-BArch, DY 6/3940, 'Analyse über die Lage unter der Jugend . . .', 1 February 1962, fo. 9.
44 SStAL, IV A2/16/454, 'Einschätzung und Berichte zur Durchsetzung des Jugendkommuniqués, 1963–1966'; Büro Schulen, 'Meinungen zum Kommuniqué', 21 September 1963.
45 On the Deutschland-Treffen, see Kaiser, *Machtwechsel*, 159–67; also 'Sonne, Sex und Sozialismus', *Der Spiegel*, 27 May 1964.
46 Thöns, 'Jugendpolitik', 238.
47 Rauhut, *Beat in der Grauzone*, 55.
48 Wicke, 'Rock around socialism', 293–305.
49 Thöns, 'Jugendpolitik', 239, fn. 40.
50 Kaiser, *Machtwechsel*, 171, and Dieter Plath, 'Über Kriminalität und innere Sicherheit', in Agde, *Kahlschlag*, 32–8.
51 See the interview with Butlers' frontman in Hans-Dieter Schütt (ed.), *Klaus Renft: Zwischen Liebe und Zorn: Die Autobiographie* (Berlin, 1997).
52 Reproduced in Agde (ed.), *Kahlschlag*, 320.

53 Michael Rauhut, 'Der Tag an dem die Illusionen starben', *Freitag*, 48 (23 November 1990), 19. Of the forty-nine amateur groups registered in Leipzig, only five retained their licences to play. In addition to providing proof of their positive attitude to the Workers' and Peasants' State, musicians had to show that they were gainfully employed. Groups with 'American' names were rejected outright.
54 SStAL, SED IV A2/16/464, 'Analyse der Leserzuschriften zu Problemen der Jugend', 26 November 1965, fo. 163.
55 *Ibid.*, 'Information über die Aussprache mit den "The Butlers" am 22.10.1965', fos 99–101.
56 Once forcibly shorn, the demonstrators had to spend the next week wearing the clothes they had been arrested in, together with severe restrictions on their use of toilet facilities. For eyewitness accounts see Schütt (ed.), *Klaus Renft*, 58–64; Erich Loest, *Es geht seinen Gang* (Stuttgart, 1978); '"Ich war sechzehn..."': Erinnerungen von J. Wede', *Freitag*, 48 (23 November 1990), 19.
57 SStAL, SED IV A2/16/464, fo.154.
58 'Beatles, Ledernacken, Aggression', *Leipziger Volkszeitung*, 5 November 1965.
59 Erich Mielke, Dienstanweisung Nr. 4/66, 'Zur politisch-operativen Bekämpfung der politisch-ideologischen Diversion und Untergrundtätigkeit unter jugendlichen Personenkreisen in der DDR', 15 May 1966.

11

Going west: the open border and the problem of *Republikflucht*

Patrick Major

In a well-to-do suburb of East Berlin, on an autumn afternoon in 1960, six men and a woman loitered with intent outside a doctor's home. They were planning to break into the apartment of one Dr H., recently granted a visa to attend a medical congress in Karlsruhe in West Germany. H. had not returned. As the subsequent enquiry recorded:

> Towards 1 p.m. on 15.9.1960 two comrades from Criminal Investigation, the deputy director of Internal Affairs, director of administration at Oranienburg hospital, local police patrolman and mayor entered the above-named's apartment in the presence of his housekeeper. Entry was gained by the patrolman and CID comrades by means of a ladder, who then opened the terrace door from the inside to afford the other persons entry. Thereupon the apartment was jointly searched for signs of a *Republikflucht*. Apparently the television, vacuum-cleaner and other objects were no longer in Dr H.'s apartment. Dr H. had written to his housekeeper from West Germany that he had fallen ill and would probably be returning a little late. He requested the latter to keep his mail for him at a prearranged place. This mail was taken by the CID comrades during the house search and later opened at the station where some of the stamps were removed.

But then came an unexpected twist:

> On the evening of 16.9.1960 Dr H. returned from West Germany. When he found his apartment sealed and learned from his housekeeper of the previous day's events, he went with her straight to the chairman of the district council's home and complained about the illegal actions of the above-mentioned comrades. Dr H. is said to have been very upset and distraught at the measures taken against him ... Dr H. was last seen at his domicile in Lehnitz, *Kreis* Oranienburg, on 18.9.1960 and has most probably departed the GDR illegally.[1]

H. was only one of over 3.5 million East Germans to commit the crime of *Republikflucht* (literally 'flight from the Republic') by crossing the Iron Curtain into West Germany. In this case the authorities had seemingly lent an unwitting hand. It was this mass exodus which prompted the Communist leadership in August 1961 to take the drastic action of sealing off the GDR from the West with a concrete and barbed-wire barrier, the infamous Berlin Wall. Throughout the 1950s, the open border had provided a loophole to effective dictatorship, causing the SED serious economic difficulties and forcing it to make various political concessions to sections of the population at risk of absconding. Dr H. was a case in point. A travel visa was a rare privilege by 1960. Yet, for those not fortunate enough to receive official permission to leave, the sector boundary in the divided city of Berlin was comparatively easy to cross on the subway or through a thin police cordon.

We have relatively reliable figures for the total exodus, both from the West German refugee administration and East German police. The West counted 2,583,302 refugees from January 1950 to 13 August 1961; the East 2,448,671, plus 311,700 legal emigrants, who included a high proportion of children and elderly. If one adds an estimated 876,200 inhabitants who left the SBZ from 1945-49 (but ignoring the 1.5 million expellees who passed through from the former eastern territories), this yields a grand total of 3.5–3.7 million. Even deducting the 428,964 'returnees', plus 167,278 immigrants from West Germany, this still leaves a net loss of 3 out of 18 million – or one in six.[2] Whereas West Germany swelled from 47.3 to 56.2 million between 1948 and 1961, the GDR, despite new births, dwindled from 19.1 to 17.1 million. Indeed, on the eve of the Wall the GDR's economic apparatus was labelling the situation 'very serious', as the workforce threatened to shrink by almost 10 per cent over the course of the current Seven-Year Plan.[3]

For a more subtle sense of the dynamics involved see the monthly figures in Figure 1, which show *Republikflucht* peaking during the summer months, with a minor surge at Easter, as holidaytime provided an alibi for heavy luggage. Seasonal work was also a factor. There was nevertheless more than an annual rhythm to the figures. It is clear that some years were far worse than others, suggesting contingent factors. The two periods associated most closely with social conflict in the early GDR were 1952–53 – the 'building of socialism' – followed in 1958-61 by the 'transition to socialism'. 1953, the year of the abortive insurrection, seems to fit this pattern, as losses peaked; conversely, 1958–61 (apart from the very final phase) was relatively quiet. Indeed, the preceding years 1955–57 were far more costly.

How do we explain this huge absolute loss with such considerable ebbs and flows? Was it a concerted 'leap to freedom', as western commentators claimed? The motives were certainly complex, but can perhaps be broken down into three main categories: political, economic and situational. By 'political' I mean both principled anticommunism based upon an alternative

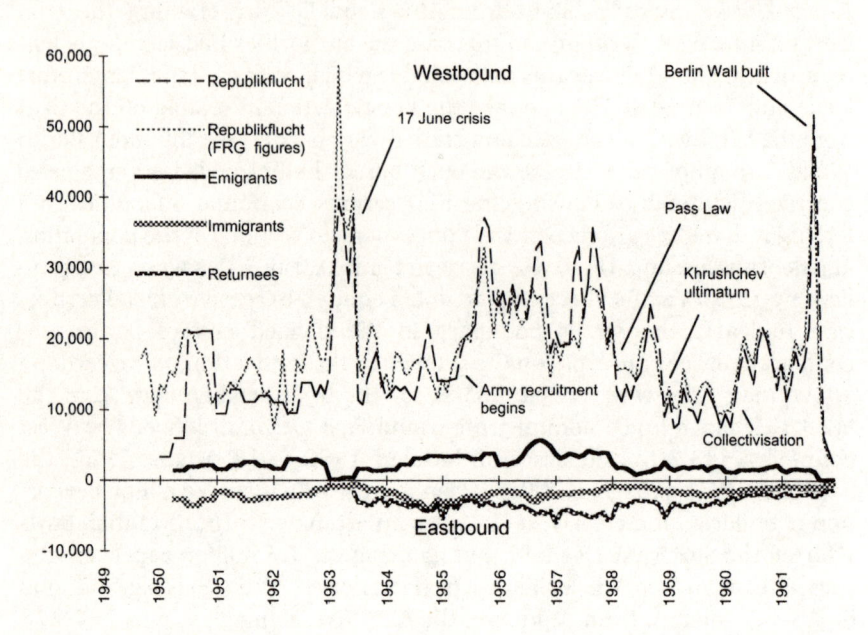

Figure 1 *Movements across the open border 1949–61 (monthly)*

[Figure shows monthly movement data from 1949-1961 with curves for Republikflucht, Republikflucht (FRG figures), Emigrants, Immigrants, and Returnees. Annotations mark: 17 June crisis, Army recruitment begins, Pass Law, Khrushchev ultimatum, Collectivisation, Berlin Wall built. Westbound movements range up to ~60,000; Eastbound movements shown below zero line down to -10,000.]

Source: Unless otherwise stated, figures are East German. See note 2.

world view, be it social democracy, nationalism or Christianity, as well as pragmatic avoidance of specific duties, such as military service or informing for the Stasi. These might also be labelled 'push factors', since they were generated within the East German system. Economic motivations have usually been viewed as 'pull factors' originating in the FRG's 'economic miracle', although, as will become evident, East German production and supply created their own share of disaffection.

More neglected perhaps was the situational predisposition of certain groups to leave. Besides personal biography and psychology, which will remain largely a closed book, there were many historical reasons why one particular worker or farmer would stay, while another would go. By the 1950s many traditional ties to *Heimat* had been considerably loosened. The Second World War had displaced about a quarter of the German population. A tangle of evacuees, retreating eastwards from Allied bombing and westwards from the Red Army, conspicuously failed to put down roots in eastern Germany. 'Resettlers' also accounted for an abnormally high proportion of *Republikflüchtige*. Under the SBZ this has been estimated at two-thirds, dipping markedly in the early 1950s, before reaching around a quarter prior to the Wall.[4] Areas of high concentration reported that many repatriated Germans were simply using the GDR as a 'springboard' to the West, where they were guaranteed financial compensation.[5] In general, it was the north which had borne the brunt of the expellee influx and which also witnessed most departures. Conversely, it may be more than a coincidence that in the Sorb areas of the south-east, with their own distinct ethnic identity, *Republikflucht* remained low.[6]

Many of the indigenous population had also lost their homes in the war. Frankfurt an der Oder was almost completely destroyed in ground-fighting; two-thirds of Dresden had been razed by fire-bombing; half of Berlin was devastated.[7] Rebuilding proceeded slowly in the East, but faster in the West. This partly explains why in the 1950s a steady stream of family reunions occurred, as easterners received residence permits to join western relatives. As well as family cohesion, marital breakdown could cause footlooseness, with some estranged partners seeking refuge beyond the Iron Curtain. Moreover, many young people had lost parents in the war. Among one sample of 550 young refugees in the mid-1950s, 40 per cent had lost one or both parents (in nearly all cases the father).[8] As family members departed, a chain reaction could develop, as kin left behind were discriminated against for having so-called 'grade-1 western relatives', prompting their own departure. At the Leuna chemical works in Merseburg around 30 per cent of employees had western friends and relations with whom they regularly corresponded. Nearly a third of these made annual western visits, giving them ample opportunity to experience the FRG, where relatives were suspected of encouraging them to stay.[9] From 1950 to 1961 there were 13.5 million such trips by East Germans to West Germany, with over 9 million in the opposite direction.[10] While prospects of national reunification receded, many private reunions clearly continued unabated.

Situational factors are perhaps more obvious with hindsight. At the time, both Cold War camps favoured political explanations, largely as a form of propagandistic point-scoring. In the West it was expedient to stress the political nature of departures as a way of delegitimising the GDR. The failures of socialism were measured by those 'voting with their feet' to abandon it.[11] Former GDR citizens' groups labelled themselves 'refugees', and parliament and press reinforced the terminology, resisting later attempts to normalise communist dictatorship by redefining newcomers as 'migrants'.[12] There is no doubt that among the first to leave the SBZ were leaders of non–Communist parties – in the first wave former National Socialists, followed from 1946 by Social, Christian and Liberal Democrats at odds with Stalinism. Marxist–Leninist ideology had also identified various 'natural' class enemies, such as industrialists and landowners, unwelcome in the antifascist–democratic order. Yet, upon arrival at reception camps in the West, it was in refugees' interests to play up the political circumstances of departure. If they could convince interview panels that they had been politically or religiously persecuted, they might receive the coveted C-Certificate, entitling them to financial compensation and housing assistance.

Nevertheless, interviewers soon became sceptical of many claims of persecution in the SBZ. Indeed, in the early years, over half of asylum-seekers were turned away, and all told only 14.2 per cent fulfilled the legal definition of political duress, with a further 10 per cent receiving discretionary C-Certificates.[13]

The GDR authorities had even more of a tendency to politicisation. The term *Republikflucht* itself had deliberate connotations with *Fahnenflucht*, or military desertion, implying abandonment of the socialist cause in the face of the capitalist enemy. Indeed, SED functionaries entertained elaborate conspiracy theories of an omnipresent Cold War 'Adversary'. Rather than suggest that refugees had gone of their own volition, they had instead been 'recruited' by the Adversary. Voluminous Stasi dossiers documented the head-hunting activities of western Allied espionage agencies and West German companies as part of a 'master plan of international reaction'.[14] According to one Volkspolizei commander, the Bonn leadership was manipulating the refugee flood to sabotage the socialist experiment. Those claiming that departures were apolitical were morally blind, since *Republikflucht* was objectively 'betrayal of the GDR'.[15] Young men were thus reminded of their military pledges to the socialist fatherland, and doctors of their Hippocratic oaths to patients. Nonetheless, although there is no doubt that some talent-spotting was occurring, it was probably in thousands rather than millions, not enough to account for the mass scale of the exodus.

What the eastern authorities found more difficult to admit was that some of their own policies might be at the root of many departures; instead, poor implementation – so-called 'heartless bureaucratism' – was alienating the populace. However, the fact that heavy losses among certain groups occurred at times of socio-economic upheaval was hardly a coincidence. For instance, in spring 1953, as tensions mounted before the 17 June uprising, *Republikflucht* reached epidemic proportions. The number of '*kulak*' farmers fleeing was tenfold what it had been the previous autumn. Nearly as many factory owners left in the first half of 1953 as in the whole remaining decade. Small businessmen and artisans, but also intelligentsia and white-collar workers, were also fleeing in above-average numbers. It is difficult to escape the conclusion that the confrontational politics associated with 1952's 'building of socialism' were taking their toll. The collectivisation of agriculture had begun; higher taxes were being levied against businesses; and artisans were being encouraged into Production Cooperatives. On top of this came blanket resentment of price and work norm rises threatening the general standard of living. Rather than take to the streets, many simply left the country. At times of heightened class struggle the state also criminalised target groups, replacing fines with custodial sentences. Whereas in 1949 only 341 persons had fled to avoid prosecution, in 1953 it was estimated at 13,060.[16] Although the New Course, designed to placate the population with reforms, reduced the refugee flow by around 80 per cent in the first few days, the uprising itself led to another massive haemorrhage, requiring temporary closure of the sector border to staunch it. Yet since numbers rose again in the autumn, the police had to concede that it was not simply a case of 'only provocateurs leaving our Republic in fear'.[17]

Indeed, the regime continued to alienate even potential allies. As Volker Ackermann has pointed out, flight did not have to spring from a principled stand against Communism, but could be the evasion of a specific obligation, such as drafting into the uranium mines or Volkspolizei.[18] Taking the case of youth in the mid-1950s, when the GDR's armed forces were emerging, young men aged 18–23 were bombarded with calls to join up. Given that the next conflict would at best be civil war, and at worst nuclear armageddon, their reluctance was understandable. Despite the fact that there was no official conscription, the authorities cajoled many into 'volunteering', some of whom then fled as the call-up date approached. Recruitment reached particular intensity in the spring of 1955, when the KVP were seeking cadres for the nascent NVA. This resulted in the proportion of young male refugees leaping from 18.2 per cent in February to 48.5 per cent in June, and staying abnormally high throughout 1955–57.[19] More alarming for the authorities was the changing complexion of young absconders:

> Whereas until the recruitment for the KVP it was mainly persons blinded by trash literature, black propaganda and family members, some of whom exhibited an openly negative attitude to our Workers'-and-Peasants'-State, now it is a group sometimes reported to be diligent and disciplined. In many cases they are members of the Free German Youth or even young members of our party.[20]

This is a good example of how the SED repeatedly turned even conformist members of the citizenry into opponents by moving the goalposts of social obligation. However, recruitees could play the system too. Even a short stay in the West would render them 'contaminated' in the eyes of the GDR security services and thus unfit for military duty. The open border thus played an important role in deterring the regime from introducing full-scale conscription. Only in the shadow of the Wall was mandatory military service introduced in 1962.

Church-goers also came under mounting pressure. Although 80 per cent of the population was nominally Protestant in 1950, over the decade hundreds of thousands left the church, peaking at 158,736 in 1958 alone. In 1954 a secular rite of passage, the *Jugendweihe* (see also Merrilyn Thomas' Chapter 12 in this volume), was introduced for fourteen year-olds, in competition with church confirmation. Members of the Protestant youth group, Junge Gemeinde, were ostracised by the regime, which routinely refused to let them go on to sixth-form or university. This bureaucratic obstructionism is reflected in fleeing church officers' reports, despite the hierarchy's injunction to stay.[21] In 1958, after the Bundeswehr started recruiting military chaplains, the SED took this as further evidence that the clergy were in league with the 'other side', seeing the worst flights by priests since 1953. It was also the year of Ulbricht's 'Ten Commandments of Socialist Morality', when religious studies were effectively removed from the school curriculum.[22] It was therefore no accident that in 1958 teachers' *Republikflucht* peaked, with over 3 per cent leaving in that year alone, and many citing anticlericalism as the cause.[23]

There is also evidence that SED policy was driving away other members of the educational bourgeoisie. The 'old', pre-1945 academic intelligentsia watched with trepidation as a new generation of younger cadres graduated. At the same time, children of academics fell foul of a quota system guaranteeing working-class children university places. In 1958 the 'socialist remodelling' of higher education promised a showdown with 'petit-bourgeois' elements and the inclusion of Marxist–Leninist studies on all curricula, including the sciences. It was also the worst year by far for the defection of academics (see Table 1), when over 200 left in comparison with 58 the previous year, the worst-depleted faculty being medicine, accounting for half of all losses. The situation among general practitioners was no better, once doctors learned of plans for the expansion of the state health sector and the wind-down of private practices. The medical exodus was so marked in 1958, that for the first time the GDR lost more doctors in one year than it could train. Moreover, the disappearance of colleagues placed horrendous strain on remaining hospital wards and surgeries.[24]

As well as domestic political factors, high politics could also cause disaffection. As the prospect of national reunification dwindled, during dramatic breakdowns in East–West relations, flights tended to increase. Thus, after the outbreak of the Korean War the *Republikflucht* curve rose. During superpower rapprochement, such as at the Berlin Conference of Foreign Ministers of 1954, or the Geneva summit of 1955, it dipped.[25] In the 1950s the Cold War had not quite attained its later sense of immutability. Many East German citizens patently believed, however overoptimistically, that 'things could turn out different' and that it might be worth hanging on. The clearest evidence for the nexus between high politics and the abandonment of wait-and-see attitudes comes from the second Berlin Crisis. When the first sixth-month deadline approached after Khrushchev's ultimatum of November 1958, some intelligentsia in East Berlin decided that it was now or never.[26] Later, in 1959, while Khrushchev visited Eisenhower in the USA and hopes of a solution lingered, flight remained low, whereas the collapse of the Paris summit in 1960, after the shooting down of the American U-2 spy plane, seems to have contributed to a renewed wave. The superpowers' failure to resolve their diplomatic differences in Vienna in June 1961 triggered what even the SED Politbüro called a 'stampede panic'.[27] The Volkspolizei concluded that 'every time that the Adversary played up the West Berlin question, a rise in *Republikflucht* was ascertained'.[28] And despite the secrecy surrounding the building of the Wall, there were constant

Table 1 Republikflucht among the intelligentsia 1949–61 (absolute figures)

Year	Engineers		Medics*		Teachers		Academics		Students	
Source:	FRG	GDR	FRG	GDR	FRG	GDR	FRG	GDR	FRG	GDR
1949	1,740	n. a.	420	n. a.	1,830	n. a.	170	n. a.	1,500	n. a.
1950	1,850	n. a.	430	n. a.	1,890	n. a.	170	n. a.	1,300	n. a.
1951	1,430	n. a.	350	n. a.	1,460	n. a.	140	n. a.	1,100	n. a.
1952	1,357	n. a.	326	n. a.	1,392	n. a.	146	n. a.	942	991
1953	2,070	1,892	534	571	2,411	1,960	135	97	1,353	1,719
1954	1,624	1,155	270	201	2,045	1,498	43	50	880	891
1955	2,474	2,699	344	290	2,720	2,223	56	69	1,835	1,806
1956	2,672	2,080	467	501	2,453	1,995	43	54	1,431	1,542
1957	2,198	1,824	440	425	2,293	1,796	58	58	1,894	1,434
1958	2,345	1,679	1,242	1,271	3,089	2,611	208	235	2,522	2,043
1959	1,590	1,300	777	796	1,252	979	188	125	1,496	937
1960	2,648	2,271	1,063	1,137	2,033	1,718	142	169	1,646	1,053
1961	3,336	2,930	1,075	1,128	2,006	1,778	32	190	2,790	2,235

Source: See note 2.
* 'Medics' includes doctors, dentists and vets.

rumours beforehand that the borders would be closed one way or another. Ulbricht's famous indiscretion at a press conference in June 1961, that 'nobody intends to build a wall', only fuelled such speculation.[29]

There are nevertheless obvious limits to a politics-only interpretation of Republikflucht. As already mentioned, even the western authorities were unwilling to recognise the vast majority of asylum-seekers as political. It is perhaps also just a little too neat to view the monthly figures as a 'seismograph' of popular opinion, triggered by ideological jolts from the SED. Based on falling Republikflucht in the late 1950s, it has even been suggested that the GDR was beginning to witness a 'social consolidation'.[30] A perhaps more compelling reason for the drop in 1958 will be offered below. The political interpretation also has potentially misleading implications for those left behind. By assuming that only those with initiative and drive would leave, a popular image emerged of a docile rump population. It might just as well be argued, however, that those seeking an easy life were the first to go, while it was often the obstreperous who stood their ground. As Corey Ross has convincingly suggested, those remaining still had the trump card of potential defection to make a number of demands on the system, in letters to the local housing office and petitions to the party.[31]

The East German authorities themselves realised that there was a limit to political conspiracy theories. At a policy discussion in late 1956, voices called for a change in terminology from Republikflucht to 'emigration': 'The majority of those leaving the German Democratic Republic are doing so not because they disagree with our system, but above all for economic and other reasons. Thus, they are not fleeing but emigrating.'[32] Historically, population movements since the nineteenth century had always followed an

East–West pattern, between an underdeveloped agrarian East and an urbanising West. Clearly, the 1950s were not the 1890s, but can some, or even most, of the 3 million be explained as an internal migration, succumbing to the 'pull factor' of an economically superior West? Bonn was also beginning to reach a more differentiated picture by the mid-1950s, commissioning a public opinion agency, Infratest, to survey refugees. The researchers applied relatively sophisticated demoscopic and sociological techniques for a broader picture of the situational and behavioural pressures operating on different strata. Although 85 per cent of the intelligentsia and 68 per cent of white-collar workers still claimed politics as the main motive, rather than economics, only 28 per cent of workers did so.[33] Since workers constituted a third of all refugees, to which should be added about 15 per cent who chose not to work, this is clearly a significant group.

More recently, Helge Heidemeyer has also made the case that the majority of persons arriving from the GDR were migrants rather than refugees and were tacitly recognised as such by the West German authorities.[34] Most notably, however, Albert Hirschman has also advanced an economistic 'exit/voice' model, originally conceived to explain customers' and party members' behaviour when faced with poor service or leadership.[35] An individual might either walk away from a problem (exit) and seek better service elsewhere, or else speak out against the problem (voice). The two variants were initially conceived as diametric opposites: when the ability to opt out of a bad situation was high, protest would remain low; when the outlet was closed off, dissent would build up like a head of steam. Although later, in the light of events in the GDR in 1989, Hirschman conceded that exit and voice could operate in tandem, what is important here is his stress on the availability of an easy alternative to a difficult situation.

There was a very obvious alternative to East German Communism: the FRG. In the mid-1950s the FRG was entering a period of sustained growth in its 'economic miracle', when it was soon facing labour shortages in many key sectors, particularly of skilled workers and technicians. The generous compensation offered to expellees from the East under the equalisation of burdens legislation of 1952 was also available to GDR citizens, helping to overcome fears of starting over. By 1961 Bonn had disbursed well over a billion DM to East German refugees.[36] Some farmers were even reported to have inventorised holdings prior to leaving, photographing property in order to support claims in the West. Yet it was industry that exerted the greatest pull. If one compares the distribution of East German refugees across the West German *Länder*, 37.4 per cent went to North Rhine-Westphalia, home of heavy industry in the Ruhr, and 18.2 per cent to Baden-Württemberg with its large engineering sector.[37] This was in almost inverse proportion to the pattern of settlement of Oder-Neisse expellees, where the agricultural states of Bavaria, Lower Saxony and Schleswig-Holstein had taken most newcomers. It was thus clear that by the

1950s the FRG was in much better shape to absorb East German refugees directly into industry, and soon became dependent on them. With the building of the Wall and the damming up of the eastern labour pool, it had indeed to switch to 'guest workers' from southern Europe to maintain momentum.

As the 1950s wore on, Communist reporters also increasingly stressed material motives for leaving. The Interior Ministry commented on the impact of the FRG boom through the 'demand for specialists and other workers in trade journals and other publications and the glorification of the western way of life, imported not only by radio, film and television, but to a great extent through multifarious personal relations and other contacts to capitalist enterprises'.[38] High wages, pensions and loans, as well as consumer goods and package holidays were irresistible lures to many. Recently fled workers wrote to colleagues, itemising improvements. Among technicians in Leipzig it was reported that conversations revolved around 'the satisfaction of personal needs. Such as the supply of televisions, refrigerators, cars etc., and the price differences of consumer goods such as stockings compared with the western zones, and the fact that personal freedom is constricted since there are not enough holiday places in the GDR'.[39] In one prominent case, the director of the Buna chemical works returned from a trip in 1961, 'raving about the affluence in West Germany and telling how his sister's cleaner drove up in a car and that out of every five building workers, three are car-owners'.[40] It is thus clear that no social group was immune from material cravings, and that even for the relatively privileged intelligentsia the aspirational yardstick remained the West.

To these should be added the 50,000-60,000 so-called 'border-crossers' (*Grenzgänger*), who lived in East Berlin and its environs but commuted daily to West Berlin, earning hard currency and contributing to the high fluctuation on shopfloors in the East. They were viewed as a double threat, encouraging others to leave, but also importing western ideology into the GDR. As the SED noted: 'Owing to the especially high susceptibility to enemy arguments and influences, made inevitable by periods spent in West Berlin, and by exploiting the extortionate rate of exchange [five east marks to one deutschmark] the vast majority of *Grenzgänger* exhibit a negative and apathetic attitude to our Republic. At the same time they influence the rest of the population in their opinions.'[41] Many East German citizens, not just those in the vicinity of the capital, also visited West Berlin on a regular basis, either to go to the cinema to watch forbidden Hollywood movies, or to buy jeans, records and 'trash literature' for private consumption back home. Thus, besides providing an escape hatch from communism, the open border acted as a revolving-door into the lures of capitalism.

There were, however, economic 'push factors' too, 'Made in the GDR'. Indeed, it makes little sense to enforce a rigid separation of politics and economics in the East German context. It was a system which used economic levers to achieve political ends. The East German shopfloor was a highly politicised arena in which the 'unity of politics and economics' was supposed to guarantee higher productivity through ideological clarity in the head. If we take the example of the technical intelligentsia, although the SED recognised that it could not do without experts to run a modern industrial economy, it was these elites who paid if things went wrong. Infratest noted a spectrum of pressure, ranging from low among the artistic intelligentsia, rising through the medical, pedagogical and technical intelligentsias, with administrative cadres most exposed. Two-thirds of bureaucrats who fled claimed to have lived in fear of severe sanctions, for failings which were often not of their own making.[42] At one power-plant in Berlin, for instance, engineers felt 'constantly threatened' following the arrest of the technical director, which prompted the pre-emptive defection of two other section heads.[43] With Ulbricht's announcement of the 'Economic Main Task' in 1958, to overtake West German *per capita* consumer production by 1961–62, those expected to deliver the GDR's economic miracle were planning functionaries and engineers. In September 1960 the SED added another self-imposed burden, the so-called 'undisruptability' campaign (*Störfreimachung*), designed to make the GDR economically autarkic in the event of an FRG trade embargo. Many specialist steels and chemicals were still imported from the West, but without them some plan quotas became unfeasible. Much valuable time was wasted preparing for a contingency which never materialised. Looking at Table 1, whereas the number of engineers had dropped steadily from 1955 and seemed immune to the pressures of 1958, by 1960-61 the technical intelligentsia were taking pole position. The ready availability of jobs in the West, coupled with the SED's tendency to turn every economic drive into a political campaign, conspired to accelerate the brain-drain.

It was not just elites who were driven from the shopfloor. Fleeing workers complained of bottlenecks in raw materials which frequently left production lines idle. For those paid at piece rates, this meant wage losses. Many factories in fact hoarded labour, with skilled trainees employed far below their ability. One young mechanic at VEB Elektro-Projekt in Berlin complained in his letter of resignation of 'being on perpetual stand-by, during which I joined in all the jobs of an unskilled worker, from storage, potato haulage, driver's mate, mail-order, coal haulage, furniture delivery and transport, to navvying'.[44] The problems were particularly acute in the VEBs in the state sector, where the *Republikflucht* rate was double that of the private sector in the mid-1950s.[45] Consequently, many skilled workers, who would otherwise have stayed in the GDR, were forced onto an all-German job market by economic mismanagement.

Workers were mobile because they could take their skills with them. Farmers were tied to the land, and knew, moreover, that land in the FRG was becoming ever scarcer. The agrarian pull factor was thus weak. Indeed, the eastern land reform of 1945 had been a popular measure, creating a new

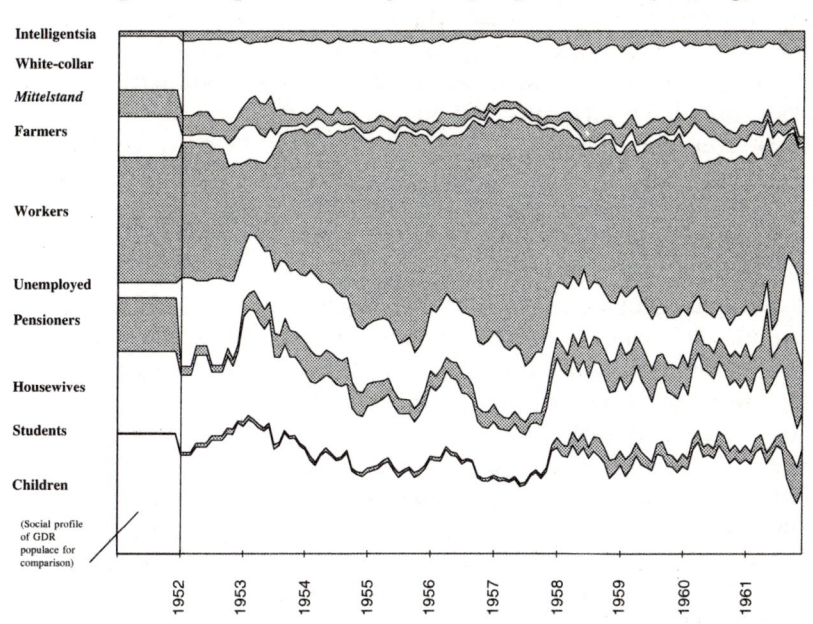

Figure 2 Republikflucht *by social group 1952–61 (monthly)*

Source: East German figures; see n. 2.

class of smallholders. As Figure 2 shows, for most of the 1950s far fewer farmers committed *Republikflucht* than other members of society. However, the collectivisation of agriculture, tentatively begun in 1952 but rushed through in the spring of 1960, unsettled many. Internal reports from 1960 show that, unlike 1952–53, when '*kulak*' farmers predominated, now smallholders were abandoning their farms in the immediate wake of collectivisation and heading west.[46] The former latifundia in the north were particularly badly affected. Some who had worked on the big estates before 1945, had no wish to return to the status of agricultural labourers in 1960. Moreover, since the countryside was already underpopulated, *Republikflucht* was far more visible than in industry, demoralising other sections of the population.

If changes in the means of production drove some producers away, consumption played an indirect but perhaps more pervasive role. Collectivisation was widely held responsible for the food shortages of 1960–61, above all of dairy products. Yet, whitewash, nappies and shoes were also in chronic short supply, to name but a few items. The lifting of rationing in 1958 had created a run on certain products, overwhelming the state distribution apparatus. Most vexing to the population was the shortage of housing, which accounted for the lion's share of petitions to the government. One chemicals worker, writing from his new workplace in West

Germany, explained to his mother how he and his wife had spent nine months looking for an apartment in Halle: 'We really tried everything, being sent all over the place. We even wrote to Berlin but it didn't help one jot.'[47] There is also evidence that some overburdened housing authorities quietly conspired in the disappearance of troublesome applicants. From all of this, it is clear that economic 'push' and 'pull factors' worked together. The boom in West Germany would no doubt have attracted a substantial portion of the GDR population whatever the situation at home. Yet, given that the East German economy was perceived to be getting worse rather than better, even more decided to seek their fortunes in the 'Golden West'.

However, as with politics-only interpretations, *Republikflucht* does not fit all the characteristics of classic economic migration. Where one might expect a substantial number of single males to be going on ahead, with family members following, only marginally more males left in the early 1950s, with a reverse trend in the second half of the decade. It is true, however, as Figure 2 reveals, that the proportion of pensioners leaving grew throughout the decade, suggesting that a demographic 'tail' was following on. But there the evidence ends. Nor should it be forgotten that the FRG spent the first half of the 1950s actively discouraging economic migrants, concerned at the burden on housing and employment. What marks out *Republikflucht* from other forms of internal migration, indeed, is that it was a criminalised act incurring confiscation of property and sanctions against remaining relatives. Unlike Hirschman's idealised model, there could be no 'free market' on the frontline of the Cold War.

In most cases a complex cocktail of motives was at work; the historian cannot neatly disaggregate them. If we take the case of Dr H. again, what caused his decision to flee? The theft of his stamps? Almost certainly not. The sealing of his apartment? Perhaps. Yet, we must distinguish between catalysts and causes. GDR reporters tended to focus on the former, since it was taboo even indirectly to criticise the basic tenets of Communism. There is no doubt that slights against individuals and bureaucratic insensitivity played an important part in breaking through the carefully cultivated veneer of conformity, which often involved years of lipservice and kowtowing. Infratest labelled this the 'short circuit reaction'. At a certain point the discrepancy between suppressed beliefs and conformist behaviour would become intolerable and it would take only a small 'spark' to blow the fuse.[48] Yet beyond this we must ask whether Dr H. was being overworked at the hospital. Apparently not a party member, was this damaging his career? Had he been offered a job at the congress in Karlsruhe? Did he have relatives in the West who could help him to start over? Although *Republikflucht* was a mass phenomenon, it was simultaneously an intensely personal action, prepared in isolation and often leaving few clues.

What could the state do to combat the exodus? The SED had two basic options: either to take a hard line and limit mobility, the most extreme variant of which was the building of the Berlin Wall in August 1961; or it could liberalise travel in the hope that this would compensate for other shortcomings, which is in essence what lay behind the gamble to open the Wall in November 1989. The Communist leadership had to walk a tightrope between repression and reform, since both, if taken to extremes, could lead to accelerated losses. To this extent it was a no-win solution and a test of the party's pragmatism. One must also recognise that individual GDR citizens, based on psychology and situation, might react differently to a hard or soft line. Repression might immobilise some, while driving others away; the legalisation of travel, on the other hand, might be exploited by the faint-hearted to abscond, while for others, the knowledge that they could come and go might persuade them to stay. For instance, taking Figure 2 again, it seems clear that the intelligentsia were less likely to flee during liberal periods, but that restrictions triggered an instinct to leave permanently. Workers, on the other hand, departed as a matter of opportunity, yet were more susceptible to obstacles placed in their way.

Early SED policy was for an aggressive defence. The most dramatic border operation before the building of the Wall was the closure of the Demarcation Line between the GDR and FRG in May 1952. A 5 kilometre exclusion zone was introduced, including a 100 metre control strip at the actual border, cleared of vegetation. Border guards had orders to shoot 'border violators' who failed to halt. A few weeks later, 'unreliable elements' in the border population were forcibly relocated to the interior of the GDR, and from then on the exclusion zone required a permit.[49] At the same time West Berlin was further cut off from its hinterland when 200 of its 277 access routes were severed.[50] In September of that year the Politbüro also instituted a Commission against *Republikflucht*. Rather fancifully, it recommended counter-recruitment of intelligentsia and skilled workers in the West. It also looked to propaganda measures, such as factory noticeboards, brochures and radio plays, to convince GDR citizens of the callous treatment they might expect there.[51]

Yet, after the New Course of June 1953, including an amnesty for *Republikflüchtige*, and again in 1956, following destalinisation, liberalisation at home was accepted as part of the solution. Yet the GDR had to ration its favours. The intelligentsia were the chief recipients of cars, consumer goods and western visas, much to the irritation of other groups. Thus, in September 1958 and December 1960, doctors were the object of SED solicitations; in November 1960 teachers received similar promises; and in February 1961 it was youth's turn.[52] Attempts to retain wavering academics could reach grotesque proportions, for instance when one professor of paediatrics at Berlin's Charité hospital threatened to accept a chair in West Germany. Repeated personal entreaties by the Minister of Education and the promise of a new car and a large villa were not enough to deter him.[53] After June 1953 there was also a massive liberalisation in issuing western visas. Indeed, as

Interior Minister Maron confirmed, these measures had contributed 'substantially to the calming of the situation in the population'.[54] At the same time, the police were all too aware that large numbers of travellers were abusing visas to flee permanently, amounting in 1957 to over half of all *Republikfluchten*. It was therefore no surprise when the Interior Ministry started pressing for a harder line. Already during the summer of 1957 trips to the West by those in the public sector were being restricted, but in December the Pass Law was tightened up with a paragraph punishing actual, attempted or abetted *Republikflucht* with up to three years' imprisonment. The number of visas issued was also drastically reduced: from 2.8 million in 1957 to just over 600,000 in 1958, and those exploiting visas to flee fell correspondingly from 171,674 to 16,644.[55] This more stringent gate-keeping, surely, must account for the bulk of the dip in the *Republikflucht* curve in the late 1950s, not an incipient sense of socio-economic well-being.

The result of the travel restrictions was instead a steadily rising wave of discontent. Whereas in the first quarter of 1957 only a quarter of complaints to the Volkspolizei related to visas, by the last quarter it was two-thirds and by 1960 over 90 per cent.[56] As one irate citizen explained: 'I was at the interzonal pass office in Erfurt yesterday. The amount of aggravation caused among the population at not being issued visas is indescribable.'[57] Petitions to the Council of State also took the authorities to task over the lack of freedom to travel. By July 1961 travel petitions had even caught up with the populace's chronic bugbear, housing. The new hard line also altered the pattern of *Republikflucht*. Unlike the mid-1950s, when half of flights had occurred 'legally' across the inner-German border, during 1958-61 the sector boundary in Berlin became the increasingly favoured point of exit, just as it had in 1952–53.[58] *Republikflucht* thus became a crime of opportunity, concentrated in areas adjacent to West Berlin. The authorities resorted to ever more desperate measures to seal off the city from its hinterland. The police established 'train escort kommandos' which patrolled the corridors of Berlin-bound expresses, on the look-out for younger persons, families and those with heavy luggage. The Border Police recruited more auxiliary volunteers. Road blocks were also set up on the approaches to the capital. The Stasi became more heavily involved. New categories of informers were created among taxi drivers, postmen and railway ticket personnel. Security checks were carried out on all those withdrawing large sums from bank accounts or selling cars. Customs were also under orders to monitor packages to West Germany for personal effects being sent on ahead.[59] In this way, between May 1960 and the building of the Wall, over 50,000 persons were detained on suspicion of *Republikflucht*, although in the same period six times as many successfully eluded the cordon.[60] The tighter the regime squeezed, the greater became the pressure to leave.

What was required was a more total solution, which would require Soviet acquiescence. Yet the decision for an actual wall came very late – certainly later than the Warsaw Pact meeting in March 1961, at which some sources still have Ulbricht laying out detailed variants of border closure. The sparsity of SED documents reflects the high level of secrecy surrounding preparations. There had, of course, already been a number of sector border closures, notably in June 1953, but also in October 1957 when a new currency was introduced in the GDR, and in September 1960, when checks were temporarily introduced for West Berliners. All of these relied on a heavy deployment of manpower and could not be regarded as permanent solutions. The pressure for something more concrete came from the East German leadership, keen to extract something from the Berlin Crisis which was threatening to become a diplomatic dead-end. According to one Soviet envoy's memoirs, in late June or early July 1961 Ulbricht informed the Soviet amabassador that with the continuing losses the collapse of the GDR was inevitable and that an 'explosion' was imminent.[61] The Kremlin probably recognised this as overdramatisation on the SED leader's part, but Khrushchev was now looking for a way out of a heavy economic commitment to the GDR, into which raw materials were poured at one end, while human resources disappeared out of the other. If the latter could be plugged, then Moscow would be able to cut its subsidies. Shortly after this meeting Khrushchev evidently gave the green light for a total border closure.

Only a select few SED leaders were initiated into the secret. The element of surprise had to be maintained at all costs in order to avoid disturbances in the GDR. At the beginning of August the Interior Ministry began surreptitiously removing stockpiles of barbed wire and concrete posts from the inner-German border to the outskirts of East Berlin.[62] A few days later Ulbricht received Warsaw Pact assent and on 9 August chief-of-staff Erich Honecker began drawing up a plan of operations. During the night of 12–13 August 1961 three concentric security rings – the first of border police, the second of East German motorised army divisions, and the third of Red Army units – converged on the edges of West Berlin. Against the hammer of pneumatic drills and the glare of welding equipment, streets were torn up, barbed-wire entanglements deployed and the first concrete slabs of the Berlin Wall put in place. The constellation of power had altered decisively to the SED's advantage, and the following months and years were a period of coming to terms with Communism for large parts of the captive populace now enclosed within the GDR. Nevertheless, the fundamental problems of convincing East Germans of the benefits of socialism remained. When the iron curtain was breached by the Hungarians in May 1989, the exodus resumed immediately.

Notes

1. Stiftung Archiv der Parteien und Massenorganisationen der DDR im Bundearchiv (SAPMO-BArch), DY 30/IV 2/19/56, 'Ungesetzliche Handlungen gegenüber Herrn Dr. H.', 30 September 1960.
2. West German figures: BAK, B 136/821, 2719, 2722; B 50/4157, 6449, 8137; East German figures: BAB, DO-1/8/290(1)-302(1), DO-1/11/960-7; BStU-ZA, ZAIG 186, 247, 412.
3. SAPMO-BArch, IV 2/2.101/25, Wirtschaftskommission/SPK meeting, 17 June 1961.
4. Federal figures in BAK, B 136/2718-19.
5. Bundesarchiv Berlin (BAB), DO-1/11/964, HVDVP, 'Republikfluchten: Auswertung des Berichtsmonates September', 2 November 1957, fos 193–01.
6. BAB, DO-1/34/54134, HVDVP (Abt. Innere Angelegenheiten) to SED-ZK, 21 January 1961.
7. Christoph Kleßmann, *Die doppelte Staatsgründung: Deutsche Geschichte 1945–1955* (5th edn, Bonn, 1991), 354.
8. Infratest (ed.), *Jugendliche Flüchtlinge aus der SBZ* (Munich, May 1957), 35.
9. Landesarchiv Merseburg (LAM), BPA SED Halle, IV/412/235, SED-KL Leuna (KPKK), 'Analyse über den politisch-moralischen Zustand der Kreisparteiorganisation', 10 July 1961, fos 118–25.
10. BAB, DO-1/11/964, HVDVP, 'Interzonenverkehr', n.d. [1957], fo. 117; BAB, DO-1/11/967, HVDVP, 'Vorlage für die Mitglieder des Kollegiums ...', 1 June 1961, fos 93–122.
11. Erika von Hornstein, *Die deutsche Not: Flüchtlinge berichten* (Frankfurt/Main, 1992).
12. Helge Heidemeyer, *Flucht und Zuwanderung aus der SBZ/DDR 1945/49–1961: Die Flüchtlingspolitik der Bundesrepublik Deutschland bis zum Bau der Berliner Mauer* (Düsseldorf, 1994).
13. Ibid., 46.
14. BStU-ZA, ZAIG 72, MfS, 'Bericht über die Organisierung der Republikflucht als wesentlicher Bestandteil der aggressiven NATO-Politik', 22 October 1958, fos 16–61.
15. BAB, DO-1/11/965, HVDVP, 'Warum ist Republikflucht Verrat an der Deutschen Demokratischen Republik?', fos 15–17.
16. BAB, DO-1/11/962, HVDVP, 'Abwanderung aus der DDR nach Westdeutschland und Westberlin aus den Jahren 1950–1953', fos 159–60.
17. SAPMO-BArch, DY 30/IV 2/13/394, 'Kurzbericht über die Entwicklung der Bevölkerungsbewegung', 26 October 1953.
18. Volker Ackermann, *Der 'echte' Flüchtling: Deutsche Vertriebene und Flüchtlinge aus der DDR 1945–1961* (Osnabrück, 1995).
19. Landesarchiv Berlin, Rep. 4/Acc. 1650/Nr. 39, Senator für Arbeit und Sozialwesen, 'Jahresbericht über die Entwicklung der Berliner Flüchtlingsituation im Jahre 1955'.
20. BAB, DO-1/11/963, untitled report, 1955, fos 70–99.
21. Landeskirchliches Archiv Berlin-Brandenburg, Rep. Gen. II/ F7, Bd. IV, Gerhard S., 'Fluchtbericht', n.d. [September 1961].
22. Robert F. Goeckel, *The Lutheran Church and the East German State* (Ithaca and

London, 1990), 40–55.
23 Joachim S. Hohmann, '"Wenn Sie dies lesen, bin ich schon auf dem Weg in den Westen": "Republikflüchtige" DDR-Lehrer in den Jahren 1949–1961', *Zeitschrift für Geschichtswissenschaft*, 45 (1997), 311–30.
24 SAPMO-BArch, DY 30/IV 2/19/53, SED-ZK (Gewerkschaften), 'Die Lage unter der medizinischen Intelligenz', 21 June 1958.
25 Heidemeyer, *Flucht und Zuwanderung*, 60–1.
26 SAPMO-BArch, DY 30/IV 2/19/53, 'Analyse über die Republikflucht ...', [1959].
27 SAPMO-BArch, DY 30/J IV 2/2/780, SED-PB, 28 July 1961.
28 BAB, DO-1/11/967, 'Stand und Entwicklung der Bevölkerungsbewegung im Jahre 1960', 13 February 1961, fos 37–60.
29 *Neues Deutschland*, 17 June 1961, 5.
30 Dietrich Staritz, *Geschichte der DDR* (2nd edn; Frankfurt/Main, 1996), 169.
31 Corey Ross, '"... sonst sehe ich mich veranlaßt, auch nach dem Westen zu ziehen": "Republikflucht", SED-Herrschaft und Bevölkerung vor dem Mauerbau', *Deutschland Archiv*, 34 (2001), 613–27.
32 SAPMO-BArch, DY 30/IV 2/13/397, SED-ZK (Leitende Staatsorgane), 'Niederschrift über die Sitzung der Kommission zu den Fragen der Republikflucht am 23.11.1956', 4 December 1956.
33 Infratest (ed.), *Die Intelligenzschicht in der Sowjetzone Deutschlands*, ii: *Analyse der Fluchtgründe* (Munich, 1959), Schaubild 1; Viggo Graf Blücher, *Industriearbeiterschaft in der Sowjetzone* (Stuttgart, 1959), 9.
34 Heidemeyer, *Flucht und Zuwanderung*.
35 Albert O. Hirschman, 'Exit, voice, and the fate of the German Democratic Republic: an essay in conceptual history', *World Politics*, 45 (1993), 173–202.
36 BAK, B 136/2719, fo. 181 and B 136/2720, fo. 25.
37 Statistisches Bundesamt (ed.), *Statistisches Jahrbuch für die Bundesrepublik Deutschland: 1962* (Stuttgart and Cologne, 1963), 68.
38 BAB, DO-1/34/21723, 'Analyse über die Entwicklung der Republikflucht in den Jahren 1954–1955 u. 1956', 3 May 1956.
39 Staatsarchiv Leipzig, BT/RdB Leipzig, 1629, RdB Leipzig (Inneres), 'Bericht über den Stand der Bevölkerungsbewegung ...', 19 May 1960, fos 139–42.
40 LAM, SED-BL Halle, IV 2/6.01/1084, Arbeitsgruppe Chemie to Koenen, 15 April 1961, fo. 11.
41 SAPMO-BArch, DY 30/J IV 2/202/65, SED-ZK (Sicherheitsfragen), 23 July 1961, fos 85–92.
42 Infratest (ed.), *Intelligenzschicht*, ii, Schaubild 5.
43 BAB, DO-1/34/21721, MdI (Innere Angel.), 'Vermerk zur Fragen der Bevölkerungsbewegung im PKB-Kohle Berlin ...', 10 July 1959.
44 BAB, DO-1/11/967, 'Stand und Entwicklung der Bevölkerungsbewegung im Jahre 1960', 13 February 1961, fos 37–60.
45 BAB, DO-1/11/963, 'Bericht über die Republikfluchten aus der Deutschen Demokratischen Republik für die Zeit vom 1.1.1954 bis 31.12.1955', n.d., fos 100–29.
46 SAPMO-BArch, DY 30/IV 2/7/120, SED-ZK (Landwirtschaft), 'Einschätzung der Republikflucht auf dem Gebiet der Landwirtschaft', 1 June 1961, fos 19–43.
47 LAM, BPA SED Halle, IV/425/115, SED-BPO Farbenfabrik Wolfen,

'Monatsbericht', 15 November 1960, fos 219–27.
48 Infratest (ed.), *Intelligenzschicht*, ii, 28.
49 Inge Bennewitz and Rainer Potratz, *Zwangsaussiedlungen an der innerdeutschen Grenze: Analysen und Dokumente* (Berlin, 1994), 13–65.
50 Bundesministerium für innerdeutsche Beziehungen (ed.), *Die Sperrmaßnahmen der DDR vom Mai 1952* (Bonn, 1987), 88–9.
51 SAPMO-BArch, DY 30/IV 2/13/393, SED-ZK (Staatl. Verwaltung), 'Vorschläge für Maßnahmen gegen die Republikflucht und zur Werbung von Fachkräften in Westdeutschland', 22 September 1952.
52 SED-ZK (ed.), *Dokumente der Sozialistischen Einheitspartei Deutschlands* (Berlin, 1961/1962), vii, 348–52, viii, 298–301, 303–6 and 367–75.
53 SAPMO-BArch, DY 30/IV 2/19/56, 'Information über die Republikflucht von Prof. Dr. D.', 5 January 1960.
54 BAB, DO-1/11/964, HVDVP (Hauptabt. PM), 'Vermerk', 13 March 1957, fos 93–8.
55 BAB, DO-1/11/967, fos 93–122.
56 BAB, DO-1/11/49-50.
57 SAPMO-BArch, DY 30/IV 2/5/253, *Eingaben* report for third quarter of 1958, 29 October 1958, fos 1–70.
58 Gerd Wendt, *Fluchtziel Berlin: Erinnerungsstätte Notaufnahmelager Marienfelde* (Berlin, 1998), 19–22.
59 BStU-ZA, MfS-ZAIG 247, MfS, 'Bericht über die Entwicklung der Republikflucht . . .', 1 July 1960, fos 39–58.
60 BAP, DO-1/11/1128, HVDVP (Operativstab), 'Aufstellung über die Verhinderung von Republikfluchten', 23 September 1960, fos 132–4.
61 Julij A. Kwizinskij, *Vor dem Sturm* (Berlin, 1993), 179.
62 Bundesarchiv-Militärisches Zwischenarchiv Potsdam, Strausberg, AZN 32588, NVA (Inst. f. Deutsche Militärgeschichte), 'Die Nationale Volksarmee in der Aktion vom 13. August 1961', 20 February 1964, 35.

III
Culture

12

The evangelical church in the German Democratic Republic

Merrilyn Thomas

Communism and Christianity make uneasy bedfellows. Nevertheless history has dictated that they have frequently been forced to cohabit. The possibilities exist for a relatively harmonious relationship, both sets of believers sharing creeds, such as a desire for peace and the need to care for the world's less fortunate. But the relationship founders on Marxist dogma which is overtly hostile to the Church, famously describing religion as the opiate of the people, and predicting that under the Marxist theory of historical inevitability the Church is bound to wither away and die in a socialist state. Not unnaturally the Church has difficulties coming to terms with a dogma which predicts its demise and demands total obedience to secular government rather than to God.

Circumstances, however, can blur the borders of most philosophical arguments. Given the peculiar conditions pertaining in the GDR at its birth, it was by no means a forgone conclusion that the Church and the atheist state would be at daggers drawn. Indeed, pragmatism dictated otherwise. Throughout the Ulbricht era, in fact, Church and state managed to coexist despite extreme provocations on both sides at various times. Notwithstanding infiltration of the Church by agents of the MfS (Stasi); the persecution, imprisonment and expulsion of some of the more irksome clergymen; and the tendency of some Church leaders to act as advocates for the capitalists across the Iron Curtain – the two sides continued to maintain a dialogue. Dogma was defeated by a combination of realism and common goals.

Since the demise of the GDR in 1990 there has been a frequently bitter debate about the role of the Church in the Communist state. How far did Church leaders actually support the regime and give it the authority to continue, rather than act as the opposition force which they claimed to be when the Berlin Wall came down? As the files of the Stasi and other government departments have revealed the extent of Church infiltration, the charge has been made that, as in the 1930s, the German Evangelical Church colluded with a totalitarian regime. The German historians Gerhard Besier and Stephan Wolf have led the way in cataloguing the intrigue and deceit which existed within the Evangelical Church.[1]

On the other hand the argument can be made that, despite the presence of many rotten apples in the Christian basket, the Church as a whole did stand up for what it believed in with considerable courage and strength, given that there was a constant threat of overt opposition being quelled by force, as in 1953, and that from 1961 onwards the GDR had become a virtual prison. Citizens, including Christians, learned the art of muted and subtle opposition, which in its way was more deadly. As Mary Fulbrook states: 'East Germans came to terms with the pressures and demands of their regime by leading a double life of outward conformity combined with private authenticity.'[2] The ability to express oneself in a manner open to interpretation and read between the lines is common to most politicians, but in the GDR it became an art form for the population at large. In addition, when examining the charges that some Church leaders colluded with the Communists, it must be borne in mind that a sympathy for socialism or even Communism is not in itself a crime (despite the fact that the Communist Party was outlawed in West Germany). Moreover, that those who criticise come from a culture committed to the GDR's downfall during the Cold War, and that, after reunification, many East Germans who thirsted for the benefits of capitalism now believe that perhaps there was some truth in the claims of the socialist regime.

The GDR was not alone in having to resolve the problematic relationship between Church and Communist state but, unlike some of its Eastern bloc neighbours, the situation was compounded by peculiarities of history and geography. Only four years had passed since the defeat of Hitler and fascism when the socialist republic was officially founded. Memories of the struggle waged by both Communists and some Christians against the Nazi regime were still fresh. During the 1930s, German Communists had provided the main opposition to Hitler and been persecuted for their pains, most of them either fleeing east to the Soviet Union or west to countries such as France. Those who remained were executed or imprisoned. Hans Seigewasser, for example, who was to become Secretary of State for Church Affairs in the GDR in 1960, was one of those who spent the war in a concentration camp. Some of those in prison formed bonds with members of the Confessing Church who faced similar fates. The Church had been established in 1934 in direct opposition to Nazism by Protestant leaders such as Karl Barth and Martin Niemöller.[3] With Communists and some Christians sharing a common enemy and past, it was not altogether unreasonable for the new leaders of the Communist state and their counterparts in the Evangelical Church in eastern Germany (most of whom professed to have been members of or associated with the Confessing Church) initially at least to have seen each other as potential allies rather than enemies. 'Let us remember', says John S. Conway, 'how readily some Christians in the former German Democratic Republic believed that this dictatorship represented a real form of Christian socialism'.[4] Ulbricht's view on Christianity was spelled out in a speech to the Volkskammer in 1960. Christianity and the humanist aims of socialism are not opposites, he said. It is just that Christianity has been abused for centuries by the ruling classes:

> Today it is being abused in West Germany by the powers of militarism, this time for nuclear rearmament policies which are hostile to mankind. The old yearning of Christian people, who pray for peace on earth and goodwill to all mankind in their gospel, can only find fulfilment through the realisation of the high ideals of humanism and socialism.[5]

In this chapter I propose to concentrate on the Protestant Evangelical Church to which most of the population of the GDR belonged in 1945. For Ulbricht and his colleagues, waging outright war on the Evangelical Church was not a realistic option even if they had wished to do so. It was far too powerful an institution to be removed. The infant Communist state was faced with the fact that about 80 per cent of its people were card-carrying members, not of the Party, but of the Protestant Evangelical Church.[6] At the end of the Second World War, 15 million of the 17 million people in the Soviet Zone (SBZ) were Protestants. The Church's many institutions were an integral part of the GDR's social fabric. In 1960 it was reckoned that the Evangelical Church ran fifty-five hospitals and clinics providing more than 9,000 places, fifty-nine homes for the mentally and physically disabled with more than 4,500 places, and hundreds of children's day nurseries and old people's homes, not to mention numerous community projects.[7] Amid the devastation and chaos following the end of the war, people needed the Church to provide them with physical as well as spiritual support. The SED's decision to tolerate the Church is reflected in the GDR's first constitution drawn up in 1949. Articles 41 and 42 provided for freedom of worship and conscience and stipulated that no-one would be discriminated against in their private and public lives for religious beliefs. The reality often differed from the theory, but the clauses provided the regime with a defence when needed. By 1968, however, when the GDR's second constitution was drawn up, the SED line against the Church had hardened. On this occasion the constitution made clear that the Church's freedom of action extended only as far as it conformed to the demands of the socialist state. But, on paper at least, persecution or discrimination for religious reasons did not exist.

The SED was stuck with the legacy of the Protestant Church, from its deeply engrained Lutheran roots to its less than glorious record during the Third Reich. However, the geography of the situation was another matter. The Evangelical Church was a pan-German organisation (the only such body intact after 1945) and its presence as such was a constant irritant to the GDR regime, undermining its struggle to gain international recognition as an independent state. As the Cold War intensified, the fact that the Church was administered by a central body representing both eastern and western Germany became an increasingly bizarre anomaly. How could Soviet-bloc Christians regard themselves as being at one with the citizens of a NATO ally? How could the GDR assert its independence when, on a daily basis, the Church was conducting itself as though Germany were one nation? According to the German theologian Jürgen Moltmann, until the building of the Berlin Wall in 1961, the 'churches were certainly the strongest organisation for the unity of the German people'.[8] The SED felt that, in this matter at least, it could take control of events. One of the main areas of conflict between Church and state became the ever-intensifying desire of the SED to split the eastern Church from its western cousins, a battle which was eventually won in 1969 when the Church in the East broke away from the pan-German organisation and formed its own administrative body, the Bund der Evangelischen Kirchen.

The dilemma of how to handle Church–state relations was not confined to the government side. Evangelical Church leaders, too, were uncertain how to proceed. Some postwar Church leaders were all too sensitive to charges that the Church as a whole had failed to put up an effective opposition to fascism. They did not wish to be accused of caving in to another totalitarian regime, albeit of a different hue. On the other hand, among some clergy there was a genuine sympathy for the aims of the socialist government, plus a belief that compromise and co-operation were more productive than conflict. As the years went by the two sides became increasingly entrenched. The gap between them widened, helped to a large extent by the machinations of the regime, which by the 1960s had decided that its most successful policy was that of divide and rule.

But for the Church the matter was not simply one of survival. For Christians there were major theological questions at stake. One wing held to the traditional Lutheran view that it was possible for two sources of authority, the secular and the spiritual, to exist side by side, and that it was a Christian's duty to support the authority of the state in its governance of the country. The other wing, with its roots in Calvinist Protestantism, was prepared to question the authority of rulers and argued that the Church had a duty to oppose a government which acted against the will of God.[9] The manner in which the Church was structured allowed the two conflicting views to develop independently. Although the Evangelical Church was a unified body, it maintained a considerable amount of democracy within its constituent parts. This factor also worked to Ulbricht's advantage, allowing him to play one bishop off against another. But the dispersal of power also made the Church more difficult for the regime to control.

The governing body of the Evangelical Church, the Evangelische Kirche in Deutschland (EKD), had been set up in 1948. It was an umbrella organisation which united the churches in the various *Länder*, or states of the GDR and the FRG, while still allowing them the autonomy they valued and to which they had become accustomed before the Third Reich and Hitler's attempts to subsume the Church into the state under one bishop. This was a return to the days of the Weimar Republic which recognised the differing historical backgrounds and traditions of the German Protestant Church. Although the Church functioned under a hierarchical structure with bishops at the head of each diocese, they were elected rather than appointed. The democratic elements of the system entailed the laity electing representatives to the various governing bodies, which in turn went on to elect the bishops. This ensured a strong grass-roots influence.

Within the GDR there were eight dioceses or *Landeskirchen* – Anhalt, Berlin-Brandenburg (a diocese which crossed the Berlin east/west divide), Saxony (Magdeburg), Görlitz, Greifswald, Mecklenburg, Saxony (Dresden) and Thuringia. Of these, the first five had Prussian traditions and formed the Evangelische Kirche der Union (EKU). The latter three practised a purer form of Lutherism and were loosely linked in the United Evangelical Lutheran Church (Germany) (VELK(D)). The bishops within these Landeskirchen were powerful within their areas. Those who were most influential from a political point of view during the Ulbricht years were Otto Dibelius (Berlin-Brandenburg), Moritz Mitzenheim (Thuringia), Friedrich Krummacher (Greifswald) and Gottfried Noth (Saxony, Dresden). Dibelius and Mitzenheim represented the two contrasting views of how the Church should accommodate itself to operating under a Communist regime. Dibelius was a thorn in the flesh of the Ulbricht regime, using his position to preach that man's first duty was to God. In 1959 Dibelius wrote an open letter under the title of 'Obrigkeit' (authority), in which he argued that the Christian duty of recognising state authority did not apply in a totalitarian state.[10] The Ministry of Church Affairs quoted Dibelius' view that if state authority claimed to be outside God's given law, then it lost its legal status.[11] To the SED this amounted to incitement to GDR citizens to disobey or disregard the law of the land and Dibelius was branded a lackey of the imperialist and aggressive West. Mitzenheim, on the other hand, was the conciliator, advocating co-operation. In a discussion with Ulbricht in 1964, known as the Wartburg Conversation, Mitzenheim gave his support to Ulbricht's views on Church–state relations, and claimed that the relationship between the eastern and western parts of the Church had been broken.[12] Subsequently, with the demise of the GDR, it became known that Mitzenheim had been encouraged in his pliancy by a senior colleague, Oberkirchenrat Lotz, who had been recruited by the Stasi, and over many years influenced the bishop to take the 'correct' line.[13] Manipulation of this type was not uncommon. Such was the intrigue that characterised relations between Church and state within the GDR from the late 1950s onwards, it is wise to take little at face value.

Both Mitzenheim's and Dibelius' declarations were used by opposing factions in battles for the moral high-ground and the philosophical argument about the right course of action. For, in this socialist state with its German history of philosophical discourse, the 'Church question', at least in the early years, was not to be solved simply by force and repression. It was important for all sides that the argument was also seen to be won. Repression itself was relatively low-key. Young people with Christian connections, for example, were more likely to find it difficult to obtain an education or a job than face imprisonment. Words were the main weapon in this conflict and it was the hidden significance behind words and actions that really mattered in the GDR.[14] Senior churchmen at the sharp end, those with regular contact with government and party officials, often walked a tightrope. Nuance was everywhere present. Moves and words were analysed for hidden meaning, often to the point of the ridiculous. In 1965, for example, the Secretary of State for Church Affairs, Hans Seigewasser, celebrated his sixtieth birthday. The two leading bishops within the GDR at that time, Krummacher and Noth, agonised at length over how this birthday should be marked. Should they send a present or just a card? Should one of them present it personally, or should the task be performed by a deputy? Too much and it might appear that they were currying favour. Too little and they could cause offence. It was eventually agreed to send a letter of congratulations, jointly signed by Krummacher and Noth.[15] The incident also highlights the institutionalised double life, some might say hypocrisy, which became a norm in the GDR. Despite the spying and betrayal that permeated society, nowhere more than in Church circles, Church leaders and members of the regime attempted to maintain a semblance of normality and common courtesy in their day-to-day relationships.

The history of Church–state relations during the Ulbricht years reflects the history of both domestic and international events and, in those terms, can be divided into two periods. During the first, from the inception of the state in 1949 to about 1957, minds tended to be concentrated on domestic matters. It was, on the whole, internal rather than external events which influenced Church policy. Thus, the abortive uprising of 1953 brought about a slight relaxation in policy towards the Church, as the regime realised that some appeasement of the population was necessary. Church youth groups, Junge Gemeinde for example, were no longer regarded as illegal organisations.[16] But the period is also punctuated by critical moments, in which the Church was the central figure rather than a mere bystander reaping the benefits or otherwise of the actions of others. One such moment was the government's introduction in 1954 of the *Jugendweihe*, a ceremony for children of early secondary school age to mark the start of their transition from childhood to maturity. The Party held that this socialist rite of passage was merely the reintroduction of a ceremony begun during the days of the Weimar Republic. But Church leaders saw things differently. For them it was a direct challenge to the Christian service of Confirmation which took place at around the same age. Children were prepared for the *Jugendweihe*, just as they were for Confirmation, only in the case of the *Jugendweihe* the aim was to win their allegiance to the atheist socialist state. This, the Church said, was incompatible with Confirmation. Children could not vow to be both atheist and Christian at the same time. Protests at first were heated. According to Mary Fulbrook and Robert Goeckel, schools were accused of putting pressure on children and parents to take part in the *Jugendweihe*. The state claimed that it was entirely voluntary.

However, judging from a complaint by a priest in Freiberg in 1958, four years after the introduction of *Jugendweihe*, if coercion was present it had not become so commonplace that it was taken as the norm. Superintendent Cornelius Kohl of Freiberg Cathedral was outraged when parishioners complained to him that their children were to be barred from secondary school if they did not take part in the *Jugendweihe*. Having first written a letter demanding an explanation from the Freiberg local council chairman and received no response, Kohl sent a telegram to the man at the top, Max Hartwig, deputy to the Secretary of State for Church Affairs. Kohl did not mince his words. He was certainly not cowed by authority. He told Hartwig what parents had said and continued: 'I think this is blackmail and cannot believe that it is in the interests of the government of the GDR.'[17] It is worth quoting some of the correspondence which ensued because it illustrates not only the attitude of a middle-ranking priest to what has been seen as a critical political issue, and the government's way of handling tricky situations, but also the ulterior motives and suspicion that lurked behind the words and deeds of both Christians and Communists.

Hartwig was looking for hidden agendas. At first he suspected the complaint might be deliberate disruptive action prior to the EKD's annual synod. Meanwhile Kohl had enlisted the local bishop, Gottfried Noth, who also telegrammed Hartwig concerning the 'disquieting' news about the children. Kohl then elaborated on the charges. It appeared that the local primary school head had asked all children applying to secondary school to stand. Then he asked all those taking part in the *Jugendweihe* to remain standing. All sat down except one. The head then explained how important the *Jugendweihe* was for acceptance at secondary school. Kohl asked Hartwig: 'Please do something to make sure that the impression that Christians are second-class citizens does not continue. It is intolerable that these things can be done so silently'.[18] Hartwig's tone became more conciliatory. A cordial meeting took place three weeks later at which Kohl made other complaints, enquiring if there was an order forbidding people whose relatives had fled illegally to the West from receiving exit permits.[19] Hartwig's suspicion that Kohl had things other than the *Jugendweihe* on his mind was confirmed when the latter, by now in regular contact, wrote that he had been invited to West Germany for a Church conference. Unfortunately he had never been allowed an exit permit because his son had emigrated to the FRG two years before.[20] Although Hartwig declined to use his influence, this episode illustrates the personalisation of Church–state relations in the GDR.[21]

Over the years the Church relaxed its line on the *Jugendweihe* and it became quite acceptable for children to take part in both Christian and Communist ceremonies. It was events outside the GDR which further soured Church–state relations in the late 1950s. In the context of international affairs, the relationship between the Evangelical Church and the regime was never going to be easy. In the 1950s West Germany's rearmament and the basing of NATO's nuclear weapons on its soil fuelled GDR fears of an aggressive capitalist West. Meanwhile GDR Church leaders continued their close association with colleagues in the West, many of whom appeared to support their government's anticommunist posturing. Matters came to a head in 1957 when the EKD ratified an agreement that the Evangelical Church should provide chaplains to FRG forces. This agreement, known as the Military Chaplaincy Agreement (*Militärseelsorgevertrag*), was seen by the SED as little short of treason. How could the leading Churchmen of the GDR give their support to providing spiritual succour for troops whose enemy, if they ever were called into action, would be the Church leaders' own flock in the GDR? It was a bizarre situation, souring relations between Church and regime, which intensified its efforts to split the two geographical wings of the EKD. The GDR accused the FRG of preparing for war, and of West German imperialism and militarism threatening world peace for a third time. The ruling CDU was a party of reaction and aggression, the GDR claimed, misusing Church institutions for its own ends.[22] GDR Church leaders, on the other hand, argued that the agreement applied only to West German members of the EKD, as well it might, since it was unlikely that NATO would encourage chaplains from across the Iron Curtain to minister to its soldiers.

However, the episode highlighted the need to clarify the situation *vis-à-vis* the GDR and the Church, and the EKD's role within the GDR Church. A series of meetings was held between East German Church and state leaders in order to resolve the problems. It resulted in the Joint Declaration of 1958 in which Bishops Krummacher and Mitzenheim and other Church leaders formally stated that the eastern Church was not bound by the Military Chaplaincy Agreement and that it had no legal validity within the GDR. The bishops also said that their aim was to maintain peace between peoples and that they therefore supported the government's peace efforts.[23] The latter concession was particularly politically charged. It may seem obvious that Christians would be for peace, but in GDR propaganda the word 'peace' was a potent weapon and much effort was put into winning the 'peace battle'. In current jargon, it was considered important that Christians should be 'on message'. One weapon in the 'peace battle' was the setting up of the Prague Christian Peace Conference in 1958. The GDR played a leading role in this organisation which, according to Gerhard Besier, was established as a counterweight to western ecumenical bodies.[24] The GDR set great store by it. Its discussions centred on the Cold War, rearmament and nuclear weapons but, seen as an instrument of anti-Western propaganda, it was supported only by pro-Marxist Christians.

EKD unity eventually fell victim to the Berlin Wall, although its death throes took several years. The Wall, built in the summer of 1961, not only made prisoners of the GDR population but also effectively made it impossible for the EKD to function as a single administrative body. Church leaders, like everyone else, were no longer allowed to cross from east to west other than in exceptional circumstances, and those did not include attending meetings of the EKD. The diocese of Berlin-Brandenburg was particularly badly affected, since its territory included both East and West Berlin. One man, Präses Kurt Scharf, president of the EKD synod and chief administrator of the Berlin-Brandenburg diocese, personified the Church's struggle to maintain its unity following the closing of the border and the state's equal determination to make things as difficult as possible. Scharf belonged to the anti-GDR 'Dibelius camp' and was mooted as the bishop's successor. A few days after the Wall went up he further angered the regime by being the chief signatory to a telegram to Ulbricht and the East Berlin mayor, Friedrich Ebert, pointing out the grief the Wall would cause to Berliners cut off from family and friends. The telegram provoked an angry reaction and the Politbüro immediately expelled Scharf from the GDR. His enforced exile in West Berlin, where he eventually became Bishop of the western part of the Berlin-Brandenburg diocese, aggravated Church–state relations for several years.[25]

The building of the Wall threw the Church into confusion. Opinions differed as to how the new situation should be handled, some Church leaders feeling that toeing the line would be more productive than opposition, others determined to maintain links with the West. A Ministry of Church Affairs report on an extraordinary meeting of the Berlin-Brandenburg diocese noted that 'reactionary' Church leaders would not accept the GDR's 'preventative measures' of August 1961 (the building of the Wall) and wanted to carry on with a united Church as before, ignoring the fact that the GDR was a legal German state and West Berlin's role as a front-line city.[26] The divisions within the Church were demonstrated when Scharf failed to be elected bishop, losing the vote among the eastern delegates, while the western members refrained from voting. Voters for Scharf did so, in the eyes of the government, because he represented Church unity. Not voting for him would sanction his expulsion and might lead to others, when the Church needed to demonstrate that the state border was not a Church border. The reporter, department head Hans Weise, went on to spell out the new Church policy of driving a wedge between the two camps. Our aim, he said, was

> to deepen and exploit the existing inner contradictions in the Church and the synod so that the provocations of reactionary forces are stopped and an improvement in Church–state relations is reached. To this end, opposition forces will be supported and helped in all ways to further their work.[27]

In particular, he added, special support should be given to Superintendent Albrecht Schönherr, who indeed went on to be elected bishop of the eastern part of Berlin-Brandenburg in 1972.

Tensions between Church and state increased during the two years following the building of the Wall. Church leaders seen by the regime as conservative struggled to assert their independence and arrive at a *modus vivendi* for both themselves and their parishioners in the new GDR state from which there was no escape and which now looked like being a permanent fixture rather than the temporary arrangement for which many had prayed. At the forefront of these moves were Bishops Krummacher and Noth, who in 1962 had been elected chairman and vice-chairman, respectively, of the eastern Conference of Evangelical Church Leaders (Konferenz der Evangelischen Kirchenleitungen in der DDR), the body which represented GDR Church leaders with the government. In 1963, after lengthy deliberations, the bishops led by Krummacher drew up a series of guidelines upon which both clergy and laity could base their behaviour in a hostile environment. It was felt that, following the building of the Wall, it was especially necessary to offer guidance to Christians now living in a state of virtual isolation from the West. Known as the Ten Articles, the guidelines called in general for more obedience to Church ordinances and a distancing from the obedience demanded by the state – once again raising the issue of what exactly one should render unto Caesar. Some commentators have seen the Ten Articles as an example of the Church's gradual move towards compliance within a socialist state. Goeckel, for example, claims that they 'reflected a considerable distancing from Dibelius'.[28] Some Western theologians at the time criticised the guidelines for being weak and inconsistent. For Besier, the Ten Articles revealed a Church in distress, one which neither wished to give up its independence in the service of the state, nor to call the Church to arms or compare the SED to the Nazis.[29] However, the official reaction supports the interpretation of a contemporary British GDR-watcher who described the Articles as striking 'a Communist reader as being, in essence, intensely subversive' and 'a courageous restatement of the Christian's duty *vis-à-vis* the State'.[30] The SED leadership attacked them as contrary to the principles of the 1958 Joint Declaration and an incitement to Christians to distance themselves from the construction of a socialist state and the GDR's quest for peace.[31]

At around the same time the synod of the diocese of Saxony in Dresden went a step further. It instructed Christians not to allow themselves to be used for political propaganda purposes or become involved in the making of political statements. Known as the Order for Silence, this demand for political abstinence was interpreted by the regime as a sign of support for the FRG and NATO on the basis that those who are not with us are against us. Noth, the Bishop of Saxony, was regarded as *persona non grata* and a concerted and strongly worded attack was mounted on him and his followers. A Ministry of

Church Affairs report described the Order for Silence as an attempt to obstruct the comprehensive building of socialism through a loosening of economic and cultural responsibilities. It went on to say that this attack on the free perceptions of the fundamental rights of citizens was contrary to the constitution. A direct component of the Order, said the report,

> is the call to say nothing on NATO's policy of preparing for war and the division of the nation by those in power in Bonn. The demand to remain silent about barbarity and inhumanity is in direct contradiction to the basic clauses of the constitution, which has always stood up for the rights and freedom of mankind, for public justice, social progress, peace and friendship with all people. The diocesan synod expects its church members to be implicated once again in the cruel barbarity, inhumanity and lawlessness, devastation and mass death caused by German fascism, as did the greater part of our people in the years 1933 to 1945 ... With this order the synod disregards the will of thousands of Christians, members of church community councils, priests and so on, who through their work make a valuable contribution to the building of socialism and because of a deep Christian belief support the humanist policies of the GDR.[32]

It was just at this moment, when Church–state relations seemed to be hitting a new low, that Ulbricht demonstrated a hitherto unexpected characteristic – flexibility. Although conventional thinking has Ulbricht as an extreme hardline dogmatist in the Stalin mould, an analysis of him in the 1960s has revealed a man with the ability to adapt and, at this juncture, briefly take on the mantle of reformer.[33] In 1963, Ulbricht introduced his New Economic System (NÖS) which acknowledged the existence of profit and market forces. It was designed to raise the GDR's standard of living to a point where it could compete with the West. At the same time he began to relax some of the constraints which had so inhibited society by, for example, taking a more liberal view of such capitalist iniquities as pop music.

Regarding Church matters, there were signs that, despite the overriding objective of splitting the Evangelical Church into its eastern and western parts, and the hostility aroused by recent Church declarations, Ulbricht was prepared to countenance a reduction in the isolation that had been imposed by the Wall. In 1963 Krummacher was allowed to spend two weeks in Britain as the guest of the British Council of Churches. In return, in 1964, a delegation from the British Council of Churches visited the GDR as guests of Krummacher. The visit was significant as the first official visit by a Christian group from Britain and was seen on both sides as the forerunner to an extension of relations.[34] One of the organisers and a member of the delegation spoke of the sense of isolation felt by Christians in the GDR and the value attached to such contacts.[35] An indication of further liberalising tendencies can be seen in the 1964 government order which allowed conscientious objector status for young people opposed to conscription. Compulsory conscription had long been criticised by the Church. The order meant that young people, for reasons of conscience, would now be able to opt to do construction work instead.[36]

Perhaps the most unexpected act of this liberalising phase in relation to Church matters was the GDR's agreement to a British Christian-based project of international reconciliation taking place within the GDR. Although there were good reasons for allowing the project to proceed, the risks attached were also very great. The philosophy of reconciliation did indeed fit in well with the GDR's 'peace policy', but the downside was that by allowing such a major gesture from a Western power the morale of GDR Christians would be raised – as indeed it was. In political terms, the project was seen by the GDR as another step forward in its battle to gain international recognition. But, on the other hand, the project was not sanctioned by the British government and, therefore, bore no official weight. In addition, those involved were openly liaising with both eastern and western Church leaders, contrary to expressed GDR policy. There can be little doubt that there were those within the SED Politbüro who were opposed to the project taking place. Contrary to common mythology, GDR Communist leaders were not united although they may have liked to give that impression. The history of the project and the machinations which surrounded it provide a good illustration of the complexity of Church–state relations in the GDR, and the manner in which attempts were made to manipulate people and ideas for political ends. The waters are so murky that, even though archive material is now available, it is almost impossible to be certain of unravelling the intrigue.

The project emanated from Coventry Cathedral in Britain. The city's medieval cathedral had been destroyed during a wartime bombing raid and the new cathedral was renowned for its Christian message of reconciliation. The plan was for a group of young British volunteers to go to Dresden, a city devastated during the war and twinned with Coventry, and help to rebuild an Evangelical Church hospital which had lain largely in ruins since 1945. The project would last for at least eight months and would be an act of reconciliation between the British and all German people, with the emphasis on the 'all'. It seemed at the time that it would founder on two counts at least – first that, as a western Christian act, it would not find favour with the GDR government, and secondly that the GDR would not accept the pan-German element of the project. In addition the GDR had been almost closed to westerners other than organised groups of fellow travellers since the building of the Wall. Both the British and West German governments were opposed because they feared it would lend credence to Ulbricht's aim that the GDR should be given legal recognition as an independent state, an event which did not finally occur until 1973 when the GDR was accepted into the United Nations (UN).

The negotiations which preceded the project took two years and were carried out on two levels. The discussions which both sides were prepared to document, although they were kept secret at the time, were held between Seigewasser, the Secretary of State for Church Affairs, and the Provost of Coventry Cathedral, the Very Reverend H. C. N. (Bill) Williams.[37] The cloak-and-dagger negotiations were conducted by Präses Lothar Kreyssig and a shadowy figure called Hans Seidowsky. Kreyssig was a leading GDR Church figure, a member of the EKD synod and founder of Aktion Sühnezeichen, an organisation set up for young Germans to take part in acts of atonement for the Nazi past. Kreyssig was deeply unpopular with the GDR regime, regarded as a leader of the reactionary, pro-Western group.[38] The GDR also did not believe that it needed to atone for fascism. The guilt lay with the West where, according to the GDR, fascism still held sway. Nevertheless it was agreed by both Seigewasser and Williams that Kreyssig should be the intermediary for the practical organisation of the project. Seidowsky was a senior Stasi agent.[39] Kreyssig, unaware of this, was under the impression that his interlocutor was a representative of the Ministry of Church Affairs. It was, therefore, in some consternation that Kreyssig sent a secret letter by courier to the Provost in September 1964, after several months of negotiations, to say that he had just discovered Seidowsky did not work for the Ministry but was acting for 'someone more important'.[40] It appears that the project was riddled with Stasi informers from top to bottom. One of the ministerial representatives in Dresden, responsible for handling the project at local level, was a Stasi informer, as was his opposite number, the clergyman administering the project on behalf of the diocese. According to Besier, Oberkirchenrat Ulrich von Brück often worked for the state during the 1960s and became an official informer in 1971.[41] The Ministry of Church Affairs representative, Horst Dohle, became a Stasi informer in 1963, according to Michael Kubina.[42] Another Stasi agent within the Ministry, Hans Wilke, was also closely involved in the 'official' negotiations.[43]

The question of whether the Stasi accumulated information that was of any real importance remains to be answered. The secrets lie in the Stasi archives. But it is almost certain that the security service could only have been acting on direct orders from Ulbricht. Whatever he hoped to gain from allowing this project to go ahead, it is unlikely that he achieved his end. But it is clear that the honeymoon between Church and state, if such it was, was short lived. By 1966 the climate was changing, not only in Church–state relations, but throughout society as a whole. This change, which according to Kaiser was a reflection of the power battle taking place between Ulbricht and his successor, Erich Honecker, is well illustrated in the contrasting line taken to a proposed second visit to the GDR by a delegation from the British Council of Churches.[44] On this occasion the welcoming flags had been put back in the cupboard. The British wished to send a youth delegation to the GDR, hoping for Krummacher to issue a formal invitation as he had done before. Krummacher, however, was forced to tell the British that circumstances had changed. 'I ask you to kindly understand that we cannot invite this youth group to the GDR in the same way as previously the British Council of Churches was officially invited by the Conference of Church Leaders', he wrote in a letter to Paul Oestreicher, international department secretary of the British Council of Churches.[45] If he were to do so, things would 'not go well', he went on, because 'the position had changed'. Quite what had changed was not spelled out. But it was apparent that the Church was no longer being encouraged to extend its international contacts. The visit did take place, but the group went through the channels reserved for so-called tourists, was at all times accompanied by official minders, and had minimal contact with other than hand-picked Christians.

Difficulties were also put in the way of further youth groups from Coventry Cathedral continuing the project in Dresden, although a small group was allowed in for a couple of weeks in 1966. As early as May 1965, though, it had become obvious that some GDR leaders wanted the project closed down. An order to expel the group from Dresden was made by the Central Committee Church Affairs Working Group as a tit-for-tat measure when the British government refused to allow the Lord Mayor of Dresden to visit Britain.[46] On this occasion the project's opponents lost the battle. The expulsion order was rescinded. But the brief welcome given to Western Christians in 1964 and 1965 was not to be repeated.

In 1968 the chill which had returned to Church–state relations was apparent in a keynote speech by Seigewasser. The almost cosy relationship between Church leaders and Church Ministry officials had ceased. The tone was aggressive. 1968 would see an acceleration of the socialist development of all members of society, said Seigewasser. Citizens and society as a whole shared common interests in a socialist state, and clergymen were not excluded from this, regardless of whether they agreed to or even rejected it.[47] Seigewasser ended by announcing that things had 'got to change from the bottom up' and listed ten objectives which had the ring of orders about them. They included instructions that the Church must provide ideological support for civil thought and clergymen must condemn American aggression in Vietnam. The final point read: 'Make sure that in all areas the policies of the clergy, Church workers and their allies are in accordance with the total policy of socialist development and the broadening of a socialist world outlook.'[48] Whereas between 1963 and 1965 the emphasis had been on nurturing support from Church leaders through a combination of persuasion and liberalisation, policy in the dying days of Ulbricht's era had reverted to the traditional inflexibility of a state which regarded socialist indoctrination as the key to the future. It seems likely, although the question remains open, that in the second half of his rule Ulbricht, the supreme tactician, may have recognised that an alliance between Communists and Christians would be an unstoppable force and was therefore prepared to tone down traditional Communist dogma in order to achieve this. If so, his plan failed because he no longer had the political strength to push through such radical policies. Honecker was waiting in the wings.

The debate about the role of the Church in the GDR focuses on whether or not it acted as an oppositional force, as seemed at first to be the case when the Wall was breached in 1989, or whether it had in fact given the Communist state the recognition and authority it needed to rule. The answer is both, although opportunistic complicity between Church and state was probably greater in the post-Ulbricht years when a new breed of Churchmen came to the fore, younger men who had not experienced the 1930s or the Second World War and who may well have been more willing to bend with the wind than those who had had to fight for their beliefs on more than one occasion.

The most damning evidence against the Church has been its connections with the Stasi. The main charges against the GDR regime, *à propos* the Church, have been its use of Stasi infiltration. Sinister though these circumstances may appear, they should be seen in the context of the time, when in the West, particularly the USA, left-wing leanings were regarded as being as suspect, or more so, as being a Christian was in the GDR. The GDR may well have feared that Christians were potential traitors in their ranks, but the same mindset applied in the West to Communists. McCarthyism in 1950s America was merely the most extreme example of this paranoia. Western intelligence systems made sure that they knew what was going on within Communist ranks just as the Stasi did among Christians. Where there are security services, there are informers. Christians have more to lose in the moral stakes in that their treachery appears greater than that of non-believers. The jury is still out on the case of the Church and its relationship with the GDR regime; more evidence needs to be extracted from the mountains of files that were the GDR's lasting legacy to the world. However, evidence which has emerged is beginning to indicate not only that the Church struggled hard to maintain its integrity within the circumstances in which it found itself, but also that Ulbricht's relationship with the Church, when compared with some of the anticommunist excesses of the West, could be seen as positively benign.

Notes

1 Gerhard Besier and Stephan Wolf, *Pfarrer, Christen und Katholiken: Das Ministerium für Staatssicherheit der ehemaligen DDR und die Kirchen* (Neukirchen, 1991).
2 Mary Fulbrook, *Anatomy of a Dictatorship: Inside the GDR 1949–1989* (Oxford, 1995), 129.
3 Besier and Wolf, *Pfarrer, Christen und Katholiken*, 12. Heinrich Grüber, the official representative of the EKD to the GDR government from 1949 to 1958, had been in the same concentration camp as Werner Eggerath, the first Secretary of State for Church Affairs.
4 John S. Conway, 'Interpreting the German church struggles 1933–1990',

German History, 16 (1998), 3.
5   BAB, DO-4/2526, Ulbricht's speech on the relationship between state and Church, 4 October 1960.
6   Robert Goeckel, *The Lutheran Church and the East German State* (New York and London, 1990), 9. In 1946, 80.9 per cent of the GDR population claimed to be members of the Evangelical Church; 12.1 per cent were Roman Catholics; and 1 per cent belonged to minority faiths. By 1964, the figure for the Evangelical Church had dropped to 59.3 per cent.
7   BAB, DO-4/2526, draft Ministry of Church Affairs (SfKF) report on the position of religion and the Church in the GDR, 10 August 1962.
8   Jürgen Moltmann, 'Religion and state in Germany: West and East', *Annals of the American Academy of Political and Social Science*, 483 (1986), 110–17.
9   Goeckel, *The Lutheran Church*, 18–19.
10 Ibid., 62 and Besier and Wolf, *Pfarrer, Christen und Katholiken*, 14.
11 BAB, DO-4/2526, SfKF report on the position of the Church in the GDR, 1962.
12 Gerhard Besier, *Der SED-Staat und die Kirche: Der Weg in die Anpassung*, (Munich, 1993), 575.
13 Fulbrook, *Anatomy*, 98.
14 In 1965, for example, a British clergyman, the Reverend Martin Turner, on a visit to the GDR was surprised to be asked by party officials for his views on British school hours: whether afternoon school was a good idea. It turned out that the government was considering extending school hours, a measure which would have hampered the Church's religious instruction for children which often took place in the afternoon. Religious instruction in schools themselves had been banned in 1946. The question about school hours was a political question; if Turner had approved of longer school hours he would have been seen to have been supporting the state against the Church.
15 Evangelisches Zentralarchiv, Bestand 102/373, Krummacher-Pabst correspondence, 1965.
16 Fulbrook, *Anatomy*, 94.
17 BAB, DO-4/2477, Kohl to Hartwig, 30 January 1958.
18 Ibid., Kohl to Hartwig, 4 February 1958.
19 Ibid., Hartwig's report of meeting with Kohl, 26 February 1958.
20 Ibid., Kohl to Hartwig, 19 March 1958.
21 Ibid., Hartwig to Kohl, 26 March 1958.
22 BAB, DO-4/2526, SfKF report on the position of religion and the Church in the GDR and the abuse of Church and religion in West Germany, 1962. The report quotes Adenauer that God had given the German people the special task of guarding the West against the East.
23 Ibid., statement by the Prime Minister's press office, 21 July 1958.
24 Besier, *Der SED-Staat*, 442.
25 For an account of Scharf's exclusion from East Berlin see Besier, *Der SED-Staat*, 423–30.
26 BAB, DO-4/369, SfKF report on an extraordinary meeting of Berlin-Brandenburg Synod, 7–9 December 1962.
27 Ibid.
28 Goeckel, *The Lutheran Church*, 63.
29 Besier, *Der SED-Staat*, 546.

30 Public Record Office, FO 371/169324, British Foreign Office report on Church–state relations in the GDR, 10 August 1963.
31 SAPMO-BArch, DY 30/IV A2/14, SED church affairs working group report, 23 July 1963.
32 BAB, DO-4/369, SfKF report on the synod of the Saxony diocese on 27 March 1963.
33 Monika Kaiser, *Machtwechsel von Ulbricht zu Honecker: Funktionsmechanismen der SED-Diktatur in Konfliktsituationen 1962 bis 1972* (Berlin, 1997).
34 *Sonnabend*, 16 January 1965.
35 Report of the associate secretary of the British Council of Churches international department, the Reverend Paul Oestreicher, October 1964. He also mentioned that the visit was given top billing in a GDR newspaper (unnamed) – a sure sign of official government approval.
36 Hartwig Bögeholz, *Wendepunkte – die Chronik der Republik: Der Weg der Deutschen in Ost und West* (Hamburg, 1999), 309.
37 The negotiations are recorded in the archives of Coventry Cathedral, the MfKF and the British Foreign Office.
38 BAB, DO-4/2955, SfKF report on Kreyssig, 25 May 1963.
39 Bernd Schäfer, *Staat und katholische Kirche in der DDR* (Cologne, 1998), 111.
40 Coventry Cathedral archives, Kreyssig to Williams, September 1964.
41 Besier, *Pfarrer, Christen und Katholiken*, 26.
42 Klaus Schröder (ed.), *Geschichte und Transformation des SED-Staates* (Berlin, 1994), 133.
43 Schäfer, *Staat und katholische Kirche*, 96.
44 Kaiser, *Machtwechsel*.
45 Evangelisches Zentralarchiv, 102/268, Krummacher-Oestreicher-Pabst correspondence.
46 BAB, DO-4/650, SfKF report, 18 May 1965.
47 BAB, DO-4/2526, Seigewasser, 'The basic problems of state policy and church affairs, with special consideration of the crucial tasks for 1968', 12 February 1968.
48 *Ibid*.

13

The fifth column: dance music in the early German Democratic Republic

Toby Thacker

There is only a short entry under the heading 'dance music' in the official history of music in the GDR. It describes the development of an alternative to the products of the 'bourgeois-capitalist entertainment industry', giving examples of the new kinds of text, music and dances developed during the 1950s. The authors describe the collective work of the SED, Ministry of Culture, Composers' Association and State Radio Committee, and praise the 'high artistic level' that the best of their efforts reached.[1] The reader might infer from the brevity of the article, only a few pages in a multi-volume history, that this was a matter of minor importance in the cultural life of a state committed to elevating the artistic taste of the masses, but this would be mistaken. GDR leaders, cultural officials and composers recognised the enormous influence of dance music as a medium of suggestion, and in the first decade of the GDR's existence, an unrelenting struggle was waged against its westernised forms. This campaign was conducted with the committed support of the SED leadership, and the involvement of many government departments and mass organisations. Sustained theoretical analysis was matched with a range of practical initiatives; repression and censorship were accompanied by a studious cultivation of new songs and dances. And, however the GDR's own historians tried to cover this up, it failed completely. Much has been written on the role of popular music in the *later* GDR, and on the oppositional youth cultures that centred on rock and punk music there.[2] I will analyse here the struggle for a socialist dance culture in the 1950s, and argue that in fact the battle against western popular music was fought and lost before the Wall was built.

The context: pluralism and confusion

Perhaps the damage was done in the five years before the resolution of the third SED congress in July 1950, which announced an offensive against

'American cultural barbarism'. Jazz, never entirely suppressed by the Nazis, enjoyed a resurgence of popularity in the cities of eastern Germany after they were occupied by the Red Army in 1945. The Radio Berlin Dance Orchestra was the first German band to start broadcasting after the war, with the permission of the Soviets. In the relative cultural pluralism of the SBZ, the enthusiasm spread. Leipzig quickly gained a reputation as a centre for jazz, and as we shall see, a notable taste for this music also developed in surrounding cities. Although the passion for genuine American jazz was only a minority interest, by 1950 no part of the GDR was immune to the characteristic form of the postwar West German hit song, or *Schlager*, typified by a dreamy sentimentality and escapism. At no time in the next decade was there any indication that the enthusiasm for jazz, for West German hits and their various hybrid forms, was in any way diminished. By 1949, however, when the GDR was founded, the Soviet Union's hostility towards all expressions of cultural modernism was being felt in Eastern Europe; this music was now seen as the decadent expression of late bourgeois society, cynically used as an imperialist tool to destroy the taste and culture of the masses.

This hostility was articulated by the GDR's leading musical theoretician, Ernst Hermann Meyer, at the founding conference of the Association of German Composers (*Verband Deutscher Komponisten*, or VDK) in April 1951. Addressing an audience which included Pieck, Grotewohl, Ulbricht and Paul Wandel, as well as a Soviet delegation, Meyer devoted much of his opening speech to what he described as 'American entertainment kitsch', or 'boogie-woogie'. This was 'a channel through which the poison of Americanism penetrates and threatens to anaesthetise the minds of the workers', 'just as dangerous as a military attack with poison gases'. It was, Meyer argued, part of a wider American scheme to 'conquer the musical markets of countries' and 'to undermine their cultural independence'. He stressed the role of mass media: 'Through radio, films, and records a veritable tide of boogie-woogie is let loose on the German people'. West German publishers and record companies were the 'people-hostile' agents of this American offensive. According to Meyer, dance music was part of 'the degenerate ideology of American monopoly capital with its lack of culture, ... its empty sensationalism, and above all its fury for war and destruction'. Summing up, he said: 'We should speak plainly here of a Fifth Column of Americanism. It would be wrong to misjudge the dangerous role of American hit music in the preparation for war.'[3] This perception did not change over the next decade; it resulted in a systematic effort to stop this kind of music from being played in the GDR and to replace it with 'socialist realism'.[4]

Control of music was not clearly demarcated in the early GDR. A number of state and party organisations, including the Kulturbund, the Gewerkschaft Kunst and the FDJ, contributed to policy-making. The Academy of Arts, formed in March 1950, and authorised to act as supreme arbiter of taste, had a Music Section, which pursued its own enquiry into the problem of dance music in 1952, headed by the composer Max Butting. The VDK was founded in April 1951, and was centrally involved with dance music from then on. Nominally, music fell within the orbit of Paul Wandel's Ministry of Education; at the top of this bureaucratic pyramid was the Central Committee's Department of Culture. However, licensing of musicians, and supervision of their programmes, was in practice carried out by local party officials, often following their own regulations. This situation was clearly intolerable, and in March 1951 the Central Committee called for a commission with complete control of culture. The State Commission for Artistic Affairs (or 'Stakuko', as it became known within the party), named after the similar organisation formed in the USSR in 1936, was established in August 1951, and given wide-ranging powers to control all musical activity. Rudolf Hartig, an old KPD fighter, was put in charge of music. Ironically, although Stakuko was intended to bring order where there was chaos, almost everything it did was tinged with ineptitude, and its many different strategies one by one ran into trouble.[5]

'An order which creates disorder'

Stakuko had two approaches to dance music. The first was repressive, and consisted of a series of measures, administrative and practical, to prevent any music deemed 'unacceptable' from being played. The second was more creative, and involved a range of efforts to promote new dance music in the GDR. Both were underpinned by close theoretical analysis, and carried out in the style of 'collective work' developed at the SED conference of July 1952. As far as can be judged from surviving Stakuko files, this resulted in terrible confusion; frequently, the reality of 'collective' and 'planned' work was the very opposite of what was intended.

As a first step, Hartig met in October 1951 with representatives from government ministries, trade unions and the Volkspolizei, to discuss the control of dance music.[6] After this, he was ordered by Holtzhauer, the chairman of Stakuko, to produce a directive to ensure uniform control over the employment of all performing musicians in the GDR. Before acting, Hartig decided to take stock of the situation. Measures reported from Saxony clearly impressed him. The regional government there had a concise regulation for licensing dance musicians and controlling their programmes. This stressed the importance of education in developing good taste, and highlighted the responsibility of all party organisations, including the FDJ, Stakuko, the radio, composers and the Volkspolizei, to work actively in the struggle against Americanised dance music. Dance bands were to be prevented from playing if they did not support these goals, and proprietors of dance halls made aware 'that they were also responsible for the purity [*Sauberkeit*] of their dance bands'.[7] Hartig expressed full agreement with this approach, and sent copies to all other *Länder*, asking them to report on their own efforts.[8]

The responses from around the country were dismaying. Clearly there was no uniformity of either theory or practice. Even where there were harsh rules on paper, implementation of licensing, and control of performance were inconsistent.[9] Reporting to the Central Committee, Hartig wrote that 'as far as the employment of musicians was concerned', there was 'an apparent chaos' in all parts of the GDR.[10]

Two administrative measures were central to Stakuko's plans. The first, a crudely worded prohibition of the performance of jazz, was ready by December 1951, stating that: 'it is now time . . . to find an appropriate form of dance music for our changed societal development . . . The performance of all jazz music is to cease. In all public dance events there should only be music played which is essentially stressed by melody and not rhythm.'[11] Implementing the ban was more difficult. Hartig's plan was simple in conception, but proved unworkable in practice. He intended, by determining *who* was allowed to play, to control *what* was played. In January 1952 he had a draft 'order' ready, according to which all musicians would have to seek a permit from a local licensing commission. To do this they would have to pass an exam with a practical, a music theory and a general educational component.[12] The employment of musicians without a permit was to be punished by a fine of up to 500 marks, or by arrest. Any private engagement of musicians was to be forbidden.[13]

This fantastically complicated structure of committees and examinations was obviously impractical, and over the next few months Hartig received suggestions for amendments. At the same time, complaints about the situation in the provinces poured in. As Hartig produced revision after revision, his patience began to wear thin. He wrote a long letter to Holtzhauer in June 1952, complaining about the time it was taking. He was now working on an eighth draft, and the prestige of Stakuko was at stake.[14] By July, a much-abbreviated version of the original was sent to various ministries and the Central Committee.[15] This brought a storm of criticism down on Hartig. Roman Chwalek, Minister of Labour, demanded a ruling from the President's office on whether or not the FDGB should be involved in issuing permits for musicians.[16] In August he wrote angrily to Stakuko that the 'unclarified situation for professional musicians had become unacceptable'.[17] The Ministry of Justice, and various *Länder* governments quite sensibly pointed out that Stakuko's proposed regulations were unworkable; they would for instance prevent somebody from playing music informally at a wedding party. A Berlin trade union leader wrote to Hartig, telling him that efforts to deal with the situation locally had made him a laughing stock.[18] There was open criticism of Stakuko in the GDR press. The FDJ later called it an 'order which creates disorder'.[19] And still further revisions were passed from one office to another. In October, Hartig was at work on a fourteenth draft, by December the sixteenth. Finally, a much abbreviated version was sent to the government in March 1953. Hartig must have breathed a sigh of relief when it was published in April.[20]

It is interesting to compare this bureaucratic activity with the reports reaching Stakuko from around the GDR. Party officials at local and national level were inundated with complaints about the music being played and the effect it was having on audiences. A selection from 1952 and 1953, *after* Stakuko's prohibition on jazz, is revealing. A local official, Federbusch, wrote from Jena in October 1952 about the Horst Hartmann Melody and Rhythm Band. He noted with dismay that towards the end of their first set they had played 'particularly American hot music', and so complained, only to be told that bands had to make concessions to the public and 'that in other towns, it was passed over with a smile'. Hartmann had then gone on to direct the band's second set, which allegedly descended into 'shrillest atonality', and became 'a primitive, sanctimonious prating'. Slipping easily into Nazi terminology, Federbusch demanded that 'such degeneracies' (*Entartungen*) should not be tolerated.[21]

Another example suggests that this casual disregard for party authority was widespread. The Hans-Georg During Dance Orchestra had been banned from playing in Liebenwerda on 8 September 1952 by a local official. During then apparently announced in the local newspaper that the orchestra would play on 18 September in the Liebenwerda Kurhaus. A local education officer had gone along with a Volkspolizei officer to observe. Their shocked description was mailed to Stakuko two days later. The band had started the evening with a RIAS-style medley of American hits, sung in German. They had then stopped playing, and a member of the band had read out the party's ban, which was greeted by an 'ear-splitting chorus of whistles'. He then read two letters of praise for the band from other local party organisations. Worse followed. The audience was told that the band could play 'respectable music', which they demonstrated with a medley of waltzes, again greeted with whistles and jeers. After this display of sarcasm, the band went back to playing 'wild' American music to great applause and acclaim.[22] Nor was this kind of display confined to the cities. An official of the State Radio Committee had spent an evening in the tiny village of Regis Breitingen, in Saxony, and was shocked by what he saw at a local dance evening, describing 'torrents' and 'wild cascades of sound at high volume' which provoked many to 'wild bodily dislocations'.[23]

Unrestrained dancing was not the end of it. Other reports confirm that dance evenings were often accompanied by violence and rioting. At regional conferences in Gera and Chemnitz, dance band leaders described 'the wildest dancing, amidst the smashing of beerglasses'. They reported that 'chairs were frequently smashed up'. Apparently bands were unwilling to play too 'hot' in case they were unable to escape the ensuing chaos with their instruments intact. One band leader told how a policeman had danced so shamelessly in front of the audience that he had not wanted to go on playing.[24] From Leipzig, a succession of letters in 1953 reported terrible scenes in the Felsenkeller, where before 1914 Rosa Luxemburg and Karl Liebknecht had spoken to earnest audiences. FDJ evenings there had ended with 'bloodied heads and smashed-up cloakrooms'.[25] Thus, even representatives of the regime could 'go native', leaving officials divided about the proper course of action.

The case of the Karl Walter Dance Orchestra from Chemnitz, one of the GDR's most popular bands, provides an example of this confusion and its consequences. Like During, Walter had been reported to Stakuko in 1952 for playing unsuitable music. In 1953 he was several times banned from performing by local officials, but like During and Hartmann, was not intimidated. According to the *Volksstimme*, this 'propagandist for American unculture' encouraged his audiences to drink beer from buckets, and even appeared on the podium with rolled-up shirtsleeves. Claiming that it was reacting to widespread local protest, 'in particular from young people', the council of the newly-named Karl-Marx-Stadt took the radical step in March 1954 of banning Walter permanently, and forbidding his musicians from appearing together in any other group.[26] Other local officials objected, but before the issue was resolved, Walter and his colleagues simply fled to West Germany, where their *Republikflucht* was much celebrated. Hartig, who made an immediate journey to Karl-Marx-Stadt to investigate, was furious with the insensitivity of local officials, clearly regarding the propaganda aspects of the case as more damaging than the actual performance of the band.[27] We can imagine how much more frustrated he would have been had he known that Walter's fans were writing to the BBC in London to contradict the official line being given out by the SED, and to ask for regular broadcasts of his music. They were looking forward to his reappearance in the GDR, when 'we won't only drink beer out of buckets, there will be mugs on the table, because that will be the day which we all yearn for, the day of "freedom" for the Eastern Zone'. In fact within only days of Walter's arrival in West Germany, the BBC was considering making recordings of his band for broadcast 'back to the Zone in the "Jazz with Joe" programme'. AFN and RIAS apparently already had recordings ready for use.[28]

Creating realist alternatives

It was obviously important for the authorities to generate alternatives to the Americanised kitsch currently on offer. This involved an offensive on several fronts. The State Radio Committee had a role to play in supervising broadcasting in the GDR. Radio signals from the West would have to be jammed as far as possible. Composers, arrangers, and songwriters had to be encouraged to write 'progressive', 'realistic' music reflecting everyday life, which would help the workforce to relax after its daily exertions. Above all, the state publishing house and the state record company had to react quickly, and get sheet music and records to the public. As an immediate measure, Stakuko announced a competition in May 1952 for composers and writers of dance music, with prize money of up to 1,000 marks. The results were announced in November. Apparently the entries received had not contributed to 'a new German dance music', and only 'consolation prizes' could be awarded. The development of dance music was at a 'complete standstill'; GDR music production could be summed up as a 'dream factory'.[29] Stakuko published its own damning verdict: 'Almost all the compositions sent in showed melodic, harmonic, and rhythmic poverty, and displayed sickly-kitschy sentimentality in the texts.' The seeming inability to publish songs written in the GDR quickly was also identified as a critical problem.[30]

In the longer term, it was important to establish structures for the collective work needed to produce new music. Hartig's plan here was to create a 'Dance Music Commission' which could deal with all ramifications of the problem, and bring the different party bodies together with composers and authors. Although, typically, the organisation for the first meeting in December 1952 was chaotic, it did take place.[31] Excerpts were published, together with a unanimous resolution, which typically strayed from its immediate purpose and linked the creation of 'a melodically healthy and rhythmically expressive dance music' with the wider political situation, and ended up rambling about the 'war politics of the Adenauer Clique'.[32]

By the end of 1952, the failure of all efforts to improve the situation was obvious, and was discussed in the highest party echelons. Leaving Stakuko to continue its vain efforts at regulation, the Central Committee sought in early 1953 to build on the theoretical work of the preceding year, and get on with the creation of an alternative dance culture. Hans Lauter, who ran the Central Committee's Department of Culture, expressed concern about the instrumentation and arrangements used by many dance bands, and noted that the main problem was 'the development of new dance movements'.[33] His intervention was followed by a conscious effort to produce new dance steps and song texts. The Berlin branch of the VDK had already suggested to Stakuko that local composers should work with a dance-partnership, the Kornills, to develop new dances; these could then be popularised with a booklet containing various sheet music arrangements, and a card with details of the new dance steps. Foreshadowing later initiatives of this kind, they suggested that the new dances could be publicised on radio, television and records.[34] A similar initiative was undertaken in Dresden, but neither appears to have led to anything.

The Dance Music Commission turned to the thorny question of new texts, and made a concerted effort in early 1953 to improve on the incredibly slow publication of sheet music for new songs. Typically, German hits in the early 1950s were written on one or more of three themes: sentimental love, nostalgia for an idealised *Heimat*, or an escapist vision of Mediterranean or South Sea sunshine. None of these was in any sense helpful in positively reflecting existing conditions in the new socialist state. Reviewing new texts, the Commission suggested that a song about Hawaii could be altered to refer instead to Lübeck.[35] Many, though, were beyond redemption. Hans-Joachim Fleischer had written a song called 'Rosalinde' which prompted this reaction:

> Why texts, which stand in relationship to nothing? For a progressive text, for instance with relevance to a tractor driver, a foxtrot is out of the question. The tractor driver must have music which is full of life and zest. A foxtrot, a leftover from the time of the bourgeoisie, simply won't do for someone who stands firmly in our new world.[36]

Ominously, the Commission proposed to hold further discussions with Comrade Fleischer. It was more enthusiastic about 'Coffee Beans', but even with this apparently excellent text there were potential difficulties: 'In the interests of quick popularity we advise rapid publication, as long as the import of coffee beans holds out.'[37] One song could be unreservedly recommended: 'We are dancing only for joy.' Others were missing the point. 'In the little pavilion by the sea' was scornfully rejected.[38] In this prescriptive climate it was, unsurprisingly, very difficult to get writers to submit texts, and harder still to find texts acceptable for publication.

Stakuko and the Central Committee had also long been aware that sheet music for GDR-produced songs was virtually unobtainable; this had been highlighted by complaints from the regions and previous analyses.[39] Although West German hits were publicly characterised in the GDR as the weapons of monopoly capital, internal reports contradicted this. There were in the early 1950s over a thousand small West German publishers pouring out a flood of songs. Their release was typically accompanied by a free distribution of sheet music arrangements to dance bands, in the GDR and in West Germany. The songs had only an ephemeral popularity, and this worked against the GDR publishing house VEB 'Lied der Zeit', which despite its claim to contemporaneity, took many months to publish arrangements, usually for a large ensemble such as a 16-piece orchestra. Most bands were much smaller though, typically consisting of five or six musicians. There were simply no GDR arrangements available for them. In the circumstances, they played what the public wanted, and what they could get free from the West.

The Ministry for Culture: a 'New Course'?

In November 1953 Stakuko was disbanded by order of the Politbüro. In the wider reappraisal of the party's role after the failed uprising of 17 June, it had been publicly criticised for its bureaucratic intervention in artistic affairs. If there had to be a scapegoat for the cultural failings of the party, Stakuko would do. In the specific field of dance music, it had already been criticised, and certainly its record here was one of utter futility. In January 1954 the SED created a new Ministry of Culture, and declared that artists would be called upon to take more responsibility for their own affairs.[40] Initially, the struggle for a new dance music was carried on by more or less the same people. Rudolf Hartig was put in charge of music in the new Ministry, and the Dance Music Commission continued its work. The mood of the so-called 'New Course' did engender some clearer thinking though, and gradually a subtle change in policy emerged.

A report to the new Minister of Culture, Johannes R. Becher, was frank. The discussion on dance music in expert circles had so far produced nothing worthy of mention. It still took between twelve and eighteen months to produce sheet music after GDR songs first appeared on records and on the radio. Obviously by this time, any popularity the songs might have had, had long since evaporated. The reason given for this incredible slowness was, ironically, 'shortage of paper'.[41] The Ministry's response was complacent. Yet another committee was formed to look into the printing problem. This body typically lost its focus, and highlighted musical and textual problems. Its ideas on 'themes for a dance song' are interesting, however. They included, uncontroversially, 'seasons of the year, the joy of creation, affirmation of our life, sport, travel, holidays, conviviality', and 'the beauty of *Heimat*'. The 'beauty of foreign lands' was only acceptable, however, if 'this also communicates a subjective reality of their pleasures', and the troublesome area of 'dreams', only 'as far as they are generally possible and recognisably attainable'. 'Lecherousness, pornography, obscenity, filth and trash', the committee added, 'do not belong in a dance song'.[42]

By the end of the year, the luckless Hartig had been taken off the case. The poisoned chalice was passed to Hans-Georg Uszkoreit, who tried to combat the undertone of resignation that had crept into the debate. In the mid-1950s, the principal concern of the SED was not with the performance of real American jazz, but with the widespread popularity of West German kitsch. Jazz in the 1950s was never more than a minority interest even in West Germany, and was by the middle of the decade achieving a degree of academic and artistic respectability there, just as in the USA and in Britain. This was reflected in the GDR, where a more discriminating approach was being taken, both in public, and in internal party discussions. Unfortunately there is not scope here for a full discussion of the unique case of Reginald Rudorf, that unusual animal, an SED activist who was also a genuine jazz lover. Rudorf, after graduating from the University of Leipzig, was accepted by the GDR musical authorities in 1952 as an expert on jazz, and allowed to speak and write about it. By 1954 he was openly critical of the party line, arguing that jazz had become the legitimate voice of the international proletariat. Rebukes from the SED did not dampen his enthusiasm, and he continued to lecture throughout the GDR, often speaking at jazz concerts; he also appeared in West Germany, and became involved in the production of a DEFA jazz film. Uszkoreit reported him to the Stasi in 1955. Undeterred, Rudorf even spoke at a jazz performance in a church in Halle. Finally, after a lecture in Leipzig, he was denounced by FDJ zealots, arrested in April 1957, charged under the notorious 'boycott-hate' law of 1951, and sentenced to two years' imprisonment. Paradoxically, during the Rudorf debate, the party was gradually softening its line on jazz.[43]

The GDR was in the mid-1950s more preoccupied with West German hits, and with their imitation. There was now a degree of public acceptance that this was unavoidable, and that perhaps the best that could be done was to encourage the performance of more acceptable music alongside this decadent sentimentality. In May 1957 the GDR's leading musical journal published an article from a 'reader' about the outcome of recent efforts at reform. Heinz Lehmann described the dance music produced in the last three years as 'hardly encouraging, if not shameful', bitterly criticising 'the texts and the way they are sung'. He wrote scornfully of 'Hawaii guitar twanging' and 'shallow male whingeing', and asked, 'what is going on in the minds of these artists? Is it somehow the purpose of this kind of dance music, that the public, after the strains of its daily work, should be tastefully narcoticised?'[44]

There was of course another new factor. Rock 'n' roll arrived in Germany in the early months of 1956, and the listening habits of young people changed almost overnight. Elvis Presley and Bill Haley songs were spread through West Germany largely through the medium of film. This was obviously not accessible in the GDR; it was in West Berlin though, in cinemas near to the boundary with East Berlin, and large numbers of young people from East Berlin and the surrounding areas visited them there. Broadcasts from Radio Luxembourg, the British Forces Network and Radio in the American Sector (RIAS) made sure that rock 'n' roll was widely heard in the GDR. Censorship was more subtle than with jazz, but equally ineffective. At a meeting of dance band leaders in Berlin, Uszkoreit 'recommended' them not to play the new craze.[45] He instructed the record industry not to produce any rock 'n' roll recordings. In practice, evidence suggests that the situation deteriorated noticeably. West German musicians appeared at a festival in Magdeburg playing rock 'n' roll,[46] and a stallholder at a market in Halle was blamed for inciting a riot there in August 1957 by playing rock 'n' roll records.[47]

An internal analysis of broadcast dance music provides a picture of the popular music being played in the GDR in early 1957: 'Many hits have English texts and above all English titles. In numerous cases they ... originated in English-speaking countries.' One 30-minute programme on Radio-DDR apparently consisted exclusively of English titles. Deutschlandsender's 40-minute 'Youth and Jazz' on 19 January had played eight songs, seven in English. Reviewing the musical aspect of the songs, the report was equally critical, and mentioned a new problem: 'There are many primitive texts which often don't contain a single word but are made up of a stammering of individual sounds.' Other difficulties identified back in the early 1950s were highlighted again. GDR publishers were now producing about fourteen new songs monthly. In the same period, over 2,000 West German publishers were pouring out as many as 4,000 new songs. Sheet music for many of these was reaching dance bands in the GDR free of charge in only a few days. A similar situation prevailed in the recording industry, where the GDR label Amiga had signed an agreement with Polydor from West Germany, and was producing mainly records of western hits, performed by western artists. Recent offerings from Amiga included songs like 'Come back to Sorrente', 'Jeepers Creepers', 'Fifty-Fifty', 'Walkin' Shoes', 'She Sleeps', and 'Swedish Pastry'. Radio stations in the GDR could choose from a huge selection of western hits, but had so few new GDR records that they had to play them all, including such classics as 'Dear Little People's Policewoman'.[48] The GDR's technical backwardness was made even more painfully apparent when Max Butting, the Academy's expert on dance music, discovered that despite all the good intentions of Stakuko and the Ministry of Culture, the GDR was still not capable of producing long-playing records, which all had to be imported from West Germany and Czechoslovakia, obviously at great expense.[49] It was thus no huge sacrifice for Költzsch, in charge of the record industry, to agree with Uszkoreit not to produce any rock 'n' roll records.[50]

'A new action'?

The GDR's efforts to generate socialist alternatives to 'Americanised kitsch' in the early and mid-1950s had created clear battle-lines, between puritans, mostly from the Ministry of Culture and the VDK, who rejected any compromise with western music, and pragmatists who advocated the absorption and use of elements from the West. By 1958 it appeared that a compromise had been reached, when it was decreed that radio stations and dance bands might play 40 per cent western titles, so long as the remaining 60 per cent were from the GDR, Soviet Union or other 'people's democracies'.[51] Yet, new popular cultural challenges in the shape of rock 'n' roll and the dance craze unleashed by the 'Twist', were to revive the internal debate. Subsequent attempts to ride these new waves, while at the same time trying to force them into socialist channels, degenerated into bitter farce.

The creation of the 'Lipsi' in 1959, apparently a kind of calypso named after the Latin word for Leipzig, drew selectively on western elements to appeal specifically to younger audiences; it was closely followed by the 'Pertutti', described in the files as a 'community dance'. It was decided, with the support of the Central Committee, to popularise these as rapidly as possible, using all the media available to the GDR.[52] Even while they were being developed though, the co-ordinated effort was collapsing. Clearly the most progressive voices, concentrated in the recording and broadcasting sectors, were chafing under party restrictions, aware that the cumbersome processes of 'collective work' made it impossible to compete with the West. The unimaginative half-way house represented by the 'Lipsi' and the 'Pertutti' did not help, and in the summer of 1960, even as they were supposed to be popularising the new dances, a group of officials from Radio-DDR decided to act on their own initiative and get on with producing and broadcasting western-style music. The plan reached the ears of the VDK, which promptly informed the Central Committee. Clearly there was by 1960 a situation of virtual breakdown in the GDR's music industry, at a time when the SED leadership was deeply and publicly concerned by the influence of western popular music.[53] According to Gerhard Bab, Secretary of the VDK, the governing body of Radio-DDR had decided to start 'a new action', as current production of dance music was 'boring and uninteresting'. It intended to commission hits using 'modern rhythms', in order 'to reach the level of Radio Luxembourg'.[54] Bab named a Comrade Spielhaus[55] as the architect of this plot, abetted by officials from the film and recording industries; one had apparently already written a 'slow rock' number. The response of the party was not to condemn Spielhaus or his colleagues, but characteristically to call for more documentation. Spielhaus was asked to produce 'an analysis of the situation in the area of dance music, with conclusions'.[56] His response in August 1960 was unusually perceptive and honest. He defended the influence of jazz as 'full-blooded' and 'vital', described recent GDR production as 'boring', and argued that the recent initiative was intended to raise the GDR's recordings to a 'technical world-level'.[57]

This is not the place to consider the slow and painful liberalisation that followed, as the GDR reacted to successive waves of popular music from Britain and America in the 1960s. I will conclude by looking at the fate of the 'Lipsi' and the 'Pertutti' while officials wrangled about the way forward. Spielhaus' report included a statistical analysis of the sad progress of the 'Lipsi' towards obscurity. Of 389 titles produced in the GDR since 1 January 1960, a mere fourteen, or 3.6 per cent, were 'Lipsis'. As for the 'Pertutti', an anguished Bab wrote to the Central Committee in September about 'the necessity to popularise the new "Pertutti" dance as quickly as possible'. The whole process was, he said, 'going very slowly'. In fact things were worse than that. Although the VDK had primed the record industry, publishers, radio and television about the new dance months in advance, they had all done nothing. Bab warned, unconsciously summarising the work of the previous ten years, 'and so arises the danger, ... that our efforts to carry through new ideas in the area of dance music ... come to naught'.[58]

Living with the enemy

Why was the GDR's campaign for an alternative dance music such a dismal failure? Commonly it is assumed that, since the GDR could not seal itself off from the capitalist world, it was fatally handicapped from the start. It is clear from the files, however, that the authorities in the early GDR were far more concerned with the live performance of American jazz and West German hits, and with their own broadcasts, than with those reaching them from outside. The 'inundation' argument also assumes that western popular music had some intrinsic attraction that made it irresistible, regardless of geography or social context, and this is demonstrably untrue. Certainly, inept leadership and the constant bungling of officials involved did not help the GDR's cause. The application of the principles of 'collective' and 'planned' work resulted in the haphazard and inconsistent application of the GDR's own censorship, and ended in the creation of music by committee, which could not match the casual style and easy spontaneity of the best western offerings. The GDR's creative effort was earnest and thoughtful, and this may have been quite inappropriate in working with musical forms that were typically light-hearted and vacuous. This gulf was also reflected in the musical interests of the officials and musicians involved. Typically they were serious composers and musicologists whose conception of dance music started with Johann Strauss and Offenbach; they were increasingly out of touch with changing public tastes.

The root causes for the failure of the GDR's campaign are to be found in the thinking behind its creative effort, and in particular in the two main demands it made of songwriters in the 1950s. These were that songs should be 'realistic', and should draw on the people's own musical heritage. We have seen some of the absurd themes used, and they are indeed easy targets for satire, but what were songwriters expected to write about? Should they try to portray the conditions in a uranium mine in the Erzgebirge? Or rows of elderly men in drab suits sitting in interminable meetings before giving unanimous assent to a previously drafted resolution? How could they 'positively reflect' the physical or psychological reality of life in cities that had been reduced to rubble by British bombers, and seen many of their women raped by Red Army soldiers in 1945? Even the enforced jollity of a party rally, or the constructive pleasure of comradely work in building a new society, was apt to produce songs that were wooden and tedious.[59] The very essence of the American and West German music so popular in the GDR was escapism. Whether the music conjured up images of affluence and glamour in the USA, or warm sunshine and easy living under southern skies, its lack of contact with any kind of reality in postwar Germany was its greatest attraction.

The demand for an organic connection with the rhythms and melodies of the people was less damaging; after all, as GDR analysts pointed out, jazz was originally the genuine folk expression of oppressed black slaves in the American South, and West German hits drew constantly on folk rhythms and tunes. Musically though, this demand prevented songwriters in the GDR from using the new instruments and arrangements which characterised music from the West. It led to a preference for strings and accordions rather than the drums, saxophone, trumpet and trombone which led American jazz, and made it quite unthinkable that artists in the GDR should exploit the electric guitar. The GDR's dance music was condemned to archaism in a world embracing modernity. When, towards the end of the 1950s, some exploitation of contemporary western musical elements was permitted, it was always too little, too late, and never carried conviction.

Even in censorship and repression, the GDR was ineffective. We have seen how GDR officials used the Nazi vocabulary of denigration in their own descriptions and analyses of western music, and it may be that some of those who railed against jazz in the 1950s had said much the same thing in the 1930s and 1940s. Yet, whereas the Nazis had attempted to prevent the performance of authentic jazz, Goebbels had encouraged the production of bland, commercialised dance music, particularly during the war. The GDR tried not only to outlaw real jazz, but fought in addition against precisely the kind of 'perfumed hits' the Nazis had popularised. Indeed, they sometimes accused West German hits of carrying Nazi meanings.[60] It is important to discriminate, however. Only rarely were officials in the GDR racist in their attacks on jazz. Typically, they took care to distinguish between 'original jazz', the legitimate expression of an exploited sub-proletariat, and the subsequent commodified product of the American entertainment industry. Only less thoughtful local officials, often not musically trained, allowed racist undertones to slip into their denunciations of jazz and 'boogie-woogie' with the use of adjectives like 'primitive' and 'wild'.[61] When it came to censorship, there was nothing in the GDR in the 1950s to compare with the physical brutality of Nazi repression. Musicians were not beaten up, imprisoned, or killed. Performance licences could be withdrawn, and thus a musician's ability to earn a living was easily threatened, but even this punishment was used sparingly.[62]

In one respect though, as the case of the fleeing Karl Walter had shown, the GDR's leaders and theorists were absolutely right. Dance music was a 'Trojan Horse', a 'Fifth Column'. Its whole culture, and the behaviour and attitudes associated with it, were profoundly antithetical to the values of the GDR. The continued performance and popularity of this music in the 1950s constituted a victory of escapism and individualism over 'realism' and 'collective work', and left a significant aspect of most people's lives that the SED could never reach. This recognition, and the accompanying frustration, were reflected in the continued hostility of the party towards western popular music after 1961, as is evident from Mark Fenemore's Chapter 10 in this volume. Although various forms of censorship and repression continued until the collapse of the GDR, there was never again the conviction of the early 1950s that this enemy within could be defeated.

Notes

1 Autorenkollektiv, *Sammelbände zur Musikgeschichte der Deutschen Demokratischen Republik*, v: *1945–1976* (Berlin, 1979), 189–92. Although there had been earlier treatments: Peter Czerny and Heinz P. Hoffmann, *Der Schlager: Ein*

Panorama der leichten Musik (Berlin, 1968).
2 Michael Rauhut, *Schalmei und Lederjacke: Udo Lindenberg, BAP, Underground: Rock und Politik in den achtziger Jahren* (Berlin, 1996); Roland Galenza and Heinz Havemeister (eds), *Wir wollen immer artig sein ... : Punk, New Wave, HipHop, Independent-Szene in der DDR 1980–1990* (Berlin, 1999); Michael Rauhut, *Beat in der Grauzone: DDR-Rock 1964 bis 1972 – Politik und Alltag* (Berlin, 1993). Uta Poiger, *Jazz, Rock, and Rebels: Cold War Politics and American Culture in a Divided Germany* (Berkeley, 2000), has more on the 1950s.
3 Ernst Meyer, 'Realismus: die Lebensfrage der deutschen Musik', *Musik und Gesellschaft* (hereafter *MuG*), 1951/2, 38–43: 42.
4 A term first taken from literature, its application to music was always difficult, and tended to focus in the GDR on discussion of ideas like 'accessibility' and 'simplicity'. This problematic was absent from the application of the idea to dance music; for examples, see Max Butting, 'Zur Situation der Tanzmusik', *MuG*, 1951/3, 77–9; Hanns Eisler, 'Brief nach Westdeutschland', *Sinn und Form*, 1951/6, 14–24; Reginald Rudorf, 'Für eine frohe, ausdrucksvolle Tanzmusik', *MuG*, 1952/8, 247–52; 'Prof. Hans Pischner über Unterhaltungs- und Tanzmusik', *MuG*, 1952/11, 367–70. The unpublished analyses in SED files tend to repeat the ideas here.
5 For a detailed analysis of GDR musical bureaucracies, Daniel zur Weihen, *Komponieren in der DDR: Institutionen, Organisationen und die erste Komponistengeneration bis 1961* (Cologne, 1999).
6 BAB, DR-1/6137, 'Protokoll über die Besprechung am 10.10.1951 wegen der Vermittlung von Musikern'.
7 BAB, DR-1/6133, 'Resolution über Verbesserung der öffentlichen Tanzmusik', 16 August 1951.
8 *Ibid.*, Hartig to Landesregierungen, 21 February 1952.
9 In Mecklenburg, for example, there were local commissions to oversee dance programmes and prevent 'western Hot music'. BAB, DR 1/6137, 'Richtlinien für die Kreis-Prüfungs-Kommission für Tanz- und Unterhaltungsmusiker des Landes Mecklenburg', 1 August 1950.
10 *Ibid.*, Hartig to Seidel, 27 February 1952.
11 Rudolf Käs, 'Hot and sweet: Jazz im befreiten Land', in Hermann Glaser *et al.* (eds), *So viel Anfang war nie: Deutsche Städte 1945–49* (Berlin, 1989), 250–5: 225.
12 Violinists, for instance, would be expected to play scales and arpeggios of three octaves, a study at the level of one by Mazas or Kreuzer and one of the 'easier' concertos. The resemblance to Associated Board Grade 8 in this country is striking.
13 BAB, DR-1/6137, 'Entwurf einer Verordnung zur Sicherung der Qualität der kunst. Veranstaltungen...', 9 January 1952.
14 *Ibid.*, Hartig to Holzhauer, 11 June 1952.
15 *Ibid.*, 'Verordnung zur Ausübung von Unterhaltungs- und Tanzmusik', 10 July 1952.
16 *Ibid.*, Chwalek to Staatssekretär beim Präsidenten der DDR, 17 July 1952.
17 *Ibid.*, Chwalek to Stakuko, 15 August 1952.
18 *Ibid.*, Gew. Kunst-KV Teltow (Kolinski) to Stakuko, 9 August 1952.
19 'Eine Anordnung, die Unordnung schafft', *Junge Welt*, 10 May 1953.
20 'Anordung über die Befugnis von Ausübung von Unterhaltungs- und Tanzmusik

vom 27.3.1953', *Zentralblatt der DDR*, (11), 4 April 1953. The matter was far from settled, though. The decree's central provision was immediately challenged by the FDJ, querying how young musicians could play, at informal or even party events, if not sufficiently competent to qualify for permits. After further alterations and drafts, shuffled from one desk to another, Hartig was still negotiating with the Office for Youth Questions when Stakuko was disbanded in November.

21 BAB, DR-1/6133, RdS Jena (Volksbildung/Kunst) to Stakuko, 25 October 1952.
22 *Ibid.* RIAS was the American radio station in West Berlin; evidently these two officials were listeners.
23 BAB, DR-1/6137, 'Unkultur in Regis Breitingen', 19 September 1952.
24 BAB, DR-1/6133, Butting to Staatliches Rundfunkkomitee (Pischner), 14 November 1952.
25 *Ibid.*, Roll to Hartig, 10 May 1953. See also his letters to Hartig of 4 January, 19 March, 18 and 20 September 1953.
26 *Volksstimme*, 30 and 31 March 1954.
27 BAB, DR-1/7, 'Bericht zur Sache Tanzkapelle Karl Walter', 12 April 1954.
28 BBC Written Archive, Caversham, E1/753/4, A B C D 225 10 28 to Londoner Rundfunk, 18 April 1954. Intriguingly these anonymous fans mentioned that they received the BBC 'almost without disturbance', and much preferred it to the 'Russian broadcasts from Leipzig'. See also BBC German Representative, Berlin to O'Rorke, 23 April 1954, in the same file.
29 'Ergebnis des Preisausschreibens für Tanz- und Unterhaltungsmusik', *MuG*, 1952/11, 384–5.
30 'Um eine neue Tanzmusik', *MuG*, 1953/2, 69–70.
31 BAB, DR-1/240, 'Protokoll der ersten Tagung der Kommission "Tanzmusik" am 17.12.1952'.
32 'Aus der Arbeit unserer Kommissionen und Sektionen', *MuG*, 1953/2, 70–3.
33 SAPMO-BArch, DY 30/IV 2/9.06/284, Lauter to Schlieder, 24 February 1953.
34 *Ibid.*, VDK-BV Berlin to Stakuko, 17 January 1953.
35 BAB, DR-1/240, 'Protokoll der 2. Sitzung der Kommission "Tanzmusik" ...', 17 March 1953, 31.
36 *Ibid.*, 'Protokoll über die Sitzung der Kommission "Tanzmusik" am 8.4.1953', 2–3.
37 *Ibid.*
38 *Ibid.*, 'Protokoll über die Sitzung der Kommission "Tanzmusik" am 16.4.1953'.
39 For example, BAB, DR-1/6133, RdB Halle to Stakuko, 30 March 1953, complaining that only western music was available locally.
40 'Programmerklärung des Ministeriums für Kultur zur Verteidigung der Einheit der deutschen Kultur', *Sinn und Form*, 1954/2, 277–321.
41 BAB, DR-1/240, VDK and Gewerkschaft Kunst to Becher, 10 May 1954.
42 *Ibid.*, 'Anlage zum Protokoll 29.6.1954. Richtlinien für die Auftragserteilung für Tanzmusik'.
43 BAB, DR-1/243; see also BAB, DR-1/236. He subsequently left the GDR and wrote *Jazz in der Zone* (Berlin, 1964). On Rudorf, and changing attitudes to jazz in East and West Germany, see Poiger, *Jazz, Rock, and Rebels*, 137–67.
44 'Tanzmusik – einmal so betrachtet', *MuG*, 1957/5, 282–3.
45 BAB, DR-1/236, HA Kulturelle Massenarbeit, 'Protokolle über die Aussprache mit Leitern bekannter Tanz- und Unterhaltungskapellen am 24 Juni 1957', 4.

46 BAB, DR-1/243, Uszkoreit to Griffaton, 21 August 1957.
47 *Ibid.*, Bezirksverwaltung Halle, 3 September 1957.
48 SAPMO-BArch, DY 30/IV 2/9.06/293, 'Zu einigen Fragen der Tanzmusik im Rundfunk'.
49 Stiftung Archiv der Akademie der Künste, Max-Butting-Archiv, Korrespondenz, Mappe 2: 1952–6, Betriebsleiter VEB Deutsche Schallplatten (Költzsch) to Butting, 7 December 1956.
50 BAB, DR-1/243, Költzsch to Uszkoreit, 25 March 1957.
51 'Anordnung über die Programmgestaltung bei Unterhaltungs- und Tanzmusik', *Gesetzblatt der DDR*, 1958/1, 38. It also tried to stem the tide and contain the outflow of royalties. Enforcement was half-hearted at best. In the first four months only two performance bans were served, in Jüterbog and Leipzig, and one 10 mark fine, in Annaberg. BAB, DR-1/241, Morsche to Uszkoreit, 9 May 1958.
52 The VDK gave whole-hearted support to the plan, claiming implausibly that the 'Lipsi' had found 'a wide international resonance'. *MuG*, 1960/6, 275.
53 The leadership's concern came to a head in 1961, when the internal *Informationsdienst* Nr. 48/IV was dominated by the article 'NATO-Politik und Tanzmusik'. Ulbricht had spoken to the VDK about the problems of dance music in April 1960 – *MuG*, 1960/5, 257–8.
54 SAPMO-BArch, DY 30/IV 2/9.06/293, Bab to Czerny, 8 June 1960.
55 Spielhaus was in charge of music at Radio-DDR; through his earlier association with Rudorf he had identified himself as a progressive.
56 *Ibid.*, Abt. Kultur und Agit.-Prop. to Spielhaus, 11 July 1960.
57 *Ibid.*, Radio-DDR (Musikalische Leitung) to Wagner, 8 August 1960.
58 SAPMO-BArch, DY 30/IV 2/9.06/285, Bab to Czerny, 21 September 1960.
59 GDR composers achieved much more success with 'realistic' themes in 'mass songs' and 'fighting songs'. By the mid-1960s theVDK had published no fewer than 225,000. See VDK *et al.*, *Komponisten und Musikwissenschaftler der Deutschen Demokratischen Republik* (Berlin, 1965), 10.
60 Songs like 'Es waren drei Kameraden', 'Der Legionär', and 'Kamerad, wo bist du?' were accused of pandering to SS veterans' nostalgia, and 'Heimatlos' and 'Zurück in die Heimat' of fostering révanchism.
61 A eugenicist discourse continued in the 1950s GDR which had dominated cultural analysis in Germany from 1933–45. Uta Poiger, noting this, also argues that the characterisation of western popular music as 'cosmopolitan' carried clear anti-Semitic overtones, but this should be qualified. Two of the GDR's principal theorists of dance music, Meyer and Knepler, were themselves Jewish.
62 Often, performance bans applied only to a given town, leaving bands free to play elsewhere in the GDR. Typically, bans were for a short period, usually three months, acting as a warning, but allowing musicians to fine-tune their programme to a level of acceptability.

14

National paradigm and legitimacy: uses of academic history writing in the 1960s[1]

Stefan Berger

Introduction

After the collapse of the GDR in 1989 GDR historiography came under sustained criticism from younger historians in East Germany as well as from established scholars from the Federal Republic. The Independent Historians' Association of the GDR, established in 1990, accused GDR historians of total moral failure, political opportunism and scientific (*wissenschaftlich*) bankruptcy.[2] In September 1990, the West German Historians' Association (VDH) published a resolution which condemned GDR historiography as a 'governmental science, whose task was above all to legitimate the SED regime'.[3] Even those who had previously espoused the importance of keeping track of GDR publications revised their opinion after 1990. So, for example, Hans-Ulrich Wehler announced that 'maybe two dozen historians [in the former GDR] ... do justice to the assessment principles that are regarded as normal in the West ... One can forget tons of East German literature.'[4]

GDR historians, confronted with widespread dismissals and checks on their political and moral suitability as well as their scientific qualifications, tried, in the words of Hans Schleier to 'account to themselves and the scientific community for the degree to which the misuse of history as legitimating the politics of the SED regime has deformed their own work'.[5] Werner Bramke's attempt in the summer of 1996 can be seen as, in many respects, typical of the kind of argument presented by GDR historians. He does not deny the strong political functionalisation of GDR historiography, but he sees the emergence of autonomous spaces for GDR historians from the early 1970s onwards. A more liberal SED regime allowed for the establishment of a 'discursive process of communication' between party officials and historians which resulted in a 'professionalisation' (*Verwissenschaftlichung*) of GDR historiography.[6] This, in fact, describes what increasingly had become common sense among West German historians in the 1980s.[7]

By the mid-1990s, however, many West German historians had reverted to an assessment of GDR historiography which had been prevalent in the 1950s. It stressed the partisanship (*Parteilichkeit*) of GDR historiography which ruled out any scientific merits of GDR research. Academic history writing in the GDR was reduced to political propaganda.[8] So, for example, Ilko-Sascha Kowalczuk's study on the historical profession in the GDR from 1945 to 1961 perceives GDR historiography only in terms of it being 'part and parcel of the SED dictatorship'. As a 'state historiography' it was characterised by its partisanship, its high degree of ideologisation and its legitimation of the SED regime.[9] Hence, the current debate about GDR historiography is often taking place within the dichotomous construction of 'legitimatory science' (*Legitimationswissenschaft*) versus the notion of 'professionalisation' from the early 1970s onwards. A third position seeks to understand the historical sciences in the GDR as a discipline which followed a different logic to that prevalent in the West. Martin Sabrow in particular has argued that scientific standards and partisanship were not opposites in the self-understanding of GDR historians; rather they were perceived as mutually compatible (*Wissenschaftlichkeit in der Parteilichkeit*).[10] Such an approach distances itself from apologias as well as condemnations, and thus successfully avoids the dichotomous structure of the debate.

With Sabrow one can start from the contention that GDR historians were neither simply total political opportunists, nor did they struggle against a small minority of dominant party officials and 'unscientific' party historiographers in an heroic attempt to establish history as a science in the GDR.[11] In this chapter I would like to look at the way in which GDR historians constructed national identity in an attempt both to overcome the traditional national paradigm dominant in German historiography at least until 1945[12] and lay the foundations for a different sort of a national tradition. The focus will be on GDR historiography in the 1960s. At this time the first generation of historians trained under Marxist–Leninist auspices, came into its own. The transformation process of the historical profession was largely completed in 1958 when the GDR's own historical association was set up. The years 1953–58 had seen a massive extension of the system of higher education in the GDR, which was paralleled by an increasing insistence that those who taught within the system should be SED members. In 1961, 90 per cent of all university historians were members of the SED.[13] By the 1960s, the GDR had successfully nurtured its own intelligentsia to maturity.

GDR historiography after 1945: moving towards new shores?

In 1946 Anton Ackermann, a leading SED official, drew a direct line from the dominant nationalist historiography of the nineteenth and early twentieth century to the victory of National Socialism in Germany, and – in line with Alexander Abusch, Ernst Niekisch and W. von Hanstein – called on historians to investigate the specifically German reasons for National

Socialism. In practice this amounted to a *de facto* reversal of the old German *Sonderweg* thesis.[14] From a positive source of national identity it was now turned into a negative one: German history became the prehistory of National Socialism.

Calls to abandon the tradition of historiographic nationalism coincided with the development of whole areas of historical research which had been neglected by German historiography before 1945, and hence excluded from the canon of what was regarded as 'proper history'. Three brief examples will serve to demonstrate how GDR historiography could in effect act as a serious challenge to its Western counterpart in the 1960s. First, I will consider labour history; secondly, social and economic history more generally; and finally, research on revolutions.

Labour history had been a non-topic in German universities before 1945.[15] In the GDR, by contrast, labour history received the greatest possible attention. In line with SED party doctrine, a finalistic narrative of a 'forward march of labour' was developed which drew a red line from the social revolutionaries of 1848 to the left wing of the SPD in Imperial Germany to the foundation of the Communist Party in 1918–19 and on to the SED. The GDR as a socialist 'workers' state' represented the apogee of the struggles of the class-conscious proletariat. After 1954 Leo Stern and a group of historians working at the University of Halle published prolifically on the emergence of the industrial world in the nineteenth century and the rise of the labour movement.[16] In September 1958, the leadership of the SED commissioned an eight-volume *History of the German Labour Movement* which was eventually published in 1966. More than 200 historians contributed and their names read like a who's who of GDR historiography: Horst Bartel, Günter Benser, Lothar Berthold, Stefan Doernberg, Ernst Engelberg, Dieter Fricke, Heinz Heitzer, Werner Horn, Annelies Laschitza, Walter Schmidt, Albert Schreiner, Wolfgang Schumann, Walter Wimmer and Hanna Wolf. One of the doyens of GDR historiography, Jürgen Kuczynski, who had returned from exile in Britain to settle in the GDR, wrote prolifically on German and international labour history.[17] After 1959 the history of the labour movement had its own separate GDR journal – the *Beiträge zur Geschichte der deutschen Arbeiterbewegung* – which published a steady stream of research on the topic. Stern and Kuczynski had been socialised and trained during the Weimar Republic, but the GDR was to produce its own labour historians such as Dieter Fricke, Horst Groschopp, Werner Kowalski, Annelies Laschitza, Dietrich Mühlberg, Jutta Seidel and Hartmut Zwahr (by no means an exhaustive list), who all wrote important works on German labour history.

Not only was the history of the German labour movement receiving major attention. The same was true for social and economic history more generally.[18] In the early 1930s, Eckart Kehr had famously remarked that social history in Germany was largely socialist history. Putting to one side the racist and nationalist *Volksgeschichte* of the 1930s, GDR historiography was first in prioritising the systematic investigation into social and economic processes in modern German history.[19] Economic history was widely regarded as 'the foundation of history-writing generally'.[20] In particular Kuczynski did not tire of reminding his fellow historians of the special importance of economic and social history for the GDR.[21] Although much of the GDR's social history remained heavily indebted to political history, research on class and social stratification was pioneered, new quantitative techniques tested and particular attention given to the close relationship between the economy and political developments. In medieval history, the history of the city states and the *Hanse*, in agrarian and economic history, the 1960s saw a flowering of social history approaches which focused on the struggle of the oppressed and which sparked off some important controversies, such as on the genesis of feudalism or on the character of the bourgeoisie in feudal society. As Helga Schultz remarked: 'The historiography of the GDR, where it was truly Marxist, that is historical, materialist and dialectic, was necessarily always also social history.'[22]

Finally, the history of revolutions was given much attention in the GDR.[23] In particular, Walter Markov and Manfred Kossok at the University of Leipzig established a comparative historiography of revolutions which quickly won international recognition.[24] Markov's studies on the left in the French revolution of 1789 were a milestone in GDR historiography of the 1960s.[25] Research on the revolutions of 1848–49 was also very prominent from early on.[26] The origins of the labour movement in the 1848 revolution was given much attention, as was the part of peasant radicalism and revolt. Furthermore, GDR research on colonialism and on various national liberation movements in Africa, Asia and Latin America had already won much international acclaim by the 1960s. In the second half of the 1960s, GDR historiography expanded these research fields in the newly established interdisciplinary 'area studies' with its institutional centres at the universities of Berlin, Rostock and Leipzig.

Overall, these three brief examples illustrate that GDR historiography achieved considerable results in areas which had hitherto been neglected by mainstream German historiography. A new generation of West German scholars hoping to establish social history in the historical profession of the FRG explicitly referred to these achievements of the other German historiography. So, for example, Jürgen Kocka, writing in 1972: 'what, in the West, is either done or has been demanded under the banner of social history has already been incorporated in the work of socialist historians.'[27]

The re-affirmation and reconstruction of the national paradigm after 1951

As Matthias Middell has argued, it looked as though a 'democratic, humanistic historiography which was European in character' would replace the old fixation with national history and national identity in the second half of the 1940s.[28] In this period, many GDR historians were tempted to look across national borders, particularly towards the French Annales school and Soviet historiography. Yet around 1950 the agenda was firmly reset in the direction of national history and the history of the labour movement in the national context.[29] GDR historians now specifically concentrated on the positive traditions in German history which would eventually come to fruition in the foundation and development of the GDR. Special 'Institutes for the History of the German People' were founded after 1951 at the universities of Berlin, Halle and Leipzig. Under the headship of Alfred Meusel (Berlin), Leo Stern (Halle) and Ernst Engelberg (Leipzig), they rapidly began to dominate the historical research agendas in the GDR. All other, non-German history was moved to departments of general history or Eastern European history.

In 1952, the Museum for German History was opened in East Berlin. Like the Institutes, it was to be a major research centre for diverse aspects of German history and it helped 'to create the foundation for an East German national identity'.[30] The Institute of History at the German Academy of Sciences, founded in 1956, also was to focus on German history, in particular under the chairmanship of Engelberg between 1960 and 1969. Within the central research plans, adopted since the early 1950s, German history dominated the agenda. In 1951 leading East German historians formed an authors' collective to prepare a multi-volume German history which was supposed to retell the German story from a Marxist–Leninist perspective. Over the next decades vast resources were absorbed in this attempt to produce a new national master narrative.[31] In 1955 the SED Politbüro even adopted a history resolution which called on GDR historians to develop lessons from German history which could be used in contemporary political struggles and which could underpin the socialist society in the GDR. When, from the second half of the 1950s onwards, contemporary history was prioritised within the GDR, it was once again a national perspective which held sway.

Despite political pressure from the SED to draw firmer boundaries to the bourgeois historiography of West Germany, many leading GDR historians, including Meusel, believed that the superiority of the Marxist–Leninist paradigm could be proven in an open dialogue with western historiography. It was not until the aftermath of the Hungarian uprising of 1956 that the SED adopted a harder line against non-Marxist historians and insisted on the theory of two separate historiographies in Germany. Henceforth, FRG historians were constructed as 'the enemy' which had to be combatted rather than convinced.[32] In March 1958 a separate GDR historians' association was set up. The institutionalised division of German historiography did not mean, however, an abandonment of the national paradigm. In the GDR, throughout the 1960s, the 'basic national concept' (*nationale Grundkon-*

zeption) sought to portray the SED and the revolutionary German labour movement as representing the true national interests of the German people. At an historical conference organised by the SED in 1958, Walter Ulbricht had defined the main task of GDR historians as that of developing a national counter-concept to the history of the FRG. Historical works were to concentrate on the national question and seek to portray the foundation of the GDR as the logical outcome of the progressive forces in modern German history. During the 1960s, the concept of the nation was closely intertwined with the class antagonisms in German history. There were now two distinct lines: one represented by the revolutionary labour movement, whose interests were closely identified with those of the nation, culminating in the foundation of the GDR. The other line was linked to bourgeois forces and imperialism, betraying the national interest and epitomised by the FRG.[33]

Which national paradigm? The example of the *Kleine Enzyklopädie Deutsche Geschichte*

One could choose many examples to illustrate the specific perspective on German national identity prevalent among GDR historians in the 1960s. I will concentrate here on the *Kleine Enzyklopädie Deutsche Geschichte* (EDG), published in Leipzig in 1965 and edited by Eckhard Müller-Mertens, Erich Paterna and Max Steinmetz. Additionally I will augment a close analysis of this text with topical articles from the *Zeitschrift für Geschichtswissenschaft* (ZfG) which published widely on the 'basic national concept'.

In the preface to the EDG, the editors argued that the necessary victory of socialism 'requires a strong national and socialist consciousness'. This set the tone for an identification of socialism and nation which is a constant in the book and provided a closed and finalistic historical narrative, tracing the 'good' nationalism of the progressive class line in German history and juxtaposing it with the 'bad' nationalism of the reactionary class line. An ahistorical view projecting modern national identity backward in history prevailed. The Franconian Reich of the ninth century was seen as the first powerful expression of 'the development of the German people and state' (p. 18). The 'consciousness of community' among the East Frankian people in particular was perceived as 'one of the most important preconditions for the formation of a German nationality' (p. 28). The East Frankian state unequivocally was the 'first German state' (p. 32).

From the earliest 'national struggles' onwards, the sympathy of the authors lay with the forces representing central power versus particular power. Like the nineteenth-century Prussian historians, their GDR counterparts castigated the medieval German monarchs for pursuing 'utopian plans for power in Italy and the Mediterranean' (p. 78). The German monarchy failed to fulfil its 'historic mission to assist and nurture the growing nation'. This was the first but not the last instance when the German ruling classes failed to live up to their national task.

The reformation was interpreted as a failed German social revolution. Its international dimension was sidelined and instead the national perspective foregrounded. The absence of a 'national monarchy' was perceived as one of the 'deepest reasons why Germany could become the site of a European war' (p. 163) in the seventeenth century. The 'development of the German nation' was held back by a 'crippled absolutism' (p. 176). The anti-national politics of Prussia and of Frederick II in particular remained beyond historical redemption. We also find much national indignation when we come to the French occupation of the German lands after 1806: 'The struggle against foreign rule became an historical necessity due to the vital interests of the German people' (p. 216). The Prussian myth of the German people demanding an independent nation state after 1807 was repeated uncritically (p. 221). The 'Prussian party of patriots' created a 'united front encompassing all classes and strata' which worked tirelessly 'towards a unifying national policy' (p. 222 f.).

Post-1815 the question of national unity became 'the central question and the key to social progress' (p. 245). 1848 was interpreted as the 'first truly national uprising of the people' in which 'the working class proved itself for the first time as a most decisive national force' (p. 273). If the bourgeoisie failed to live up to its 'national task' in 1848, it did so again in the early 1860s. The exclusivity of the National Association meant that 'the bourgeoisie once again put their egotistical class interests above those of the whole people and acted in an anti-national manner' (p. 286). The author thus unproblematically posited a national interest which transcended class. The class character of the nation vanished from sight. The nation became a category which stood outside the ongoing class struggles.

Although the way unity was finally brought about through Prussian wars meant 'victory for the anti-national path' (p. 279), the Franco-Prussian war was described as serving 'a just aim: national unity'. It was 'a just defensive war', at least until Sedan (p. 295). In the newly created nation state, the labour movement was assigned a 'national task', namely to unite all democratic forces against Prussian militarism. In this way, the labour movement 'served the interests of the nation' (p. 302), while 'the imperialists and militarists were and are the arch-enemies of the nation' (p. 314). The move to the present tense in the latter sentence was highly significant. It already indicated that the dichotomy which allegedly had such deep roots in German history was held through to the present time: the revolutionary German labour movement came to stand for the true national interest whereas imperialists and militarists from Bismarck to Adenauer were the enemies of the nation.

Reformist Social Democrats were also identified as antipatriots. The policies of Majority Social Democrats and the ADGB trade union leadership in the First World War was described as 'anti-national' (p. 337). By contrast, the foundation of the KPD 'corresponded to the interests of the nation' (p. 343). Time and again, whether in the Ruhr struggle of 1923 or the fight against the economic depression and National Socialism, it was the KPD which alone 'represented the national interests' (p. 352). This theme was repeated in the passages dealing with the Communist resistance against National Socialism: 'Antifascists, under the leadership of the KPD which proved itself as the true national force of our people, saved the honour of the German nation.' The category of the nation thus remained unproblematical throughout the text, and the GDR was portrayed as the state in which the long struggle between patriots (the revolutionary labour movement and its allies) and antipatriots (militarists and imperialists) had finally been resolved in favour of the former.

Which national paradigm? The example of the *ZfG*

The overriding concern for and commitment to the national principle in history was also visible from the many articles in the *ZfG* which dealt with this topic in the 1960s. The *ZfG* was founded in 1953 as the key historical journal for the whole of the profession and an explicit alternative to the West German *Historische Zeitschrift*. It was the most representative of GDR historical journals. Although several contributions by foreign historians can be found, German historians and German topics dominated the pages of this journal. It rapidly became an 'instrument in the formation of a national master narrative'.[34]

The GDR was portrayed as representing the realisation of all progressive ideas and revolutionary traditions in the German past.[35] As Albert Norden, one of the chief SED ideologues, explicitly stated in 1967: 'The flag and the leadership of the nation today lies in the hands of the German working class'.[36] The GDR had become, according to Stefan Doernberg, 'the model for any solution to the most essential questions facing the whole of our nation'.[37] Rolf Rudolph, the *ZfG*'s chief editor at the time, emphasised in 1962 that it had been 'the Communists alone – ever since the foundation of the party of Communists in 1847/48 – [who] consistently stood for the national and social interests of the German people'.[38] For Lothar Berthold the German working class, in its 120-year history, had developed a consistent 'national concept' which culminated in the current position of the SED.[39] Merging the concepts of class and nation in this way, the SED and its historians were in fact de-emphasising the importance of class. Communists did not represent sectional class interests, but the interests of the whole nation. This then becomes an interesting variant to western Social Democrats' attempts to tone down the concept of class in the 1950s. The transformation of the SPD into a people's party, culminating in its Bad Godesberg programme, found a parallel in the transformation of the SED from a class to a national party.

The history of the SED was written in such a way that the party's interest always coincided with the German national interest.[40] This, in turn, had major repercussions for labour movement history in the GDR more generally. It became a state historiography focused on national organisations, leaders and ideologies. Its innovative potential was soon lost, and by the 1970s it often looked stale and conservative in its approaches and its research objectives.[41] Marxist–Leninist historiography in the GDR, just as its nineteenth-century Prussian counterpart, sought to develop an historical consciousness which legitimated a particular political regime by identifying it with the national interest.

The imperialist bourgeoisie, by contrast, was associated with 'antinational class politics': 'In the interest of their class position, they drop German national history, openly abandon the nation state', thereby manipulating the perception of European history. While the historians of the FRG wrote 'the history of reaction', GDR historians were allocated the central task of defending 'the socialist fatherland' and promoting 'socialist patriotism' by portraying 'the proletariat as the most decisive national force in Germany'.[42] Ignoring the many continuities of the national framework of interpretation in West German historiography after 1945,[43] GDR historians accused their West German colleagues of carrying on the antinational tradition of the German ruling classes.[44] A 'German national renaissance' was possible only if the 'enemies of the nation', that is, West German finance capitalism and world imperialism, had been defeated.[45] Norden, on the occasion of the GDR's fifteenth anniversary, confirmed the SED's theory of the two class lines 'going back to the foundation of the medieval German empire'. In a wide-ranging historical survey Norden contrasted the repeated betrayal of the nation by the ruling classes with the efforts of the working class 'to make the fatherland the property of the people'.[46] Time and again we find this manichean construction: 'The shame lies with the behaviour of the ruling classes, the glory with the resistance of the oppressed classes.'[47]

Allocating historical guilt to the ruling classes created major problems for GDR historiography only when it came to the history of National Socialism. It led historians to construct a narrative in which the majority of Germans appear as victims of the evil Nazis and capitalists pulling the wires in the background: 'never before has a nation been led by its ruling classes into a bigger catastrophe ... One look at the endless gravesites, at the heaps of rubble across Europe ... demonstrates just how much the haute bourgeoisie and its fascist and militarist accomplices have harmed the German people.'[48] The wider responsibility of Germans for National Socialism and its crimes was thus removed from sight. Like the West German historiography of the 1950s, the problem was limited to a small group of individuals. Thus German nationalism could be rescued from the ruins of National Socialism in both Germanies.

The GDR, as Günter Benser insisted, was no Soviet import. Dismissing the 'legend of a Sovietisation of central Germany', he affirmed the GDR's roots in German history and German traditions.[49] Joachim Streisand's survey of the development of German historiography was full of righteous indignation about Hegel's enthusiasm for Napoleon 'at the moment of national repression'. National unity was described as 'economic necessity', and the Marxist labour movement in the nation state was the 'consistent guardian of the progressive national heritage'. The GDR thus represented 'the best from the German past and the future of our nation'.[50] History, as Lothar Berthold emphasised, had many 'national lessons' in store for the people. 'National historical consciousness,' he argued, 'belongs to those social ideas which, when the masses and especially the working class take possession of it, help to bring about social progress.' That German national historical consciousness for vast periods of the nineteenth and twentieth centuries had a singularly destructive effect on developments and that national consciousness is at the very least a deeply ambiguous affair remained hidden behind the assumption of a positive national tradition to which the GDR traced its heritage. Instead Berthold praised history-writing which 'promotes pride in the historical achievements of the German working class' and 'love for the GDR'.[51]

The GDR's 'socialist human community' (*sozialistische Menschengemeinschaft*) was described as the 'conscious co-operation of allied classes and strata which, under the leadership of the working class and its Marxist–Leninist party, shape the social system of socialism'.[52] It thus resembled the concept of the 'levelled middle-class society' popular in 1950s West Germany.[53] Although the specific content of both ideas differed substantially, in both concepts class antagonisms were denied and social conflict harmonised. Working class and middle class in the GDR were assumed united by a common interest, and all patriotic Germans found themselves at one with the GDR.[54] As Albert Norden stressed in 1964: 'The people find the nation only through socialism; only socialism merges the nation and the people into one.'[55]

Socialist nationalism did not equal 'national egotism'.[56] Quite the contrary: 'socialist patriotism' was diametrically opposed to 'bourgeois and petty-bourgeois nationalism'.[57] According to Engelberg, 'the socialist patriot fights for the victory of world historical progress in his own country and perceives himself ... as the ally of all progressive forces in other countries'.[58] Such 'patriotism of a new kind' was remarkably similar to Second International internationalism before 1914, which had also shied away from juxtaposing nationalism and internationalism and instead favoured an uneasy compromise between the two.[59] Furthermore, this Marxist–Leninist version of nationalism was not so different from its liberal Western variant which distinguished between a benign patriotism and its nasty cousin, nationalism. Whereas the former simply rested on the recognition of difference, only the latter was based on the explicit construction of enemies.

However, apart from the fact that GDR nationalism certainly knew its enemy, such a theoretical distinction time and again collapsed in real historical situations when nationalism tended to follow the lowest common denominator.

For GDR historians the nation was one of the basic structures of society. Apart from its connections to class the nation was also linked to other 'given elements which build community' such as 'language, territory, the economy and psychologial peculiarities'.[60] On this definition, the nation was understood not as a constructed concept but as a given, almost natural force. Such essentialist notions of the national in GDR historiography were sometimes mixed up with a rather ambiguous use of the term 'people' (*Volk*). Peter Lambert has drawn attention to the multi-faceted use of the term in the work of Fritz Rörig, the eminent historian of the German *Hanse*. Whereas it had democratic connotations before 1933, Rörig shifted the emphasis of the term to fit the more ethnic and racialised meaning adopted by the Nazis after 1933, and in the GDR he could still use the term, this time in a manner coinciding with official SED usage.[61] Engelberg also at times used the term in a way which made it very difficult to distinguish the ethnic from the democratic political element. So, for example, in 1954 he could speak about the 'healthy people's sentiment' (*gesundes Volksempfinden*) of the nineteenth-century miners in the Erzgebirge.[62]

The linguistic emplotment of the GDR's national paradigm showed the same manichean construction of good socialist nationalism versus bad capitalist nationalism already encountered above. It led to passages where the revolutionary labour movement acted 'decisively' or in a 'determined manner'. They formed a 'strong national power-centre' and their analyses were always characterised by 'wisdom' and far-sightedness'. The workers demonstrated 'high levels of consciousness', they were willing to 'devote all their energies', and their 'constant efforts' were invariably 'glorious'. By contrast, the ruling classes were described as 'treacherous' and 'cowardly'. Their 'weakness' and 'selfishness' led to 'betrayals of the nation' at several turning-points in German history. A highly dramatised language thus adopted an heroic register in order to allow for a direct identification of the reader with the forces of light and an imminent revulsion against the forces of darkness.[63]

Nationalism in GDR historiography fulfilled two important functions: first, it was a useful tool to justify the GDR's existence as a state at a time when the FRG was still largely successful in denying the GDR international recognition,[64] and, secondly, it was a kind of putty to hold the diverse interests in the state together. The 'national mission' of the GDR always also meant a call on GDR citizens to recognise their 'prime task of strengthening the economic foundations of the GDR'.[65] GDR historians aimed to contribute to the 'glowing boost of socialist will-power which brings about the economic miracle that everyone talks about in today's world'.[66] After all, as

Günter Benser and Heinz Heitzer put it, 'the construction of socialism in the GDR has become the most pressing task of the future national struggle'.[67] History thus becomes a moral force which uses the well-established national paradigm in a modified form so as to boost identification with the GDR. As Walter Schmidt was to emphasise in 1970, the 'main function of history as science' was to contribute to the 'development of socialist consciousness' and the 'stability of the socialist system'. History-writing was to make people 'proud of the GDR' as 'the present high point of German history'.[68]

We have noted above the tendency of GDR historiography to reject all those historical forces opposed to an effective centralisation of power in the nation-state. Consequently, the tradition of *Landesgeschichte* was replaced by research on regionalism (*Regionalismusforschung*).[69] Regional historians such as Max Steinmetz adhered to the centralising features of GDR historiography.[70] Germany's fragmentation was classified as 'disastrous'. Small-state absolutism was 'a deformity directed against the interests of the nation' and a 'deviation from normal development'. Steinmetz's plea not to neglect regional history any further was not based on an attempt to present it as an alternative history to the national paradigm (as was sometimes the case with West German regional history). Rather, he argued, regional history could complement national history. After all, the everyday life of the people had been shaped by the regions and regional cultures shaped German national culture. Regional history could foster feelings of 'pride in the Heimat and in the fatherland' and contribute to an 'education in socialist patriotism'.

Conclusion

Four basic principles structured the narratives of the national paradigm in the GDR. First, a finalistic narrative portrayed the progressive traditions of German history as culminating in the GDR. The antagonistic alternative tradition was personified by the FRG. Secondly, GDR historians reclaimed national identity by constructing a class-based national paradigm which distinguished between a good progressive national identity championed by the revolutionary German labour movement and the SED, and a reactionary national identity linked to the German ruling classes before 1945 and then to the FRG. Such a clear-cut juxtaposition of the two German national traditions stood in marked contrast to the obvious similarities between the two German states in their attempts to reconstruct national identity. Both Germanies witnessed concerted efforts to de-emphasise the class societies of the past. Instead homogenising concepts such as the 'socialist human community' (GDR) and the 'levelled middle-class society' (FRG) enjoyed much popularity. Additionally both national historiographies of the GDR and the FRG made much of the distinction (albeit differently defined) between a positive patriotism and a negative nationalism. The notion of homogeneous national communities was an effective weapon against the representation of any rival interests to the one propagated by the SED. The category of 'class' replaced categories such as 'language', 'culture' and 'race' as the guiding principle of narrating the story of the German nation, but the borderline between these categories was often quite blurred. Essentialist notions of the national were by no means uncommon among GDR historians. Thirdly, the insistence on a progressive national identity meant that the category of the national and the concept of national identity remained unproblematical and unproblematised in GDR historiography. Hence, many of the old nationalist myths continued to be conveyed and upheld by GDR historians well into the 1960s – at a time when, ironically, many of these myths became deeply problematical in West Germany.[71] Finally, the conceptualisation of centralisation as progress did not allow for the full investigation of the rich alternatives to the national discourses presented by strong regional and local identities in Germany, as well as the complex interplay between local, regional and national discourses. On the whole, there can be no doubt: the national paradigm continued to form a key characteristic of GDR historiography throughout the 1960s. Only after 1971 did GDR historians tone down their national(ist) orientation and begin instead to emphasise internationalism and the GDR's rootedness as a separate German nation in the east European bloc of Communist nation-states. Yet in the 1980s GDR historians began to rediscover national history in the context of the 'heritage and tradition debate'. Once again 'historians in the GDR ... stress the positive quality of national values'.[72] However, viewed from the 1960s, the ground had been prepared earlier.

Notes

1 I would like to thank Heiko Feldner and Martin Sabrow for their helpful suggestions and comments on a draft of this chapter.
2 Rainer Eckert *et al.* (eds), *Hure oder Muse? Klio in der DDR: Dokumente und Materialien des Unabhängigen Historiker-Verbandes* (Berlin, 1994).
3 Reprinted in Rainer Eckert *et al.*, *Krise – Umbruch – Neubeginn: Eine kritische und selbstkritische Dokumentation der DDR Geschichtswissenschaft* (Stuttgart, 1992), 228–30.
4 Hans-Ulrich Wehler, 'Hart widersprechen und mit dem Unfug stets konfrontieren', *Frankfurter Rundschau*, 24 September 1992.
5 Hans Schleier, 'Vergangenheitsbewältigung und Traditionserneuerung? Geschichtswissenschaft nach 1945', in Walter H. Pehle and Peter Sillem (eds), *Wissenschaft im geteilten Deutschland: Restauration und Neubeginn nach 1945* (Frankfurt/Main, 1992), 219.
6 Werner Bramke, 'Freiräume und Grenzen eines Historikers im DDR-System: Reflexionen sechs Jahre danach', in K. H. Pohl (ed.), *Historiker in der DDR* (Göttingen, 1997), 35, 38.
7 Alexander Fischer and Günther Heydemann (eds), *Geschichtswissenschaft in der DDR* (Berlin, 1988), i, 15 f.

8 A typical example of this perception is Hermann Weber, 'Manipulationen mit der Geschichte: Der Stalinismus herrscht nach wie vor in der östlichen Geschichtsschreibung', *SBZ-Archiv*, 8 (1957), 275–82.
9 Ilko-Sascha Kowalczuk, *Legitimation eines neuen Staates: Parteiarbeiter an der historischen Front. Geschichtswissenschaft in der SBZ/DDR 1945 bis 1961* (Berlin, 1997), 9 and 13 f. See also Ulrich Neuhäußer-Wespy, *Die SED und die Historie: Die Etablierung der marxistisch-leninistischen Wissenschaft in den fünfziger und sechziger Jahren* (Bonn, 1996).
10 Martin Sabrow, *Das Diktat des Konsenses: Geschichtswissenschaft in der DDR (1949–69)* (Munich, 2001); Martin Sabrow, '"Beherrschte Normalwissenschaft": Überlegungen zum Charakter der DDR-Historiographie', *Geschichte und Gesellschaft* (*GG*), 24 (1998), 412–45; see also many of the contributions in: Georg G. Iggers et al. (eds), *Die DDR-Geschichtswissenschaft als Forschungsproblem* (Munich, 1998); Martin Sabrow (ed.), *Verwaltete Vergangenheit: Geschichtskultur und Herrschaftslegitimation in der DDR* (Leipzig, 1997); Martin Sabrow and Gustavo Corni (eds), *Die Mauern der Geschichte: Historiographie zwischen Diktatur und Demokratie* (Leipzig, 1996); Martin Sabrow and P. T. Walther (eds), *Historische Forschung und sozialistische Diktatur: Beiträge zur Geschichtswissenschaft der DDR* (Leipzig, 1995).
11 For the latter view see Joachim Petzold, 'Die Auseinandersetzung zwischen den Lampes und den Hampes', *ZfG*, 42 (1994), 101–17.
12 Stefan Berger, 'The German tradition of historiography, 1800–1995', in Mary Fulbrook (ed.), *German History Since 1800* (London, 1997), 477–92.
13 Kowalczuk, *Legitimation*, 245. On the extensive exchange of elites at GDR universities in the 1950s see Ralph Jessen, 'Diktatorischer Elitewechsel und universitäre Milieus: Hochschullehrer in der SBZ/DDR (1945–1967)', *GG*, 24 (1998), 24–54.
14 For a good introduction to the concept of the German *Sonderweg* see Helga Grebing, *Der 'deutsche Sonderweg' in Europa 1806–1945: Eine Kritik* (Stuttgart, 1986).
15 See Stefan Berger, *Social Democracy and the Working Class in Nineteenth and Twentieth Century Germany* (London, 2000), 12–14 and 154–77 on the GDR.
16 See the series published under the general direction of Leo Stern entitled *Archivalische Forschungen zur Geschichte der Deutschen Arbeiterbewegung* (Berlin, 1955 ff.). See also the series published later on under Werner Kowalski entitled *Hallesche Studien zur Geschichte der Sozialdemokratie* (Halle, 1977 ff.).
17 See especially Jürgen Kuczynski, *Die Geschichte der Lage der Arbeiter unter dem Kapitalismus*, 38 vols (Berlin, 1961–72); the impact of exile on Kuczynski is discussed in Mario Keßler, *Exilerfahrungen in Wissenschaft und Politik: Remigrierte Historiker in der frühen DDR* (Berlin, 2001).
18 Carl-Ludwig Holtfrerich, 'Zur Position und Entwicklung der Wirtschaftsgeschichte in der DDR seit 1960: Das "Jahrbuch für Wirtschaftsgeschichte"', in Fischer and Heydemann (eds), *Geschichtswissenschaft*, i, 423–34; Manfred Straube, 'Sozial- und Wirtschaftsgeschichtliche Forschungen zum Mittelalter und der frühen Neuzeit an den Universitäten der DDR: Anspruch und Ergebnisse', in Eckart Schremmer (ed.), *Wirtschafts- und Sozialgeschichte: Gegenstand und Methode* (Stuttgart, 1998), 57–71.
19 See, for example, Hans Mottek, *Wirtschaftsgeschichte Deutschlands: Ein Grundriss*, 2 vols (Berlin, 1957 and 1964).

20 Walther Eckermann and Hubert Mohr (eds), *Einführung in das Studium der Geschichte* (2nd edn, Berlin, 1969), 76.
21 Jürgen Kuczynski, 'Warum studieren wir deutsche Wirtschaftsgeschichte?', *Aufbau*, 2 (1946), 356–61; Jürgen Kuczynski, 'Betrachtungen zur deutschen Geschichtsschreibung', *Aufbau*, 2 (1946), 742–7.
22 Helga Schultz, 'Was bleibt von der Geschichtswissenschaft der DDR?', in Eckert *et al.* (eds), *Krise*, 453.
23 Matthias Middell, 'Die Revolutionsforschung in der DDR', in Rainer Eckert (ed.), *Wer schreibt die DDR Geschichte?* (Berlin, 1995), 37–49.
24 See, for example, the *ZfG*'s special 1965 volume on *Evolution und Revolution in der Weltgeschichte*; Manfred Kossok (ed.), *Studien zur vergleichenden Revolutionsgeschichte: 1500–1917* (Berlin, 1974).
25 Walter Markov, *Jacques Roux*, 4 vols. (Berlin, 1965–69). See Walter Markov, *Jakobiner und Sansculotten: Beiträge zur Geschichte der französischen Revolutionsregierung 1793/94* (Berlin, 1956). On Markov see Manfred Neuhaus and Helmut Seidel (eds), *'Wenn jemand seinen Kopf bewußt hinhielt...': Beiträge zu Werk und Wirken von Walter Markov* (Leipzig, 1995), and Walter Markov, *Zwiesprache mit dem Jahrhundert* (Berlin, 1989).
26 Karl Obermann, *Die deutschen Arbeiter in der Revolution von 1848* (Berlin, 1953); Helmut Bleiber, 'Literatur zur Geschichte der Revolution von 1848/49', *ZfG*, 8 (1960), 212–28; Gerhard Schilfert, *Sieg und Niederlage des demokratischen Wahlrechts in der deutschen Revolution 1848/49* (Berlin, 1952).
27 Jürgen Kocka, 'Zur jüngeren marxistischen Sozialgeschichte: Eine kritische Analyse unter besonderer Berücksichtigung sozialgeschichtlicher Ansätze in der DDR' [1972], in Fischer and Heydemann (eds), *Geschichtswissenschaft*, i, 400. On the innovative potential of sections of GDR historiography see also Georg Iggers (ed.), *Ein anderer historischer Blick: Beispiele ostdeutscher Sozialgeschichte* (Frankfurt/Main 1991).
28 Matthias Middell, 'Jenseits unserer Grenzen? Zur Trennung von deutscher und allgemeiner Geschichte in der Geschichtswissenschaft und Geschichtskultur der DDR', in Konrad H. Jarausch *et al.* (eds), *Nach dem Erdbeben: (Re-)Konstruktion ostdeutscher Geschichte und Geschichtswissenschaft* (Leipzig, 1994), 88–120.
29 This national turn had already been observed by Fritz Kopp, *Die Wendung zur 'nationalen' Geschichtsbetrachtung in der Sowjetzone* (2nd edn, Munich, 1962).
30 H. Glenn Penny III, 'The Museum für deutsche Geschichte and German national identity', *Central European History*, 28 (1995), 343.
31 A detailed analysis of the history of those volumes is provided by Martin Sabrow, 'Planprojekt Meistererzählung: Die Entstehungsgeschichte des "Lehrbuchs der deutschen Geschichte"', in Martin Sabrow (ed.), *Geschichte als Herrschaftsdiskurs: Der Umgang mit der Vergangenheit in der DDR* (Cologne 2000), 227–86.
32 Martin Sabrow, 'Die Geschichtswissenschaft der DDR und ihr "objektiver Gegner"', in Iggers *et al.* (eds), *Die DDR-Geschichtswissenschaft*, 53–91. On the German–German meetings of historians at the conferences of the historians' association see Martin Sabrow, 'Ökumene als Bedrohung. Die Haltung der DDR-Historiographie gegenüber den deutschen Historikertagen von 1949 bis 1962', in Gerald Diesener and Matthias Middell (eds), *Historikertage im Vergleich* (Leipzig, 1996), 178–202.
33 This notion of the two traditions in German history and of the close identification

between class and nation already can be traced back to the classics of Marxism. See Jan Herman Brinks, *Die DDR-Geschichtswissenschaft auf dem Weg zur deutschen Einheit: Luther, Friedrich II und Bismarck als Paradigmen politischen Wandels* (Frankfurt/Main, 1992), 31–90.

34 Matthias Middell, 'Autoren und Inhalte: die Zeitschrift für Geschichtswissenschaft, 1953–1989', in Matthias Middell (ed.), *Historische Zeitschriften im internationalen Vergleich* (Leipzig, 1999), 293 f. On the national master narrative of GDR historians see also Konrad Jarausch, 'Die DDR-Geschichtswissenschaft als Meta-Erzählung', in Sabrow (ed.), *Verwaltete Vergangenheit*, 26 f.

35 Joachim Streisand, 'Progressive Ideen der deutschen Vergangenheit und ihre Verwirklichung in der DDR', *ZfG*, 12 (1964), 1335–40.

36 Albert Norden, 'Die DDR weist den sozialistischen Weg der Nation', *ZfG*, 15 (1967), 1141.

37 Stefan Doernberg, 'Die volksdemokratische Revolution auf dem Gebiet der DDR und die Lösung der Lebensfragen der deutschen Nation', *ZfG*, 8 (1960), 549.

38 Rolf Rudolph, 'Die nationale Verantwortung der Historiker in der DDR', *ZfG*, 10 (1962), 253.

39 Lothar Berthold, 'Zur Geschichte der nationalen Konzeption der deutschen Arbeiterklasse', *ZfG*, 11 (1963), 7. To emphasise the point about the revolutionary German working class being the only truly national force in modern German history, the *ZfG* published a special volume. See *Beiträge zum nationalen Geschichtsbild der deutschen Arbeiterklasse*, *ZfG*, Special Volume 10 (1962). Of particular interest are the keynote articles by Ernst Engelberg, 'Probleme des nationalen Geschichtsbildes der deutschen Arbeiterklasse', 7–49, and Leo Stern, 'Die westdeutsche imperialistische Geschichtssschreibung und die Frage der Nation', 50–69.

40 Günter Benser and Heinz Heitzer, 'Die nationale Politik der SED 1945–1955', *ZfG*, 14 (1966), 709–31.

41 Alf Lüdtke, 'Wer handelt? Die Akteure der Geschichte: Zur DDR-Geschichtsschreibung über Arbeiterklasse und Faschismus', in Iggers *et al.* (eds), *Die DDR-Geschichtswissenschaft*, 369–410. Of course, there were exceptions, for example the research unit on 'Cultural history of the German working class' discussed in the same volume by Adelheid von Saldern, 'Eine soziale Klasse ißt, trinkt und schläft nicht: Die Arbeitsgruppe "Kulturgeschichte der deutschen Arbeiterklasse"', 241–60.

42 Rudolph, 'Die nationale Verantwortung', 257–65.

43 Stefan Berger, *The Search for Normality: National Identity and Historical Consciousness in Germany since 1800* (Oxford, 1997), 40–76, where I argue that one can speak only about a 'delayed break' in West German historiography after 1945.

44 See, for example, Gerhard Lozek and Horst Syrbe, 'Die moderne Epoche, die Perspektive der deutschen Nation und die Sorgen imperialistischer westdeutscher Historiker', *ZfG*, 11 (1963), 1229–51.

45 Doernberg, 'Die volksdemokratische Revolution', 549.

46 Albert Norden, 'Die Nation und wir', *ZfG*, 12 (1964), 1113 and 1115.

47 Norden, 'Die DDR', 1141.

48 'Die geschichtliche Aufgabe der Deutschen Demokratischen Republik und die

Zukunft Deutschlands', *ZfG*, 10 (1962), 765.
49 Günter Benser, 'Die nationale Konzeption der deutschen Arbeiterklasse. Kernfragen des sechsten Bandes der 'Geschichte der deutschen Arbeiterbewegung (1945–49)', *ZfG*, 14 (1966), 1456 f.
50 Joachim Streisand, 'Progressive Traditionen und reaktionäre Anachronismen in der deutschen Geschichtswissenschaft', *ZfG*, 9 (1961), 1781, 1784 f., 1788.
51 Lothar Berthold, 'Ein geschlossenes Bild der Geschichte der deutschen Arbeiterbewegung', *ZfG*, 14 (1966), 1209.
52 Joachim Streisand, 'Geschichtsforschung und Geschichtsschreibung auf dem Wege zur sozialistischen Menschengemeinschaft', *ZfG*, 17 (1969), 1529.
53 For a critical evaluation, see Hans Braun, 'Helmut Schelskys Konzept einer "nivellierten Mittelstandsgesellschaft": Würdigung und Kritik', *Archiv für Sozialgeschichte*, 29 (1989), 199–223.
54 Thus explicitly Horn, 'Der Kampf der SED um Frieden, Sozialismus und die Lösung der nationalen Frage 1956–63: Zum achten Band der "Geschichte der deutschen Arbeiterbewegung"', *ZfG*, 14 (1966), 1491.
55 Norden, 'Die Nation', 1116.
56 *Ibid.*, 1117.
57 Stefan Doernberg, 'Proletarischer Internationalismus und Geschichtswissenschaft', *ZfG*, 17 (1969), 87.
58 Engelberg, 'Probleme', 15 f.
59 Stefan Berger and Angel Smith, 'Between scylla and charybdis: nationalism, labour and ethnicity across five continents', in Stefan Berger and Angel Smith (eds) *Nationalism, Labour and Ethnicity 1870–1939* (Manchester, 1999), 9–21.
60 Ernst Engelberg, 'Über Gegenstand und Ziel der marxistisch-leninistischen Geschichtswissenschaft', *ZfG*, 16 (1968), 1136.
61 Peter Lambert, 'From antifascist to Volkshistoriker: demos and ethnos in the political thought of Fritz Rörig, 1921–1945', in Stefan Berger *et al.* (eds), *Writing National Histories: Western Europe Since 1800* (London, 1999), 137–49.
62 Cited in Brinks, *Die DDR-Geschichtswissenschaft*, 127.
63 On the language of GDR historiography see Konrad Jarausch, 'Historische Texte der DDR aus der Perspektive des linguistic turn', in Iggers *et al.* (eds), *Die DDR-Geschichtswissenschaft*, 261–80.
64 The political functionalisation of 'national history' by the SED is emphasised by Klaus Erdmann, *Der gescheiterte Nationalstaat: Die Interdependenz von Nations- und Geschichtsverständnis im politischen Bedingungsgefüge der DDR* (Frankfurt/Main, 1996), esp. 121–54, on the 1960s.
65 Berthold, 'Zur Geschichte der nationalen Konzeption', 27.
66 Norden, 'Die Nation', 1122.
67 Benser and Heitzer, 'Die nationale Politik', 727.
68 Walter Schmidt, 'Geschichtsbild und Persönlichkeit in der sozialistischen Gesellschaft', *ZfG*, 18 (1970), 149–62.
69 On the fate of Landesgeschichte in the GDR see Katrin Keller, 'Landesgeschichte zwischen Wissenschaft und Politik: August der Starke als sächsisches 'Nationalsymbol'', in Jarausch and Middell *et al.* (eds), *Nach dem Erdbeben*, 195–218; for a very critical account of a self-declared 'bourgeois historian' in the GDR see also Karlheinz Blaschke, 'Die "marxistische" Regionalgeschichte. Ideologischer Zwang und Wirklichkeitsferne', in Iggers *et al.* (eds), *Die DDR-*

Geschichtswissenschaft, 341–68.
70 Max Steinmetz, 'Die Aufgaben der Regionalgeschichtsforschung in der DDR bei der Ausarbeitung eines nationalen Geschichtsbildes', *ZfG*, 9 (1961), 1735–74.
71 On the failure of the national cult in West Germany in the 1960s including some perceptive comments on East Germany see Edgar Wolfrum, *Geschichtspolitik in der Bundesrepublik Deutschland. Der Weg zur bundesrepublikanischen Erinnerung* (Darmstadt 1999), Ch. 3, 124–257.
72 Georg G. Iggers, 'New directions in historical studies in the German Democratic Republic', *History and Theory*, 28 (1989), 68.

15

History in the academy: objectivity and partisanship in the Marxist historiography of the German Democratic Republic[1]

Heiko Feldner

This chapter looks at the relation between objectivity and partisanship as discussed in the GDR historiography of the Ulbricht era. It investigates whether, and to what extent, East German Marxist historians subscribed to a mode of academic knowledge-making characterised by the properties of objectivity and scientificity. In pursuing this question, I shall be arguing against two equally ahistorical perspectives: the nostalgic transfiguration of academic history in the GDR on the one hand, and its denunciation from the viewpoint of innocent western universalism on the other.

The discursive field

The relation between objectivity and partisanship in GDR historiography is obvious. At least, that would appear to be the case. The discursive field of the recent German discussion of East German academic history in the 1950s and 1960s is structured by a clear-cut pattern. The basic oppositions configuring the field are partisanship versus professionalism, politics versus science, value-laden reasoning versus scientific objectivity.[2] The dichotomous simplicity of this pattern resembles in many respects the prevailing historical discourse in the FRG of the 1950s and early 1960s. As late as 1965, Reinhart Beck argued:

> The ideal of the free, creatively working historian of the western world, who does research of his own accord and on his own responsibility, is confronted with a different type of historian in the East. The latter is a functionary who writes history just on behalf of the ruling party, which dictates purpose and method to him.[3]

More succinctly, Walther Hofer had argued ten years before in 1956: 'The Soviet ideal of science is determined by the concept of *partisanship*, the occidental ideal by the concept of *objectivity*.'[4]

The 1970s and 1980s brought a significant shift towards a more differentiated view of GDR historical writing. The temporary hegemony of social–liberal discourse in the FRG encouraged a number of accounts that put the historiographies in both Germanies in a more comprehensive historical perspective. Best known is the two-volume guide to East German historical science (*Geschichtswissenschaft*), edited by Alexander Fischer and Günther Heydemann, which largely avoids simplistic juxtaposition.[5]

By contrast, the 1990s were again marked by a discursive arrangement which reduces both the range and scope of possible subject positions available to historians to a dichotomising minimum. While East German historiography was based on 'unscientific partisanship'[6] that produced power knowledge (*Herrschaftswissen*) and was therefore legitimatory science, western historiography was obliged to scientific objectivity, critical method and fact-based truth. Whatever case individual historians may wish to present, they are anticipated in this discursive field and have to deal with its restrictive implications.[7] This holds by no means only for the margins of the field or especially poor and equivocal contributions, but above all for the intellectual centre ground of the discussion. The controversy between Martin Sabrow and Ralf Possekel in Germany's leading social-historical journal *Geschichte und Gesellschaft* exemplifies this.[8]

Sabrow, who has published extensively on GDR historiography in recent years,[9] adopts the viewpoint of an ethnologist who sets out to explore an unfamiliar culture. Positing GDR historical science as an idiosyncratic other that followed its own operating logic, he suggests not measuring it by the yardstick of universal standards of scientificity but describing its discourse in its own terms. In so doing, Sabrow protects his analysis from three fallacies: first, from the 'evaluative perspective' that views GDR historiography through the grid of FRG historiography and, thereby, inevitably misrepresents its object; second, from a model of interpretation which in the name of compatibility neglects analysing the difference between East and West German historiographies; and finally, it rejects from the analysis the journalistic short-termism of the day. All in all this is an impressive methodological manoeuvre which leads to an informative portrayal of historiography in the GDR.

However (and this is also the starting point of Possekel's criticism), what else do we accomplish by setting apart East German historiography from universal standards of scientificity but reproduce the dichotomous pattern once more, this time as a systematic prerequisite? The replication in discourse–analytical terms of the simplifying dichotomy does not only remove GDR historiography from immediate criticism, as Possekel rightly remarks. It also renders the universal standards of scientificity virtually immune. Those universal standards – and let us be clear here: western-white-liberal-male standards – run through Martin Sabrow's account like a hidden agenda. They are the yardstick which is rendered invisible. They represent the Same in opposition to the Other, the order in contrast to the deviation. At the end of the day, analysing GDR historiography has become a challenge of great historical interest, though, it will not teach us anything meaningful to our own historiographical practice – except, perhaps, that deviation leads us nowhere.

This latter aspect is clearly seen in Ralf Possekel's response. He reproaches Sabrow for turning GDR historiography into a 'gallery of curios' instead of exploring it, through a *universal* conception of science, as part of the history of science. Analysing the academic practice of GDR historians *as scientists*, Possekel argues, would teach us something about the temptations and dangers inherent in modern science.[10] There is no doubt about that. But does it not tell us something about the *nature* and *properties* of modern science too? Implicitly in Sabrow, explicitly in Possekel: in both cases GDR historiography is gauged by the criterion of universal scientificity. The criterion itself, however, is beyond analysis and remains untouched by it.

It goes without saying that a brief synopsis does not do justice to the complexity of subtle accounts like those of Sabrow and Possekel. What I want to show is how the dichotomous structure of the discourse on GDR historiography restricts the field of significant subject positions. At the very heart of this dichotomous arrangement lies the relation between scientific objectivity and political partisanship. It seems as if there was some kind of repressive hypothesis[11] underlying the discussion of GDR historiography, suggesting that objectivity was not only being repressed – this was unquestionably the case – but that repression was the fundamental link between scientific objectivity, historiography and power. The historiographic equation reads as follows: scientifically objective history *minus* repression by state and party *equals* partial historiography (in the double meaning of the word).

My argument, however, is that the relationship between objectivity and power in GDR historical writing was not primarily characterised by repression. Scientific objectivity was neither simply absent from East German Marxist historiography nor does repression account for the particular relation between objectivity, historical knowledge-making and power. As an institutional code of practice and professional attitude, as a methodological principle and regulative idea, scientific objectivity was rather part and parcel of the same operating logic of the same discursive network of the same institutional set-up as the power it wished to denounce.

I want to demonstrate my argument through the analysis of a sample text. A more extensive analysis would have to consider at least three aspects or analytical levels: (1) the level of theoretical reflections, (2) the level of historiographical discourse and (3) the level of the institutional setting. Dealing with the question of objectivity and partisanship as a matter of theoretical debate, this chapter is confined to the first aspect.

The controversy on defining objectivity and partisanship of 1956–58: the case of Jürgen Kuczynski

It is easy to make light of the first generation of GDR Marxist historians. Yet, I am more inclined to applaud their seriousness. Discussing the relation between objectivity and partisanship, they took up a matter of central importance to historical science that mainstream German historiography tended to avoid. Enclosed in this discussion – for some its core, for others its blind spot – was the possibility of a new type of historical science, a science which did not place itself above social struggles but raised the question of history from an explicitly interventionist standpoint. That is to say, a science which would no longer endow the many with historical traditions that mirrored and served the interests of the few, but a science that equipped the hitherto underprivileged with a history that justified and guided their commitment to a better future. So the question of objectivity and partisanship was not just a matter of epistemological interest. At stake was rather the very possiblity of a historical science that intentionally presented things in a certain perspective as part of a political project, without renouncing modern standards of scientificity. In the 1950s and 1960s, however, overcoming the traditional ways of historical knowledge-production in Germany seemed to many academic activists in the GDR synonymous with establishing a historical science of Marxist or Marxist–Leninist design.

The first explicit controversy about objectivity and partisanship in the GDR was instigated by Jürgen Kuczynski in 1956. Kuczynski (1904–97) was one of the most eminent East German historians[12] and at that time a leading member of the academic establishment. His article 'Partisanship and objectivity in history and historiography', published in the GDR's foremost historical journal *Zeitschrift für Geschichtswissenschaft* (ZfG),[13] was a well-calculated advance towards more scientificity in Marxist–Leninist historiography. It was directed against the erosion of scientific standards in the name of political conformism. Kuczynski's stance embodies the most challenging, flexible and far-reaching position in the entire controversy. I want to retrace his argument here, as it marks the scope of the historians' discourse on objectivity and partisanship within the framework of Marxism–Leninism.

Kuczynski discriminates between two different concepts of partisanship within Marxist–Leninist discourse: 'The first one developed in confrontation with the bourgeois pseudo-concept of "objectivity". This concept of partisanship says that impartial ideology is something impossible, that any ideology implies partisanship and judgement.'[14] He illustrates this as follows:

> While, in Ranke's view, the ideal historiography 'shows impartially how it actually was', while Max Weber advocates the ideal of a 'value (judgement)-free science' that represents 'objectively' the social relations and their development, Marxist scientists oppose such misleading talk. We point out that in reality scientists cannot, did not, and must not avoid taking a stand.[15]

This kind of partisanship may be conscious or unconscious, Kuczynski continues, and he concludes: 'From the proposition that every historiography is partial it follows conversely that "objective" historiography, in the meaning of impartial historiography, is impossible.'[16]

Partisanship in this sense denotes a general attribute of the cognitive subject as such. It says that any speaker speaks from a certain viewpoint which is predicated on a number of features such as origin, education or religion. Any cognitive interest is therefore particular, biased or party. Moreover, partisanship in this sense implies that in a world of antagonistic class relations the idea of writing impartial history is a mere chimera. Kuczynski calls this 'the more general concept of partisanship' and specifies it as 'partisanship for some class'.[17]

In a second step, he makes plain that this is not a specifically scientific concept of partisanship. He does so by setting apart from it a second concept which represents, as it were, the dictates of science itself: 'To say that the development of [historical] science demands partisanship does not mean, of course, that we are supposed simply to take a stand.'[18] In other words, scientific historiography requires more than active partisanship in the general meaning of class standpoint. Consequently, Kuczynski proceeds:

> The development of [historical] science demands rather a *specific partisanship*. It demands partisanship for progress: at the beginning of the 19th century partisanship for capitalism and the bourgeoisie, today partisanship for socialism and the working class. It demands *partisanship for the new and the progressive to which society advances*. To be partisan for reality – that is the literal meaning of the word objectivity.[19]

That is to say, the development of historical science itself demands partisanship, but *partisanship of a different type*. Why, though, does historical science require this? Because, Kuczynski answers, its task is to explore historical reality; yet, historical reality features a particular trait, which he describes as follows:

> That trait consists in the fact, that the process of social motion is a process of development, not an anarchic or circular motion ... but a progressive movement, a movement in ascending line, from lower to higher stages of society. It is a law-governed [*gesetzmäßig*] and elemental process.[20]

Whence Kuczynski concludes: 'Thus reality itself is partisan! Partisan for the modern and the new as against the ancient and the obsolete, partisan for higher stages of development as against lower ones.'[21] The fact, though, that there is 'partisanship of reality for the new',[22] Kuczynski argues, entails two things on the part of the cognitive subject. First, that only the attitude of specific (scientific) partisanship for the new and the progressive ensures realistic objectivity.[23] Kuczynski explicitly underlines here that this is meant to be a universally valid prerequisite of any scientific research on society.[24]

Secondly, the attitude of specific partisanship helps to optimise the use of science in the interest of the new and the progressive. To this effect, he sums up:

> We demand partisanship – in the sense of taking sides with the new – for two reasons: firstly, in order to guide the process of scientific thinking, so that it leads to an adequate understanding of the process of social motion and its lawfulness [*Gesetzmäßigkeit*]. Because this process is objectively, lawfully and elementally partisan for the new. Secondly, in order to change [social] reality by applying the results of scientific research, so that we can accelerate the process of social progress in the interest of the people.[25]

In other words, on the basis of Lenin's theory of cognition which presumes a homologous relation between historical reality and its adequate representation, Kuczynski speaks up for an attitude that brings this homology about, in order to turn historical science into a productive force that operates in the name of progress. And Kuczynski resumes: 'There, in the reality of the process of social motion, lies the fundamental reason for partisanship in the societal sciences.'[26]

Eventually, he concludes his argumentation by drawing his fellow historians' attention to the underlying but hitherto unspoken issue that had made him write his article, namely:

> that partisanship is not required of them 'as a result of a resolution of the Socialist Unity Party of Germany' or 'in the interest of a uniform working-class ideology'. It is reality itself, the material process of social development, that demands partisanship. That is to say, partisanship is required of them in the interest of the objectivity and reality of science.[27]

In rephrasing Kuczynski's argument, we may summarise: since every historiography is partial, objective historiography in the meaning of impartial is impossible. *Realistic objectivity* requires partisanship, though not in the simple meaning of class standpoint or party-political conformity, but in the meaning of being partisan for the new and the progressive in a historical reality which is, as a law-governed progressive process, itself inescapably partisan for the new and the progressive. In a nutshell, realistic objectivity requires *objective partisanship*, an attitude corresponding to the course of history. Conversely and as a result of this, objective partisanship is the condition of possibility of realistic objectivity and hence the universal prerequisite of any scientific research on history.

Kuczynski was subjected to a welter of criticism for his account. The *Zeitschrift für Geschichtswissenschaft* alone published nine articles against him in 1957–58.[28] The polemic ranged from 'unprincipled eclecticism' and having 'not resolutely argued on the basis of Marxist partisanship', to 'bourgeois objectivism', an 'attempt to undermine proletarian class partisanship' and 'revisionism'.[29] His advance was all the more remarkable as it followed the History Resolution of the Central Committee of the SED of 1955, a resolution that had been designed to ultimately establish in academic history the dominance of Marxism as understood by the Central Committee.[30] Indeed, from a party-political standpoint Kuczynski's concept of partisanship was certainly not partisan enough. His article symbolised the short period of 'thaw' following the twentieth party congress of the Communist Party of the Soviet Union in February 1956, which had announced the new course of destalinization. By the beginning of 1957, however, the Central Committee headed by Walter Ulbricht had already replaced the modest attempts at overcoming '[Stalinist] dogmatism' by a fierce campaign against '[bourgeois] revisionism'. Critical left-wing intellectuals such as Fritz Behrens, Ernst Bloch, Hermann Klenner, or Hans Mayer were now denounced as revisionists.[31] Kuczynski, defending himself against the verdict of revisionism, underwent a gruelling marathon of disciplinary actions.[32] However, unlike less fortunate academics such as the historian Günther Mühlpfordt, who had his academic career forcibly terminated,[33] Kuczynski did not face any serious consequences either personally or professionally.[34] The effect of his advance was rather different. It was to incite a process of rethinking the question of objectivity in an academic discipline that was intentionally designed not to abstain from political practice, yet had come to defend itself from being reduced to it. The vehement but short-lived polemical campaign amplified this effect still more. The controversy of 1956–58 revealed, finally, that there was a problem at all. This precisely had been Kuczynski's intention.[35]

Helmut Rumpler suggested an interesting explanation for the absence of an effective rebuttal of Kuczynski's theses. Kuczynski's approach, he argued, was in the long term far less problematic to the political leadership than the attempts to pin historical science down to subjective class partisanship of his opponents, such as Joachim Höppner, Ernst Hoffmann and Josef Schleifstein. Partisanship as a political creed might have been more easy to handle. Yet, the authority of a political system that rested on the ideology of Marxism–Leninism did not derive from professing one's belief in socialism but from taking recourse to objective laws of social evolution. After all, Rumpler concluded, the belief in the superiority of Marxist–Leninist partisanship was ultimately founded on the idea that the subjective interests of the proletariat would coincide with the objective laws of history.[36]

This is a forceful argument and, yet, it overstates the ability of the SED leadership to be aware and in control of both the logic and the effect of discourse. Political management of the kind of the History Resolution of 1955 suggests that this is rather unlikely.[37] Far from excluding the positions of his opponents, Kuczynski's reformulation of partisanship and objectivity overarched the spectrum of positions within Marxist–Leninist historical discourse and thereby opened up a space to accommodate the more critical contemporaries who were, regardless of sometimes considerable friction, not inclined to abandon the platform of Marxism–Leninism altogether. Despite the fact that the polemical campaign against Kuczynski was targeted at his theses on history, a great deal of the polemic was meant to attack his very personality. The extrovert style of his writing, the provocative banality of his arguments, the air of distinction and cheerful vanity about him – all revealing the bourgeois-scholarly background which had equipped him with that kind of capital which is invisible only to those who possess it. But that is another story. The theoretical design of Kuczynski's theses was Marxism–Leninism par excellence.[38]

During the later 1950s, 1960s and early 1970s many GDR historians made their statement on objectivity and partisanship. Joachim Streisand, for example, who was to become one of the leading East German historians in the 1960s and 1970s, largely agreed with Kuczynski in a review article of 1956. Like Kuczynski, but more explicitly, he criticised the 'fetishisation of partisanship' among fellow historians, arguing that a theory's partisanship was not sufficiently ensured by the mere fact that its proponents felt partisan.[39] At the same time Streisand made it quite plain that it would take practical partisanship or commitment for the cognitive potential of the Marxist perspective to be actualised. He viewed the two concepts of partisanship, which Kuczynski had drawn attention to, as two sides of the same coin.[40]

Ernst Engelberg, who was by this time already a key figure, stressed on various occasions the particular value of the correspondence between partisanship and objectivity in Marxism–Leninism. At the founding conference of the German Historians' Society of the GDR in 1958, as well as in his report to the International Historians' Congress in 1960 on the achievements of East German historiography, he drew a direct line from proletarian class interests and Marxist partisan objectivity to scientificity, truth, vitality and historic future prospects.[41] Simultaneously, though, he emphasised the significance of professionalism, insinuating that the potential advantage arising from the correspondence between partisanship and objectivity could be put into historiographical practice only where professional research techniques such as the procedures of source criticism were appropriated and applied.[42]

In the course of the 1960s, then, defining the central methodological terms of Marxism–Leninism became the monopoly of other academic disciplines. It became in particular the domain of dialectical and historical materialism, the reorganised disciplines of academic philosophy. This was mirrored in the first edition of the GDR's Marxist–Leninist historical primer *Einführung in das Studium der Geschichte* of 1966 and the leading historical handbook *Kritik der bürgerlichen Geschichtsschreibung* of 1970. Whereas both contained just a few lines on objectivity and partisanship, the first comprehensive Marxist–Leninist philosophical dictionary of the GDR in 1964 dealt with the concepts in extensive articles.[43]

A basic theoretical debate on specific meta-historiographical questions was established in the 1970s. Initiated and primarily driven by historians of the Department of Methodology and History of Historical Science at the Central Institute of History at the Academy of Sciences in East Berlin, such as Ernst Engelberg, Wolfgang Küttler and Hans-Peter Jaeck, the debate was part of an international trend towards the theorisation of historical writing.[44] In this context Gerhard Brendler discussed in a 1972 article what part partisanship played in the cognitive process of the historian.[45] Arguing that Marxist–Leninist partisanship is not merely a personal creed but first and foremost the 'social quality of [a] subject' that – informed by the 'explanans of a philosophical theory' – accords with the objective course of history,[46] Brendler's article reflects at what level of conceptualisation the methodological discussion had arrived by the early 1970s. More important, it indicates that, much as the concepts of partisanship and objectivity had been elaborated since Kuczynski's advance in 1956, the scope of his notion of realistic objectivity via objective partisanship was not expanded upon. The questions that had driven the controversy of 1956–58 remained much the same: how could historiography get involved in political practice without inexorably getting reduced to it? Were historians able to present things in a certain perspective as part of a political project without renouncing standards of scientificity? Conversely, were detachment, systematic self-distancing, disinterestedness and impartiality the indispensable conditions of objectivity and scientificity, or did they represent one possible case of scientific rationality among others?

Jürgen Kuczynski and Max Weber

Kuczynski's text is in many ways archetypical of Marxist historical discourse in the GDR of the later 1950s and 1960s. It is worth returning to it once again in order to compare some of Kuczynski's arguments to those developed by Max Weber in his essay on '"Objectivity" in social science and social policy'.[47] Weber is of particular interest here, as he is the classical exponent concerning objectivity and value-free science; furthermore, he was explicitly opposed by Kuczynski and, not least, he was to become of central importance to the paradigm shift towards social history in the FRG of the late 1960s and 1970s. So he, too, is in many respects archetypical.

Kuczynski, we recall, had started out from 'the more general concept of partisanship' which was directed against 'the bourgeois pseudo-concept of "objectivity"'. Rejecting Ranke's notion of objective historiography and Weber's concept of value-free science as misleading talk, Kuczynski had underscored 'that in reality scientists cannot, did not, and must not avoid taking a stand'.

Ironically, Weber could not have said it any better, as he also opposed pseudo-objectivity, which means here basically indifference and neutrality. In Weber it reads: 'An attitude of moral indifference [*Gesinnungslosigkeit*] has no connection with scientific "objectivity".'[48] He criticised the 'illusion of the self-evidence of normative standards of value' and claimed that: 'Normative standards of value can and must be the objects of [scientific] dispute.'[49] As for the value-free character of social science, Weber made it quite clear that this does not simply mean indifference to value-ideas as such.[50] To this effect he could well have subscribed to Kuczynski's conclusion that '"objective" historiography, in the meaning of impartial historiography, is impossible'.[51]

What Weber really meant as disinterest in and indifference to value-assumptions concerns the logic of the scientific procedure itself. The means, as it were, are neutral. For Weber scientific action is and has to be of purely *instrumental character*. Empirical science has to analyse the 'appropriateness of the means for achieving a given end'; it can test 'the internal consistency of the desired end'; and it should make the cultural values underlying the concrete end explicit and intelligible.[52] To appraise the rationality of the ends themselves (or to judge the validity of the underlying values), however, is not its business. This is beyond 'the boundaries of a science which strives for an "analytical ordering of empirical reality"'.[53]

This leads us back to Kuczynski's text. Turning to Leopold von Ranke, Kuczynski pays tribute to his historical method and praises his 'technique of research': 'No doubt, Ranke uses the new *instrument* in the interest of the ruling classes ... But how much closer have we come in *technical* terms to an adequate understanding of the past through Ranke! ... Any *means*, however, that help us to understand reality better ..., are of importance to social progress'.[54] To underpin his argument, he claims that: '"techniques in themselves" [are] neutral. They can be applied in support of progress as well as against it.'[55]

In themselves neutral, scientific methods are treated by Kuczynski as devices or instruments which have to be directed to the proper ends. This clearly suggests an instrumental concept of scientific reason too. In other words, it indicates traditional theory in contrast to critical theory in the sense of Max Horkheimer and the Marxist discourse of the early Frankfurt School.[56]

Yet what about Weber's notion of value-judgement-free science, that Kuczynski had rejected? According to Kuczynski's concept of historical science, are the rationality of ends and the validity of values subject to evaluation? The answer is: only in a very selective fashion. Most notably, his critical-interventionist approach does not apply to the version of Marxist conception of history he advocates himself. As we could see from his argument on objective partisanship, the ends and value-assumptions underlying this conception of history are given and remain beyond the scope of historical science. They are anchored in an historical reality which is, as a law-governed progressive process, itself inescapably partisan for exactly these ends and values. They are in line with the historical process itself and therefore indisputable.[57]

This leads us to a further correspondence between Kuczynski and Weber.

In distinguishing between value-judgements and empirical knowledge, Weber presupposes 'the existence of an unconditionally valid type of knowledge in the social sciences'.[58] Indeed, he asserts that the objectivity of – faultless – scientific research entails the universal validity of its results, which he illustrates as follows:

> It has been and it remains true that a systematically correct scientific proof..., if it is to achieve its purpose, must be acknowledged as correct even by a Chinese... Furthermore, the successful *logical* analysis of the content of an ideal and its ultimate axioms and the discovery of the consequences which arise from pursuing it, logically and practically, must also be valid for the Chinese. At the same time, our Chinese can lack a 'sense' for our ethical imperative and he can and certainly often will deny the ideal itself and the concrete value-judgement derived from it. Neither of these two latter attitudes can affect the scientific value of the analysis in any way.[59]

This again refers us back to Kuczynski, who considered objective partisanship the universally valid prerequisite of any scientific research on society, because it ensured realistic objectivity:

> Our demand for partisanship in historiography is a *postulate*, which is the *indispensable condition of any scientific research on society whatsoever*. It is impossible to develop an adequate attitude to the reality of social development, without taking sides with the new and the progressive produced by that reality. The demand for partisanship, that we make today, is therefore nothing else but the demand for *realistic objectivity*.[60]

That is to say, in Kuczynski as well as in Weber the concept of objectivity backs the claim for universal validity, which entails their mutually exclusive claim to scientific truth. Common to either concept is the specific blindness against social space and time in general, and against culture, gender, race and partly against class in particular. The difference consists here basically in the respective instances that may ensure objectivity: Weber anchors his claim in the specific rationality ('logic') of the scientific procedure, Kuczynski in the particular rationality ('lawfulness') of the historical process. This, however, refers us back to different value-ideas and partisanships rather than to notions of objectivity and scientificity in themselves.

Some conclusions

My initial question was whether and to what extent the GDR Marxist historiography of the Ulbricht era subscribed to a mode of academic knowledge-making characterised by the properties of objectivity and scientificity. The answer is 'yes', and to a large extent. The analysis suggests that historians in the GDR did not simply deny scientific objectivity. Rather they attempted to develop their own concepts. Traditional versions were resumed and redefined in line with the new constellation and new aspirations. This implied theoretically the possibility of a new type of historical science that would help develop the cultural capacity for action from below. This potentially emancipatory element, however, was not actualised. In one of its most flexible versions, in Kuczynski, Marxist–Leninist historical science was conceptualised as traditional theory, which meant occupying and defending a privileged social space of relative autonomy within the frame of given political ends.

The hypothesis I started out with was that repression cannot in adequate terms account for the relation between scientific objectivity and political power in GDR historiography. Without a doubt, East German Marxist historiography lent itself to the purposes of the authoritarian state and its ruling party, but it was not primarily the repression of scientific objectivity that made it so susceptible to legitimatory purposes. The case study of Jürgen Kuczynski indicates a more complex and less palpable power mechanism which enabled historians as academics to accommodate the demands of the regime.

Kuczynski's concept of realistic objectivity, like much scientific discourse, claims a code of conduct that guides the particular practice of academic institutions: a code of conduct which does not allow for a statement that cannot prove its proper objectivity. It is on this basis that Marxist–Leninist historiography made its claim to universally valid truth. It offers stability and evades questions of conflicting interests. Resistance within the terms of this discourse is impossible because it denies any alternative position from which to speak. Whoever seeks to challenge the assertions about history, progress, the new, etc. argues against the course of history itself. Ultimately, the claim for realistic objectivity appears as an institutional attempt to impose and monitor an all-encompassing perspective on social reality that conveys, transposes and amplifies the effects of domination. In other words, like much scientific discourse it organises the way of experiencing social relations *from above*.

The controversy of 1956–58 reveals furthermore that Marxist–Leninist historians, while being alert to the socio-structural roots of ideological thought as regards 'bourgeois science', were not much concerned about their own institutional anchoring within the political system and the system of the social division of labour. Most notably, the discussion about partisanship in historical science did not challenge the demarcation that separates academia from other forms of social labour. Conceived as interventionist discourse, yet bereft of any alternative agency owing to its detached socio-structural position and the absence of effective institutions of a civil society, the Marxist historiography of the GDR construed the Communist state-party as the institutional condition for transcending the academic limitations of its area of practice. It produced historical knowledge in a form which predestined it for the appropriation by the apparatuses of state and ruling party. However, the state-bound historiography of the GDR produced power knowledge neither as a deviation from the paths of modern Western scientificity, nor simply as a corollary of the fact that the historians concerned were by definition and expressly partisan. There is absolutely no reason to misread the story of GDR historiography as a plea for the externalisation of commitment from historical science. It is the way in which academic historiography was inscribed within the social structure of knowledge-production in the GDR that put its results spontaneously at the disposition of the ideological powers of vertical socialisation.[61] And it is the consent to this – unwitting, tacit or explicit – that made historians part and parcel of an operative network of mental socialisation from above.

Notes

1 I would like to thank Karen Adler, Stefan Berger, Patrick Major, Franziska Meyer, Jonathan Osmond and Helmut Peitsch, whose ideas and comments have fed into this chapter.
2 Konrad H. Jarausch (ed.), *Zwischen Parteilichkeit und Professionalität: Bilanz der Geschichtswissenschaft der DDR* (Berlin, 1991); Ulrich Neuhäußer-Wespy, *Die SED und die Historie* (Bonn, 1996); or Ilko-Sascha Kowalczuk, *Legitimation eines neuen Staates: Parteiarbeiter an der historischen Front* (Berlin, 1997).
3 Reinhart Beck, *Die Geschichte der Weimarer Republik im Spiegel der sowjetzonalen Geschichtsschreibung* (Bonn and Berlin, 1965), 66.
4 Walther Hofer, *Geschichte zwischen Philosophie und Politik* (Stuttgart, 1956), 146, emphasis is added.
5 Alexander Fischer and Günther Heydemann (eds), *Geschichtswissenschaft in der DDR*, 2 vols (Berlin, 1988–90); see also Helmut Rumpler, 'Parteilichkeit und Objektivität als Theorie-Problem der DDR-Historie', in Reinhart Koselleck *et al.* (eds), *Objektivität und Parteilichkeit in der Geschichtswissenschaft* (Munich, 1977), 228–62; Jürgen Kocka, 'Parteilichkeit in der DDR-marxistischen Geschichtswissenschaft', *ibid.*, 263–9; or Günther Heydemann, *Geschichtswissenschaft im geteilten Deutschland* (Frankfurt/Main, 1980).
6 Jürgen Kocka, 'Nachwort', in Rainer Eckert *et al.* (eds), *Krise, Umbruch, Neubeginn* (Stuttgart, 1992), 470.
7 For the political dimensions, see Heiko Feldner, 'Politischer Umbruch und Geschichtswissenschaft in Deutschland', *Geschichte und Gesellschaft*, 22 (1996), 90–7.
8 Martin Sabrow, '"Beherrschte Normalwissenschaft": Überlegungen zum Charakter der DDR-Historiographie', *Geschichte und Gesellschaft*, 24 (1998), 412–45; Ralf Possekel, 'Kuriositätenkabinett oder Wissenschaftsgeschichte? Zur Historisierung der DDR-Geschichtswissenschaft', *ibid.*, 446–62.
9 Martin Sabrow and Peter Thomas Walther (eds), *Historische Forschung und sozialistische Diktatur* (Leipzig, 1995); Martin Sabrow (ed.), *Verwaltete Vergangenheit* (Leipzig, 1997); Martin Sabrow, *Das Diktat des Konsenses: Geschichtswissenschaft in der DDR 1949–1969* (Munich, 2001); or Martin Sabrow, 'Klio mit dem Januskopf', in Gerald Diesener *et al.* (eds), *Historische Zeitschriften im internationalen Vergleich* (Leipzig, 1999), 235–66.

10 Possekel, 'Kuriositätenkabinett', 448.
11 I draw here on Michel Foucault's rearrangement of the question of repression in *The History of Sexuality*, i (New York, 1978).
12 The most referred-to works among his over 3,000 publications are *Die Geschichte der Lage der Arbeiter unter dem Kapitalismus*, 38 vols (Berlin, 1961–72); *Studien zu einer Geschichte der Gesellschaftswissenschaften*, 10 vols (Berlin, 1975 ff.); and *Geschichte des Alltags des deutschen Volkes*, 5 vols (Berlin, 1980 ff.).
13 Jürgen Kuczynski, 'Parteilichkeit und Objektivität in Geschichte und Geschichtsschreibung', *Zeitschrift für Geschichtswissenschaft* (*ZfG*), 4 (1956), 873–88. About the journal, on whose editorial board Kuczynski sat at the time, see Sabrow, 'Klio'; and from the angle of its general editor in 1956, Fritz Klein, 'Dokumente aus den Anfangsjahren der ZfG 1953–1957', *ZfG*, 42 (1994), 39–55.
14 Kuczynski, 'Parteilichkeit', 873.
15 *Ibid.*
16 *Ibid.*, 875.
17 *Ibid.*, 886.
18 *Ibid.*, 875.
19 *Ibid.*, emphasis added.
20 *Ibid.*
21 *Ibid.*
22 *Ibid.*, 877.
23 *Ibid.*, 875 f.
24 *Ibid.*, 875.
25 *Ibid.*, 876.
26 *Ibid.* The term 'societal sciences' (*Gesellschaftswissenschaften*) refers to both humanities and social sciences. It was used in the GDR – and not only there – to contrast with the traditional German paradigm of *Geisteswissenschaften* (sciences of the spirit).
27 *Ibid.*, 888. See, by contrast, Walther Hofer's analysis in *Geschichte zwischen Philosophie und Politik*, 146: 'The ideal of objectivity – in the meaning of rising above day-to-day politics and party-political interests and purposes – is even theoretically denied by the Soviet concept of partisanship.'
28 *ZfG*, 5 (1957), 456 ff., 1217 ff.; *ZfG*, 6 (1958), 169 ff., 304 ff., 313 ff., 558 ff., 562 ff., 578 ff., 1049 ff. Besides Kuczynski's essay on partisanship and objectivity, the criticism applied to the following texts in which he defended, further specified and developed his views on history and historiography: 'Soziologičeskie sakony', *Voprosy Filosofii*, 11/5 (1957), 95–100; 'Der Mensch, der Geschichte macht', *ZfG*, 5 (1957), 1–17; 'Meinungsstreit, Dogmatismus und "liberale Kritik"', *Einheit*, 12/5 (1957); *Der Ausbruch des ersten Weltkrieges und die deutsche Sozialdemokratie* (Berlin, 1957).
29 Joachim Höppner, 'Zur Kritik der Geschichtsauffassung von Jürgen Kuczynski in den Fragen des Klassenkampfes und der Parteilichkeit', *ZfG*, 6 (1958), 562–77: 571, 573, 577; 'Gegenwartsaufgaben der Geschichtswissenschaft in der Deutschen Demokratischen Republik', *ZfG*, 5 (1957), 449–55: 454; Ernst Hoffmann, 'Über Tendenzen, die den weiteren Fortschritt unserer Geschichtswissenschaft hemmen', *Einheit*, 12/9 (1957), 1150–66: 1153, 1161; and 'Für die Festigung der sozialistischen deutschen Geschichtswissenschaft',

ZfG, 6 (1958), 457–67: 460, which concluded the controversy. The party-political implications of Kuczynski's position are discussed at length in Rumpler, 'Parteilichkeit', 231–40.

30 'Die Verbesserung der Forschung und Lehre in der Geschichtswissenschaft der Deutschen Demokratischen Republik', ZfG, 3 (1955), 507–27. For the context of the origin and impact of the History Resolution, see Horst Haun, *Der Geschichtsbeschluß der SED 1955* (Dresden, 1996).

31 For a graphic description of the situation at universities, see Armin Mitter and Stefan Wolle, *Untergang auf Raten* (Munich, 1995), 231–6, 260–71; Guntolf Herzberg, *Aufbruch und Abwicklung* (Berlin, 2000), 34–50; and Hermann-Josef Rupieper (ed.), *Erinnerungen an die Martin-Luther-Universität* (Halle, 1997), 102 ff.

32 Culminating in his ritual self-criticism at the Third University Conference of the SED (28 February to 2 March 1958), *Neues Deutschland*, 12 March 1958; for the preceding ritual debate, see *Sonntag*, 9 March 1958.

33 Mühlpfordt, from 1954 head of the Department of the History of the Soviet Union at the University of Halle-Wittenberg, was expelled from the SED and suspended from academic duty in 1958. In 1962, he was dismissed without compensation, and it was not until 1990 that he was rehabilitated. See Erich Donnert (ed.), *Europa in der Frühen Neuzeit: Festschrift für Günther Mühlpfordt*, Vol. 4 (Cologne and Weimar, 1997), 679–732.

34 From 1956 until his retirement in 1968, Kuczynski ran one of the most productive research institutes of the GDR, the Institute of Economic History at the Academy of Sciences, while at the same time maintaining an enormous output as a much-published author himself. Of course, he could not possibly have known this at the time he took the step of writing his article.

35 For Kuczynski's account, see Jürgen Kuczynski, *Frost nach dem Tauwetter* (Berlin, 1993). In the course of the 1950s Kuczynski ignited several other controversies in various academic disciplines. Indeed, he complied with things his way, like a 'loyal dissident', Jürgen Kuczynski, *Ein linientreuer Dissident* (Berlin and Weimar, 1992) and *Ein Leben in der Wissenschaft der DDR* (Münster, 1994).

36 Rumpler, 'Parteilichkeit', 238–41.

37 For a subtle discussion of the range of the regime's power within the academy during the Ulbricht era, see Ralph Jessen, *Akademische Elite und kommunistische Diktatur* (Göttingen, 1999).

38 For the impact of exile in Britain 1936–45 on Kuczynski, see Mario Keßler, *Exilerfahrungen in Wissenschaft und Politik* (Cologne, 2001), 91–145.

39 Joachim Streisand, 'Kategorien und Perspektiven der Geschichte', ZfG, 4 (1956), 889–8: 890–3.

40 Ibid., 892 f. See also Joachim Streisand, 'Brief an die Redaktion', ZfG, 5 (1957), 619 f. In the same issue Eric Hobsbawm argued that 'much academic history is present politics dressed up in period costume. Whether he likes it or not, the work of the academic historian reflects the attitudes and views of his class.', Eric Hobsbawm, 'Wohin gehen die englischen Historiker?', ZfG, 4 (1956), 950–63: 950.

41 Ernst Engelberg, 'Politik und Geschichtsschreibung', ZfG, 6 (1958), 468–95: 469 f., 472 ff., 482, 494 f.; Ernst Engelberg and Rolf Rudolph, 'Zur Geschichtswissenschaft der Deutschen Demokratischen Republik', ZfG: Sonderband (Berlin, 1960), 7–22: 13 ff.

42 Engelberg, 'Politik und Geschichtsschreibung', 469; see also Ernst Engelberg, 'Parteilichkeit und Objektivität in der Geschichtswissenschaft', *ZfG*, 17 (1969), 75–91.
43 Walther Eckermann and Hubert Mohr (eds), *Einführung in das Studium der Geschichte* (Berlin, 1966); Gerhard Lozek et al. (eds), *Kritik der bürgerlichen Geschichtsschreibung* (Cologne, 1970); Manfred Buhr and Georg Klaus (eds), *Philosophisches Wörterbuch*, Vol. 2 (Leipzig, 1964), 803, 819 ff.; see also Wolfgang Eichhorn et al. (eds), *Wörterbuch der marxistisch-leninistischen Soziologie* (Berlin, 1969), 310 ff., 331 ff.
44 Ernst Engelberg (ed.), *Probleme der Geschichtsmethodologie* (Berlin, 1972); Ernst Engelberg and Wolfgang Küttler (eds), *Probleme der geschichtswissenschaftlichen Erkenntnis* (Berlin, 1977).
45 Gerhard Brendler, 'Zur Rolle der Parteilichkeit im Erkenntnisprozess des Historikers', in Engelberg (ed.), *Probleme der Geschichtsmethodologie*.
46 *Ibid.*, 112 ff.
47 Max Weber, '"Objectivity" in social science and social policy' (1904), in Max Weber, *Max Weber on the Methodology of the Social Sciences* (New York, 1949), 49–112. Kuczynski – who, as a student in Heidelberg in 1923–4, had been a member of the Weberian circle still assembled at the time by Weber's widow Marianne – referred to Max Weber as 'Germany's greatest bourgeois societal scientist' of the century, and 'the last, truly important societal scientist of the bourgeoisie'. Jürgen Kuczynski, *Memoiren* (Berlin, 1973), 60 f., 410; Jürgen Kuczynski, *Zum Briefwechsel bürgerlicher Wissenschaftler* (Berlin, 1976), 148.
48 Weber, 'Objectivity', 60. See also 67 and 71 f., where he discusses why 'one-sidedness of viewpoint' would not simply contradict scientific objectivity.
49 *Ibid.*, 56.
50 *Ibid.*, 110 f.
51 Kuczynski, 'Parteilichkeit', 875.
52 Weber, 'Objectivity', 52 ff.
53 *Ibid.*, 52 ff., 58, 63, 111: 54. See also 61, where Weber portrays 'the framework of scientific discussion' as 'the possibility of coming together freely with one's political opponents in a neutral forum' for 'the sharpest factual, scientific criticism ... in the service of scientific knowledge'.
54 Kuczynski, 'Parteilichkeit', 887, emphasis added.
55 *Ibid.* Kuczynski speaks here also of the 'technique of historiography'.
56 See Max Horkheimer, 'Traditionelle und kritische Theorie' (1937), in Max Horkheimer, *Traditionelle und kritische Theorie: Vier Aufsätze* (Frankfurt/Main, 1973), 12–65.
57 Kuczynski, 'Parteilichkeit', 875 f., 888.
58 Weber, 'Objectivity', 63.
59 *Ibid.*, 58 f., emphasis added. See also 76 f., 110 f., where Weber emphasises that the *validity* of scientific knowledge is not to be confused with the belief in its *significance*, which presupposes a specific 'value-orientation' and is 'the product of certain cultures' alone.
60 Kuczynski, 'Parteilichkeit', 875 f., emphasis added.
61 For a fuller account, see Heiko Feldner, *Das Erfahrnis der Ordnung* (Frankfurt/Main, 1999), 7–16, 25–35.

IV
Conclusion

16

Retheorising 'state' and 'society' in the German Democratic Republic

Mary Fulbrook

The history of the GDR remains a highly controversial area of contemporary history.[1] Interpretations of the past have very clear implications in the present, in a whole variety of ways. These obviously include major juridical issues, such as bringing to justice those who played a major role in the murkier aspects of the regime (such as shootings at the Wall), as well as the much larger problems associated with the massive 'restructuring' of institutions and turnover of personnel, so intimately linked with the Stasi informant witchhunt. There are also personal implications for each and every East German over a certain age: whether they are able to retain their jobs, their self-respect, or the respect of colleagues, friends and neighbours; how they interpret past experiences, successes, their own life-histories or biographies; whether, in short, they feel they can salvage a degree of personal authenticity in their own life histories, or whether 1989 has to be a new *Stunde Null* in modern German history, comparable to the caesura in consciousness at 1945.

These political and personal considerations have directly affected the ways in which GDR history has been written. Most interpretations are in some way 'betroffen': affected by and morally responding to the subject matter under discussion. Even those approaches which seek a degree of neutrality or objectivity are often castigated for failure to condemn, and hence implicit support for the regime.[2] Many critiques of certain interpretations of GDR history are couched in terms of their political or moral stance and implications, rather than their empirical or theoretical content. Some views are considered more 'right-wing' or 'left-wing' and adjudicated accordingly. Where does this leave the supposed scientific validity of interpretations – or is such a thing an intrinsically unrealisable goal? In short, to what extent are theoretical debates over the past on a par with the practical political struggles of the past?

This chapter seeks to explore a little more the issue of approaches to state and society in relation to the question of value neutrality in historical analysis.[3] I shall present a brief survey of types of approach to GDR history, although I shall clearly not be able to provide a comprehensive, let alone exhaustive, coverage. In the light of this, we can return to the questions of adjudicating among different approaches to state–society relations in the GDR, and working towards a new approach.

State–society and value neutrality

Current approaches to GDR history may be grouped under a variety of headings. For present purposes, we shall look at approaches as they fall along the major fault line relating to conceptions of state and society. It is interesting to note, as we go along, that the divisions in no way correspond to 'western' versus 'eastern' (or, more colloquially, *Wessi/Ossi*) approaches. Each of the following positions has exponents from both sides of the fallen Wall. It is also interesting to note the ways in which moral and political preconceptions colour, shape and contaminate or render sensitive each theoretical approach.

Focus on state and power: condemnatory–exculpatory modes

Oddly, when we look at approaches to state and society in the GDR, we find that there is a degree of conflation between *focus of inquiry*, on the one hand, and *assumed moral–political implications* on the other. The overlaps are not neat or symmetrical, but they are quite striking. First, there are those – probably the vast majority of works on the GDR – which focus primarily on the state, or which, in precisely not focusing on the state, nevertheless essentially constitute their object of enquiry as it is shaped by or responds to the state. The focus is thus essentially on structures of power, repression, domination; and on associated patterns of resistance and opposition.

The condemnatory mode   Many approaches emphasising the state tend to fall into the condemnatory mode. There are many theoretical variants within this area of substantive focus. A very large number of early post-1989 publications were, quite understandably, determined both to explore the apparatus of repression which had so recently been overthrown, and on which there was now such an unexpected wealth of material, and at the same time to vent pent-up feelings of emotion and anger. This type of *betroffene Literatur* (victim literature) was not, and did not intend to be, explicitly theoretical. It was quite happy to be consciously condemnatory in tone and also, for many authors and readers, to some extent emancipatory (or at least cathartic).

As illustrations we may take, for example, the early works of Mitter and Wolle: their edited collection of Stasi documents from the closing months of the collapsing GDR, *'Ich liebe Euch doch alle!' Befehle und Lageberichte des MfS*; or their archivally rich, but theoretically ill-conceived and awkwardly written book, *Untergang auf Raten*.[4] Leaving aside the theoretical problems with the assumptions on which the latter work was based, it clearly performed a major service in 'writing oneself free' of a hated regime.

There was also a plethora of accounts of the Stasi as an organisation, and of Stasi informants, including general academic overviews, journalistic revelations, biographical explorations, and other reflections.[5] The moral and political issues are extraordinarily hard to disentangle with respect to the Stasi, representing arguably the epitome of evil in GDR colours. A similar depth of feeling is evident, again for perfectly understandable reasons, in the wide range of autobiographical works of dissidents, or the collections of materials relating to the 'gentle revolution'.[6] Many of these accounts have to be treated rather in the nature of primary sources than as candidates for major interpretive frameworks.

There are also a relatively large number of academic accounts of particular topics, such as church–state relations, by both western and eastern scholars, which are also highly coloured by a sense of moral outrage. A classic example of this would be the works by Gerhard Besier on the church, seeking not only exhaustive scholarly documentation but also sharp indictment of Stasi infiltration and SED distortion of the East German churches.[7] From an East German perspective, we have the works of Ehrhart Neubert on both the churches and opposition.[8]

The bulk of publications on the GDR in the early 1990s probably fell within these sorts of category. By the mid-1990s, a growth industry in a new – but at the same time very old – paradigm of interpretation was emerging, threatening to become a hegemonic discourse about the GDR. This is the rather stridently resurrected theory of totalitarianism, which sets out with an explicit theoretical agenda.[9] This claims to achieve three objectives in one: to typologise the GDR as an instance of a particular type of twentieth-century dictatorship; to explain its internal dynamics of development; and at the same to time to condemn it. In my view (which there is not space to develop in detail here) it fails on all three counts.[10]

For present purposes, there are two points of importance. First, a major problem with totalitarianism theories is that the overall concept is too all-encompassing: it tries to typologise, to explain and to provide some form of exhaustive analysis. Although there have been attempts to introduce a degree of dynamism and capacity to account for changes over time, the explanatory emphasis is necessarily on the combination of repression and indoctrination. There are problems too with even the middle-level concepts, the vocabulary of description. The conceptual net is not appropriate to a comprehensive, nuanced and differentiated capturing of reality, but rather represents a Procrustean bed. Not all areas of life can be adequately captured in terms of power and oppression and resistance; but there is no vocabulary, no space in the conceptual apparatus, for dealing with other areas within an integrated theoretical framework. We shall return later to the explicit claim that the vocabulary of power (*Macht*) is more appropriate than any concept suggesting a degree of internalisation of authority (*Herrschaft*).

Finally, there is an exclusionary moral problem: the totalitarianism framework is not merely implicitly, but rather explicitly and wilfully condemnatory. If, however, we wish to retain any notion of historical analysis as the pursuit of some version of 'truth' which can be shared across political differences, then this pursuit must be phrased in some way that all participants – whether for or against – can share debate on. This cannot be achieved by the use of essentially contested concepts such as totalitarianism. There are even problems with the morally less unambiguously laden concept of dictatorship, given the very different meanings of this term within the Marxist–Leninist and western liberal–democratic interpretations of the term. The fact that there is not a common ground of terminology renders pluralistic debate in pursuit of more appropriate interpretations of the past, which can be adjudicated on rational criteria irrespective of protagonists' political or moral preferences, exceedingly problematic.

In any event, not all approaches to the GDR have been subsumed under this general heading. In particular, two quite different sorts of reproach have been levelled against those works with a primary focus on power and repression. Neither, as yet, appears to have solved the bigger problems, to which we shall return in a moment.

The exculpatory mode   The first type of reproach to the condemnatory mode might be termed, very simply, the exculpatory mode. Many protagonists of this approach are very clearly political actors in the drama they are seeking to interpret. We have, for example, the SED successor party, the PDS, producing its own 'reckoning with the past' as an answer to the official parliamentary inquiry, the Bundestag's Enquete-Kommission.[11] We have the various generally self-serving memoirs of former prominent individuals in the regime: Günter Schabowski or Egon Krenz were two prominent early contributors to this mode of self-exculpation.[12] There are of course also less luminary figures, as well as a variety of political sympathisers who never held positions of prominence.

The exculpatory approach too appears in a variety of versions. First of all, there is the overtly political response which seeks to retain elements of the original vision. This it refuses to condemn in principle, while seeking to explain the perversions in practice. Hence, it is possible to say that the project, the cause, remains good, while the conditions under which it had to be attempted were such as to produce unacceptable distortions in the way it was pursued. Here, there is a clear prioritisation of ends over means. If the goal is an equal society, and the means are essentially nasty – expropriation of the previously propertied and powerful – then these means must be used, however unpleasant for those affected (hence the 'dictatorship of the proletariat'). If the Wall is the essential prerequisite for the functioning of the East

German economy, then the curtailment of human rights in the here and now (to travel, to move west) must be undertaken in the interests of the more perfect society in the future. If the competition with and threat of undermining from the West, the Class Enemy, is the prime danger to the achievement of utopia on earth (in the form of the GDR), then the surveillance and repression of the Stasi is the essential and acceptable means.

While in power, such analyses were strictly speaking simply political legitimations of what was being put into practice, rather than interpretations of the regime. After the *Wende* – the 'turn' of 1989 – they have become arguments about 'what went wrong' and, as such, constitute a mode of highly politicised 'reckoning with the past'. However, they also contain elements of an explanatory framework about the character and reasons for the development of the regime.

There is a rather different variant of the exculpatory approach which focuses on the internal structures of power. This essentially starts from the same premise: that the original vision was good. It then goes on to say that the real problem lay not – or not only – with the conditions of realisation of the project, but rather – or also – with the concentration of power at the top, the *Machtspitze*. There were of course good reasons for this 'democratic centralism' in the Leninist version of Marxism, but such reasons are usually conveniently forgotten in this post-*Wende* self-exculpation. Thus, we have a curious symmetrical inversion of totalitarian theory. The power structure is seen as a clean pyramid, with only a handful of men (in the 1980s, the gerontocratic triumvirate of Honecker, Mielke and Mittag) at the top holding all the reins of power in their hands, with a few more powerful barons in the Politbüro having wide latitude to dictate policy in their particular areas of power. Below or beyond these tightly drawn circles, the vast army of functionaries were, to adapt the title of one collection of accounts, 'without power'.[13]

Leaving aside the moral issues, on which there can be no academic means of adjudicating (the absolute beliefs and prior values attached to rationality of means or ends, to use the Weberian terms), there are historical paradigms and *Geschichtsbilder* proposed here which are, I would suggest, in principle amenable to empirical analysis. For example, to take the last illustration relating to the *Machtspitze*, it should be possible to analyse the concentration and extent of power and leeway that was or was not available, was or was not utilised, by those lower in the power hierarchy. One does not have to accept self-exculpations at face value.

Again, in many instances here we may be dealing with a body of literature that may have to be treated more as primary source material than as serious candidates for interpretation. Given, however, that in the practical political arena the 'west has won', it is easier to recognise this when the interpretations emanate from the side of the historical losers than when, as is the case with totalitarianism theory, it comes from the winners' quarters.

Focus on society: Ostalgie, *everyday life and social history*

There is however also a quite different form of reproach to the condemnatory focus on the structures of power and repression: the reproach from those who lived through it and who do not recognise their own private pasts in the accounts they are being presented with. Quite apart from the fact that there was, in the uncertain conditions of the 1990s, a noticeable wave of '*Ostalgie*' or nostalgia for the East, there has also been a clearly registered dissonance between the accounts of historians and the remembered experiences of contemporaries. Many former citizens of the GDR feel there was somehow more – or possibly less – to life in the GDR than suggested in accounts focusing primarily on the state and power structures; that, in fact, they were able to lead what they perceived at the time as 'perfectly ordinary lives'. Alternatively, if they accept the analyses of domination and opposition, they feel they have metaphorically to rewrite their own autobiographies; they have to reinterpret their own lives, incorporating a personal *Stunde Null*, with a concomitant crisis of continuity in personal identity, a lack of authenticity.

This almost schizophrenic sense of two very different pasts has been captured, in different ways, in several academic analyses. The East German authors Mitter and Wolle, for example, perceive this as a rift in East German memories themselves. They suggest that, listening to former GDR citizens, it often seems as if they had lived in very different countries from one another: while some remember the politically repressive and economically miserable aspects, others think rather of security of employment and career prospects, state guarantees of child care provision, low rents and cheap bread.[14] For the West German scholar Ulrich Mählert, by contrast, the rift is rather one between western historical analyses and East German memories. He states that:

> Characteristic for today's situation is an ignorance – present on both sides – of the history of the German–German division in general and the history of the GDR in particular. In the West the focus on the GDR as an 'unconstitutional state' distorts the picture of the lived reality of the alienated neighbour. In the East it is the fixation with the everyday, whose injustice increasingly pales in the memory, which obscures the dictatorial and inhuman praxis of rule by the SED.[15]

In this context, according to Mählert, 'the work of historians' acquires a significant social relevance: 'It is their responsibility to attempt to reconstruct the past in all its multiplicity, on the basis of the vast array of sources available.'[16]

In my view, the rift in focus and emphasis is not an East–West distinction, as Mählert represents it, nor is it purely one of East German memories, as Mitter and Wolle suggest. It both cross-cuts the inner-German border, and, more importantly for present purposes, it is a feature not only of memory and ill-informed popular perceptions (to which Mählert's 'historians' work' is the proposed solution) but rather one of historical theory. Let me briefly comment on several current historical approaches to dealing with this clearly identified schizophrenia.

Alltagsgeschichte *approaches*

Some historians have suggested *Alltagsgeschichte* as the way to reconstruct life as it was actually lived and experienced in the GDR. What precisely is *Alltagsgeschichte*? To some extent it is self-defining in terms of subject matter, or object of inquiry: literally, the history of everyday life. However, there are (as with many other paradigms in history) a bundle of associations or connotations, which may or may not be intrinsically or essentially connected, but which have tended to hang together, at least as far as most (metaphorically) paid-up practitioners are concerned. To take the formulations of two key German proponents, Alf Lüdtke and Thomas Lindenberger, one may perhaps summarise these as follows:[17]

Topic   There is a tendency to focus on the 'masses', the 'kleine Leute', the 'little people' who are not the major actors on the political stage of history, and who in the accounts of both conventional political and structural societal historians have tended to remain faceless and nameless; in other words, the previously marginalised objects, rather than subjects, of historical accounts. They are now to be reconstituted as actors in history. There may or may not also be a tendency to focus on previously marginalised aspects of their lives not captured in the accounts of organisations and movements (leisure, consumerism, popular culture, and so on).

Aim of history   There is a tendency to query the totalising, synthesising goal of both the 'grand narrative' tradition of history and of the societal structural history which had displaced grand narratives in the 1970s. In place of synthesis and the search for 'one' history, there is an emphasis on the multiplicity of possible histories which can be reconstituted from the 'same' past. In this sense, it is explicitly and self-consciously 'post-modern'.

Politics of history   There is a notion that history may be a communicative and emancipatory endeavour carried out at the grass-roots, assisting in the recovery of multiple pasts and the construction of new identities in the present, irrespective of one's place in the establishment hierarchy of the academy.

There are a series of points with which one could take issue in this list. As far as the first element is concerned, even the constitution of the substantive topic – what is 'everyday life'? – poses some problems. Practitioners may look at any substantive areas, such as, for example, relationships in the workplace, which are also in principle open to those working from quite different theoretical perspectives (such as, in this case, labour history). Nor are they the first to claim that human beings should be treated as agents acting within given circumstances, rather than objects constituted by structures. (The 'structure–agency' problematic cross-cuts a number of theoretical approaches.)

This ambiguity with respect to the first point might not matter much were it not that there is a degree of self-contradiction with respect to the next claim. To construct as one's subject of study any aspect of 'the whole of life' presents no explicit principle of selection: hence, the *actual* selection of specific problems or areas for analysis imports implicit assumptions about priorities within a wider – and hence totalising – body of knowledge and set of aims of inquiry. Interestingly, in practice *Alltagsgeschichte* does actually presuppose some form of totalising historical synthesis. The generally unspoken premise is at least in part that some crucial pieces in the overall picture have previously been left out: subjective experiences and perceptions (*Erfahrungen* and *Wahrnehmungen*), in particular of those on the social margins. It also, to some extent, has to take for granted the structural context, or *Rahmenbedingungen*, of contemporaries' experiences and actions. However, against the suggestions of, among others, Jürgen Kocka, that it is therefore symbiotic with a new, more culturally sensitive, version of societal history, many practitioners would still explicitly resist the claim that its aim is historical synthesis.

Thirdly, the political issue is one of 'taking sides'; again a long-standing and thorny issue for historians. For reasons which are unclear, many German historians – on both left and right – have tended to confuse empathy (or what Weber called 'interpretive understanding', a necessary tool of the historian) with 'sympathy'. Whether the historically contingent political sympathy of many 'barefoot historians' with the (re-?)construction of micro-specific and local identities is a necessary feature of their theoretical approach is open to question. Much of this research has pointed up, for example, the less pleasant aspects of popular apoliticism and antisemitism in the Third Reich, a precondition of the removal of Jews from civil society and eventually life itself. Nevertheless, it is this focus which has in part roused the ire of such notable critics as Hans-Ulrich Wehler, with his diatribes against the romanticisation of the underdog and the trivialisation of what is truly important in history.

Political social history?

A very explicitly formulated alternative – or possibly, depending on one's definition of *Alltagsgeschichte*, complementary – approach is that of a 'political social history'.[18] This has been championed by proponents from what used to be known as the Bielefeld school of societal history (*Gesellschaftsgeschichte*), particularly Jürgen Kocka. In some respects it suggests a softening of approach towards at least some aspects of

Alltagsgeschichte, notably its emphasis on subjective experience (though not the full theoretical bundle sketched above).

'Political social history' is explicitly *not* social history in the classical sense of 'history with the politics left out': rather, it focuses precisely on the ways in which it is not possible to analyse society in the GDR without considering politics. A central concept here is that of the 'durchherrschte Gesellschaft' – interestingly, picked up by Kocka, doyen of *Gesellschaftsgeschichte*, from an essay by Alf Lüdtke, a key proponent of *Alltagsgeschichte*.[19] This notion sought to draw attention to the ways in which the state 'drenched', or 'seeped through' the whole of society. It sought to bring together the previously separate elements of 'politics', 'society' and 'everyday life, subjective experience and perception'. Thus, in many respects it represents a rapprochement of previously separate and often mutually hostile theoretical approaches.

The approach has led to many valuable contributions and highly promising on-going projects on particular topics: women, youth, workers, to name but a few of the early fruits. However, beyond the claim that the GDR was a *durchherrschte Gesellschaft*, it has not as yet led to a synthesis which brings together social and political history. Some have even suggested that it is essentially a left-liberal, 'politically correct', means of reimporting (under camouflage) the notion of totalitarianism: that the state in some way does grasp the whole of society under its all-encompassing control, but that one cannot use the politically laden vocabulary of the Cold War for describing this.

Not surprisingly, this approach has also not gone without criticism in the expected conservative quarters. A major proponent of the totalitarianism thesis, Klaus Schroeder, pokes considerable fun at it: 'The characterisation of the GDR as a "durchherrschte Gesellschaft" enjoys great popularity especially among some social historians. Nevertheless, there is as yet no empirically-founded or even theoretically-deduced definition of this term.'[20] After a slightly confused remark about the alleged lack of clarity in relation to Weber's conception of *Herrschaft*, Schroeder goes on to point out – quite rightly – that democratic systems are also 'durchherrschte Gesellschaften'.[21] From this he concludes, with an extraordinary lack of intellectual logic, that, for political reasons, the concept of a *durchherrschte Gesellschaft* cannot be applied to the GDR:

> This indirect equation or at least analogy suggests, moreover, that both systems of rule are legitimated, albeit in different ways. The decisive difference between rule legitimated by the consent of the majority and rule based on force or ideological claims, can easily be overlooked in the process.[22]

In place of *Herrschaft*, therefore, Schroeder wishes to talk of power: a 'vermachtete Gesellschaft', in which power was used to effect policies against the will of others. *A priori*, in Schroeder's view, power is used in dictatorships; authority in democracies; and the distinction between Bad and Good must be upheld by the use of sharply contrasting, black and white vocabulary. We are back more or less where we started this section on approaches to state and society in the GDR: the political implications of a concept seem to determine its analytical acceptability or otherwise.

Towards a new conceptual framework for state and society

How should one proceed? This depends in part on quite extraneous metatheoretical assumptions about the nature of history: if, for example, one holds that in principle there cannot be a value-free historical science, or that there can be no point in searching for a synthesis which provides a closer approximation to past realities than other (more or less fictional) constructions, then we might as well give up. If, however, one retains any belief in the notion of greater or lesser degrees of empirical validity and approximation to historical adequacy (irrespective of political views), then it seems to me we have to re-examine the concepts of, and relations between, state and society in the GDR. What follows are some tentative, essentially preliminary, ruminations.

First of all, beyond the very simple everyday usage of the terms, I think we have to cease to see 'state' and 'society' as such watertight separate entities. Of course, if we are undertaking an organisational history of state institutions, we know what we are talking about, what is included and what excluded. But if we are talking about something altogether more difficult to define, namely the 'boundaries of the political' in the GDR, then a radical rethinking may be in order. In other words, if we are seeking to present a more comprehensive history of the GDR than that provided by a straight history of the party and political structure, without simply 'tacking on' a few themes in 'economic and social history' (as Schroeder actually does), then we have to think harder not about the 'relations' between, but rather the '*inter*-relations' between, the overlapping and mutually informing elements of state and society. Whether or not the interrelations are similar to or different from the patterns in capitalist and/or democratic societies is quite beside the point, and is not a relevant criterion for deciding on the validity of a conceptual framework with respect to the GDR.

The issue here may be in part a failure to theorise society as both constituted by, and constituting and/or limiting state. Part of the problem with the approaches outlined above may be the assumption of a clear difference, entailing an associated set of assumptions about repression, collaboration or the leading of a double life (the celebrated *Nischengesellschaft* or 'niche society'). This problem is not, it should be noted, solved by those who follow 'modernisation' theory's assumption of the 'de-differentiation' (*Entdifferenzierung*) of spheres in the GDR, in which – as in Sigrid Meuschel's analysis – 'society' is conceived as being in some way more or less subsumed or *aufgehoben* in the Hegelian sense within the state.[23]

I would suggest that we need to retheorise both terms in this problematic. We need to think in new ways of the formation of society by the state, and indeed even the formation of social personality; we need a new historical anthropology or social psychology. But we need at the same time also to see the state as less omnipotent, less monolithic. 'State' – or, to put it in slightly more active terms, political – projects are both informed and limited by 'society'; they are carried by individuals and groups formed under certain circumstances, interacting with contemporaries in ways which are not simply given by a reading of the ideology, propaganda, power structures, and so on.[24]

Let me tentatively suggest a new vocabulary or conceptual apparatus.

State

First of all, I would suggest we adopt a less all-encompassing notion for the political system proper of the GDR. This should be, initially, a purely classificatory concept, not entailing explanatory and condemnatory functions; it should be less essentially contested and value-laden than that of 'totalitarianism'.[25] Let me propose – purely for purposes of discussion, or freeing up our capacity to think without a trail of contemporary emotive connotations – a notion of 'modern party absolutism'. Absolutism is of course a term with a good early-modern, and particularly eighteenth-century, pedigree, connected with Frederick the Great and his contemporaries. It can be used to refer to the projects of rulers, not to the system as a whole; it does not presuppose any success on the part of rulers who attempt to rule without representative institutions as mediators between ruler and 'society'. The concept of absolutism need not be a global category, combining descriptive, explanatory and condemnatory functions, as does totalitarianism. It is to some extent typological, in that it seeks to identify key elements of a particular type of political regime, irrespective of ideology. But it is not in itself explanatory (indeed, the emergence of such systems at certain points in time itself needs explanation). To explain the success or failure of the absolutist project under different circumstances we have to look at a variety of other factors, including not only the balance of domestic forces but also the ever-changing international system and the role of individual actions and historically contingent developments.

Why, to start with, should the term 'absolutism' be applicable both to certain forms of early-modern state in which the ruler sought to abolish the institutions of the late-medieval *Ständestaat*, and to the GDR? There are clearly certain structural similarities. These include: the claim of the ruler to rule without mediating representative institutions; the reliance of the ruler on an extensive state bureaucracy; a surveillance apparatus; and a set of repressive forces for the suppression of internal dissent as well as external power political purposes.

But there are of course also numerous differences: hence the qualified term, 'modern party absolutism'. In the twentieth-century version, the Party, not an individual (in the eighteenth century, hereditary) ruler, lays claim to absolute power. Hence 'party' absolutism. Such claims are often founded in a very explicitly articulated ideology (such as Marxism–Leninism), quite different from such earlier notions as the divine right of kings. And these claims are staked in a quite different historical arena. There are major changes, often technologically founded, in the means of communication, control and repression; changes in assumptions about the internal relations between populations and governments; and in the international system. Thus we have phenomena not found, at least not on this scale, in the early–modern predecessors: the construction or presented appearance of apparent 'democracy' (the *Scheindemokratie* of the various 'people's republics') as a legitimation measure not perceived as necessary in a premodern era; and the attempted mobilisation of the masses, their incorporation into and enforced participation in mass organisations and events. The link between 'people' and ruler' is supposed to be closer (although such notions and attempts were not entirely absent in a premodern era, where religion often played the political role of modern ideologies).[26] Hence 'modern' party absolutism.

We may not wish to be committed to this concept; but it is worth at least playing with as a tool to assist clarity of thought. Democrats might not approve of party absolutism, and by definition believe in the moral superiority of representative institutions (whatever their shortcomings and failures in practice in self-professed democracies). But the notion of absolutism (particularly given its somewhat antiquarian or anachronistic flavour) would not be as immediately condemnatory as are concepts taken from a twentieth-century political vocabulary. Nor would it entail just an enumeration of the 'list of political institutions' (with concomitant holding hands up in horror at the Stasi and repression of human rights). It would have to deal seriously, and in a non-condemnatory fashion, with the extent and character of state intrusion into and shaping of society, if we may still use the terms as though they were separate, while being aware of the difficulties involved.

To take some more concrete illustrations: we could escape from the increasingly sterile, politically informed ping-pong debate about whether an emphasis on *Macht* or on *Herrschaft* is more appropriate for the GDR.[27] Instead of counterposing the two concepts and arguing for the exclusive use of one or the other for essentially extraneous political reasons, we could now look, empirically, at the peculiar *combination* – in different proportions at different times – of the two in the history of the GDR. We would clearly want to apply the term *Macht* to the undoubtedly repressive elements in the GDR: the use of the Stasi, police and army, and the abuse of the system of 'justice' to repress internal dissent; the capacity to enforce the party's will against the will of others (to put this into Weberian terminology). But we need not let it rest at that, as though this were a sufficient characterisation and explanation (as totalitarian theorists tend to do). We could go on to explore the extent and implications of *Herrschaft*, particularly as used in the genuinely Weberian sense to refer, not to the beliefs of the ruled, but rather to the claims made by rulers, and to the tendency of rulers' staffs to uphold these claims, whether or not they genuinely believed in them. Thus we can look at the establishment over time of a system of functionaries in the GDR; the difficulties experienced in securing socialism at the grass roots in the 1950s, the slow and partial process of instituting this in the 1960s, and the much more smooth and effective running of the system in the 1970s, until the functionaries themselves increasingly began to query the capacity of the gerontocracy at the top to deal with mounting economic and political issues in the 1980s.[28] The constitution and mentalities of the functionaries who struggled – often for the highest of motives, in difficult circumstances and for little reward – to improve the lot of people in the localities must be understood in a non-judgemental fashion if we are to obtain any measured understanding of the history of the GDR.

Our approach must also somehow capture the phenomena typical of 'modern' absolutism: the incorporation and mobilisation (whether into willing, unthinking, reluctant, disgruntled or forced participation) of wide sectors of the population. We need therefore to look, for example, in detail at the ways in which the system of mass organisations eventually encompassed and affected virtually all areas of social life. The youth organisations (the various branches of the Young Pioneers, FDJ) were almost inescapable whether a young person was part of the vast majority who belonged or stood out and was not; the trade union (FDGB) membership figures captured, at least in the official statistics, 100 per cent of the adult working population; there was no sphere of life or leisure activity, from domestic pursuits such as cooking, childcare and needlework beloved of the DFD to the more obviously ideological messages of the Society for German–Soviet Friendship (DSF) and the clearly paramilitary activities of the GST, that was not in some way caught by and contained within this system of organisations. To seek to depict these in terms of 'power' and 'oppression', or 'collaboration', is to fail to understand – indeed to do a blatant historical injustice to – what the vast majority of GDR citizens were doing, and often doing willingly and for their own ends, for quite substantial portions of their lives. While the history of the minority of dissidents is important, so too is the history of the majority of those who felt they were living 'perfectly ordinary lives' within this system of organisations.

We also need to look at state policies: at the ways in which the SED actively sought to change society through legislation and economic and social policies. In doing this, again we need in some way to get away from the western-centric moralising implicit in many approaches to the political sphere. One way might be to look at aspects which are at least more morally neutral, or perhaps one might say morally ambiguous, ambivalent – more open to a range of legitimate difference of viewpoint among western democrats – than are the questions of such basic human rights as freedom of speech and association. If we take, for example, the question of the emancipation of women, it is easier to read oneself into the mindset of those energetic, active, idealist SED members who were urgently and earnestly seeking to persuade teenage girls to raise their sights above a view of life as orientated towards, perhaps, a job for two or three years, but ultimately marriage and a family. Attempts to persuade girls to contemplate further and higher education, to embark on serious careers, to take on leadership roles, to combine parenting with personal career fulfilment and even service to the community, cannot be so easily written off in a framework of 'power and oppression' or 'state repressing society'.[29] Similarly, if one takes a rather different example, that of policies towards the Sorbs, it is at least more morally ambiguous than totalitarian approaches can capture: does one – should one – prioritise the preservation of what is increasingly a stagnant, crystallised version of an 'old' language and culture through the support of co-opted political and cultural institutions, festivals, print media and education; or should one prioritise economically essential energy policies requiring the exploitation of brown coal reserves and hence the removal of the very villages that formed one of the material preconditions of a homogeneous Sorb community and culture? Comparable questions could be asked about the attitudes of the SED towards other minorities, such as Jewish communities, in the GDR.

Other aspects of SED policies would be intrinsically more contentious. There is a clear problem with principled differences over means–ends rationality when one considers the issue of producing a more equal society through the forcible expropriation of the previously propertied and privileged classes, or what was effectively positive discrimination in education for children of workers and peasants in the 1950s and early 1960s. In any event, as the examples of mass organisations, of policies towards women, or the 'acceptable' cultural minority of Sorbs may perhaps suggest, there is a lot more to a societal history of the GDR than can be captured if one wants to talk (for extraneous political reasons) purely in terms of *Macht* rather than *Herrschaft*, viewing these as mutually exclusive alternatives rather than coexisting and complementary elements in a complex and ever-changing system. Moreover, as we have seen even in these last few brief illustrations, it does seem, conversely, more or less impossible to speak of 'society' without reference to politics. How then should we conceive of 'society' in the GDR?

Society

Here I would argue that we need some notion of the constitution of social beings through power relationships, institutional structures, selected patterns of social behaviour, cultural tides and so on. 'Society' does not simply 'pre-exist' as separate from – even when 'setting limits to' – the 'dictatorship';[30] nor, however, is it completely subsumed under politics, as totalitarian theory suggests. We need somehow to think in new ways of the changing patterns of mentalities. There is, for example, a failure of conceptualisation on the part of those who talk in terms of allegedly 'frozen' nationalisms in eastern Europe, the return of what had been 'repressed for forty years', and so on, as though the state had acted as a lid on a saucepan which was still boiling the same brew as half a century earlier. The problem is basically one of a failure of historical imagination or empathy. One has to take a view on whether historians should seek to understand and reconstruct particular mindsets 'as they actually were' (again, drawing on the notion of empathy in the sense of 'interpretive understanding', not 'sympathy'); or whether historians are so deeply rooted in their own prejudices about what it is possible or reasonable to believe that they have to write off other views as evidently the products of repression or indoctrination, fear and brainwashing (as is often effectively the case in totalitarian theory, which ironically operates with an implicit notion of what a Marxist would call 'false consciousness').

Successive generations, growing up within different institutional and ideological frameworks, with different formative experiences, in social groups and strata which are constituted in different ways over time, become very different social beings from the (internally variegated) generations of their parents and grandparents. It seems to me quite urgent for historians to take more seriously the need for a historical social psychology.

The problem is that this is an area not well addressed theoretically by historians. There is, it seems to me, no readily available theoretical framework for this kind of historical social psychology. Historians have rightly critiqued those few attempts at historical psychoanalysis of individuals to have come to critical attention (Erikson on Luther) but have not so far thought seriously about the historical and social constitution of typical personality patterns, behaviour orientations, aspirations and so on. A bowdlerised version of mass Freudian psycho-analysis, as for example presented rather cathartically in the now renowned work of Hans-Joachim Maaz, is far from adequate: authoritarian and collectivised potty training cannot explain the orientations and actions of both those sustaining the regime and those rebelling against it, as Maaz would have us believe.[31] Whatever we make of this highly readable, but utterly unconvincing account, it is clear that we need something a little more historically sensitive and situationally variable than a 'general social psychology' of whatever theoretical flavour – whether Freudian, Jungian, Piagettian, or even Lacanian – and yet at the same time more prepared to entertain the notion of the creative, acting individual than is evident in the works of those theorists favouring some notion of 'decentring'.[32]

There is a further problem here (much beloved of historians): that of sources. How does one get at the essentially intangible elements relating to emotions, interpersonal behaviour patterns, body language, assumptions of communality rather than individualism, and so on? Novels, by virtue of their power to entice the reader into an imaginative world, compel the reader to believe in their construction of reality; but it has to be remembered that even the often explicitly social–critical creative writings of *Leserland DDR* were precisely constructions of, interventions in and critiques of, rather than uncontaminated reflections of, 'social reality as it really was'. Other sources – Stasi, SED, and trade union reports, for example, as well as opinion poll surveys – have to be read with considerable caution when we are looking at facets of personality and aspiration, as do the more obviously personal oral history accounts and 'protocol literature'. However, it seems to me that these essentially methodological problems are less insurmountable, less difficult in principle, than the more general theoretical issues about our conceptions of the individual and the historical construction of characteristic personality types.

What, then, might a new social history of the GDR look like? Herewith some modest suggestions for a framework of interpretation. We need to look not only at specific social groups in isolation (as is often the case in practice with works claiming to be a 'social history'), but also at changes over time in the overall shape of society. Here, we need also to free ourselves somewhat of the polarised debates sketched above, and take a more open look at long-term trends as well as short-term politics and specific, often politically relevant and controversial, debates. The general framework of state–society relations entailed by a notion of 'modern party absolutism' was clearly not a static one, as purely classificatory concepts often tend to suggest. Let me suggest three major forces which intertwined and mutually interacted in different ways over time:

- First, we need to be aware of long-term *secular trends* of major importance: processes of industrialisation, urbanisation, competition within global socioeconomic and political–military and cultural systems.
- Secondly, we need of course to analyse *politically determined policies*: we need to look at the aims, policies and practices of the SED in its fundamental, ideologically driven attempts to transform society and personality into a new mould (and, incidentally, at the areas of contradiction among these aims and policies).
- Thirdly, we need to be sensitive to patterns of persistence and transformation in pre-existing mentalities, beliefs, interpersonal behaviour, and so on. We need to explore, for example, whether the 'private sphere' – such as the gendered division of labour in the home – was more affected by secular trends such as shift-working in factories than by state policies towards women.

We could then, through detailed empirical analyses of a range of facets, attempt to put together a complex and multi-faceted historical social anthropology of the GDR. This would not only cut across traditional disciplinary boundaries, but also might help to lower the political temperature of current theoretical controversies and provide a historical picture of the GDR which can perhaps be recognised as empirically adequate, both by those who want explicitly to remind us of the GDR's repressive features and those who want to rescue some memory of 'perfectly ordinary lives'.

Notes

1 For the longer discussion see Mary Fulbrook, *Interpreting the Two Germanies, 1945–1990* (2nd edn, Basingstoke, 1999).
2 Jens Hacker, *Deutsche Irrtümer: Schönfärber und Helfershelfer der SED-Diktatur im Westen* (Frankfurt/Main and Berlin, 1992).
3 Clearly, there are several related issues which need to be addressed. We need to have an explicit understanding of what is meant by 'objectivity' or 'value neutrality' in historical analysis; we need to decide whether we think this is possible in principle; if so, whether we think it is A Good Thing; and, if so, how if at all it should be pursued. For differences among historians on these issues, see my book, *Historical Theory* (London, 2002).
4 Armin Mitter and Stefan Wolle (eds), *'Ich liebe Euch doch alle!' Befehle und Lageberichte des MfS* (Berlin, 1990); Armin Mitter and Stefan Wolle (eds), *Untergang auf Raten* (Munich, 1990); see also my review of this in Mary Fulbrook, 'Methodologische Überlegungen zu einer Gesellschaftsgeschichte der DDR', in Richard Bessel and Ralph Jessen (eds), *Die Grenzen der Diktatur* (Göttingen, 1996).
5 For a selection of early post-*Wende* examples, see for example, Karl Wilhelm Fricke, *MfS Intern* (Cologne, 1991); Joachim Gauck, *Die Stasi-Akten* (Hamburg, 1991); David Gill and Ulrich Schroeter, *Das Ministerium für Staatssicherheit* (Berlin, 1991); Erich Loest, *Die Stasi war mein Eckermann* (Göttingen, 1991).
6 There is not space for a comprehensive list here: examples would include works by Michael Beleites, Wolfgang Rüddenklau and Vera Wollenberger. For fuller references, see the bibliography in *Interpreting the Two Germanies*; see also my discussion in 'Heroes, victims and villains in the history of the GDR', in R. Alter and P. Monteath (eds), *Rewriting the German Past* (Atlantic Highlands, NJ, 1997).
7 Gerhard Besier, *Der SED-Staat und die Kirche* (Munich, 1993); Gerhard Besier and Stephan Wolf (eds), *'Pfarrer, Christen und Katholiken': Das Ministerium der ehemaligen DDR und die Kirchen* (2nd edn, Neukirchen, 1992).
8 Ehrhart Neubert, *Vergebung oder Weißwäscherei: Zur Aufarbeitung des Stasiproblems in den Kirchen* (Freiburg im Breisgau, 1993); Ehrhart Neubert, *Geschichte der Opposition in der DDR, 1949–1989* (Berlin, 1997).
9 See Klaus Schroeder and Jochen Staadt, 'Die diskrete Charme des Status Quo' in Klaus Schroeder (ed.), *Geschichte und Transformation des SED-Staates* (Berlin, 1994); Klaus Schroeder, *Der SED-Staat* (Munich, 1998), 621–48.
10 My own views on this are developed in Mary Fulbrook, 'The limits of totalitarianism: God, state and society in the GDR', *Transactions of the Royal Historical*

Society (Cambridge, 1997); see also my comments in *Interpreting the Two Germanies*; and in 'Aufarbeitung der DDR-Vergangenheit und "innere Einheit" – ein Widerspruch?', in Christoph Kleßmann *et al.* (eds) *Deutsche Vergangenheiten – eine gemeinsame Herausforderung* (Berlin, 1999).

11 Deutscher Bundestag (ed.), *Materialien der Enquete-Kommission 'Aufarbeitung von Geschichte und Folgen der SED-Diktatur in Deutschland'*, 9 vols (Frankfurt/Main, 1995); PDS/Linke Liste im Bundestag (ed.), *Ansichten zur Geschichte der DDR* (Bonn and Berlin, 1993).

12 Egon Krenz, *Wenn Mauern fallen* (Vienna, 1990); Günter Schabowski, *Das Politbüro* (Hamburg, 1990) and *Der Absturz* (Berlin, 1991).

13 *OhnMacht. DDR-Funktionäre sagen aus* (Berlin, 1992). See also for example, Manfred Uschner, *Die zweite Etage* (Berlin, 1993).

14 Mitter and Wolle, *Untergang*, 7.

15 Ulrich Mählert, *Kleine Geschichte der DDR* (Munich, 1998), 8.

16 *Ibid.*, 9.

17 See particularly: Alf Lüdtke, 'Introduction: what is the history of everyday life and who are its practitioners?' in Alf Lüdtke (ed.), *The History of Everyday Life* (Princeton, NJ, 1995); Thomas Lindenberger, 'Alltagsgeschichte und ihr möglicher Beitrag zu einer Gesellschaftsgeschichte der DDR', in Bessel and Jessen (eds), *Die Grenzen der Diktatur*, 298–325.

18 See particularly Hartmut Kaelble *et al.* (eds), *Sozialgeschichte der DDR* (Stuttgart, 1994).

19 See Lüdtke's and Kocka's essays in Kaelble *et al.* (eds), *Sozialgeschichte*.

20 Schroeder, *Der SED-Staat*, 632.

21 Schroeder fails to notice that Weber uses 'Herrschaft' in both the senses that Schroeder seeks to distinguish, not only the one he attributes to him (on Weber, see further below). Schroeder's suggestion that contemporary social historians are unclear about their own usage may or may not be apposite but has little to do with his ill-informed comment on Weber. *Ibid.*, 633.

22 *Ibid.*, 633.

23 Sigrid Meuschel, *Legitimation und Parteiherrschaft in der DDR* (Frankfurt/Main, 1992); Sigrid Meuschel, 'Überlegungen zu einer Herrschafts- und Gesellschaftsgeschichte der DDR', *Geschichte und Gesellschaft* 19(1), 1993.

24 For an interesting attempt to represent the SED as a relatively powerless puppet between Moscow on the one hand, and the practical veto power of the working class on the other, see Jeffrey Kopstein, *The Politics of Economic Decline* (Chapel Hill, 1997). On the interplay between 'state' and 'society' at the grass roots, see Corey Ross, *Constructing Socialism at the Grass Roots: The Transformation of East Germany, 1945–65* (Basingstoke, 2000).

25 One might have thought that 'communist dictatorship' would do; but even this seems to be an essentially loaded term, given the different theoretical understandings of 'dictatorship' as well as its generally negative connotations with respect to the issue of popular opinion. Hence my speculative venture into less emotive, historically distanced terminology.

26 See Mary Fulbrook, *Piety and Politics: Religion and the Rise of Absolutism in England, Württemberg and Prussia* (Cambridge, 1983).

27 Cf. the discussion of Schroeder, in n. 21 above.

28 Mary Fulbrook, *Anatomy of a Dictatorship* (Oxford, 1995). See also Mark

Allinson, *Politics and Popular Opinion in East Germany, 1945–68* (Manchester, 2000); Ross, *Constructing Socialism*.
29 Unless of course one is a principled antifeminist.
30 Here I find the approach in Bessel and Jessen – for all the valuable contributions made by this book in a variety of ways – slightly ill-conceived.
31 Hans-Joachim Maaz, *Behind the Wall* (London, 1995).
32 I do not think, incidentally, that Foucault provides the answer here.

Index

The index refers readers from subject to text and also provides supplementary information where available. In the case of individuals, it highlights the most relevant and/or the most important role played. Unless noted otherwise, positions cited refer to the GDR, and 'Politbüro' and 'Central Committee' refer to those of the Socialist Unity Party of Germany (SED). Dates of birth and death are based on the latest material readily available. Note: 'n.' after a page number indicates the number of a note on that page. Page numbers in **bold** refer to main entries. Readers seeking fuller information are referred to the following volumes, which are acknowledged here with gratitude: Martin Broszat and Hermann Weber (eds), *SBZ–Handbuch: Staatliche Verwaltungen, Parteien, gesellschaftliche Organisationen und ihre Führungskräfte in der Sowjetischen Besatzungszone Deutschlands 1945–1949* (Munich, 2nd edition 1993); Günther Buch (ed.), *Namen und Daten wichtiger Personen der DDR* (Berlin and Bonn, 1979); Andreas Herbst, Winfried Ranke and Jürgen Winkler (eds), *So funktionierte die DDR*, 3 vols (Reinbek bei Hamburg, 1994); Helmut Müller–Enbergs, Jan Wielgohs and Dieter Hoffmann (eds), *Wer war wer in der DDR? Ein biographisches Lexikon* (Bonn and Berlin, 2001); Hartmut Zimmermann, Horst Ulrich and Michael Fehlauer (eds), *DDR Handbuch*, 2 vols (Cologne, 3rd edition 1985).

Abakumov, Viktor (1908–54) Soviet Minister of State Security (1946–51) 44
Abusch, Alexander (1902–82) Minister of Culture (1958–61) 245
Ackermann, Anton (1905–73) Politbüro candidate (1949–54) 22–3, 27, 35, 245
Adenauer, Konrad (1876–1967) Chancellor of Federal Republic (1949–63) 28, 101, 173, 233, 250
Agricultural Production Co–operatives (LPG) 9, 139–47
Alltagsgeschichte (history of everyday life) 286–8
Association for Mutual Peasant Aid (VdgB, 1947–90) 137–45
Association of German Composers (VDK, founded 1951) 228–9, 233, 238
Axen, Hermann (1916–92) Politbüro candidate/member (1963/1970–89) 39

Bab, Gerhard, Secretary of VDK 238
Bartel, Horst (1928–84) Director of Institute of History at Academy of Sciences (1969–84) 246
Barth, Karl (1886–1968) theologian 211
Bauer, Leo (1912–72) chair of Hesse KPD faction (1946–49) 35
Beatles, the (1959–70) musicians 13, 181–2, 184
Bebel, August (1840–1913) social democrat 23
Becher, Johannes R. (1891–1958) Minister of Culture (1954–58) 235

Behrens, Friedrich 'Fritz' (1909–80) head of State Central Statistical Administration (1955–57) 268
Benjamin, Hilde (1902–89) Minister of Justice (1953–67) 156
Benser, Günter, historian 246, 252, 255
Berger, Wolfgang (1921–94) adviser to Ulbricht (1953–71) 30, 33–4
Beria, Lavrenti (1899–1953) head of Soviet secret police (1938–53) 1, 35
Berlin
  Berlin–Adlershof 47
  Berlin–Karlshorst 51
  Berlin–Lichtenberg 43
  crisis (1958) 6, 196
  Quadripartite Accord (1971) 31–2
  Unter den Linden 89
Berlin Wall (1961–89) 6, 15, 52–3, 99, 172–4, 196–7, 204–5, 218
Berthold, Lothar (b. 1926) Director of Institute for Marxism–Leninism (1964–68) 246, 251, 253
Biermann, Wolf (b. 1936) writer and musician 185
Bismarck, Otto von (1815–98) Chancellor of Germany (1871–90) 250
Bloch, Ernst (1885–1977) philosopher 268
Brandenburg 131
Brandt, Willy (1913–92) Chancellor of Federal Republic (1969–74) 30, 105
Brendler, Gerhard, historian 270
Brezhnev, Leonid (1906–82) Soviet leader (1964–82) 14, 30–1, 34

299

Brück, Ulrich von (b. 1914) churchman 222
Butlers, the, musicians 182–3
Butting, Max (1888–1976) composer 229, 237

Christian Democratic Union (CDU, founded 1945) 3, 50, 97, 135
churches 10–11, 29, 87–8, 195–6, **210–24**, 282
Chwalek, Roman (1898–1974) Minister of Labour (1950–53) 230
cinema 12–14, 176
collectivisation (1952–60) 9, 104, 130, 144–7, 201
Communist Party of Germany (KPD, founded 1918, refounded 1945) 2–4, 22, 124–5, 131, 135
constitution (1968) 105
Coventry Cathedral 221–3
Credo, Renate (b. 1920) Central Committee member (1963–71) 151
Czechoslovakia (1968) 30–1, 52, 99, 103–7

Dahlem, Franz (1892–1981) Politbüro member (1950–53) 27, 33, 35
Democratic Peasants' Party of Germany (DBD, 1948–90) 3, 97, 138, 143–4
Democratic Women's League of Germany (DFD, 1947–90) 154, 292
Dertinger, Georg (1902–68) Foreign Minister (1949–53) 46
Dibelius, Otto (1880–1967) Bishop of Berlin–Brandenburg (1945–66) 214, 218–19
Doernberg, Stefan (b. 1924) historian/diplomat 246, 251
Dohle, Horst, functionary for Church Affairs 222
Drechsler, Heike (b. 1964) athlete 13
Dresden 4, 193, 221–3
DSF *see* Society for German–Soviet Friendship
Dubček, Alexander (1921–92) Czechoslovak leader (1968–69) 25, 30–1, 105–7, 126
During, Hans–Georg, musician 231–2
Dzerzhinsky, Feliks (1877–1926) head of Russian secret police (1917–26) 42

Ebert, Friedrich (1894–1979) Mayor of [East] Berlin (1948–67) 218
Eggerath, Werner (1900–77) State Secretary for Church Affairs (1957–60) 224n.3
Eisenhower, Dwight (1890–1969) US President (1953–61) 196
EKD *see* Evangelical Church in Germany
elections 3, 29, 153
Engelberg, Ernst (b. 1909) President of Historians' Association (1958–65) 246, 248, 253–4, 269–70

Engels, Friedrich (1820–95) political philosopher 29
Evangelical Church in Germany (EKD, founded 1948) 213–14

FDGB *see* Free German Trade Union Association
FDJ *see* Free German Youth
Fechner, Max (1892–1973) Minister of Justice (1949–53) 50
Federal Republic of Germany (FRG, founded 1949) 27, 30, 42, 198–9
Field, Noel H., director of Unitarian Service Committee 45
Fischer, Kurt (1900–50) head of People's Police (1949–50) 64
Fleischer, Hans–Joachim 'Fips' (b. 1923) musician 234
Fomferra, Heinrich (1895–1979) official in Ministry of State Security (1950–59) 46
Frederick II 'the Great' (1712–86) King of Prussia (1740–86) 250, 290
Free German Trade Union Association (FDGB, 1946–90) 3, 292
Free German Youth (FDJ, 1946–90) 13, 83, 86, 97, 176, 181, 228, 292
Fricke, Dieter (b. 1927) historian and chief editor of *ZfG* (1957–60) 246
Fröhlich, Paul (1913–70) Politbüro member (1963–70) 119

Gagarin, Yuri (1934–68) Soviet cosmonaut 13
Gniffke, Erich (1895–1964) SPD/SED politician (1945–48) 24
Goebbels, Joseph (1897–1945) National Socialist Minister of Propaganda (1933–45) 240
Gomulka, Władysław (1905–82) Polish leader (1956–70) 126
Gorbachev, Mikhail (b. 1931) Soviet leader (1985–91) 25
Groschopp, Horst, historian 246
Grotewohl, Otto (1894–1964) Prime Minister (1949–64) 23, 27, 35, 44, 140–1
Grüber, Heinrich (1891–1975) EKD plenipotentiary to GDR government (1949–58) 224n.3
GST *see* Society for Sport and Technology

Haas, Frieda, VdgB functionary (1946–48) 137
Hager, Kurt (1912–98) Politbüro candidate/member (1958/1963–89) 39, 182
Haley, Bill (1927–81) musician 236
Hallstein Doctrine (1955) 31

Index

Hamann, Karl (1903–73) Minister for Trade and Supply (1949–52) 45
Harich, Wolfgang (1923–95) philosopher 50
Hartig, Rudolf, Stakuko official 229–35
Hartmann, Horst, musician 231–2
Hartwig, Max, deputy to State Secretary for Church Affairs 216–17
Hegel, Georg Wilhelm Friedrich (1770–1831) philosopher 253
Heitzer, Heinz (1928–93) historian 246, 255
Herrnstadt, Rudolf (1903–66) editor of *Neues Deutschland* (1949–53) 25, 27, 33–5, 48
Hilferding, Rudolph (1877–1941) social democrat 23
Hindenburg, Paul von (1847–1934) soldier and *Reich* President (1925–34) 90
historians in the GDR **244–56, 262–74**
Hitler, Adolf (1889–1945) Chancellor and *Führer* of Germany (1933–45) 31, 64, 103, 211, 214
Hoernle, Edwin (1883–1952) President of German Agricultural Administration (1945–49) 148n.6
Hoffmann, Ernst (b. 1912) historian and political philosopher 268
Hoffmann, Heinz (1910–85) Minister of National Defence (1960–85) 86–7
Holtzhauer, Helmut (1912–73) chair of Stakuko (1951–53) 229–30
Honecker, Erich (1912–94) SED First/General Secretary (1971–89)
  and Beat music 182–3
  and Berlin Wall 205
  and churches 222, 224
  and deposition of Ulbricht 11, 28–30, 34, 54, 222, 224
  and Ministry of State Security 47, 54
  and nudism 13
  and policing 72
  and SED leadership 43, 284
  social policy 53, 91, 166–7
  youth policy 182–5
Honecker, Margot (b. 1927) Minister of Education (1963–89) 185
Höppner, Joachim (b. 1921) philosopher/historian 268
Horkheimer, Max (1895–1971) philosopher/sociologist 271
Horn, Werner (b. 1926) historian 246
Hungarian uprising (1956) 50, 71, 99, 102–3

Jaeck, Hans-Peter, historian 270
Janka, Walter (1914–94) head of *Aufbau* publishers (1952–56) 50
Jugendweihe (secular confirmation ceremony) 11, 195, 215–17

June uprising (1953) 25, 49–50, 69–70, **112–26,** 156–7, 234

Kautsky, Karl (1854–1938) social democrat 23
Kehr, Eckart (1902–33) historian 246
Kern, Käthe (1900–85) SED/DFD politician 154, 161
KGB (Soviet Commissariat of State Security) 43, 51
Khrushchev, Nikita (1894–1971) Soviet leader (1953–64) 6, 25–6, 33–4, 50, 53, 102, 108, 196, 205
Klemperer, Victor (1881–1960) philologist/author 86
Klenner, Hermann (b. 1926) legal philosopher 268
Kohl, Cornelius, churchman 216
Költzsch, Harri (b. 1927) Director of VEB Deutsche Schallplatten (1954–88) 237
König, Georg (1886–1965) police chief in Saxony–Anhalt (1945–47) 59
Kossok, Manfred (1930–93) historian 247
Kostov, Traicho (1897–1949) Bulgarian communist 35
Kosygin, Alexei (1904–80) Soviet Prime Minister (1964–80) 34
Koval'chuk, Nikolai, Soviet Deputy Minister of State Security 43
Kowalski, Werner, historian 246
KPD *see* Communist Party of Germany
Kreikemeyer, Willi (1894–c.1950) head of railways (1947–50) 45
Krenz, Egon (b. 1937) SED General Secretary (1989) 43, 283
Kreyssig, Lothar, lawyer and church official 222
Krummacher, Friedrich-Wilhelm (1901–74) Bishop of Greifswald (1955–72) 214–23
Kuczynski, Jürgen (1904–97) historian 246–7, **265–74**
Küttler, Wolfgang (b. 1936) historian 270
KVP *see* People's Police in Barracks

land reform (1945–46) 4, 9, 134–7
Lange, Inge (b. 1927) SED women's leader (1961–89) 159, 161–2
Laschitza, Annelies, historian 246
Lauter, Hans (b. 1914) Central Committee Secretary for Culture (1950–53) 233
LDPD *see* Liberal–Democratic Party of Germany
Leipzig 4, 70, 117–22 *passim*
Lenin, Vladimir (1870–1924) Russian/Soviet leader (1917–24) 23, 29, 86, 89–90, 131, 139, 267, 284
Leonhard, Wolfgang (b. 1921) KPD/SED activist (1945–49) 93

Index

Liberal–Democratic Party of Germany (LDPD, 1945–90) 3, 97, 135
Liebknecht, Karl (1871–1919) social democrat/communist 23, 231
Linse, Walter, jurist 45
Loest, Erich (b. 1926) author 135–6
Lotz, Gerhard (1911–81) church official and Volkskammer member 214
LPG *see* Agricultural Production Co–operatives
Ludendorff, Erich (1865–1937) soldier/politician 90
Ludwig, Werner, police *Oberkommissar* 71–2
Luxemburg, Rosa (1870–1919) social democrat/communist 231

Maaz, Hans–Joachim (b. 1943) psychotherapist 294
Markov, Walter (b. 1909) historian 247
Maron, Karl (1903–75) head of People's Police (1950–55) Minister of Interior (1955–63) 7, 64–8, 204
Marx, Karl (1818–83) political philosopher 23, 29
Matern, Hermann (1893–1971) Politbüro member (1950–71) 52
Mayer, Hans (b. 1907) literary scholar 268
Mecklenburg 131, 133
men 42, 54, 135, 153, 157–8, 179, 195
Merker, Paul (1894–1969) Politbüro member (1946–50) 33, 35, 45, 50
Meusel, Alfred (1896–1960) historian 248
Meyer, Ernst Hermann (1905–88) composer 228
Meyer, Julius (b. 1909) president of [East] Berlin Jewish community (1946–53) 46
MfS *see* Ministry of State Security
Mielke, Erich (1907–2000) Minister of State Security (1957–89) 35, 41, 44, 48, 50–5, 65, 185, 284
Mikołajczyk, Stanisław (1900–66) Polish politician 4, 27
militarisation 79
Ministry of State Security (MfS or Stasi, 1950–53, 1955–89) 7, **41–55**, 281–2
Mittag, Günter (1926–94) Politbüro candidate/member (1963/1966–89) 284
Mitter, Armin (b. 1953) historian 7, 109, 113, 116–17, 281–2, 285
Mitzenheim, Moritz (1891–1977) Bishop of Thuringia (1947–70) 214, 217
Möbis, Harry, State Secretary and economic adviser to Council of Ministers (1967–73) 53
Molotov, Vyacheslav (1890–1986) Soviet Foreign Minister (1939–49, 1953–56) 26
Mühlberg, Dietrich (b. 1936) historian 246

Mühlpfordt, Günter (b. 1921) historian 268, 276n.33
Müller, Kurt 'Kutschi' (1903–90) deputy chair of West German KPD (1948–50) 35, 45
Müller–Mertens, Eckhard (b. 1923) historian, editor of EDG 249
music 6, 12–13, 105–6, 178, 181–5
dance music **227–40**

National Democratic Party of Germany (NDPD, 1948–90) 3, 97
National People's Army (NVA, 1956–90) 31, **78–91**
National Socialists 3, 9, 44, 48, 86, 97, 102, 134, 193, 240
NDPD *see* National Democratic Party of Germany
Neumann, Alfred (1909–2001) Politbüro candidate/member (1954/1958–89) 39
New Course (1953) 5, 25, 28, 112, 194–5, 235
New Economic System (NÖS, 1963–67) 11, 33–4, 53, 179, 220
Niekisch, Ernst (1889–1967) historian 245
Niemöller, Martin (1892–1984) pastor 211
NKVD (Soviet People's Commissariat of Internal Affairs) 43
Norden, Albert (1904–82) Politbüro member (1958–81) 251–3
NÖS *see* New Economic System
Noth, Gottfried (1905–71) Bishop of Saxony (1953–71) 214–16, 219
Nuschke, Otto (1883–1957) CDU leader (1948–57) 45
NVA *see* National People's Army

Oelßner, Fred (1903–77) Politbüro member (1950–58) 26, 33, 35, 114, 144
Oestreicher, Paul (b. 1931) Director of International Ministry of Coventry Cathedral (1986–97) 223, 226n.35
Ostalgie (nostalgia for the East) 11, 104, 285–6

Paterna, Erich (1897–1982) historian, editor of EDG 249
Paulsen, Herbert (1900–79) police chief in Saxony–Anhalt (1950–52) 70
peasants **130–47**, 194, 200–1
People's Police (DVP, 1945–90) 7, 44, **59–72**, 145, 195
People's Police in Barracks (KVP, 1952–56) 65–6, 80
Pieck, Wilhelm (1876–1960) President (1949–60) 26–7, 35, 44, 80, 132, 142, 228
Plekhanov, Georgi (1856–1918) political philosopher 23

Index

popular opinion 7–8, 82, **96–110**, 131–2
Potsdam Agreement (1945) 26, 96
Presley, Elvis (1935–77) musician 236
Prussia 2, 88–90
Puhdys, the (1969–) musicians 13

Radio in the American Sector (RIAS) 232, 236
Rajk, László (1909–49) Hungarian communist 35
Ranke, Leopold von (1795–1886) historian 265, 270–1
refugees 3, 133, 137, 153, 193–4
Republikflucht (flight from the Republic) 101, 144–5, **190–205**
Reschke, Erich (1902–80) DvdI President (1946–48) 63–4
RIAS *see* Radio in the American Sector
Rörig, Fritz, historian 254
Rostock 8
Rudolph, Rolf, chief editor of *ZfG* 251
Rudorf, Reginald, jazz writer 235–6

Saxony 2, 4, 64, 131, 135–6
Saxony-Anhalt 4, 131
SBZ *see* Soviet Occupation Zone
Schabowski, Günter (b. 1929) Politbüro candidate/member (1981/1984–89) 283
Scharf, Kurt (1892–1990) Bishop of Berlin–Brandenburg (1966–1972/1976) 218
Schenk, Fritz, SED functionary 117
Schirdewan, Karl (1907–98) Politbüro member (1953–58) 26–7, 33, 35, 50
Schmidt, Elli (1908–80) leader of DFD (1949–53) 154
Schmidt, Walter (b. 1930) historian 246, 255
Schönherr, Albrecht (b. 1911) Bishop of Berlin–Brandenburg (1972–81) 219
Schreiner, Albert (1892–1979) historian 246
Schumacher, Kurt (1895–1952) leader of West German SPD (1946–52) 24
Schumann, Wolfgang, historian 246
Schur, Täve (b. 1931) cyclist 13
Schürer, Gerhard (b. 1921) chair of State Planning Commission (1965–89) 34
SED *see* Socialist Unity Party of Germany
Seidel, Jutta, historian 246
Seidowsky, Hans, functionary 222
Seifert, Willi (1915–86) DVdI Vice-President (1946–48) 63
Seigewasser, Hans (1905–79) State Secretary for Church Affairs (1960–79) 211, 215, 222–3
Selbmann, Fritz (1899–1975) Central Committee member (1954–58) 26, 34–5
Semionov, Vladimir (1911–92) political adviser to SMAD (1946–49) 2
Serov, Ivan (1909–90) Soviet secret service head in SBZ (1945–47) 43
Sindermann, Horst (1915–90) Politbüro member (1967–89) 31
Slánský, Rudolf (1901–52) Czechoslovak communist (1945–51) 35
SMAD *see* Soviet Military Administration in Germany
Social Democratic Party of Germany (SPD, founded 1875, refounded 1945) 2–3, 22, 123–5, 131, 135
Socialist Unity Party of Germany (SED, 1946–90)
  foundation 22
  June uprising 112–26
  leadership 22–40
  party of a new type 64, 137
  Stalinisation 22–4
  and *passim*
Society for German–Soviet Friendship (DSF, founded 1949) 97, 292
Society for Sport and Technology (GST, founded 1952) 13, 78, 83, 86
Soviet Military Administration in Germany (SMAD, 1945–49) 1–3, 60–2
Soviet Occupation Zone (SBZ, 1945–49) 1–4 and *passim*
SPD *see* Social Democratic Party of Germany
sport 13, 41
Springer, Axel (1912–85) West German publisher 183
Stakuko (State Commission for Artistic Affairs) 229–34
Stalin, Joseph (1879–1953) Soviet leader (1924–53) 4–5, 23–7, 32–5, 44, 50–1, 70, 80–2, 89–90, 102, 118, 131, 139, 175
Stasi *see* Ministry of State Security
Steinhoff, Karl (1892–1981) Minister of Interior (1949–52) 44–5
Steinmetz, Max (b. 1912) historian, editor of EDG 249, 255
Stern, Heinz, *Neues Deutschland* correspondent 182–3
Stern, Leo (1901–82) historian and Rector of Halle University (1953–59) 246, 248
Stoph, Willi (1914–99) Politbüro member (1953–89) Minister of National Defence (1956–60) 83
Streisand, Joachim (1920–80) historian 253, 269
Strittmatter, Erwin (1912–94) author 147

television 12, 42, 72, 98, 174

Tereshkova, Valentina (b. 1937) Soviet cosmonaut 13
Thuringia 104, 131, 133, 137
Tito, Josip (1892–1980) Yugoslav leader (1945–80) 5, 45, 102
Tiul'panov, Sergei (1901–84) leader of Propaganda/Information Administration in SMAD (1945–49) 3, 24
totalitarianism 282–3
Turba, Kurt (b. 1929) editor of *Forum* (1953–63) 178, 180

Ulbricht, Walter (1893–1973) SED General/First Secretary (1950–71)
  abortion policy 153
  agricultural policy 138–9, 144
  and Berlin Wall 197, 205
  and churches 212, 214, 220–4
  deposition from power 11, 28–30, 34, 54, 222, 224
  economic and social policy 5–6, 11, 15, 45, 53, 66, 91, 164, 200
  and historians 249, 268
  and June uprising 112–13, 116, 119, 123, 126
  and Kremlin 96, 112
  and military 80, 85, 89
  and Ministry of State Security 43–8, 51–5, 85
  and music 228
  and policing 65–6
  popular attitudes towards 97, 116, 119, 123, 176
  and SED leadership 22–36, 43–5
  tattoo of on buttock 176
  Ten Commandments of Socialist Morality (1958) 196
  youth policy 171–3, 176–9, 182
Uszkoreit, Hans-Georg (b. 1926) Rector of Music High School Dresden (1963–68) 235–7

VdgB *see* Association for Mutual Peasant Aid
VDK *see* Association of German Composers
Walter, Karl, musician 232, 240
Wandel, Paul (1905–95) Minister of Education (1949–52) 23, 228–9
Warnke, Herbert (1902–75) chair of FDGB (1948–75) 151
Weber, Max (1864–1920) sociologist 265, 270–2, 284, 287, 291–2
Wilke, Hans, functionary for Church Affairs 222
Williams, H. C. N. 'Bill' (1914–90) Provost of Coventry Cathedral (1958–81) 222
Wimmer, Walter, historian 246
Witt, Katarina (b. 1965) skater 13
Wolf, Christa (b. 1929) author 12
Wolf, Hanna (b. 1908) head of Party University (1950–83) 246
Wolle, Stefan (b. 1950) historian 7, 109, 113, 116–17, 281–2, 285
Wollweber, Ernst (1898–1967) Minister of State Security (1953–57) 26, 35, 47–8, 50
women 9–10, 82, 116, **151–67**
  abortion 152–4, 160–2
  in agriculture 132–40
  employment 155–60
  family 160–2, 164–6
  girls 176–7, 179
  housework 157, 163–4
  rape 152–3
workers 5, 42, **112–26**, 200

young people 81, 83, 87, 105–7, 144, **171–86**

Zaisser, Wilhelm (1893–1958) Minister of State Security (1950–53) 25, 33–5, 44, 46–8, 50, 69
Ziller, Gerhart (1912–57) SED Secretary for the Economy (1953–57) 26, 50
Zwahr, Hartmut (b. 1936) historian 246